God's Patience and Our Work

For Mum and Dad

God's Patience and Our Work

*Hans Frei, Generous Orthodoxy
and the Ethics of Hope*

Ben Fulford

scm press

© Ben Fulford 2024

Published in 2024 by SCM Press
Editorial office
3rd Floor, Invicta House,
110 Golden Lane,
London EC1Y 0TG, UK

www.scmpress.co.uk

SCM Press is an imprint of Hymns Ancient & Modern Ltd
(a registered charity)

Hymns Ancient & Modern® is a registered trademark of
Hymns Ancient & Modern Ltd
13A Hellesdon Park Road, Norwich,
Norfolk NR6 5DR, UK

British Library Cataloguing in Publication data
A catalogue record for this book is available
from the British Library

ISBN: 978-0-334-05928-8

Typeset by Regent Typesetting
Printed and bound in Great Britain by
CPI Group (UK) Ltd

Contents

Acknowledgements

I have accrued many debts of thanks over the several years of this project.

I am grateful to funding from the Santander International Research Excellence Awards, at the University of Chester, and from the University's Faculty of Humanity, towards the costs of two research trips to the archives at Yale University and Yale Divinity School in February and June 2015.

I am grateful to Martha Smalley and her colleagues in the archives of Yale Divinity School, for their assistance; likewise to Elizabeth Dunn and her colleagues at the Rubenstein Library at Duke University, Jennifer Hadley at Wesleyan University and Christopher Pote at the Bishop Payne Library at Virginia Theological Seminary. Christopher Fiorillo, of the Sterling Memorial Library at Yale, was very helpful in arranging loan of microfilms of the New Haven Register. Betsy Goldberg and her colleagues found useful sources on Project Concern for me in the collections of the Whitney Library in New Haven. Julie Hulten, volunteer archivist for the North Haven Historical Society, was also very helpful. Daniel Driver and Mike Higton kindly made their own copies of texts by Frei available to me. I am grateful to the Fortunoff Video Archive at the Sterling Memorial Library, Yale, for permission to cite and quote from Frei's Holocaust Video Testimony.

A number of people generously gave of their time to talk with me about this research. Cal Vinal of the Connecticut Housing Investment Fund spoke with me about the history of CHIF in New Haven and I'm grateful to him and those who put me in touch with him. Several of Frei's former colleagues and students allowed me to interview them about him, including Margaret Farley, David Ford, Alex Garvin, David Gouwens, Serene Jones, Wayne Meeks, Gene Outka, Michael Root and Sib Towner.

The Department of Theology and Religious Studies at the University of Chester granted me research leave during the autumn of 2018 and I am thankful for the support of Wayne Morris and then Hannah Bacon as Heads of Department, and of colleagues who picked up my responsibilities. The Department has been a supportive and encouraging place to pursue research amid the pressures of academic life today. I am especially grateful to conversations with David Clough and Dawn Llewellyn. David Shervington has been a supportive and patient editor.

I have also benefitted from the opportunity to present parts of this argument at the Research Institute in Systematic Theology at King's College London, at the Society for the Study of Theology and at Trinity College, Bristol. I have benefitted from conversations about Frei and the argument of the book with many theological colleagues, and in particular Drew Collins, Mike Higton (who kindly read several draft chapters) and Susannah Ticciati.

Finding time to write in academia is more difficult than it used to be. Writing while carrying managerial responsibilities in an academic department is even more difficult. I am so thankful for supportive friends and family. Brett Grey, Julie Gittoes and Gabby Thomas have provided constant encouragement, as has my sister, Nancy. My wife, Alison, has constantly believed in my ability to finish this project and been hugely supportive, encouraging and patient with me. Our boys, Matthew and Nathan, have been very patient too!

I dedicate this book with great love to my parents, Mike and Charlotte Fulford, who have been faithfully supporting my writing and research ever since my teenage years.

Introduction

How far can one combine faithful Christian discipleship and the pursuit of social justice or orthodox Christian belief with solidarity with the marginalized? What role do churches have in pluralistic societies in the light of their faith in Jesus Christ and their hope in his eschatological future? On what terms can a public account of that faith and hope be given? And for what can they hope in history, in the face of the entrenched power of unjust structures, the apparent weakness of many movements for change? The main thesis of this book is that the theology and ethics of Hans W. Frei (1922–88), who was Professor of Religious Studies at Yale University, can help us with all these questions (and more). In so doing, I offer a new interpretation of Frei's theology and ethics, its development and coherence in context.

In his mature writings, Frei developed an increasingly subtle and flexible account of the essence of Christianity, a Christology in which Jesus Christ's irreducible, particular identity grounds both his universal significance, his enduring solidarity with the poor, the oppressed and the marginalized, and his living presence in them, to the church and to wider history. He espoused a non-triumphalist vision of the church's witness and service, combining devotion to Christ and passionate concern for justice and being receptive to enrichment from without. He sought to recover the practical and theological conditions for an ethics of responsibility and articulated terms of the publicness of theology and ethics hospitable to those practices. He offered an understanding of collective and individual discipleship shaped according to Christ's compassionate humanity and solidarity, characterized by generous, reconciliatory love of the individual and a ministry of penultimate reconciliation and justice in the context of social sin and the structural divisions it engenders and thrives upon. And he outlined a theology of God's patience and providence to frame a hopefully realist, contextually pragmatic, progressive engagement of Christian communities with politics and hope of the ultimate meaningfulness and fulfilment of humanistic projects and struggles for dignity, justice, liberation and reconciliation. In all these ways, I argue, he articulates a rich, complex and profound vision of a generous orthodoxy and makes an important contribution to Christian political theology and ethics.

Frei is not widely recognized as a theologian with something significant to say about these issues. He is known variously as a 'narrative theologian', a kind of Barthian or post-liberal theologian, a hermeneutical thinker about narrative and biblical interpretation and a historian of modern biblical hermeneutics. Indeed, he has been described as having more to say about Christian self-understanding in a secularizing world than how his approach 'generates distinctive forms of action'.[1]

Where he is recognized as an important historical and constructive theologian, thanks to the considerable work that has been done to recover and evaluate his contributions to theology and the study of theology, little has been said about his ethics or the political character of his theology.[2] That gap remains even as studies proliferate of aspects of Frei's thought and its application to various areas of contemporary theology.[3] Nor does Frei feature in surveys of Christian political theology and ethics.

At one level, this omission is not surprising. Frei never published a work of ethics or political theology. Yet ethical and political concerns and reflections pervade his mature work, and grow out of its central and celebrated insights, as we shall see, indicating a little noticed and even less examined fruitfulness. This book therefore offers a study of Frei as a political theologian and ethicist.

This material in Frei's work and its potential has not gone wholly unnoticed. Frei's colleague Gene Outka offered a careful analysis of how Christ's identity governs the ethical orientation of the disciple in the midst of their circumstances, drawing inferences from Frei's *The Identity of Jesus Christ*.[4] David Ford claimed that Frei should be recognized as having eventually arrived 'at the beginnings of a first-order political theology'.[5] Ford has also noted a 'condensed Jesus-centred practical wisdom' marked by 'radical respect for "otherness"' in the later chapters of Frei's posthumously published lectures on his typology.[6] In the fullest treatment of this topic, Mike Higton has argued that Frei calls for and clears theological space for patient, reconciliatory work and realistic, strategic political engagement in the messy public world, framed by a Christocentric understanding, and figural reading, of God's providential involvement in the contingent events of human history.[7] These insights support the plausibility of this project and I will build on them to give a fuller account of the political and ethical dimensions of Frei's theology and its significance in its context and for today.

Frei's biography offers further support and context for the project. His early life shaped an acute political awareness and sensitivity, marked by experiences of anti-Jewish violence, intimidation and legislation in Berlin in the 1930s, by the tearing asunder of a German Jewish identity, the loss of a future and the dislocation of flight to the United States in the summer of 1938. Frei belonged to a family of middle-class Jewish professionals (his mother, Magda, was a paediatrician; his father, Wilhelm, was an eminent dermatologist, known for inventing a skin test for a sexually transmitted disease), whose ancestors had been in Germany for generations on both sides of the family.[8] They thought of themselves as 'utterly patriotic' and 'deeply indigenous in German culture'.[9] They saw themselves as Jews in the sense of being German citizens of Jewish religion, whose Jewish distinctness did not interfere with their being German citizens, first and foremost.[10] Frei describes them as 'secularized Jews' whose cultural formation was in the German classics.[11] Like many German Jews, they were wholly assimilated, to the extent of having all their children baptized, and sending Hans to a church school where he received Christian instruction.

The Frei family moved to Berlin in 1929 so Wilhelm could take a post as head of the dermatology department at the municipal hospital Berlin-Spandau.[12] In 1933, Frei's sister had plans to go to medical school, his brother was nearing the end of high school, and his parents hoped that Hans would pursue an academic career.[13] For this family, the ascent of Adolf Hitler and the Nazi party to power in Germany in 1933 and the increasing restrictions and intimidation of Jewish businesses and the forced dismissal of many Jewish professionals (including in medicine), followed by the near-total prohibition of Jews' participation in professions under the Nuremberg race laws of 1935, represented, as Frei put it, the robbery of their primary, national identity and the abrupt end of the futures his parents projected for their children.[14] That sense of rupture is an important part of Frei's sense of his own biography. The life and identity his family had inhabited was, as he put it in a set of 'Autobiographical notes' written in his hand in 1983, a 'world left behind'.[15]

Early in his Holocaust testimony, Frei describes being politicized early on in his life by an awareness of what was going on in Germany and a sense of anticipation of what was about to happen. He talks of being politicized by the age of 8 (so by April 1930), by which time he had begun reading the *Vossische Zeitung*, a liberal daily Berlin newspaper.[16] He refers to having seen 'Brownshirts tyrannising small clumps of people and clashing with small groups of communists on the streets'.[17] In his 'Autobiographical notes', Frei identifies Hitler's accession to power as a 'decisive moment' in his lived experience, and seems to link it to the propaganda and violence directed against Jews in that year at locations not far from the family home.[18]

Frei's testimony mixes recollections of his own experiences in Germany in this period with an analysis of Nazi organizing and activity and of their effects on German Jews in Berlin in the early 1930s, repeatedly drawing out the wider political lessons he learnt from those episodes and sometimes applying them to current affairs. For example, in relation to the violence perpetrated by the SA, Frei recalled the real terror of witnessing the beating of a Jewish newspaper vendor across the street from their apartment and realizing that the Brownshirts assaulting him represented, in effect, not the weakness of the law but its actuality.[19] This terror, he adds, 'is what blacks must feel when they experience police terror, in South Africa, and sometimes in this country'.

Frei also offers recollections and analysis of Nazi organizing and the insinuation of the party into Germany society. As a child in the 1930s, and despite being Jewish, he attended, once or twice, a Hitler Youth mass meeting for his area of the city and age, at a stage when people still attended in ordinary clothing as well as in the organization's uniform.[20] He recalled in the interview the way the speeches would appeal to idealism at a surface level while their stronger undercurrent appealed to hatred of 'those who were not part of "us"'. The biggest political lesson he learned in Germany, he comments, is to beware when politicians 'appeal to the instinctive hate in you'. He also noticed the mesmeric effect of martial music at these events, and the way that organizing the group to chant slogans robbed the participants of their minds and swept them 'into the current', a tactic whose practice in the present still retained its capacity to terrify him. He also noted how the Hitler Youth were able to exploit the pervasive romantic atmosphere of German youth culture of the time.[21] And he recalled the systemic organization of Nazi groups for children and adults of both sexes in each area of a town, and its efficacy once the party was in power: the pervasiveness of the organization, the enormous pressure to join (backed by the threat of social ostracization and damage to career prospects if you did not), combined with the attraction of the appeal to an ideology of national renewal.

Most striking are Frei's observations of the complex effects of Nazi pressure and anti-Semitic persecution on him and other Jews, and their complex responses. He remembered, for example, the powerful appeal of the Hitler Youth and their ideology of national renewal, despite knowing that he himself could not belong to it and that it was wrong.[22] He drew broader lessons from these observations too. He recalled the overwhelming effect of anti-Semitic propaganda, even on the Nazis' political opponents and also on Jews. It took 'an awful lot, as a Jew, to be able to say to yourself, "I'm not really what they're making me out to be"'.[23] This dynamic was, he reflected, 'a ... kind of symptom which you find among oppressed peoples, that they tend to adopt the image that their oppressors impose on them – the image of themselves. And that happened to an awful lot of Jews.' That few of them held tightly to their Jewish heritage, he reasoned, left them with no cultural background to hang on to and strengthen their collective resistance to the image of themselves. Frei's description here resonates with W. E. B. Du Bois' analysis of the double consciousness of black people in America: the sense 'of always looking at one's self through the eyes of others' and measuring oneself by their attitudes.[24] Despite the differences between the two sets of historical experience of African Americans and German Jews, it is not difficult to imagine, given that he draws other comparisons in his testimony between his own experiences and those of black people in the United States and elsewhere, that Frei saw the analogy too.

In a similar vein, Frei recalled the transformation in the way non-Jewish friends would treat his family in 1933, from a 'genteel anti-Semitism' to either cutting them off or distinguishing between their particular Jewish acquaintance, 'one of the good Jews', who were all right, and Jews in general, who were evil.[25] It was an attitude Frei saw on the part of white Americans towards black people, especially in the South, when it was still acceptable at the time he emigrated (Frei went to college in North Carolina). One could be friends with individual black persons, but 'the race as a whole had to be kept in its place'.[26] Frei also reflected on the contempt German Jews felt for the Eastern Jews who came to Berlin in the early 1930s, seeing it as 'almost like a form of Jewish anti-Semitism', a painful, shameful reaction (which, in fact, had a longer history).[27] Again, he saw this as an instance of a wider phenomenon among minority populations, that within an atmosphere of oppression, one group within the minority sees itself as superior to another.[28]

Frei's conversion to Christianity took place in the context of this traumatic experience and its politicizing effects, a context that seems to have shaped Frei's religious sensibility and quest. As early as 1933 his parents had had 'the uneasy feeling that it was the beginning of the end of our citizenship in Germany' and, terrified, sought to get the children out of the country and to keep a low profile in it.[29] By early 1935 they were hearing rumours of concentration camps, even concentration camps for children, but had probably already made their decision. In January 1935, Hans was first sent to school in England, returning home in the holidays.[30] The danger of the children being abducted to a concentration camp was clearly behind the decision, for that was their fear when he once missed a train returning home to Berlin. They chose a Quaker school because the Quakers were one of the few groups that facilitated their going to England, something that currency regulations made very difficult, and because they had come to know and like the Quakers whom they met when Hans had attended a Quaker youth group.[31] In England Frei learnt

English, became an Anglophile, but suffered from anxiety and a sense of isolation; nevertheless, sensing the approach of war, he wanted to stay.[32]

The school is the probable setting for Frei's conversion to an espoused Christian faith.[33] His student, William C. Placher, recalls Frei telling the story of seeing Jesus on the cross 'and suddenly "knowing that it was true"'.[34] As a graduate student, he recalled how, like many of his contemporaries, he 'had a feeling that *history* and *impersonal fate* were hemming me in', that they were '"ruthless and no respecter of persons"'.[35] He felt '"divided against himself by the weight of prejudice against him"'.[36] His reading of Kierkegaard, moreover, impressed on him an understanding of the human condition as one of loneliness. He felt that liberal Judaism had no answer to either problem. Eventually, he recounted, he found he could not wait and, having adopted Christianity, felt he had arrived at '"a God who is really a God ... in the Orthodox Jewish sense"'.[37]

Frei's conversion addressed his religious needs to some extent but further complicated his identity. He remained, he related to Vlock, someone who, like Saul Friedländer in *When Memory Comes*, struggled to integrate the two halves of his personality, Jewish and Christian, except tenuously.[38] Insofar as he did so, his dominant personality was Christian and secular. His sense of fatedness remained too; his natural bent, he would tell his friend John Woolverton, was 'very pessimistic'.[39] The development of his faith and its theological articulation would be shaped by his education at Yale Divinity School.

Frei's path to Yale began with his family's emigration to New York in 1938.[40] Their financial circumstances meant that Hans had to rely on a scholarship in order to go to college. It seems all that was available to him was one to study textile engineering at North Carolina State University, which he had seen advertised in a newspaper.[41] The most decisive thing that happened to him there was hearing an invited lecture from H. Richard Niebuhr.[42] Frei was so impressed that he started a correspondence with him that evening, which led to Niebuhr advising him to study theology at Yale Divinity School, advice that Frei followed.[43] Yale Divinity School (YDS), in Frei's 'Autobiographical notes', is the 'world *not* left behind'.[44] It was at Yale that he first encountered the generous orthodoxy of his teachers: a strong, open-ended, hospitable, living tradition, rooted in traditional dogma yet confident in the confluence of divine grace and human reflection, realistic in its convictions both as to God's providence and human finitude and frailty.[45] Here, not least in the public theology of H. Richard Niebuhr, he found the resources to articulate a Christological doctrine of a gracious providence that was more than fate and could inform a public, political theology and ethics.[46]

In this book, I show how he did so, and the significance of that achievement, in two parts. Part I focuses on the context and content of Frei's Christological essays, first published in 1966 and 1967, some of which were republished in *The Identity of Jesus Christ*, in 1975, and related writings from this period.

Chapter 1 focuses on features of his involvement in institutional change and political protest at Yale and Civil Rights activism in New Haven in the 1960s and early 70s, which provide a context for the political strands and echoes in these texts. It also begins the contextualization of Frei's thought, its development and political character that I continue throughout the rest of the book, extending and thickening the work of John Woolverton and Mike Higton in this regard.[47] To that end, I have drawn on archival sources, principally in Frei's papers at Yale Divinity School, New Haven; on his Holocaust Testimony from the Fortunoff Video Archive at Yale; on close reading of contemporary newspaper articles, and contemporary theological works; and on my transcripts of several semi-structured interviews I conducted with some of Frei's colleagues and students.[48]

Chapter 2 examines the theological context of Frei's Christological essays and their political theological outworkings in some of the post-liberal thinkers to whom Frei was responding: Rudolf Bultmann and Karl Barth; the 'post-Bultmannians', Günther Bornkamm, James Robinson and Schubert Ogden; and the theologians of hope, Wolfhart Pannenberg and Jürgen Moltmann. This survey highlights the currency of the questions Frei faced and some of the salient alternatives his response is in dialogue with. Those questions have to do with the meaning and significance of modern (that is, historically conscious) Christocentric Christian faith. What is the significance of Jesus Christ today? What does it mean to believe in his presence? How should we interpret the miracle-strewn, eschatologically charged New Testament texts that speak about him? What does faith in Christ and his contemporary presence mean for the Christian life and to what extent or in what way does it entail political engagement for believers?

In Chapter 3, I offer a fresh reading of those Christological essays and related texts, as responses to both Frei's political and theological contexts. I show that Frei explains the self-focused freedom of Christ's contemporary presence, in the church and the world, and his universal significance by an analysis of his identity as given in the narrative structure of the Synoptics. Jesus Christ emerges as a figure whose unsubstitutable singularity, inseparable from God's identity and presence, entails his living presence in the church and providentially; the salvific, vicarious character of his death and resurrection; and his redemptive inclusion of all human beings in himself. Frei's interpretation of Christ's presence and of the discernment of its figural traces in certain political events, I argue, amounts to a political theology intended to orientate the church's political responsibility to and reciprocity with the wider world.

Part II charts the evolution of the constructive arguments of Frei's unfinished project on the history of modern Christology and its political, theological and ethical dimensions, culminating in the more overt political theology of some of his last writings.

In Chapter 4, I offer an original interpretation of the historical and constructive argument of Frei's *Eclipse of Biblical Narrative* as a development of the argument of his Christological essays. Here Frei not only charts the course and factors contributing to the eclipse of western Christianity's focus on the narrative meaning of realistic biblical stories but offers an account of the essence of western Christianity and of the theological and hermeneutical conditions for the theological imagination that frames Christian ethics and political engagement. Indeed, I argue, implicit in Frei's argument is an account of Christian ethics as responsibility that combines aspects of the accounts of Karl Barth and H. Richard Niebuhr.

Chapter 5 examines Frei's re-conception of his project in his typology of modern Christian theology. Here he offers a more subtle, practical and historical understanding of the essence of Christianity and a stronger account of the publicness not only of Christian theology but of Christian ethics as responsibility. The sort of public theology he commends, I argue, aims to foster a social and political vocation for Christian communities after Christendom and lays the basis for a Christian humanism rooted in Christ's identity, indeed for a generous orthodoxy.

In Chapter 6, I draw my argument to a conclusion through a reading of the threads and sketches towards a political theology and ethics, to be found in Frei's later writings, to argue that Frei has at least the outline of a political theology and ethics that has a significant contribution to make to those fields. He develops his ethics of responsibility by way of the theme of discipleship, characterized by a distinctive account of generous neighbour-love and the ministry of penultimate justice and reconciliation, framed by an understanding of social sin (where he is in need of supplementation from a liberationist account) but also of divine patience, to complement his doctrine of providence. Frei's significance can be seen, I argue, in carrying forward a political theology and ethics of hope informed by an account of divine patience and providence, in continuity with H. Richard Niebuhr (over against his brother) and in a way that supplements accounts of Christ's presence in several liberationist accounts, including those of Gustavo Gutiérrez and James H. Cone. In so doing, I seek to advance the (still underdeveloped) dialogue between post-liberal and liberation theologies in a new way.[49]

Notes

1 Elaine L. Graham, Heather Walton, Frankie Ward, *Theological Reflections: Methods* (London: SCM Press, 2013), p. 100.

2 The principal landmarks in the reception of Frei as a theologian include the essays in Garrett Green (ed.), *Scriptural Authority and Narrative Interpretation* (Philadelphia, PA: Fortress Press, 1987); the articles in David Demson and John Webster (eds), *Hans Frei and the Future of Theology = Modern Theology* 8:2 (April 1992); the chapters in Giorgy Olegovich (ed.), *Ten Year Commemoration to the Life of Hans Frei (1922–1988)* (New York: Semenenko Foundation, 1999); Charles Campbell, *Preaching Jesus: New Directions for Homiletics in Hans Frei's Postliberal Theology* (Grand Rapids, MI: Eerdmans, 1997); David Demson, *Hans Frei and Karl Barth: Different Ways of Reading Scripture* (Grand Rapids, MI: Eerdmans, 1997); David G. Kamitsuka, *Theology and Contemporary Culture: Liberation, Postliberal and Revisionary Perspectives* (Cambridge: Cambridge University Press, 1999); John David Dawson, *Christian Figural Reading and the Fashioning of Identity* (Berkeley, CA: University of California Press, 2002); Mike Higton, *Christ, Providence and History: Hans W. Frei's Public Theology* (London: T & T Clark, 2004); Paul J. DeHart, *The Trial of Witnesses: The Rise and Decline of Postliberal Theology* (Malden: Blackwell Publishing, 2006); and Jason A. Springs, *Toward a Generous Orthodoxy: Prospects for Hans Frei's Postliberal Theology* (New York: Oxford University Press, 2010).

3 See, for example, my *Divine Eloquence and Human Transformation: Rethinking Scripture and History through Gregory of Nazianzus and Hans Frei* (Minneapolis, MN: Fortress Press, 2013); Tim Boniface, *Jesus, Transcendence, and Generosity: Christology and Transcendence in Hans Frei and Dietrich Bonhoeffer* (Lanham, MD: Lexington Books/Fortress Press, 2018); Daniel Shin, *Theology and the Public: Reflections on Hans W. Frei on Hermeneutics, Christology, and Theological Method* (Lanham, MD: Lexington Books, 2019); Drew Collins, *The Unique and Universal Christ: Refiguring the Theology of Religions* (Waco, TX: Baylor University Press, 2021).

4 Gene Outka, 'Following at a Distance: ethics and the identity of Jesus', in Garrett Green (ed.), *Scriptural Authority and Narrative Interpretation* (Philadelphia, PA: Fortress Press, 1987), pp. 144–60.

5 David F. Ford, 'Hans Frei and the future of theology', *Modern Theology* 8:2 (1992), p. 208.

6 David Ford, 'On being theological hospitable to Jesus Christ: Hans Frei's achievement', *The Journal of Theological Studies* 46:2 (1995), pp. 542–3.

7 Higton, *Christ, Providence and History*, and especially the thesis statements on pp. 4, 13, 89, the account of figural reading of history and his turn towards political theology on pp. 169–173. See also Shin, *Theology and the Public*, pp. 93–6.

8 Hans F. Holocaust Testimony HV 170, Fortunoff Video Archive for Holocaust Testimonies, Yale University, 1980 (from 5 minutes in). His Testimony is published online in a critical edition with introduction by Ion Popa and transcript

here: https://editions.fortunoff.library.yale.edu/essay/hvt-0170. For a rich and sensitive analysis of the long, complex and troubled history of assimilation to which Frei's ancestors belonged, see Deborah Hertz, *How Jews Became Germans: The History of Conversion and Assimilation in Berlin* (New Haven, CT: Yale University Press, 2007).

9 Hans F. Holocaust Testimony (from 5 minutes in).

10 Hans F. Holocaust Testimony (from 51 minutes). Frei was disciplined for using Yiddish at home. See his 'Autobiographical notes', p. 3, from Yale Divinity School (YDS) archive, Record Group 76, Series VI, Box 27, Folder 336. Henceforth, I will cite such archival records by their record group, series number, box and folder, in this form: YDS 76 VI 27-336. Where, describing his parents, he comments, 'Using Yiddish expressions -> mouth washed out'. This discipline probably reflects a long-standing antipathy towards Yiddish of emancipated German Jews who embraced the ideals of German *Bildung* and saw Yiddish as the embodiment of *Unbildung* and an impediment to assimilation. Behind their antipathy lay an anti-Semitic reality: pejorative characterizations of Jewish speech retained a currency in German culture into the Nazi period. See Steven E. Aschheim, *Brothers and Strangers: The East European Jew in German and German Jewish Consciousness, 1800–1923* (Madison, WI: The University of Wisconsin Press, 1982), pp. 7–11.

11 'Autobiographical notes', pp. 1, 3. Frei appears to have written a longer version (pp. 1–2) and shorter version (p. 3) and the two complement each other in some respects. I read them as mutually supplementary and interpretive here.

12 Hans F. Holocaust Testimony (first 2 minutes).

13 Hans F. Holocaust Testimony (at 2 minutes 50 seconds and at 6 minutes).

14 Hans F. Holocaust Testimony (at 2 minutes 50 seconds, 3 minutes 48, 6 minutes and 51 minutes). This programme of 'graduated pressure', as Frei termed it, began in 1933 and is more fully described in Christoph Kreutzmüller, *Final Sale: The Destruction of Jewish Commercial Activity, 1930–1945* (New York: Berghahn Books, 2017), pp. 151–88; and in its brutality, extensity, protean forms and intimidating, immiserating and isolating effects in daily life by Marian A. Kaplan in her *Between Dignity and Despair: Jewish Life in Nazi Germany* (Oxford: Oxford University Press), pp. 17–49.

15 'Autobiographical notes', p. 1.

16 Hans F. Holocaust Testimony (from 59 minutes). See also 'Vossische Zeitung' in *The Oxford Companion to German Literature*, Henry Garland and Mary Garland (eds) (Oxford: Oxford University Press, 1997).

17 Hans F. Holocaust Testimony (1 minute in). Brownshirts was a name given to the SA, the Sturmabteilung ('assault division'), a Nazi paramilitary organization, who were attacking people whom they took to be Jews, with increasing frequency, long before Hitler's appointment as Reich chancellor on 30 January 1933. See Kreutzmüller, *Final Sale*, pp. 100–1.

18 'Autobiographical notes', pp. 1, 3. On the first page of his autobiographical notes, Frei lists 30 January 1933 as a 'decisive moment' in his lived experience and linked the date with an arrow to 'Kudamm, "Angriff"'. In a second, very similar, shorter draft, the date is replaced by 'Hitler', whose name is followed by the same names in brackets. 'Kudamm' is an abbreviation of Kurfürstendamm, a long shopping boulevard in Berlin where many Jews lived and worked and which was a symbolic focus for targeted SA violence towards Jews and Jewish businesses in 1931 and 1933. It was at the other end of the street from Frei's home on Uhland-

strasse. *Der Angriff* ('The Attack') was a newspaper founded by Joseph Goebbels in 1927 and an instrument of Nazi party propaganda that helped stir up public hostility to Jews and repeatedly called for action against them. Frei's home address is given in Magda's entry in the database of the Deutsche Gesellschaft für Kinder- und Jugendmedizin, 'Jüdische Kinderärztinnen und -ärzte 1933–1945' (https://www.dgkj.de/die-gesellschaft/geschichte/juedische-kinderaerztinnen-und-aerzte-1933-1945), accessed 4.08.2023.

19 Hans F. Holocaust Testimony (from 18 minutes, 43 seconds).

20 Hans F. Holocaust Testimony (from 25 minutes, 29 seconds).

21 Hans F. Holocaust Testimony (from 35 minutes). Frei reflects further on how the folk ideology of that youth culture was ripe for such exploitation in his review of Wendelgard von Staden's *Darkness Over the Valley: Growing Up in Nazi Germany* (YDS 76 III 10-166), a translation about which Frei had advised the publisher (see correspondence from Chester Kerr in YDS 76 I 2-50 and pp. 197–8 of the transcription of the (possibly unpublished) review in Mike Higton (ed.), *Unpublished Pieces: Transcripts from the Yale Divinity School archive* (1998–2004): https://divinity-adhoc.library.yale.edu/HansFreiTranscripts/, accessed 29.04.2014).

22 Hans F. Holocaust Testimony (from 33 minutes, 40 seconds).

23 Hans F. Holocaust Testimony (from 14 minutes, 40 seconds).

24 W. E. B. Du Bois, *The Souls of Black Folk* (New York: Dover Publications, 1994 [originally published 1903]), p. 2.

25 Hans F. Holocaust Testimony (from 6 minutes, 25 seconds).

26 Hans F. Holocaust Testimony (at 8 minutes, 47 seconds).

27 Hans F. Holocaust Testimony (from 54 minutes). See also Aschheim, *Brothers and Strangers*.

28 There is an echo in his analysis of Paulo Freire's account of how dehumanized oppressed groups, having internalized their oppressors, adapt to the structure of oppression and strive for the model of humanity projected by their oppressors, and so become oppressors or sub-oppressors themselves. See his *Pedagogy of the Oppressed* (London: Penguin Books, 1970), pp. 19–21.

29 Hans F. Holocaust Testimony (from 8 minutes, 39 seconds). This sense contrasted with the hopes of many Jews, including Frei's grandmother, who felt that if only the Nazis could be made to understand that Jewish families had also suffered in the First World War, all the anti-Semitic persecution would stop (Hans F. Holocaust Testimony, from 8 minutes).

30 Frei gives the date in his 'Autobiographical notes', p. 1.

31 Hans F. Holocaust Testimony (from 48 minutes).

32 'Autobiographical notes', p. 1.

33 See his own account reflected in 'Frei describes his acceptance of Christianity. Christian Jew's "Odyssey." Second talk of series discussed in Hillel Forum', *Yale Daily News* 71:43, 8 November 1949, p. 1; and corrected by Frei's letter to the Chairman of the *News*, *Yale Daily News* 45, 10 November 1949, p. 4.

34 William C. Placher, 'Introduction to Frei', in Placher and G. Hunsinger (eds), *Theology and Narrative: Selected Essays* (New York: Oxford University Press, 1993), p. 5. See also Frei's 'Autobiographical notes', pp. 1, 3.

35 'Frei describes his acceptance of Christianity' and Frei, letter to the Chairman of the *News*, *Yale Daily News* 45, 10 November 1949. The italics are Frei's, intended to emphasize that it was these forces that were the subject of these remarks, and not liberal Judaism, as he had been misquoted as saying in the YDN report.

36 'Frei describes his acceptance of Christianity'.

37 'Frei describes his acceptance of Christianity'.

38 Hans F. Holocaust Testimony (from 1 hour 18 minutes, 34 seconds). *When Memory Comes* is Saul Friedländer's memoir, which switches back and forth between his experiences of fleeing Prague following the Nazi occupation, then being a refugee as a child in pre-war France, then Vichy France, and converting to Catholicism, before later recovering his Jewish identity and emigrating to Israel during the War of Independence in 1948, and his early experiences there, and the present of 1977, on the anniversary of the Six Days' War. Running through Friedländer's recollections, and expressed in the interleaving of past and present, is a persistent sense of connection and rupture with his past self, including with the Catholic faith and identity he once espoused, which he articulates explicitly at points (see pp. 100 and 136–9).

39 John Woolverton, 'Hans W. Frei in context: a theological and historical memoir', *Anglican Theological Review* 79:3 (1997), p. 374.

40 'List or Manifest of Alien Passengers for the United States. S.S. Deutschland, Passengers sailing from Southampton, 29th July, 1938', from *Findmypast*, accessed 17.08.2017. Frei himself tells us in his 'Autobiographical notes' that he was in England until August 1938 (p. 1).

41 Woolverton, 'Hans W. Frei in context', n. 36.

42 It is the chief thing he records about North Carolina State in his autobiographical notes (p. 1).

43 Placher, 'Introduction', p. 5.

44 'Autobiographical notes', p. 1; the emphasis is Frei's.

45 See Hans W. Frei, 'In memory of Robert L. Calhoun', quoted in George Lindbeck, 'Introduction', Robert L. Calhoun and George Lindbeck (eds), *Scripture, Creed, and Theology: Lectures on the History of Christian Doctrine in the First Centuries* (Eugene, OR: Wipf & Stock, 2011), pp. xix–xxi; and Higton, *Christ, Providence and History*, pp. 2–4.

46 Hans W. Frei, 'History, salvation-history, and typology', in Mike Higton and M. A. Bowald (eds), *Reading Faithfully: Writings from the Archives, vol. 1, Theology and Hermeneutics* (Eugene, OR: Wipf & Stock, 2015), pp. 159–60; Frei, 'H. Richard Niebuhr on History, Church, and Nation', in *Theology and Narrative*, pp. 214–33.

47 See Woolverton, 'Hans W. Frei in context', pp. 369–93, and Higton, *Christ, Providence and History*.

48 Ethical approval for these oral history interviews was granted by the Research Ethics Committee of the Faculty of Humanities at the University of Chester in November 2014. Interviewees were selected on the basis of their being mentioned in the sources or recommended by others, subject to their availability and the limits of my own time for this project.

49 David G. Kamitsuka's *Theology and Contemporary Culture: Liberation, Postliberal and Revisionary Perspectives* (1999) remains the key text here. See chapters 1 and 5 especially. For an excellent (but apparently rare) recent example, see Kristoffer Norris, *Witnessing Whiteness: Confronting White Supremacy in the American Church* (New York: Oxford University Press, 2020), chapters 3–4.

PART I

Christology, Providence and Politics

I

Yale, Civil Rights in New Haven

Following graduation in 1945 and a short spell in the Baptist ministry, in New Hampshire, Frei, now an ordained Anglican, returned to Yale in 1947 to pursue doctoral study under Niebuhr's supervision.[1] In 1956 he would finally complete his doctorate on 'The doctrine of revelation in the thought of Karl Barth, 1909 to 1922: the nature of Barth's break with liberalism'. Following appointments at Wabash College, Indiana, and the Episcopal Seminary of the Southwest at Austin, he returned again to Yale as assistant professor of religion on 1 July 1957.[2] Here he would produce the works for which he is best known and develop his generously orthodox approach to theology. He was, one former student recalls, 'deeply invested in life within institutions'.[3] He valued academic citizenship highly and committed a great deal of time and energy to committee work.[4] The full story of Frei's involvement in the life of Yale College and the New Haven area in this period is too large to tell here. Instead, I will focus on those aspects that help us understand the political context reflected in his theology in the latter half of the 1960s and early 70s, attending to Frei's role in the changes of institutional policy and culture and the political tumults over the Vietnam War, Civil Rights and Black Power within Yale in this period, and his participation in Civil Rights activism in the Greater New Haven area, aspects of his biography that have not featured in previous treatments of his life.

Some remarks Frei made in March 1963, in an interview for the student newspaper, the *Yale Daily News*, offer us a sense of his orientation to those contexts as a Christian theologian. In the interview, he was asked about the challenge of making religious convictions relevant to a student body indifferent to institutionalized religion.[5] Frei saw that indifference as a reflection of the exhaustion of the possibilities in Protestant Free Church tradition 'for offering profound intellectual and emotional satisfaction to its adherents and to those outside its sphere'. It was also a symptom, he thought, of Christianity's chronic decline from being the effective religion of western culture. Christianity was now likely to thrive apart from society, by which I take him to mean, apart from institutional forms fitted to that defunct social role, which was no measure of its relevance.

This decline was, he implied, a welcome development. Christianity had probably never been well suited to being the tribal religion of any group, including 'western culture'. Real Christians were, and always had been, a small minority characterized by 'a gladness of life, depth of compassion and firm conviction about Jesus Christ curiously bound together with openness and receptiveness' and marked by passion.[6] The change to become such a person was rare and nearly miraculous and could precede or follow intellectual reflection. This position, which Frei would reiterate in later writings, combined a lack of anxiety about the prospect of Christianity becoming a minority religion in western society together with an openness and receptivity towards that same society, which helps make sense of his own engagement with changes at Yale College and with Civil Rights activism in the New Haven area.

Change at Yale

When Frei returned to Yale in 1957, he re-entered an institution on the cusp of change. He would be caught up in and supportive of these changes. The post-war period had seen Yale's elitist ethos and social make-up altered by the returning war veterans who went to Yale under the terms of the GI Bill in the years 1946–50. The end to the segregation of Jewish and black students' accommodation was one product of these post-war years, and the gradual opening up of secret societies to Jews was another; overt genteel anti-Semitism was no longer acceptable.[7] In the 1950s, however, Yale's faculty and the next generation of students 'set about to reimpose the prep school ethos on Yale culture' and to reassert the traditional social constitution of Yale's student body of wealthy WASPs, often the children of alumni, through formal and informal dress codes and social snobbery.[8] Masters of colleges recruited according to their social preferences, leading to accumulations of social power, student wealth and wealthy alumni and a continued informal limitation on Jewish admissions.[9]

Gradual change towards a meritocratic, academic admissions policy and a more diverse student body came in the later years of President A. Whitney Griswold and was accelerated at the end of Griswold's tenure with the review of admissions policy by the Committee on the Freshman Year. [10] Griswold's successor, Kingman Brewster, implemented recommendations from its 1962 report, along with other changes (such as disregarding applicants' financial status, expanding scholarships, and a greatly expanded recruitment drive which focused on under-recruiting areas like inner-city and rural schools).[11] Despite opposition from trustees and alumni, those changes brought a greater number of enrolments of students from ethnic minorities from 1966 onwards. Finally, long after other Yale University institutions, Yale College first admitted women in September 1969, expanding its numbers to accommodate them.[12]

Part of the effect of Yale's changing admissions policy (together with student exposure to and participation in Civil Rights activism and Vietnam War protests) was to transform student attitudes to university authority, leading to protests about various events in the life of Yale College and to demands for student participation in decision-making. These demands led to a more consultative approach from Yale's administration and the inclusion of students (with voting rights) on some university committees, such as those responsible for teaching and learning and for discipline.[13] Frei was involved in this development as a member of the steering committee of the Faculty Coalition for a New University, a permanent group associated with its student equivalent, and committed to change at Yale.[14] They jointly proposed a plan for a Special University Commission to examine governance and decision-making at Yale as a step towards the democratizing of the university.[15] This proposal led, eventually, to reforms to Yale's governance, administration and disciplinary processes, though not to fundamental change in governance or decision-making.[16]

Frei was also supportive of women graduates who studied at Yale and in favour of the admission of women to Yale College.[17] As a member of Yale's Admissions Committee in 1971, he seems to have been in favour of Yale dropping quotas that limited the number of women it admitted and preserved a high proportion of male admissions.[18] He also questioned Yale's elitism. In making the case for dropping quotas and expanding efforts to recruit students from minority backgrounds, a contemporary report reaffirmed Yale's traditional purpose as a 'leadership-training' institution.[19] In the article, however, Frei is quoted questioning whether preparing people for elite leadership in society, the premise of the meritocratic argument for changing admissions policy in these ways, should be Yale's sole purpose. Yale should also accept some riskier cases and those whose purpose was to be trained for service rather than leadership.

The most significant area in which Frei contributed to Yale's changing culture in this period of his career, however, was as master of one of its residential colleges, Ezra Stiles. As admissions to Yale College from public high schools increased in the 1960s, and students from those schools arrived without the ready-made networks of students from preparatory schools, residential colleges grew in importance as centres of undergraduate community life, displacing the fraternities and so helping break with 'the exclusive, preppy culture that had characterized Yale'.[20] Each residential college had a dean appointed to counsel students. They became places with distinctive identities with which students self-identified. They also provided an institutional space in which students were given a greater say over what they learned in respect of new for-credit college seminars.[21] Frei served as Acting Master of Silliman College during the academic year 1970–71, and in 1972 he was appointed as Master of Ezra Stiles, where he and his family would live until Frei stepped down in 1980.[22] For the year 1975–76 he was also Chair of the Council of Masters at Yale.[23] He was recognized in the university for being 'extraordinarily effective in that role [of Master]'.[24] He saw the task of the master, together with college fellows, as one of shaping the college 'into an educationally significant community supplementing formal undergraduate instruction'.[25] For Frei, this task, requiring 'intellectual and cultural versatility and … initiative', was another aspect of academic citizenship.[26]

Vietnam and May Day

In the 1960s and early 70s, Yale was also swept up in a series of nationwide issues, as many universities were. The responses to them by students, faculty and the Yale administration helped change the culture of the university. The Civil Rights movement was one of these; the war in Vietnam was another.[27] From 1965, many Yale students and faculty were increasingly drawn into protests against the escalating participation of the United States in the Vietnam War.[28] The war polarized wider society and campuses, not least through the exemption of students from the draft, so that students were caught between duty, conscience and the instinct for self-preservation. Frei was one of those Yale faculty concerned at the escalation of US military action in the bombing of North Vietnam in Operation Rolling Thunder in February 1965. Along with his colleague James Gustafson and 177 others, he signed an open letter to President Lyndon Johnson that criticized the bombing as out of step with Johnson's stated goal of reducing international tensions, as likely to be counterproductive, to lead to further escalation and hostility towards the USA in Asia as well as further division at home and to cause great loss and injury to human life.[29] Published as an advert in *The New York Times* (as well as the *Yale Daily News*), it urged the pursuit of a negotiated settlement.[30] Like several of his Religious Studies and Yale Divinity School colleagues, Frei was also among hundreds of Yale faculty signatories to a statement supporting Yale's chaplain, William Sloane Coffin, when he (along with four others) was indicted by a Federal Grand Jury in Boston in January 1968 for conspiracy to counsel young men to violate draft laws.[31] The statement's signatories warned that by this indictment the government was attempting to coerce the conscience of many of its citizens, a course of action that risked undermining consent for democracy and the rule of law. It showed that the war was eroding 'the constitutional, moral and psychological consensus which a democracy requires'.[32]

Frei was also part of a much smaller group of faculty, including Coffin, who signed another statement in the *Yale Daily News*, announcing and encouraging participation in local and national anti-war activities comprising the second Vietnam Moratorium in November 1969 and culminating in a march in Washington on Saturday 15 November, with the aim of securing the withdrawal of US troops from Vietnam as soon as possible.[33] The statement refers to Yale students and faculty participating in local forums and programmes and we may suppose that, as part of the group commending these events, Frei himself was probably a participant. He was also among the Yale faculty who publicly supported a delegation from the city of New Haven to lobby for the 1972 Case-Church amendment to the funding bill for the US State Department, which would have removed funding for American participation in the Vietnam War four months after an agreement for the release of American Prisoners of War and an account for all Americans missing in action.[34]

In 1970, Yale was also the setting for the May Day protest at the trial of the Black Panther leader, Bobby Seale, for the torture and murder of an alleged police informant, Alex Rackley.[35] The protest was held on New Haven's central green, right next to Yale College. Over the May Day weekend, Yale hosted demonstrators in its residential college. This hospitality was a collaborative effort between Yale's administration, faculty and students. The offer of hospitality was part of a strategy by the Yale administration, coordinating with the organizers of the demonstration and New Haven police, to prevent an outbreak of violence on campus and to mitigate the perceived threat posed to Yale by radicals (in the light of rumours and injunctions to 'burn Yale'), and the dangers of violent confrontation between demonstrators and police or National Guardsmen. It also went together with an effort by Brewster and his staff to facilitate discussion at Yale of the trial, its fairness and the wider issues it raised of racial oppression and discrimination. At a meeting of faculty on 23 April, Brewster publicly questioned whether a black revolutionary could receive a fair trial in America at that time. The faculty voted to allow classes to be suspended to facilitate engagement with those issues. Lots of Yale students and faculty volunteered to help feed protesters and to be marshals, medics and day-care attendants. Frei was among them, stationed at a first-aid post in the basement of Battell Chapel at the edge of the green (where he was the recipient of a large sack of metal projectiles abandoned by a young man who had come prepared for a fight).[36]

The Shockley affair

One more angle on Frei's involvement in the political life of Yale is provided by his small role in the 'Shockley affair'. Part of the background for this episode in Yale's history was the organization of minoritized students to change Yale. In the context of civil rights campaigns and the emergence of the Black Power movement, African American students formed the Black Student Alliance at Yale. From the Alliance's conversations with the Yale administration came a whole series of actions, including a recruitment campaign to increase minority admissions, scholarships, job training programmes, racial awareness training for campus and city police, the hiring of black faculty members, a black cultural centre and an African American studies programme.[37] Right-wing student groups sought to push back at the changed composition and ethos of Yale by offering a public platform for provocative speakers to voice highly offensive, racist views, on the spurious grounds of testing the administration's commitment to free speech.[38]

Frei was also one of those who condemned an attempt by such an organization to arrange a debate between William B. Shockley, a Nobel Prize-winning physicist who publicly advocated racist, eugenicist views with respect to black Americans, including proposing voluntary sterilization, and William Rusher, the publisher of *National Review*, a highly influential conservative magazine.[39] This was the third such attempt by these groups and their alumni backers to stage a debate on Shockley's views. It was a tactic that minority groups sought to expose and oppose by public comment and protest.[40] The debate risked legitimating and promoting Shockley's views and would result in the continuation of the degradation and oppression of Third World peoples in the history of the USA and of white domination and racial polarization on campus and in New Haven. Amid this opposition and criticism from Brewster's administration, several invitations to Shockley were made and withdrawn by different student groups.[41] A further group invited Shockley to debate with William Rusher whether society is morally obliged to diagnose and treat 'tragic racial IQ inferiority', which enabled the debaters to assume as fact Shockley's unsupported assertion there were some intellectually inferior races.[42] Despite clear warnings of severe disciplinary action before and at the event, protestors effectively disrupted the debate so that it had to be abandoned.[43] In the end, 12 students were suspended for the next term with the possibility of returning if they agreed to abide by university regulations on general conduct.[44] In response to concerns among faculty about what they saw as a curtailment of free speech, Brewster set up a committee chaired by C. Vann Woodward, a Yale historian and free-speech advocate, to review 'free expression, mutual respect and charitable relations' at Yale, which reported in December 1974.[45]

The Woodward Report argued that the right of free expression was necessary to the intellectual freedom required for a university to fulfil its function of discovering and disseminating knowledge.[46] Such freedom must extend to 'the new, the provocative, the disturbing, and the unortho-dox' without regard to majority opinion. Other important values, such as 'the fostering of friendship, solidarity, harmony, civility, or mutual respect', could not trump its primacy, though anyone exercising their right to free expression should consider them. Therefore, anyone becom-ing a member of the university was obliged to permit free expression and the administration was obliged to enforce it by appropriate sanctions. In letters, opinion pieces and reports in the *Yale Daily News*, faculty and students discussed its categorical prioritization of free speech, the absence of mitigation of sanctions on grounds of provocation and Brewster's pro-posal of a mandatory minimum one-year suspension for disruptors.[47]

It was in the context of these debates that the Young Americans for Free-dom re-arranged the Shockley–Rusher debate at Yale for 17 April 1975. They focused the debate again on the question of whether government should intervene in respect of putative differences of racial intelligence, taking as read the false premise that such differences existed.[48] Frei was among several voices who publicly condemned the move and called for members of the Yale community to boycott it, a boycott being one of a number of modes of non-disruptive protest advocated and planned in the run-up to the event and on the day itself.[49] In a joint letter to students, published on the day of the debate in the *Yale Daily News*, Frei and the historian George Gaddis Smith (Master of Pierson College) dismissed Shockley's views.[50] By re-inviting Shockley and Rusher, 'a tiny group of Yale students' had callously exploited the right to free speech in order to humiliate members of the community. The YAF had attacked 'the dignity and humanity of minority members of this community'. They had thus 'imposed a sense of isolation on some of their fellow students'. Rather than contributing to the insult by attending the debate, members of Yale should demonstrate their disgust by staying away.[51]

The fragmentary picture of Frei at Yale that emerges from these sources is of someone who was deeply involved in its institutional life, adminis-tratively and pastorally, and was supportive of its inclusion of women and minorities, opposed to attempts to intimidate them and who was prepared to engage constructively in the attempt to give greater scope for student participation in its processes and decisions. Like many other faculty and students at the time, he was opposed to US involvement in the Vietnam War. This picture is complemented by the glimpses we have of his involvement in 'human relations' activism in the city of New Haven and its suburbs.

Residential segregation in New Haven

According to Douglas Rae, New Haven in the 1960s exemplified a wider pattern in urban America.[52] The city had attracted capital investment and population settlement thanks to the combination of the local availability of energy production and the railway. It gave rise to a high concentration of industries, factory owners, workers, businesses and shops in close proximity and daily interaction, supporting a rich, open-textured and democratic 'civic fauna' of organizations that offered opportunities for civic participation and the formation of social capital. It fostered what Rae calls 'urbanism': the patterns of private conduct and decision-making that make the successful governance of cities possible even where city hall is fairly weak. However, as it became possible to transmit electrical energy cheaply and instantaneously over long distances and to transport goods away from railway hubs using improved roads and vehicles with combustion engines, capital, populations and retail moved to the city suburbs and peripheries, and capital was rationalized in national corporations. A decline of voluntary organizations and civic engagement followed, leaving a hollowed-out city that mainly housed the working poor in a high concentration of public housing, with high educational failure and crime rates. This was the situation in which mass migration of African Americans from the South to New Haven (and other cities), attracted by the city's now declining industries, took place during the Second World War and in the decades following its end.

African Americans arriving in New Haven each year faced not only a declining industry but limited employment opportunities and housing options because of prejudice towards them and their lack of ready cash, Social Security, bank accounts, documented employment histories and propertied friends.[53] Other widespread factors contributed to promote the segregation of the black population in the city. Residential zoning by local government determined what land could be used for and articulated a valuation of neighbourhood quality. Zoning valued purely residential neighbourhoods with low density, single-family, detached housing most highly, and high-density, mixed-use neighbourhoods (with industry and businesses) lowest. The places in New Haven where black people were able to settle in this period were at the lower end of the scale and their presence tended to lead to the downgrading of a neighbourhood's classification.

Federal government intervention in the private housing market, initiated during the Great Depression, also helped reinforce residential segregation.[54] The Home Owners Loan Corporation (HOLC) was formed in 1933 to take on and re-finance mortgages on dwellings where either the borrower was missing payments or where the lending institution's assets (including its loans) had been frozen. It offered long-term loans that allowed the borrower to pay off both the loan and the interest on it with regular, uniform payments. It did so based on appraisals of the housing to be financed that relied on its assessors' profiles of neighbourhoods. The criteria for these assessments privileged new buildings, incomplete developments, home ownership, the exclusion of undesirable populations based on a racialized, anti-black, anti-immigrant scale of social status, neighbourhood homogeneity and single-use residential areas. The criteria reflected the prevailing segregationist prejudices of homebuyers and sellers, brokers, builders and financial institutions. The HOLC appraisals influenced the decision-making of other financial institutions, such as the Federal Housing Association, created in 1934, which insured private lenders' long-term mortgages for building and selling homes, alleviating the risks for them and so reducing the down payments they required from buyers.

As applied to New Haven, Rae shows, these neighbourhood classifications skewed federal support towards white, suburban neighbourhoods and away from mixed, urban areas, reflecting the values embedded in the criteria.[55] By signalling the undesirable quality of city neighbourhoods and their populations, they also amplified the effects of prevailing prejudices and influenced potential investors in the city: house-buyers, lenders and businesses. On those assessments, the presence of black families seems to have led automatically to the lowest 'red-lined' categorization, above all in Lower Dixwell avenue, the area of most concentrated settlement by African American migrants during and after the Second World War. For those living in the city, the classifications made it harder or, in red-lined areas, impossible, to obtain loans for repairs and renovations. In this way, HOLC classifications promoted the very decline in housing stock and neighbourhood quality its criteria predicted. They incentivized and supported white middle-class flight to the suburbs while closing them to black people and augmented existing spatial hierarchies. Zoning decisions and local opposition meant there was little scope or willingness to build low- or moderate-income housing in the suburbs to which minorities living in the city could aspire and little was available, limiting their options considerably.[56]

These effects also doomed public housing projects built in lowest-rated areas, so that white and many black households moved away, leaving 'a more homogenously impoverished population' who become trapped in an area where jobs were scarce and schools were poor.[57] Those same dynamics meant that low-income populations located in areas undergoing physical transformation by Mayor Richard Lee's famous urban renewal project tended to be displaced from them and dispersed, a movement that disproportionately affected black households, who were much more likely to end up in public housing and stay in the city.[58] Urban renewal thus may well have reinforced the movement of white families out of New Haven city to its suburbs.[59]

The residential segregation of cities in the USA isolated African Americans by limiting opportunities for employment and political alliances with other groups and reducing gain in value of their homes and the public benefits of home ownership, leading to racial disparities of wealth.[60] It constrained black people on lower incomes to neighbourhoods of concentrated poverty, which tended to have high rates of crime, drugs, teenage childbearing, and so on. It limited the ability of middle-class black people to move to more affluent areas. It also sustained racially segregated schools and poorer educational outcomes for students living in neighbourhoods with high crime rates and unusually high levels of violence.

Residential and educational segregation in northern cities, and their effects, were the target of much civil rights and social activism in the 1950s, 60s and 70s. It is significant for our understanding of Hans Frei and his theology that there is some evidence for his participation in such activism in this period in Greater New Haven, the area defined by the city and its suburbs.

Desegregating housing and education in Greater New Haven

When Frei returned to Yale with his family, they settled in the suburbs north of New Haven and Yale: first in Hamden and then a few roads away in next-door North Haven, where his wife Geraldine's parents lived.[61] At some point during the time they lived in this area, Frei became involved in an organization called the Greater New Haven Human Relations Council.

The Human Relations Council of Greater New Haven, as it was known from 1957, was a prominent Civil Rights and community relations organization that had been active in the metropolitan area of New Haven from at least the beginning of the 1950s, with a particular concern for members of New Haven's ethnic minorities.[62] It was one of a number of organizations sharing that concern in the area that also included branches

of national organizations like the National Association for the Advance-
ment of Colored People (NAACP), the Congress of Racial Equality
(CORE), local ecumenical organizations, like the New Haven Council
of Churches, and groups linked to educational institutions. There were
also a number of neighbourhood organizations such as the Hill Neighborhood Corporation, the Junta for Progressive Action and later the Hill
Parents Association, the Black Coalition and briefly the Black Panthers,
with programmes providing services and training to minority residents,
some of which were funded by the city's own anti-poverty agency, Community Progress, Incorporated.[63] Like the NAACP and CORE, it had a
constructive as well as critical relationship with the administration of
Mayor Richard Lee.[64]

Frei's diary indicates that from no later than October 1965 to October
1971, at least, he attended meetings of the Greater New Haven Human
Relations Council and of its Board and Education Committee.[65] He also
attended meetings of its North Haven branch and its Executive and Education Committees (a period of activity that may have been curtailed by
his responsibilities as Master of Silliman and then Ezra Stiles Colleges).

By the time Frei returned to New Haven in 1957, the Human Relations
Council focused its efforts on what it saw as the most pressing issues:
'more and better housing for minority families'; 'better police–community
relations'; and better opportunities for members of minority groups to
advance to higher levels of employment and gain promotions.[66]

In relation to housing, the Council was well aware of the problem
of housing segregation in the city, which it blamed on a conspiracy of
realtors, bankers and prejudiced ordinary white citizens in the city and
its suburbs.[67] It sought to remedy the lack of housing for minorities and
unfair housing practices towards them with multiple initiatives. Its Housing Committee sponsored meetings with city agency officials, housing
professionals and social workers, to address the difficulties that large
black and Puerto Rican families were having finding apartments to rent
and landlords willing to rent to them.[68] It campaigned for a municipal
fair housing ordinance and for fair housing practice state legislation.[69]
It sought to raise awareness of positive changes to regulations against
discrimination in housing, along with other local organizations.[70] It pres-
sured the Mayor's office to uphold equal housing opportunities and report
unfair housing practices, wrote to the Governor and Welfare Commis-
sioner asking them to investigate breaches of updated state legislation,
challenged the New Haven Real Estate Board to change its attitude on
restrictive housing, demonstrated outside the offices of at least one dis-
criminating realty company and surveyed housing conditions, needs and
desires in one of the main areas of minority ethnic settlement in the city.[71]

It sought to challenge beliefs contributing to the fear of white people that black people moving into a neighbourhood would lower property value.[72] It offered neighbourhood housing clinics in minority ethnic neighbourhoods.[73] It sponsored the construction of affordable housing in the city.[74] It had a voluntary listing agency for sale and rental properties, Housing Opportunity Made Equal (H.O.M.E.) which circulated its own newsletter, listing contacts in the HRC and houses and apartments for sale or rent on a non-discriminatory basis.[75] H.O.M.E. had committees of volunteers in each area who were ready to accompany prospective renters or buyers to look at houses or contact estate agents.

The HRC understood that residential segregation 'fosters educational segregation' and did so in New Haven: an observation it made in its June 1962 newsletter, one year after the first ruling against school segregation in a northern school system, by the US District Court for the Southern District of New York.[76] In the editorial of that edition, the HRC declared that the court's decision, removing residential patterns as a justification for educational segregation, meant it was time to remove the fiction of separate but equal schooling and eliminate segregated schools. In May 1963, the HRC wrote to the New Haven Board of Education pointing out 'aggravated examples of de facto segregation in New Haven's schools', and arguing it was educationally unsound and should be remedied.[77] Pressure to address racial school segregation in northern cities was building. In that context, the Board of Education appointed a special Committee on the Equalization of Educational Opportunity. The Board of Education's newly appointed Committee held hearings in July of 1963, where the HRC (alongside other organizations) advocated for desegregation of schools at a public hearing held by the New Haven Board of Education.[78] On 23 September 1963, the Board undertook to desegregate the city's schools within a year, on the basis that they were educationally unsound.[79] The HRC's Education Committee pledged to work with other organizations to ensure its realization with an adequate plan.[80]

That plan, entitled 'Proposals for Promoting Equality of Educational Opportunity and Dealing with the Problems of Racial Imbalance', was eventually proposed by the Board in June 1964. It proposed a mixture of compensatory and integratory measures, improving the quality of teaching and administration and reducing racial imbalance among teaching staff, alongside extensive redrawing of attendance zones for junior high schools so that the areas of high black population were divided more equally between them.[81] This proposal would involve some transfer (and transport) of white students to black-majority schools and vice versa. Despite vehement opposition, expressed at public meetings, by letters, petitions and public statements, and pressure through obscene phone calls and broken friendships, litigation and referenda to change its composition by election, the Board adopted the plan on 7 July with some amendments.[82] Although implemented in the face of continued opposition, the plan seems to have had little effect. According to Russell Becker of Frei's local North Haven branch of the HRC, the concentration of black school children in New Haven's black-majority schools had grown by 1967.[83] In part this failure may have been due to the difficulties of integrating schools within a city where growing minority ethnic population and continued white flight limited its impact.[84] These developments form the background to a school desegregation initiative in Greater New Haven called Project Concern, with which Frei was involved.

Project Concern

Project Concern began in 1966 in Hartford, the nearby state capital of Connecticut, as an experimental answer to the need for equal educational opportunities for disadvantaged inner-city youth in a racially segregated school system.[85] The rationale for an experiment in addressing this problem noted the disappointing results of compensatory education programmes (such as smaller classes, improving the quality of teachers, curricula, physical facilities) and the perceived danger of accelerating white flight to the suburbs by integrating inner-city schools. A report was commissioned from Harvard academics, which recommended cooperation across the metropolitan area so that two non-white Hartford children could be placed in suburban classrooms across that area. The theory behind the plan was that the social context in which learning takes place shapes how students learn; that learning in neighbourhoods with a high incidence of social problems (for example, high unemployment, family disintegration) shaped learning in ways that inhibited effective education; that compensatory programmes could not overcome the influence of social context on learning; and that its effects on students were cumulative: the longer they learnt in such contexts, the further behind their mental ability and academic achievement fell against national norms.[86] By placing children in environments with better social, physical and psychological conditions, it was hoped they would likely develop towards patterns of learning exhibited by their peers, and teacher expectations would be both raised and more effective. In this way, inner-city children would benefit from the effective way in which suburban schools seemed to transmit the skills and attitudes needed for success in American society.

Despite initial negative reactions, Hartford public schools, its Chamber of Commerce and the Connecticut State Education Department developed a plan to implement that proposal, sponsored by the State Education Department and with support from Hartford business, industrial, civic and political leaders.[87] Suburban school systems were selected on the basis of an impression of their receptivity to the idea, but the decision as to whether each of them would participate was, the State Attorney General determined, one for each local Board of Education. Letters of invitation were sent to these Boards by the State Education Department, which sparked local contests between supporters and opponents, who organized petitions, held meetings, wrote letters and threatened legal action.[88] Suburban Boards of Education held packed public meetings where feelings ran high, the predominant tone was negative and contributions were sometimes vehement and vicious.

Opponents argued that the problem should be solved by the city, and the money would be better spent there; that suburban schools were overcrowded and had no room for outsiders; that the plan threatened local autonomy; that long journeys on buses would physically damage the inner-city children; that the contrast between the suburbs and the poverty of their home environment would traumatize them; that they would lose their sense of belonging to their neighbourhoods; that 'the presence of disabled learners would result in the reduction of the quality of education in the suburbs'; that the black community would prefer to have its own schools; that inner-city families should work their way out to the suburbs as suburban families had done.[89] Most of these arguments were not overtly racist but all provided white opponents with cover for maintaining educational (and residential) segregation and keeping non-white children out of suburban schools, a tactic used by contemporary opponents of desegregation in education in other northern cities.[90] However, three out of four towns invited agreed to participate and another joined a little later.[91] It was agreed that the city of Hartford would pay suburban schools for the tuition of the children accepted, would administer the programme and organize transport and that the schools would decide where the children would be placed and would be able to withdraw from the programme with 30 days' notice. On that basis, 266 places were made available and the programme began in September 1966.

In December 1966 and January 1967, the North Haven Human Relations Council explored the possibility of North Haven's schools receiving Hartford pupils as part of the plan. Nothing seems to have come from that proposal. Nevertheless, the North Haven HRC had been in favour of an earlier desegregation plan of this kind and were clearly supportive of extending Project Concern.[92] Some of its members were to be instrumental in replicating it in the Greater New Haven area, Frei among them.

As the *Yale Daily News* would later report, Frei and another North Haven HRC member, Bernard Burg, were part of a small group of people from the suburbs of New Haven who, together with representatives of the Jewish Community Council, the New Haven Council of Churches and the Catholic Interracial Council, met on 15 December 1967 to form a steering committee for a campaign to promote Project Concern in the New Haven area.[93] In the weeks running up to that meeting, Frei's diary shows him attending meetings of the Education Committees of New Haven HRC in addition to other HRC meetings, meetings with Burg and meetings at New Haven High School, where another steering committee member, Ed Dudley, ran the Mathematics department.[94]

The North Haven HRC had been wary of campaigning publicly for a similar plan devised by two Yale members of staff a year earlier, no doubt aware of the opposition the New Haven Board had encountered when introducing its plan to mitigate racial imbalance in the city's schools, as well as anti-desegregation campaigns in other US cities.[95] The steering committee quietly worked, therefore, to build a coalition like the one that had supported the Hartford Project. It sought support from the Greater New Haven Chamber of Commerce through Yale's Secretary, Reuben Holden, who advised the group and arranged meetings with the executive editor of the *New Haven Register*, Robert Leeney.[96] Frei's good relationship with Kingman Brewster, whom Holden advised, may have been critical in obtaining Holden's mediation and guidance for this initiative.[97]

Frei's diary reveals he was closely involved in some of this activity, attending a meeting with the Chamber of Commerce alongside Burg and Dudley on 4 January.[98] Frei was also involved in meetings on 20 and 28 February between the HRC and the Black Coalition, an umbrella group of local black organizations with whom Yale was developing a relationship at the time and which it would soon agree to help fund.[99] These meetings were probably about inner-city education. In March 1968, the two organizations issued a joint statement that in effect set out the background to Project Concern, urging a public hearing into '"glaring deficiencies" in the city's school system'.[100] It is likely, then, that Project Concern would have been discussed at the meetings Frei attended, though in this respect they were not a success, for the Black Coalition would later come out against Project Concern.[101] It is not clear from the sources whether the HRC had any meetings with the grass-roots Hill Parents Association.[102] By December 1968, another black organization, the Urban League, was represented on the Steering Committee.[103]

The steering committee gained the backing of several churches and other organizations.[104] Following meetings with suburban school superintendents in April 1968, the State Education Department then issued invitations to 13 school districts, asking them to participate in the scheme, and a series of public meetings was held in the suburbs concerned.[105] Several of these meetings saw disruptive action from opponents of Project Concern. As with opposition to the Hartford scheme, some of the arguments made by opponents were overtly racist. Others expressed opposition to desegregation in terms of fears about value for money, the loss of 'the neighbourhood school' and 'reverse busing' of white suburban children to 'ghetto schools', though the proposal did not threaten the access of suburban children to schools near them nor require them to attend schools in the city.[106] Such arguments echoed the terms of other northern anti-desegregation campaigns.[107] Some opponents organized themselves into groups, like the Concerned Citizens of North Haven, in order to win others over to their stance. Some leaders of black Civil Rights and community groups (the Black Coalition, the NAACP, the Dixwell Legal Rights Organization) also criticized the proposals at a meeting in Dixwell in June, concerned that exposing children to an environment where they could never live, away from the place they would have to work, would only add to their frustrations, though they conceded the Project was probably popular with black parents.[108]

Frei was again involved in this stage too, attending public hearings on 13 May in Cheshire and on 12 June (this may have been the Dixwell meeting), a further meeting with the Black Coalition on 15 May and a meeting with parents in Dixwell, one of the main areas where African Americans lived, on 11 July, alongside Thomas Mahan of the Hartford Project Concern.[109] In those meetings, Frei may well have espoused the argument the *Yale Daily News* attributed to supporters of Project Concern – he was one of those interviewed for the piece – that the Project was only a temporary, partial solution that needed time in order to evaluate its effectiveness.[110] Indeed, Project Concern needs to be seen alongside alternative contemporary initiatives, including local projects seeking to improve urban schools and give parents greater responsibility for how they were run, such as the Hill Neighborhood Corporation's Five Year Model Cities Plan.[111]

The programme began in September 1968 with 204 children.[112] In the end, the Boards of Education from nine suburban districts signed on to New Haven's version of Project Concern, including North Haven, where Frei and Burg were active in the local HRC branch. The Boards signed a one-year contract with the New Haven Board of Education. The arrangements were designed to minimize the impact on suburban schools. Funded by the State, Project Concern paid the suburban elementary schools the tuition cost for each student plus 5 per cent to guarantee no funds raised by local taxation would be used.[113] They also provided a supporting teacher and teaching aide for each 25 children. Children from city schools were selected by lottery and two to three were assigned per class.

Frei was still involved at this stage. His calendar books record a meeting of the Project Concern committee on 17 September, along with other HRC meetings throughout the late summer and autumn.[114] The Project Concern Steering Committee resumed meeting again in December 1968 to offer sustained support for the Project in the face of sustained, aggressive, racist suburban opposition and through forthcoming struggles in the legislature, contract renewal process and school board elections in the Spring of 1969.[115] Such opposition made it much harder for suburban schools participating in the Project to achieve its aims. In January 1969, the principal of one participating school in Milford described how the League of Concerned Citizens had heightened anxieties on the part of local people, which inhibited the full acceptance of the black children from New Haven and added considerable pressure to teachers, principals and others involved with the Project.[116] The children themselves, however, had mostly fitted in and adapted to the school's pattern. Most parents of participating children were also positive about the Project at this stage.[117] A preliminary study of participating children in Cheshire schools in the first year of the Project indicated a positive trend in their attainment of basic skills compared with the average attainment of children at the same point in a national sample.[118]

Frei's calendar book for 1968 indicates he attended this meeting of the Committee on 3 December.[119] On 21 January 1969 he was at an HRC meeting concerning a legislative proposal, which may have been legislation to counteract racial imbalance in Connecticut schools.[120] Meetings recorded in his 1969 calendar book in Wallingford for 13 February, with Bernie Burg, in Milford on 27 February, and at the Education Committee of Dudley HRC on 22 April, may well have been to do with supporting HRC branches in suburbs participating in the scheme where opposition was fierce.[121] An HRC public meeting on 7 May may also have been connected with these efforts to shore up support for the Project.

Whatever contribution these efforts by Frei and his colleague made, their immediate overall aim seems to have been achieved. The Project was renewed for a second year with 277 children, despite continued opposition.[122] There continued to be different views within black communities too about the merits of integrated versus separate schools under community control.[123] Struggles over the participation in the scheme of various white-majority suburbs, including North Haven, continued in the next school year and on into the mid-1970s at least, indicating that the Project continued for at least that long. I have not been able to trace clear evidence for Frei's involvement beyond 1969, however.[124]

Fair housing

Frei may also have been involved in efforts to address, or at least mitigate the effects of the problem that underlay educational segregation in New Haven, namely segregated housing, poor access to housing for minorities and discrimination against them in the housing market. As we have seen, this issue was one of the priorities on which the New Haven HRC campaigned and sought to provide practical assistance, as did other groups and grass-roots organizations.[125] One of Frei's Yale colleagues told me that Frei had been active, along with a maverick estate agent, in an organization in North Haven that sought to help people of colour buy homes in the town.[126] That claim is quite plausible because Frei clearly worked closely with someone who fits that description, who, with Frei, was closely involved with an organization that also fits the bill, and who was a leading local figure in trying to help minority families buy suburban homes: Bernard Burg.

Burg was, as we have seen, 'particularly active' in the New Haven Project Concern Steering Committee alongside Frei.[127] Indeed, the December 1968 newsletter of the New Haven HRC describes him as heading it up.[128] He had been a member of the North Haven HRC for several years by this point, for the affiliation is mentioned in news reports dating back to 1964.[129] Opponents of Project Concern had made much of the fact that Burg had been subpoenaed by the House Committee on Un-American Activities and accused of being a Communist, back in 1956 (a fact that did not seem to have bothered Frei or others on the Steering Committee).[130] The *Yale Daily News* described him as 'intense, outspoken'.[131]

Burg was also a real estate broker and at least four contemporary reports describe him in those terms in the context of fair housing. The first of these, from February 1968, also links his interest in fair housing to his role in the North Haven HRC and his Jewish faith. When he was slated to participate in a panel on fair housing for Race Relations Sunday at First Congregation Church, Cheshire, he was announced in *The Morning Record* as 'president of the North Haven Human Relations Council, real estate broker and a member of the Congregation Mishkan Israel', a local Reform Jewish community.[132] In the second, about a talk on fair housing he was to give to women voters in North Branford in November 1968, the *New Haven Register* describes him as the director of 'the Connecticut Fair Housing Center'.[133] The third, from December 1968, links his estate agent experience to a specific fair housing initiative. In his *Yale Daily News* report on Project Concern, Alan Boles describes Burg as 'a former North Haven realtor who now heads a project to help blacks finance suburban homes'.[134]

That project is identified by the fourth report as the Connecticut Housing Investment Fund (CHIF), a non-profit private organization founded in Hartford. It had opened an office in New Haven in the summer of 1968, supported by a grant from the Ford Foundation and run by Burg (which may be what the *New Haven Register* was referring to).[135] CHIF was helping black and Puerto Rican families buy homes in the suburbs of New Haven by lending them funds for down payments, helping them secure mortgages with local banks, work out how to manage repayments alongside other financial commitments and find second jobs. Burg also sought to avoid blockbusting, the practice of estate agents helping African Americans buy homes in all-white neighbourhoods in order to provoke white flight and a collapse in house prices, so as to profit from buying houses at low prices and selling them on to African American families, desperate for housing, at inflated prices.[136] It was a practice the New Haven HRC sought to combat.[137] To minimize the risk of opening the way for such practices, Burg would help no more than one black family move into any white-majority block.[138] He was prepared to circumvent the racism of sellers and brokers by getting a white person to buy a house and sell it on to a black purchaser.[139]

Burg clearly also sought to link his work for CHIF with HRC branches in the New Haven area and to encourage them to pursue activities and advocate for practices and policies. In his capacity as Director of the New Haven CHIF, he spoke at a meeting of the Cheshire HRC in September 1969, to urge them to actively recruit minority groups to live in the town, so that they would be made to feel more welcome there.[140] He also suggested that the town 'ask the Community Development Agency to help finance the purchase of land for low and moderate income housing in town', which could be bought by black families, with low interest rate mortgages made available under recent federal housing legislation, with the help of loans from CHIF. In the context of a controversy over advice allegedly given by a state official to local government board members to use priority lists based on residency in order to exclude people from out of town, Burg called on the Cheshire HRC to give CHIF its lists of property available to members of ethnic minorities.

There are indications that the North Haven HRC, of which Burg was a member, was active on similar lines at this time. By October 1968, it had a hospitality committee to welcome minority group members to the community.[141] In December 1969, it approved resolutions to ask local government board members 'to establish a housing authority and to implement initial steps toward the establishment of a Community Development Action Plan (CDAP)'.[142] A few days later, it hosted a discussion about housing needs in North Haven, which included the prospects for black people moving into the town and participating in its life, though North Haven's political leaders, like those of other suburbs, resisted proposals like the one Burg had made in Cheshire.[143]

It seems very likely, then, that the North Haven HRC, to which Burg belonged, may have worked with Burg's New Haven CHIF office to help people from minorities to buy homes in the town and join the local community as part of a wider strategy to make more affordable homes available there to minoritized people wishing to move out of the segregated, red-lined and under-resourced neighbourhoods of the city. As an active member of the North Haven HRC, it would be quite plausible that Frei would have been involved in such activity. There are other pointers to the plausibility of his working closely with Burg on such an initiative. For one thing, the two met several times over several years in addition to any meetings of the New Haven HRC or North Haven HRC they both attended (some of which were hosted at Burg's home) and apparently in addition also to Project Concern Steering Committee meetings.[144] They met especially frequently in the summer and early autumn of 1969, when Burg's CHIF office was getting underway.[145] Some other meetings in Frei's calendar books suggest a practical interest in housing, moreover. Frei visited the building company Arbor Homes in New Haven on 12 November 1965, and Frei and Burg met with Arbor Homes at Burg's office on 2 May 1968.[146] On 22 October 1969, he visited a 'development', presumably a housing development, in Woodbridge. Though I have found no evidence yet to link Frei directly to Burg's work on housing, there is enough circumstantial evidence to support the credibility of his colleague's recollections.

Conclusion

The period from Frei's return to Yale to his tenure as Master of Ezra Stiles is, to date, the most richly documented in terms of his political activities beyond his teaching and research. It is, however, only a very partial record and gives us limited insight into the local and institutional initiatives, discussions and struggles Frei was part of, and an even more limited glimpse of his part in them. They show a deep commitment to Yale and its students, which was expressed in participation in its committees but also in efforts to transform the make-up of its student body, to change its ethos and shift the way power was distributed within it, as well as in leading and helping to support a community and its members. They gesture too at profound concerns about the conduct of the Vietnam War. They also indicate a serious, close involvement with at least one but probably two sustained attempts to promote a degree of immediate integration of suburban schools and neighbourhoods – and opportunity for inner-city minority children and households – in the New Haven area, within larger, long-term strategies for change. Both were at once principled, anti-racist and carefully calibrated, pragmatic projects that aimed to increase the opportunities available to black people in the city; which were admitted to have their problems but which Frei, Burg and those they worked with must have judged were on balance worth the risks and the vicious opposition they provoked.

My purpose in painting this picture of Frei's politics in this period is not to highlight Frei as an extraordinary figure in these stories. As the account I have given indicates, many students and faculty were involved in the transformations at Yale, many more prominently than Frei, and many were involved (and some more intensively involved) in a whole range of Civil Rights initiatives, including those in which Frei played his part. Rather, by shedding some light on these aspects of Frei's life I hope to better contextualize his mature theological project, to which I turn in the next two chapters.

Notes

1 See Mike Higton, *Christ, Providence and History: Hans W. Frei's Public Theology* (London: T & T Clark, 2004), p. 17. On Frei becoming an Anglican, see J. Woolverton, 'Hans W. Frei in context: a theological and historical memoir', *Anglican Theological Review* 79:3 (1997), pp. 377–8. Woolverton says Frei was ordained in the Episcopal Church in 1947 but must have misremembered, as Frei was ordained deacon in Crawfordsville, Indiana, on Saturday 17 November 1951 ('Wabash professor to become deacon', *The Indianapolis Star*, Saturday 17 November 1951, p. 12).

2 Higton, *Christ, Providence and History*, pp. 17–18; 'Yale adds four', *The Bridgeport Post*, 25 March 1957, p. 16.

3 Interview with Professor David Gouwens about Hans W. Frei, 6 March 2015.

4 Interview with one of Frei's Yale colleagues, 20 February 2015. This ethos is reflected in many of Frei's letters of recommendation for his graduate students in his papers at Yale Divinity School.

5 Alexander E. Sharp, 'Christianity: exhausted but not shrinking', *Yale Daily News*, 1 March 1963, p. 5.

6 Sharp, 'Christianity: exhausted but not shrinking'.

7 Dan A. Oren, *Joining the Club: A History of Jews and Yale* (2nd edn) (New Haven, CT and London: Yale University Press, 2000), pp. 172–80.

8 Oren, *Joining the Club*, pp. 178–9; Geoffrey Kabaservice, 'The birth of a new institution: how two Yale presidents and their admissions directors tore up the "old blueprint" to create a modern Yale', *Yale Alumni Magazine* (December 1999), http://archives.yalealumnimagazine.com/issues/99_12/admissions.html, accessed 21.02.22.

9 Oren, *Joining the Club*, p. 181; Kabaservice, 'The birth of a new institution'.

10 Oren, *Joining the Club*, pp. 181–216.

11 Kabaservice, 'The birth of a new institution'.

12 Women had been admitted to Yale's School of the Fine Arts since its opening in 1869, to its Graduate School from 1892, to its School of Medicine from 1916, to its Law School from 1919, to its (then all-female) School of Nursing and to its Drama School from their opening in 1923 and to its Divinity School from 1932 (https://celebratewomen.yale.edu/history/timeline-women-yale, accessed 21.02.22). For the story of the lengthy process by which Yale came to the decision to become co-educational, see Geoffrey Kabaservice, *The Guardians: Kingman Brewster, his Circle, and the Rise of the Liberal Establishment* (New York: Henry Holt & Company, LLC, 2004), pp. 293–8, 323–4, 366–9.

13 Kabaservice, *The Guardians*, pp. 285–6, 349–55, 375–8, 384–8. See also 'Students may serve on faculty committees', *Yale Daily News*, 18 September 1968, pp. 1, 6, and 'Faculty admits students to executive committee', *Yale Daily News*, 4 October 1968, p. 1.

14 'Faculty coalition for a new university', 22 April 1969 (Yale Divinity School Archive (YDS) 83 V 33-412). My account of the Student Coalition is drawn from Kabaservice, *The Guardians*, pp. 375–87.

15 'Proposal for a university commission of governance', YDS 83 V 33-412. That the proposal was a joint one between the Student and Faculty Coalitions is clear from this report: Stuart Rosow, 'Coalition meets on Yale plan', *Yale Daily News*, 28 April 1969, p. 4.

16 See George Kanmar, '1000 meet on governance; seek open decision making', *Yale Daily News*, 6 May 1969, p. 1; Charles R. Sprague, 'Brewster sets commission on governance, discipline', *Yale Daily News*, 4 November 1969, p. 1; Charles Cole, 'Governance survey reveals deep interest in curriculum', *Yale Daily News*, 25 January 1971, p. 1; D. H. Black, 'Group completes governance study', *Yale Daily News*, 3 March 1971, p. 1; John Geesman, 'Corporation votes to shorten length of trustees' term', *Yale Daily News*, 6 April 1971, p. 1; D. H. Black, 'Governance commission submits proposals', *Yale Daily News*, 30 June 1971, pp. 7, 11; Matt Coles, 'Faculty approves board for university discipline', *Yale Daily News*, 12 November 1971, p. 1; 'Taylor announces new council on Yale planning and priorities', *Yale Daily News*, 10 February 1972, p. 1.

17 Judith Plaskow took his module on Theological Hermeneutics as a graduate student and remembered Frei as seeking to be supportive of women (see her interview with the editors in Judith Plaskow, *Feminism, Theology and Justice*, Hava Tirosh-Samuelson and Aaron W. Hughes (eds) (Leiden and Boston, MA: Brill, 2014), p. 97. Wayne Meeks recalls that he and Frei both celebrated the admis-

sion of women to Yale (Transcript of Interview with Professor Wayne A. Meeks about Hans W. Frei, 6 November 2015). See also Frei's comments supportive of an increase in the number of women at the college as acting master of Silliman College in the context of plans to increase admissions of women at Yale College ('Yale plans increase in freshman women', *Yale Daily News*, 16 April 1971, p. 1).

18 See Brad Graham, 'Taylor expects sex ratio study', *Yale Daily News*, 7 December 1971, p. 1. Frei asked to join some other members of the Admissions Committee who met with the provost to discuss their request for the quota system to be reviewed and his reported comments indicate he was in sympathy with that request.

19 Brad Graham, 'Staff asks for more aid', *Yale Daily News*, 11 April 1972, p. 1.

20 Kabaservice, *The Guardians*, p. 354.

21 Kabaservice, *The Guardians*, pp. 354–5.

22 'Frei to succeed Giamatti in Ezra Stiles mastership', *Yale Daily News* 136, 10 May 1972.

23 Copy of Resolution of President and Fellows of Yale University to Frei, appointing Frei, on the President's recommendation, as Chairman of Council of Masters – effective 1 July 1975 for three years (YDS 76 I 5-114).

24 Interview with one of Frei's Yale colleagues, 20 February 2015. David Gouwens recalls being told that Frei saw Stiles as his parish (Interview with Professor David Gouwens, 6 March 2015).

25 Frei's letter to William Clebsch, 4 December 1979 (YDS 76 I 1-15).

26 In his letter to Clebsch, Frei praises Albert J. Raboteau (the historian of African American religion) for exhibiting these qualities while a residential fellow at Stiles.

27 On Yale and the Civil Rights movement, see Warren Goldstein, *William Sloane Coffin Jr.: A Holy Impatience* (New Haven, CT and London: Yale University Press, 2004), pp. 115–22, 137–40, and Kabaservice, *The Guardians*, pp. 210, 229, 347–8.

28 See Kabaservice, *The Guardians*, pp. 221–2, 233–6, 255–6, 298–304, 317–20, 375–8, 389–90, 393.

29 'An open letter to the President of the United States', *Yale Daily News*, 7 April 1965, p. 2; Dennis T. Jaffe, 'Faculty criticizes US in Vietnam conflict', *Yale Daily News*, 7 April 1965, p. 1.

30 Kabaservice, *The Guardians*, p. 301.

31 'Advertisement', *Yale Daily News*, 23 February 1968, p. 3; see also Fred P. Graham, 'Spock and Coffin indicted for activity against draft', *New York Times*, 6 January 1968, p. 1.

32 'Advertisement', *Yale Daily News*, 23 February 1968, p. 3.

33 'Statement of 29 faculty on antiwar activities', *Yale Daily News*, 10 November 1969, p. 2. The first moratorium was in October 1969.

34 'City group leads lobby effort', *Yale Daily News*, 15 May 1972, p. 1.

35 My account here is drawn from Kabaservice in *The Guardians*, pp. 1–9, 402–12, and from Brewster's then assistant, Henry 'Sam' Chauncey, and then student (and member of the Black Student Alliance at Yale), Henry Louis Gates Jr, in *May Day at Yale, 1970: Recollections. The Trial of Bobby Seale and the Black Panthers* (Westport, CT: Prospecta Press, 2016). See also Goldstein, *William Sloane Coffin Jr.*, pp. 252–8. Kabaservice and Chancey tell the story from the Yale administration's perspective.

36 Interview with Professor Wayne A. Meeks, 6 November 2015.

37 Kabaservice, *The Guardians*, pp. 327–33.

38 See Alan Astrow, 'PU invites Shockley, Innis to meet in March debate', *Yale Daily News*, 22 January 1974, p. 1; 'Debate opposition may force PU vote', *Yale Daily News*, 6 February 1974, p. 1; Debbie Cohen and Alan Astrow, 'PU ponders proposed Shockley-Innis debate', *Yale Daily News*, 21 January 1974, pp. 1, 4.

39 On Shockley, see the Southern Poverty Law Center's profile: https://www.splcenter.org/fighting-hate/extremist-files/individual/william-shockley (accessed 13.03.2022). On Rushton, see Robert D. McFadden, 'William Rusher, champion of conservatism, dies at 87', *New York Times*, 19 April 2011 (https://www.nytimes.com/2011/04/19/us/politics/19rusher.html, accessed 13.03.2022).

40 See Alan Astrow, 'PU invites Shockley, Innis to meet in March debate; "Racist, hypocritical and naïve", statement of leaders of black campus groups', *Yale Daily News*, 28 January 1974, p. 2; 'Shockley v. Innis: letters and statements Despierta Boricua', *Yale Daily News*, 30 January 1974, p. 2; 'Shockley v. Innis: letters and statements', *Yale Daily News*, 30 January 1974, pp. 2–3; 'MEChA statement', *Yale Daily News*, 6 February 1974, p. 2; 'Third World Coalition to Disinvite Shockley and Innis, "Thank You"', *Yale Daily News*, 18 February 1974, p. 3.

41 Harvey Himel, 'Shockley saga persists, twists PU disinvites Shockley, debate here still possible', *Yale Daily News*, 18 February 1974, pp. 1, 5; 'Brewster statement', *Yale Daily News*, 18 February 1974, p. 1; 'Text of statement', *Yale Daily News*, 19 February 1974, p. 1; 'L&V drops debate plan, opts for forum instead', *Yale Daily News*, 20 February 1974, p. 1; 'Statement of Lux et Veritas', *Yale Daily News*, 20 February 1974, p. 4; Daniel Rubrock, 'Calliopeans retract invitation to debate', *Yale Daily News*, 8 March 1974, p. 1. The term 'Third World' is taken from the reports of protestors' views in these sources. Its contemporary connotations for these students were probably anti-colonial and revolutionary. For background to the term, see Lilian Calles Barger, *The World Come of Age: An Intellectual History of Liberation Theology* (New York: Oxford University Press, 2018), pp. 24–5.

42 Marc Margolius, 'YAF revives Shockley for rescheduled debate', *Yale Daily News*, 5 April 1974, p. 1.

43 See Charlie Homer, 'Yale will suspend debate disrupters', *Yale Daily News*, 15 April 1974, p. 1; Alan Astrow, Lloyd Grove and Dan Rubock, 'Chauncey call for order fails to quell disruption', *Yale Daily News*, 16 April 1974, p. 1.

44 'Suspensions end affair', *Yale Daily News*, 1 July 1974, pp. 12, 21.

45 Pam King, 'Petitions readmit Shockley protest', *Yale Daily News*, 5 September 1974, p. 13; Pam King, 'Brewster charges expression group', *Yale Daily News*, 20 September 1974, p. 1.

46 'Report of the Committee on Freedom of Expression at Yale' (December 1974), https://yalecollege.yale.edu/get-know-yale-college/office-dean/reports/report-committee-freedom-expression-yale (accessed 15.03.2022).

47 See for example, Tom Alpert and Dave Scobey, 'Why free speech', *Yale Daily News*, 21 January 1975, p. 2.

48 Peter C. Neger, 'YAF reinvites Shockley, Rusher', *Yale Daily News*, 24 March 1975, p. 1.

49 A *Yale Daily News* editorial called for a boycott ('Not Again', 25 March 1975, p. 2), as did a coalition of minority ethnic, Third World, radical and anti-racist student groups (John Tabor, 'Group forms at meeting on Shockley boycott plan', *Yale Daily News*, 31 March 1975, p. 1). The 17 April edition of the *Yale*

Daily News carried appeals to boycott (and peacefully protest) in its editorial ('Boy-cott', p. 2) and a number of other pieces and reports (e.g. Mindy Beck, 'Shockley protestors urge: stay away', p. 1; Tom Alpert and Dave Scobey, 'Stay home' p. 2). See also 'Students organize Shockley protests', *Yale Daily News*, 28 March 1975, p. 1; Sam Overstreet, 'Shofar echoes protest', *Yale Daily News*, 31 March 1975, p. 1.

50 'Masters' view', *Yale Daily News*, 17 April 1975, p. 1.

51 It is very likely, however, that Frei himself had to attend. Brewster, despite protests, requested masters to do so. The *Yale Daily News* reported that 10 out of 12 heeded the request though most appeared disinterested and one read a book (Mindy Beck, 'Politeness, police mark exchange', *Yale Daily News*, 18 April 1975, p. 1). Frei is not among the two masters named in another piece who did not attend (John Tabor and Marie Lefton, 'Some choose silence, prayer; Battell forum explores racism', *Yale Daily News*, 18 April 1975, p. 11).

52 My account here is drawn from Douglas Rae, *City: Urbanism and its End* (New Haven, CT and London: Yale University Press, 2003).

53 Rae, *City*, p. 255.

54 My account here is drawn both from Rae, *City*, pp. 264–7, and Christopher Bonastia, *Knocking on the Door: The Federal Government's Attempt to Desegregate the Suburbs* (Princeton, NJ: Princeton University Press, 2006), especially pp. 60–3.

55 See Rae, *City*, pp. 264–74.

56 Walter Duda, 'Area housing shortage worsening, study finds', *New Haven Register*, 25 February 1970, p. 1.

57 Rae, *City*, p. 279. For the account reflected here, see Rae, *City*, pp. 275–82. This argument is borne out in the more detailed analysis of one public housing project in Adam Wolkoff, 'Creating a suburban ghetto: public housing at New Haven's West Rock, 1945–1979', *Connecticut History Review* 45:1 (2006), pp. 56–93.

58 Rae, *City*, pp. 318–42.

59 Rae, *City*, pp. 342–3.

60 Bonastia, *Knocking on the Door*, p. 54.

61 Frei lists his home address at 98 Knollwood Road, Hamden, Connecticut in his 1959 Calendar book (YDS 76 VI 27). In his 1962 calendar book, the address is 1 Cooper Road, North Haven. On Geraldine's parents, George and Ethel, see the obituary for Ethel Frost Nye in the *North Haven Post*, 23 July 1986, p. 16.

62 Its first newsletter, which came out in November 1957, announced this new name ('Council has New Name, New Program', *Human Relations Council Newsletter* 1:1 (November 1957), p. 1 (New Haven Memorial Library MSS 79 Box III Folders D and F)). Its newsletter from June 1963 reported on its thirteenth annual dinner, held in May of that year ('Monsignor addresses annual dinner', *The New Haven Human Relations Council Newsletter* IX:3 (June 1963), p. 1 (New Haven Memorial Library MSS 79 Box III Folders D and F)), which suggests that by 1951 the Council was sufficiently well organized and funded to hold an annual dinner.

63 On the Hill Neighborhood Corporation and the Junta for Progressive Action, see *El Boricua: The Puerto Rican Community in Bridgeport and New Haven. A Report of the Connecticut State Advisory Committee to the United States Commission on Civil Rights* (January 1973). On the Hill Parents Association, the Black Coalition and the Panthers, see Yohuru Williams, *Black Politics/White Power: Civil Rights, Black Power, and the Black Panthers in New Haven* (Oxford: Blackwell, 2008).

64 One indication of the closeness of the relationship: the Council's Newsletter in January 1964 welcomed Donald Wendell as its Executive Director, who was previously housing director for the mayor's urban renewal agency, CPI, and whose post was funded by the CPI and the New Haven Foundation. See 'New Executive Director welcomed', *The New Haven Human Relations Council Newsletter* X:2 (January 1964), p. 1 (New Haven Memorial Library MSS 79 Box III Folders D and F). The story of the relationship between the NAACP and CORE and Mayor Lee's administration is told in Williams, *Black Politics/White Power*, pp. 21–67.

65 See Frei's calendar books for the years 1965–71 (YDS 76 VI 27).

66 'Council has new name, new program', p. 1.

67 'Make dignity a reality', *The New Haven Human Relations Council Newsletter* VIII:6 (June 1962), p. 2 (New Haven Memorial Library MSS 79 Box III Folders D and F).

68 'HRC holds special meeting on housing for large families', *Human Relations Council Newsletter* 1:1 (November 1957), pp. 2–3; 'Better housing for all a major goal', *Human Relations Council Newsletter*, II:1 (April 1958), p. 2.

69 'Better housing for all a major goal', pp. 2–3; 'Housing Committee Report', *The New Haven Human Relations Council Newsletter* VIII:6 (June 1962), p. 2; 'Bills supported', *Human Relations Council of Greater New Haven Newsletter* 17:3 (May 1967), p. 2 (New Haven Memorial Library MSS 79 Box III Folders D and F).

70 John H. Lahr, 'Housing discrimination regulations amended. Rally, march to stress community importance', *Yale Daily News* 83:8, 27 September 1961, p. 1; 'Hundred rally for equality in housing', *Yale Daily News* 83:11, 2 October 1961, p. 1; 'Housing Committee Report' from *The New Haven Human Relations Council Newsletter* VIII:5 (April 1962), p. 1 (New Haven Memorial Library MSS 79 Box III Folders D and F); 'Housing Committee Report on activities and plans', *The New Haven Human Relations Council Newsletter* X:1 (November 1963), p. 2.

71 'Housing Committee Report', *The New Haven Human Relations Council Newsletter* VIII:5 (April 1962), p. 1; 'Housing Committee Report on activities and plans', p. 2; 'Ross realty discrimination demonstrated in courts & at their door', *New Haven Human Relations Council Newsletter* (December 1968), p. 3 (New Haven Memorial Library MSS 79 Box III Folders D and F).

72 'Integration and property values', *The New Haven Human Relations Council Newsletter* IX:3 (June 1963), p. 6.

73 There is an announcement of such a clinic to be held in the Bethel AME church in the Dixwell areas in 'Housing Committee Report on activities and plans', p. 2.

74 'Housing Committee Report on activities', *The New Haven Human Relations Council Newsletter* X:2 (January 1964), p. 2.

75 'Housing Committee Report on activities and plans', p. 2; 'Housing opportunities made equal newsletter #54', 12 December 1963 (New Haven Memorial Library MSS 79 Box III Folders D and F); 'Housing Committee Reports on activities', p. 2.

76 'Make dignity a reality', p. 2. See also the 'Editorial' in the same issue and on the same page. The editorial refers to *Taylor vs. Board of Education of the City School District of City of New Rochelle*, 31 May 1961.

77 William G. Buss, 'New Haven (affirmative integration: studies of efforts to

overcome de facto segregation in the public schools)', *Law & Society Review* 2:1 (1967), p. 33.

78 'Education Committee works to integrate schools', *The New Haven Human Relations Council Newsletter* X:1 (November 1963), p. 5 (New Haven Memorial Library MSS 79 Box III Folders D and F).

79 Buss, 'New Haven', p. 34.

80 'Education Committee works to integrate schools', p. 5.

81 Buss, 'New Haven', p. 36.

82 Buss, 'New Haven', p. 36. It paired the seventh and eighth grades at two schools, presumably so that an integrated seventh grade was taught at one school, and an integrated eighth grade at the other, after the model of integration at Princeton in 1948 (the 'Princeton Plan'), and withdrew Fair Haven from the plan. In the event, the pairing arrangement was quickly terminated when the black-majority school was made into an elementary school. See Alan Boles, 'City busing ghetto students', *Yale Daily News* 90:57, 5 December 1968, p. 3.

83 'Disadvantaged Children need funds, hearing told', *The Bridgeport Post*, 25 February 1967, p. 4.

84 There is some support for this hypothesis from an article in the *Yale Daily News* which claimed that the benefits of the scheme had not been realized because black and Puerto Rican children represented over 60 per cent of the elementary school population. See Boles, 'City busing ghetto students', p. 3.

85 Thomas W. Mahan, *Project Concern – 1966–1968: A Report on the Effectiveness of Suburban School Placement for Inner-City Youth. Hartford Public Schools* (Hartford, CT: August 1968), p. 7. Mahan was the director of Project Concern in Hartford.

86 Mahan, *Project Concern – 1966–1968*, pp. 7, 11–12.

87 Mahan, *Project Concern – 1966–1968*, p. 8.

88 Mahan, *Project Concern – 1966–1968*, pp. 8–9.

89 Mahan, *Project Concern – 1966–1968*, p. 9.

90 See Matthew F. Delmont, *Why Busing Failed: Race, Media, and the National Resistance to School Desegregation* (Oakland, CA: University of California Press, 2016), pp. 23–92.

91 Mahan, *Project Concern – 1966–1968*, p. 10.

92 At a hearing of the Education Committee of the Connecticut General Assembly in February 1967, Russell Becker representing the North Haven HRC expressed his support for a bill that would extend the Project Concern model. See 'Disadvantaged children need funds, hearing told', p. 4.

93 Boles, 'City busing ghetto students', p. 3.

94 Alan Boles identifies Dudley as chairman of the New Haven High School Mathematics Department in 'City busing ghetto students', p. 3.

95 See Alan Boles, 'Two at Yale urge busing of Negro pupils to suburbs', *Yale Daily News*, 28 September 1966, p. 7.

96 Boles, 'City busing ghetto students', p. 3.

97 In an interview with me, Margaret Farley recalled that at the time she joined the Yale faculty in 1971, Frei was a good friend of Brewster (interview with Margaret Farley, 13 March 2015).

98 Calendar book for 1968 (YDS 76 VI 27).

99 In the aftermath of the assassination of Martin Luther King Jr, Brewster announced, in a 'Memorandum to the Yale community' on 9 April 1968, the

setting up of a Yale Council on Community Affairs, which would help coordinate local initiatives and support them in planning and fundraising. He identified the Black Coalition in particular as a group showing the promise of being able to offer comprehensive representation of black groups, organizations and neighbourhoods and a commitment to 'local, neighborhood self-development', in which Yale was prepared to put its faith and which it was willing to provide with planning funds (from Sidney Ahlstrom's papers YDS 83 I 2-22).

100 'Public hearing on New Haven schools urged', *The Bridgeport Telegram*, 5 March 1968, p. 25.

101 Boles, 'City busing ghetto students', p. 3.

102 Yohuru Williams argues that the Black Coalition's relationship with Yale led to it rising to the forefront of black Civil Rights organizations in New Haven in 1968 at the expense of the more radical, grass-roots organization, the Hill Parents Association, which had been receiving funding from the city (Williams, *Black Politics/White Power*, pp. 92–3).

103 'More on Project Concern', *New Haven Human Relations Council Newsletter* (December 1968), p. 3.

104 Boles, 'City busing ghetto students', p. 3.

105 The *Yale Daily News* report (Boles, 'City busing ghetto students', p. 3) says the New Haven Board of Education issued the letters; another more contemporary report says it was Alexander Plante, the executive director of the State office of programme development ('School board to consider Project Concern contract', *The Morning Record*, 22 April 1968, p. 10). The latter matches the procedure in the Hartford Project Concern and seems more likely.

106 Boles, 'City busing ghetto students', p. 3.

107 In particular, the arguments about busing and the appeal to neighbourhood schools echoed prominent opposition campaigns covered in the media. See Delmont, *Why Busing Failed*. It is notable that the *Yale Daily News Article* frames the project in terms of busing rather than desegregation, which reflects the wider media trend analysed by Delmont.

108 In 'City busing ghetto students', Alan Boles mentions several speakers at a meeting in Dixwell in June 1968, including the chair of the Black Coalition, Henry Parker, the leader of the local branch of the NAACP, Courtland Wilson, and Joseph Harris of the Dixwell Legal Rights Association whose views are summarized above. Wilson was one of those who had previously proposed a similar scheme.

109 Calendar book for 1968 (YDS 76 VI 27).

110 Boles, 'City busing ghetto students', p. 3.

111 See 'Parent involvement one goal of model cities', *New Haven Register*, 12 September 1969, pp. 1, 6, and 'HNC praises school board for plan effort', *New Haven Register*, 13 September 1969, p. 34.

112 Boles, 'City busing ghetto students', p. 1.

113 See Boles, 'City busing ghetto students', p. 3, and 'School board to consider Project Concern contract', p. 10.

114 Calendar book for 1968 (YDS 76 VI 27).

115 'More on Project Concern', New Haven Human Relations Council Newsletter (December 1968), pp. 3–4. Bernard Burg described the opposition's motive as racism, noting that its tactics were confined to the one area of school policy where black children were involved. Demands for referenda on future agreements to participate in the project (which opponents described as 'busing agreements')

were among opponents' main tactics along with petitions to recall Board of Education members who voted for such agreements: see, for example, James Rose, 'Citizens May Ask for Referendum Despite Vote "Defeat"', *New Haven Register*, 22 November 1968.

116 James Rose, 'Busing referendum favored by school board', *New Haven Register*, 23 Jan 1969.

117 'Parents hail busing result, want project another year', *New Haven Register*, 30 January 1969.

118 Stephen August, Superintendent of Schools and Marily Levy, Research Specialist, *Project Concern in Cheshire: A Preliminary Report* (Department of Education, Cheshire, January 1970).

119 YDS 76 VI 27.

120 Frei's calendar book for 1969 (YDS 76 VI 27). An editorial for the *New Haven Register*, 6 September 1969, comments on powers to correct racial imbalance in schools in the state, which had been granted the State Board of Education by the state legislature. The close cooperation between the HRC and state education officials over Project Concern and their common concern about segregated schooling makes this legislation a plausible candidate for what the New Haven HRC was proposing and which it discussed on 21 January 1969.

121 Both suburbs are named as participating in Project Concern by Boles in 'City busing ghetto students', p. 1; both are also among the suburbs where Boles reports organized resistance to the Project on page 3 of his report. The Wallingford HRC had also been struggling and another member of the North Haven HRC, Ed Dudley, had attended a meeting in October 1968 to advise its members, perhaps setting a precedent for Frei's visit ('Human Relations Council enthusiasm has waned', *The Morning Record*, 5 October 1968, p. 6).

122 'Cheshire adding 23 pupils from Project Concern', *New Haven Register*, 7 September 1969, p. 9; 'Project Concern parents to discuss improvements', *New Haven Register*, 1 December 1969, p. 48.

123 See, for example, Babs Putzel, 'Integration, separation of blacks, whites argued', *New Haven Register*, 20 November 1969, p. 64. Patrick Coggins of the Hill Health Center favoured separation, Alfred Baker Lewis of the NAACP favoured integration.

124 See for example, Babs Putzel, 'Busing plan in Bethany discontinued', *New Haven Register*, 8 April 1970, p. 1; '500 attend busing panel in Wilton', *The Bridgeport Post*, 17 April 1970, p. 12; 'Busing plan for Milford schools out', *New Haven Register*, 23 April 1970, p. 50; 'Woodbridge will continue Project Concern', *New Haven Register*, 28 April 1970, p. 12; 'Reconsideration sought for Project Concern', *The Morning Record*, 13 April 1976, p. 18; 'Group opposes Project Concern', *North Haven Post*, 13 April 1977, p. 9.

125 For example, the Hill Housing Development Corporation, established by the Hill Neighborhood Corporation, began a programme to develop community and individual home ownership in the Hill area by buying houses and employing and training neighbourhood residents to repair them ('Hill Housing Unit has purchased two dwellings', *New Haven Register*, 6 February 1970, p. 34).

126 Interview, 20 February 2015.

127 Boles, 'City busing ghetto students', p. 3.

128 'More on Project Concern', *New Haven Human Relations Council Newsletter* (December 1968), p. 3.

129 A *North Haven Post* article from 12 November 1964 described him as its steering committee chairman ('Posts of the past', *North Haven Post*, 13 November 1974, p. 20). The link is also made in an article about the evacuation of residents of the Hill area of New Haven to suburban homes during the riots of August 1967: 'Bernard Burg of the North Haven Human Relations association placed 90 people in homes around that area' ('Milford Chapel shelters 50 Elm City evacuees', *The Bridgeport Post*, 23 August 1967, p. 1).

130 Boles, 'City busing ghetto students', p. 3. The hearing was reported in local newspapers at the time. See for example, '11 witnesses mum on red affiliations', *Hartford Courant*, 27 September 1956, pp. 1, 6.

131 Boles, 'City busing ghetto students', p. 3.

132 'Dr Kelsey to moderate fair housing discussion', *The Morning Record*, 9 February 1968, p. 18.

133 'Women voters plan fair housing talk in North Branford', *New Haven Register*, 18 November 1968.

134 Boles, 'City busing ghetto students', p. 3.

135 Robert Kilpatrick, 'Minority families helped to own suburban homes', *New Haven Register*, 8 December 1968. Burg is mentioned as the New Haven director of CHIF in 'Human Relations Council sets series of public programs', *New Haven Register*, 5 September 1969, p. 37.

136 Brent Gespaire, 'Blockbusting', https://www.blackpast.org/african-ameri can-history/blockbusting (accessed 13.04.2022).

137 See 'Housing Committee Report', *The New Haven Human Relations Council Newsletter* VIII:6 (June 1962), p. 2, which describes how a committee from one locale had met to plan how to deal with realtors pressurizing white homeowners to sell their property to black people, presumably to initiate blockbusting in the area.

138 Kilpatrick, 'Minority families helped to own suburban homes'.

139 'No welcome mat in Cheshire, minority housing expert says', *New Haven Register*, 11 September 1969, p. 39.

140 'No welcome mat in Cheshire, minority housing expert says'.

141 'Human Relations Council Enthusiasm has waned', *The Morning Record*, 5 October 1968, p. 6.

142 'Posts of the past', *North Haven Post*, 11 December 1974, p. 20.

143 On the meeting, see Eugene Seder, 'Housing shortage in North Haven acute: women voters report', *New Haven Register*, 21 December 1969, 8B. On contemporary resistance in North Haven to demands for low- and moderate-income housing, see, for example, '3 selectmen cool on helping New Haven housing problem', *New Haven Register*, 10 April 1970, and 'Overbrook Association blasts town's veto of public housing', *New Haven Register*, 29 April 1970, p. 20.

144 See Frei's calendar books for 1965–69 (YDS 76 VI 27), which have entries for 'Bernie Burg' or 'Bernard Burg' from July 1965. The HRC Executive Committee met at Burg's home on 7 September 1967, according to Frei's calendar book for that year, for example, and the 'HRC' met there on 28 November.

145 Frei's calendar book for 1969 shows meetings with Burg for 4 June, 24 June, 26 June, 5 September and 2 October.

146 Calendar books for 1965 and 1968.

2

The Presence of Christ in
Post-liberal Theology

In 1966, in the midst of his teaching at Yale and his developing human
relations activism in the New Haven area, and alongside his research in
the history of modern Christology, Frei published a Christological essay,
'Theological reflections on the accounts of Jesus' death and resurrection'.[1] The following year he published 'The mystery of the presence of
Jesus Christ' in two instalments, the first of which was a longer version
of his 1966 article and the second a reflection on the presence of Christ
in church and history.[2] These he would lightly edit and republish in
1975, with a new introduction and an epilogue, as *The Identity of Jesus
Christ*, his fullest constructive theological statement.[3] Here, in dialogue
with contemporary debates about theological method and theological
interpretation of the New Testament in modernity, Frei set out a bold
proposal for thinking about who Jesus Christ is and how he is present,
culminating in a doctrine of providence with a political edge.

To understand the theology of the essays and its contemporary significance, however, we need not only to bear in mind Frei's background,
doctorate and other early writings, as others have shown, or the context
of his involvement in the transformation of Yale and in human relations
activism in Greater New Haven laid out in the last chapter.[4] We also need
to appreciate them in the context of the academic theological projects to
which he was overtly responding at the time, as reflected in the essays
and named in a lecture he gave about them at Harvard in 1967.[5] In this
chapter, therefore, I will focus on the Christology of Rudolf Bultmann
and the Christologies of several thinkers who wrote in dialogue with
Bultmann (among others): Karl Barth, Günther Bornkamm, James Robinson, Schubert Ogden, Wolfhart Pannenberg and Jürgen Moltmann, all
of whom feature in Frei's Harvard lecture or the 'Theological reflections'
or both.[6] These are all thinkers who could, at the time, be broadly classed
as 'post-liberal'; that is, articulating theologies in critical continuity and
reaction to the nineteenth-century German Protestant tradition of liberal
theology.[7] Bultmann and Barth belong to the first generation of post-

liberals and the rest can be said to be in a similarly constructive critical relationship to their theologies as much as to those of their predecessors. Examining those essays in the context of those projects will bring the concerns, contours and significance of Frei's proposals into sharper relief when we turn to them in the next chapter.[8]

Rudolf Bultmann, 'New Testament and Mythology'

By the time Frei was writing these essays, the theology of the German Lutheran theologian, New Testament scholar and contemporary of Barth, Rudolf Bultmann, had been generating sometimes lively debate and constructive responses through the 1950s and into the 1960s.[9] Bultmann's now pupils dominated German academic theology, and for several academic theologians in North America at this time his thought still set the agenda for constructive theology, even if they thought one had to push beyond its limitations and problems.[10] Frei recognized Bultmann's contemporary influence and significance by devoting a week's seminar to Bultmann's *Jesus Christ and Mythology* as an example of contemporary Christology, alongside Kierkegaard and Barth, in his course on 'Contemporary Christian thought' in the autumn of 1967.[11] As James Kay rightly observes, Frei's Christology essays from the previous year are, among other things, a response to Bultmann's theological and hermeneutical project.[12] So much is evident from Frei's discussions of myth and his footnotes in the Christological essays and his Harvard lecture from 1967.

Bultmann's famous article from 1941, 'New Testament and mythology', is an apt focus for understanding Bultmann's theological programme and its significance.[13] There Bultmann lays out the problem raised for contemporary theologians by the world-picture of modern human beings and the way he thought theology had to proceed to address it, in contradistinction to nineteenth-century liberal theology and its quest for the personality or the religious and ethical teaching of the historical Jesus. The scientific outlook ingrained in our modern way of life, he argued, makes it impossible for modern humans to accept, without contradicting themselves, the mythical world-picture of the New Testament and the mythical account of the events of salvation that we find in its proclamation.[14]

The New Testament, he explains, presents the drama of salvation in an earthly setting placed between the heavenly dwelling place of God and his angels, located spatially above it, and the place of torment, underneath it. That earthly setting is a theatre for the interventions of supernatural powers (God, angels, Satan, demons) in natural occurrences, in the thoughts, willing and actions of human beings and in the direction of historical events: a cosmology derived from Jewish apocalyptic. The New Testament combines that cosmology with the Gnostic Redeemer myth to proclaim the advent of the last days and the fulfilment of time, when God sends his Son to earth as a human being, to die an atoning death for others' sin and be raised as the commencement of the cosmic catastrophe that destroys death, and then to reign until he returns to complete his work of salvation and judgement.

That world-picture, Bultmann argues, is incompatible with an outlook shaped by scientific explanation and the scientific understanding of our world embedded in a way of life built on the use of modern technology. Law-governed natural processes and causes explain the events and phenomena of our world, not the activities of supernatural powers. 'We cannot use electric lights and radios and, in the event of illness, avail ourselves of modern medical and clinical means and at the same time believe in the spirit and wonder world of the New Testament.'[15] Modern humans understand themselves as unified beings, who ascribe their feeling, thinking and willing to themselves alone; a closed system of causes excludes any vulnerability to supernatural agents. The New Testament eschatological expectation has been refuted by its own chronic disappointment. The ideas of death as a punishment for sins and of the substitutionary atonement of the guilty by the death of the innocent are all unintelligible to us, as is belief in the resurrection of a dead person and the notions of participation in someone's death and resurrection and sacramental feeding from their resuscitated body.

There is more to myth in the New Testament, however. Myths, Bultmann explains, hamper their intentions in their form. They intend to talk about faith in and knowledge of a transcendent power or ground beyond the familiar, on which we all depend, and through that dependence we may be freed from familiar powers. But they objectify that transcendent ground or power by depicting it in terms of familiar, worldly things. They demand to be understood in existentialist terms and hence provide the motive for critiquing their objectivizing representation of their subject matter.[16]

This account is consistent with Bultmann's understanding of divine transcendence, as articulated in earlier essays. God as the reality determining our existence is 'Wholly Other' and cannot be viewed external to that relationship or spoken about in neutral, universal terms abstracted from the existential position of the speaker before God (and neither can our existence).[17] God is thus not 'a given entity', a 'directly accessible object' which can be 'crystallised in knowledge', incorporated into a world view or cognitive system, even as its basic principle.[18]

In the case of the New Testament, this gap between the intention of the myth and its form is indicated by various elements in contradiction with one another, such as the idea of kenosis and the miraculous wonders that attest Jesus' Messianic status, or pre-existence and the virgin birth, but above all between the understanding of human beings as cosmically determined and as independent persons 'who can win or lose themselves by their own decisions'.[19] We need then to interpret the New Testament's mythology existentially, thus 'demythologizing' its proclamation and revealing its true intention, to see whether it offers an existential understanding of ourselves, one which 'constitutes for us a genuine question of decision'.[20] Behind this account, as Schubert Ogden explains, lies Bultmann's understanding, indebted to the philosopher Martin Heidegger, of human beings as distinguished by their concern with their own existence.[21] What they are, and who they ought to be, is always in question, as possibilities in their unique situation. They must continually take responsibility for answering those questions by freely deciding and enacting that decision, in answer to their understanding of themselves in that situation.

Elsewhere, Bultmann argues that it is this understanding of oneself and one's possibilities in a situation that makes possible the understanding of literary, philosophical and religious texts, reflecting the wider condition of all interpretation that author and interpreter share 'the same life relation to the subject matter under discussion'.[22] For Bultmann, existentialist philosophy thus provides a means of identifying that common subject matter in respect of the New Testament. It thus also furnishes conceptual language with which to restate the meaning of the New Testament in non-mythological terms.[23]

In *Jesus and the Word*, Bultmann had already offered in effect a demythologized interpretation of the eschatological message of the historical Jewish rabbi, Jesus of Nazareth, as represented in the earliest layers of Synoptic tradition.[24] In contrast to nineteenth-century German liberal theologians, Bultmann thought the Gospels tell us little of Jesus' life and personality. In any case, what matters is the cause he worked for, which in Jesus' case was encapsulated in his teaching.[25] What interests us about his teaching is his interpretation of existence and how it interrogates us about our own.[26] For Bultmann, Jesus' preaching of repentance in the face of deliverance by God's future action and his ethical teaching are irreconcilable with the liberal theological notion of the kingdom as the realization of the highest human ideal (not even a social or political one) through historical development or faith as the inner life.[27] Rather, in its Jewish context, it expressed, in a mythology contrasting the present age and the coming supernatural kingdom, the existential meaning of a call to present decision, to radical obedience in love of God and neighbour, in the face of the claim of the God whose will, in judgement and grace, determines our existence.[28]

For Bultmann, however, while the New Testament presupposes Jesus' message in its proclamation, it is that proclamation of him that is its starting point.[29] In 'New Testament and mythology', Bultmann finds an existential understanding of the human condition in both Pauline and Johannine interpretations of the proclamation of Jesus Christ, which both, to differing degrees, already interpret Jewish apocalyptic and Gnostic redeemer mythologies existentially.

Paul, for example, maintains human guilt for sin, against the current of his Adamic theory of the origin of sin. He understood that humans are burdened with care, a concern to secure our lives and the temptation to trust in and live out of what is visible and disposable ('the flesh'), including our own achievements and creations.[30] Even though the flesh is not actually secure, so we come to depend on it. From the vulnerability to transience and death that accompanies dependence on what is disposable comes the all-encompassing atmosphere of the 'slavery of anxiety', in which we seek to keep hold of ourselves and our possessions in fear that they are slipping away from us.[31] However, a genuine human life is possible by obedient trust that what invisible, unfamiliar and non-disposable encounters us as love and intends life and a future for us. Such a life is possible by faith in God's grace, which forgives our sins and frees us from our past.

> It is radical submission to God, which expects everything from God and nothing from ourselves; and it is the release thereby given from everything in the world that can be disposed of, and hence the attitude of being free from the world, of freedom.[32]

This manner of existence is eschatology, the new creation, an attitude of freedom from anxiety and freedom for others: faith working through love. By interpreting apocalyptic and Gnostic eschatologies in this way, Paul demythologizes them, interpreting salvation and the future life as something experienced in the present.[33] Similarly, by characterizing life in the Spirit as one of faith and the decision to obey in freedom, relativizing the significance of spiritual manifestations and experiences, Paul likewise interprets the mythological concept of the Spirit as a sort of supernatural force or matter existentially.

Bultmann insists that such demythologized faith remains faith in Christ, as the New Testament identifies it, and thus distinct from existentialist philosophies. For, according to the New Testament proclamation, this liberated, authentic existence of faith is not something we can achieve for ourselves, such is the desperateness of our plight, but only by an act of God in Christ. Every attempt at self-justification only perpetuates the fallen attitude of trying to secure our lives and live from our own resources. It is a refusal of the gift of existence. God must therefore free us from ourselves, for authentic, eschatological faith, by the revelation of God's love in Christ.[34]

Can that message, however, be demythologized without loss of its reference to God's eschatological action in Christ (which liberal theology had eliminated)? Bultmann argues that the New Testament is distinct from other contemporary soteriological myths because its representation of the Christ event intertwines the mythological stories of this same person (as God's pre-existent Son, born of a virgin, who performed wondrous deeds and was raised from the dead) with the story of a historical person with a human destiny, ending in crucifixion.[35] Such mythical representations express the saving significance of the historical person of Jesus for faith, a meaning which historical inquiry cannot attain.[36] They seek to express the saving significance of his historical crucifixion by representing it as an act of atonement and cosmic judgement upon us, and the worldly powers that dominate us, and cosmic liberation from them. It is these cosmic representations that express the 'decisive, history-transforming meaning' of the cross as an eschatological event that takes place in time but transcends time in its constant contemporaneity wherever it is proclaimed and its existential meaning is accepted in obedient, trusting decision (being crucified with Christ, bearing his death in our bodies).[37] As David Congdon argues, Bultmann thus distinguishes the eschatological meaning of the cross from the apocalyptic mythological form in which it was expressed.[38]

The cross is thus proclaimed not as a historical event whose significance we can know of through historical research but in its unity with the resurrection, as God's liberating and life-giving eschatological judgement on the world.[39] The resurrection here is not an authenticating miracle, for the miraculous does not express the resurrection's present existential meaning: the saving significance of the cross, which is an object of faith expressed in concrete living.[40] It is not a fact and its unity with the cross is one of simultaneity, not a historical sequence.[41] The historical event that follows the cross is not the resurrection but, rather, the emergence of this Easter faith in the first disciples, from which the proclamation of cross and resurrection originates.[42] The proclamation of cross and resurrection belongs to the eschatological event, together with faith in the proclamation (which God also actualizes) and the community where they are proclaimed and where those who believe gather: the church.[43] The proclamation makes its demand on us intelligible by asking us whether we will understand ourselves as crucified and risen with Christ. Indeed,

Christ, his cross and resurrection are present, they take place and encounter us there (and only there), in that word, which meets us as God's word and asks us whether we will believe it.[44]

In this way, Bultmann believes he has recovered the central intention of New Testament mythological themes such as the Son's incarnation, Christ's kenosis and the sending of the Son in the likeness of sinful flesh.[45] For God acts, God speaks, in the historical phenomenon of proclamation concerning a historical person and destiny, so that these phenomena are thus also eschatological events. As Ogden explains, for Bultmann, God 'acts' in a non-mythological sense that is analogous to interpersonal human communication, to create communion among human beings.[46] Like all personal acts, this action is only discernible to those who receive it in faith and love. God's transcendent Word is thus 'incarnate' in the proclamation of Christ crucified, present without becoming immanent; a paradox that faith accepts in obedience without re-mythologizing God's Word, without objectivizing God's presence. (Indeed, for Bultmann, we can only speak of God as the 'reality determining all else' from the perspective of and in relation to existence as determined by God's Word, that is, faith).[47] Thus, Bultmann contends, one may (and must) demythologize the New Testament and yet may preserve the Christocentric character of Christian faith.

Karl Barth on Christ's presence

Along with other founders of the journal *Zwischen den Zeiten* ('Between the Times'), Bultmann and Karl Barth had once been theological allies as advocates of dialectical theology in the early 1920s, but their theologies had developed in divergent ways.[48] By the 1950s and 60s, when Bultmann's influence was perhaps at its greatest in Germany and the United States, Barth's mature theological statement, the multi-volume *Church Dogmatics*, represented a substantial alternative to Bultmann's project. Frei would look to the *Church Dogmatics* as a source of inspiration in constructing his own Christology in that context, and especially to Barth's Christology in volume IV, which can be read, in part, as a response to Bultmann. As Barth explained in the Foreword to the first part of that volume, he had been in an intensive if quiet debate with Bultmann throughout it, and the same may be said for the whole of volume IV.[49]

Barth thought that Bultmann, by beginning with the subjective experience of human beings as recipients of the New Testament message, rather than with the saving action of God and the inclusion of humanity in Christ, had reversed the order of the New Testament message. He had thus fallen into the danger of an 'abstract subjectivism' that abstracted Christian existence from its foundation in God's saving act in Jesus Christ.[50] Bultmann's doctrine of the Christ event was really a doctrine of the transition from the old life to the new, which takes its title from Jesus Christ but to which he and his death and resurrection are marginal as an independent figure and events, having no existence outside the kerygma and faith. In Bultmann, Barth thought, Christology is absorbed into soteriology and faith and salvation are deprived of their basis in Christ.

At the same time, Barth argued, Bultmann's hermeneutics distorted the New Testament message. His understanding of myth was alien to it.[51] There seemed to be no place in Bultmann's interpretation of the New Testament message for the central subject matter of that message, as Barth understood it: God's loving, condescending act to redeem humanity in Jesus Christ's death and resurrection, whose saving work and contemporary reign and presence precede and are the object for human faith and discipleship.[52] Making human self-understanding, in an existentialist sense, the exclusive key to the New Testament, he added, had the same result.[53]

Barth made God's condescending, saving divine action in Jesus Christ central to his interpretation of the New Testament message in volume IV of his *Church Dogmatics*.[54] For Barth, that subject matter, 'God with us', is the origin and content of Christian faith, hope and love, and determines them.[55] They encounter something prior, different and external to them – the triune God – 'from whom they have their being, whom they can lay hold of but not apprehend or exhaust'.[56]

Rather than subject the New Testament to an existential hermeneutics that (he thought) marginalized its subject matter, Barth claimed to seek to understand the New Testament on its own terms, being open-minded about its message and flexible in seeking to interpret it, and dependent on the Holy Spirit's discipline.[57] Barth saw the New Testament writings as witnesses to this event of 'God with us', to the initiative and priority of Jesus of Nazareth as One qualitatively different from all other men, who has 'full power, against their cosmic limitation, to pronounce in His existence a final Word concerning them and all human history'.[58] They attest and recognize this person and his determinative significance for the Christian community and the world rather than express primarily that community's conceptions of him.[59] His risen presence so shapes the recollection of him in the New Testament that he dominates it; that pre- and post-Easter images of him are inseparable there.[60] He is determinative of its meanings and empowers its message, whether we accept or reject it.

In consequence, Barth's reading of the New Testament involves a very different understanding of the Christ event as historical from Bult-

mann's. For Bultmann, the eschatological event of Christ might be said
to be historical in the sense that, as God's Word, it encounters historical
human beings in their present situation. Jesus of Nazareth is merely historical background to that event. Barth, however, applies the language of
eschatological event to Jesus Christ's life and death as the history of God
with humanity, whereby God graciously takes on the human condition
and responsibility for it, reconciles us with God and, in his resurrection,
applies and proclaims that atonement to us.[61] As Barth explained earlier
in the *Church Dogmatics*, this event is historical as a singular, temporally
extended human existence, with a past and future, a section of public
history (as indicated in the Creed's reference to Pontius Pilate), of fallen
time subject to judgement and death.[62] But it is also fulfilled, transformed
time, which, by being assumed by God, partakes in God's existence and
eternity and is full of reality, and does not cease to be present for being
past; it is real time, which irrupts into our ruined, fallen time.[63] It is God's
time for us, which limits and determines our time as the centre to its
periphery and is available to us to become its contemporaries through the
witness of the prophets and apostles.[64] In his account of reconciliation in
volume IV/1, Barth says that this history, which underlies and includes
the history of every human individual, is present and happens for human
beings in the Holy Spirit, and Jesus Christ pronounces a final Word in it
on all human beings and their history.[65]

In contrast to Bultmann, the central, reconciling decision of that history is not that of the individual believer, but the decision of the Son of
God to take on the human cause, and his human decision to suffer in his
death the judgement of God on humanity, in obedience to God's will,
seen in his baptism and at Gethsemane.[66] The universal significance of
that decision emerges from the way it proceeds from, fulfils and exceeds
the history of God with Israel: a history of God's condescending faithfulness in unmitigated solidarity with this elect, representative people,
focused in a representative person.[67]

Barth's understanding of the Christ event also involves a different way
of thinking about God's transcendence, compared with Bultmann. For
Bultmann, God is transcendent in being non-objectifiable in divine action
that is analogous to human communication and which is received and
known by trusting faith rather than scientific grasp. For Barth, God's
transcendence is known in the Son of God's obedient partaking of human
nature, in his self-humiliation to death on the cross.[68] God is the One who
loves in freedom, and that omnipotent freedom with which he loves is
exhibited in his becoming human, concealing his divinity (without loss to
it) and adopting the human form and cause in time, in solidarity with the
world in its sin and lostness.[69] For Barth, such an understanding of God's

freedom in the incarnation is grounded in the ordered triune relationship of Father and Son in the Holy Spirit, the three co-equal modes of divine being.[70]

This way of thinking about the Christ event as the history of Jesus Christ involves for Barth a very different hermeneutical approach to the soteriological narrative variously told by New Testament texts from that taken by Bultmann. Barth interprets that soteriological narrative through the primary Johannine prism of God's saving action in the incarnation. God is its principal actor. Jesus Christ as the Son of God and Word, assuming and transforming our human condition, is its central character. His existence is a particular historical sequence that defines the meaning of the majestic titles by which the New Testament witnesses recognized him.[71] Above all, his atoning work, to represent humanity and bear divine judgement against them, by penitently obeying God on their behalf in this way, is enacted in his history, culminating in his passion.[72] For this reason, Barth is led to take the narrative sequence of the gospel story with great seriousness, 'emphasizing the passage from election, to rejection, to vindication'.[73]

For Barth, the New Testament's soteriological story does not reduce God to an object but witnesses precisely to God's free self-disclosure in becoming human for us as Jesus of Nazareth. For 'his concealment [in becoming this human being] … is the image and reflection in which we see Him as He is'.[74] As Barth says earlier in the *Church Dogmatics*, the Son or Word of God is God's primary objectivity by which God knows Godself. In gracious condescension, God uses Jesus Christ's human nature, by conforming it to the divine Word, as the basic creaturely veil and sign, the sacramental secondary objectivity by which God freely veils and unveils God's primary objectivity, while remaining the Subject of this act of self-revelation.[75] God thus gives Godself to be known by us in spite of our incapacity, in the Spirit and by faith, in an indirect, graced participation in God's self-knowledge, according to the measure of human cognition in time, by claiming and transforming our cognition and language in partial correspondence to God.[76] Since God reveals Godself in Jesus Christ's historical humanity, we may infer, it is fitting that that historical objectivity is attested in the derivative objectivity of the Gospels' soteriological stories.

Barth offered also a very different way of thinking about the significance of the Christ event for human beings. For Bultmann, the encounter with Christ as God's Word in the preaching of the New Testament message liberates human beings to achieve the authentic existence that existentialist philosophies prescribe for us; its meaning and significance is understood in those terms. For Barth, the significance of the Christ event is determined and revealed by God graciously raising from the dead the same Jesus who was crucified and buried and destroyed.[77] This divine action, not the faith of the disciples it evokes, is the subject of the New Testament's Easter narratives.[78] The resurrection is an objective, spatio-temporal event, although as revealed divine action it cannot be grasped in the way other historical events can. The resurrection and the 40 days of Jesus' resurrection appearances, in their unity with the crucifixion, are God's verdict of justification on Jesus Christ's obedience in assuming human plight in his incarnation and death, and God's declaration of the saving efficacy of that atoning history.[79] They reveal Jesus' beloved Sonship in unity with the Father, and God's reconciling will and justification of human beings in Jesus as the basis of a new world and the ending of the old one.[80] They mean that what Jesus Christ has done for all human beings, in his history, is the basis for their life and for the objective alteration of their situation in their having been judged, having died and having been made righteous and children of God, in Christ's obedience, death and resurrection.[81]

The resurrection reveals that the Christ event does not actualize a latent possibility in human existence but decisively alters the human situation.[82] Those accounts and the stories of the ascension also disclose the difference the incarnation makes to our human nature.[83] In the second part of volume IV of the *Church Dogmatics*, Barth argues that in freely assuming human existence as Jesus of Nazareth, the Son of God participates in every aspect of our humanity, including being formed by his own historical and cultural context, including our spiritual plight, and thereby exalts our nature to fellowship with God.[84] He does this in fulfilment of God's election of the Son to be God for us in this way as the beginning of all God's ways and works; of the human Jesus Christ and of humanity with him for fellowship with God.[85] In consequence, the Son's humanity, while remaining fully and historically human and finite, is graciously determined by the Son's mode of being.[86] It is exalted to the true freedom of obedience. It participates in the Son's share in the work of the Trinity. It is empowered to attest, and be the creaturely medium and human form of, his divine authority and mediatorial action.[87] As the Son's permanent garment, it is clothed with the Son's majesty.

The Synoptics attest this sanctification of our humanity in the history of Jesus as the 'royal man', the Son of Man. They depict the awesome impact of his presence on those who encountered him, the way he evoked decisions in them and divisions between them, shaped recollections of him, and of his complete, unique freedom to do his Father's will so that his presence is that of the kingdom of God and is active today.[88] They show forth, across the whole activity of his life, in speech and action, his conformity and correspondence to God's mode of being, purpose and work: in his humiliation by others; in his keeping company with the materially and spiritually poor; in his revolutionary freedom to cut across, interpret and invert the orders and values of the world around him, revealing their relative, transitory validity and crisis in view of the antithesis of his kingdom to them; and in being for other human beings despite their sin.[89] This history, marked by the cross, the resurrection reveals, is objective, public and both representative and universally inclusive of all human life: it is our reality as human beings.[90] Barth unfolds the significance of the Christ event not by reference to an independent understanding of the human situation but from the particularity of Jesus of Nazareth, the incarnate Son, and his history. An identifying description of him is 'logically indispensable' to Barth's understanding of his saving significance and governs the application of concepts of saving significance applied to him.[91]

Barth's understanding of the resurrection likewise involves a very different construal from Bultmann's of the presence of Christ. Barth's affirmation of the unity and irreversible sequence of Jesus Christ's crucifixion and resurrection means that for him the One who is present is Jesus Christ in his historical existence in time, including his crucifixion.[92] The resurrection accounts reveal, he argues, that Jesus who was crucified and buried is not confined by the limits of his birth and death. His historical existence has become his eternal being as Lord of time. It has become something that took place once for all and is present in all time, filling and determining 'the whole present'.[93] Christ is directly present and revealed in the Christian community in the medium of recollection, tradition and proclamation in the power of his resurrection, the Holy Spirit.[94] Christ by his resurrection also reveals our reality in him, addresses and claims us, awakens, empowers and directs us to correspond to him.[95] He calls those disturbed by his direction in their lives to fellowship with his existence, liberating them from bondage to sin, empowering them to live in conformity to his humanity.[96] He calls them to follow him in faithful obedience and to attest the coming kingdom of God realized in him.[97]

In part three of volume IV of the *Church Dogmatics*, Barth expands on the premise of these claims, in implicit contrast to Bultmann's theological procedure. As the One who lives, in freely condescending divinity and corresponding, elevated humanity, in whom God and humanity are reconciled, Jesus Christ is his own witness, creating knowledge of himself, radiating the light of his life, revealing his history, making it public and calling all humanity to the right response of obedience and affirmation.[98] We cannot prove or validate this self-revelation, for example as meeting a need of ours that we otherwise know about; to do so is to speak of something else, something doubtful.[99] The basis of the validity and eloquence of his self-revelation lies in the presence of God in him and is ultimately grounded in the self-revealing triune existence of God.[100] The real question, therefore, is of our gratitude and obedience to it and its self-validation in our lives, heeding him alone as the one Word of God freely speaking in his empowered witnesses in Scripture, church and even beyond the church, but not synthesized with or under any ideology.[101]

This prophetic work of Jesus Christ takes the form of a sovereign, dynamic, secondary repetition of his history in other times, establishing liberating knowledge of Christ in the world reconciled to God and thereby bringing about participation in that reconciliation, overcoming all resistance to that knowledge.[102] It is the middle form of his coming again, his effective presence or Parousia in the gift of the Holy Spirit, beyond all creaturely possibility.[103] It is his presence as the world's eschatological telos, in the time that remains between the resurrection and his final, definitive appearance. As Jesus Christ thus makes his way to this goal, he calls those awakened to liberating knowledge of himself and of their own reconciliation to God, into his prophetic work, as his witnesses: to be free, independently active subjects with him in that work and set in motion towards that end, bearing the promise and anticipation of that eschatological fulfilment in its universal import.[104] Here too the mythological concepts of the New Testament serve a necessary purpose for attesting the presence and call of the concrete person of Jesus Christ.[105] Jesus Christ is not made meaningful in the quasi-independent sphere of human existence but draws us into his reality, where we truly exist.[106]

In these in-between times, then, the times and events of all people, whether they know it or not, are related to, conditioned and encircled by this progress of his history passing among us, who is for them all and their hope.[107] In this context, the Christian community as the earthly-historical, visible form of Christ's existence, awakened to their reconciliation, gathered, built up by his power, the Spirit, into the provisional representation of his sanctification of humanity, assumes greater significance than it does in Bultmann.[108] For it is more than a locus for the event of Christ's presence in the Word. It is called and sent by the Spirit in and for the world as a provisional representation of the calling of all humanity in Christ and as a witness to God's reconciliation of the world to himself in Christ, and of Christ's eschatological presence as living hope.[109] It is just in this respect that Barth's doctrine of reconciliation intimates most clearly, if largely indirectly, its political character.

Barth's Christology in volume IV has political overtones, whether in the characterization of omnipotence in the humble assumption of human form in IV/1, the revolutionary attitude of Jesus Christ to worldly orders and values as the 'royal man' in IV/2, or the humanism and the language of liberation and freedom of his account of Christ as Victor.[110] Negatively, faith in Christ precludes absolute loyalty to anyone else or any ideology, as Barth's quotation and exposition of the first thesis of the Barmen Declaration of 1934 asserts.[111]

Positively, Barth's account of the Christian community's relationship to history, its orientation, task and ministry, makes it responsible for the world in a way that entails constructive political engagement within that not-yet-redeemed world that is created, preserved, accompanied and over-ruled in every event by God, who restrains its tendency to chaos and war caused by humanity's confusion of creaturely goods with nothingness.[112] To that world the Christian community proclaims the new thing that is hidden from the world and not deducible from the observation of history but is disclosed to the community: God's liberation and reconciliation of the world to himself, God's gracious address to that world, in Jesus Christ, the 'first and last thing in world-occurrence', to be manifested in the future coming of God's kingdom as the reality of all history.[113]

This knowledge conditions the community's participation in history. It understands the provisionality of all human crime and accomplishment, and so is neither enthusiastic about radical improvement in the world nor sceptical of the world's renewal, neither reactionary nor revolutionary.[114] It witnesses confidently to Christ in definite, 'resolute decisions' about available possibilities, in small, relative steps, following God's decision in Christ for the new reality of the world reconciled to God, actualized and revealed in Christ.[115] It is thus always responsible and engaged or about to engage 'in resolute action within general world-occurrence', in order to make a relative difference, the erecting of a sign, as it awaits with hope Christ's final revelation to the world of himself as its Lord and of its new reality as reconciled to God.[116] In Jesus Christ and the power of the Spirit, following and imitating Christ, it is thus the community for the world. It knows the world as it is, binds itself to the world in full solidarity, and takes responsibility for it in action that bears witness to Christ, in his likeness.[117]

The political subtext of this ecclesiology is most apparent in Barth's posthumously published exposition of the petition in the Lord's Prayer for the coming of God's kingdom.[118] Christians are commanded, by the proclamation of God's righteousness and the consequent possibility and necessity of human righteousness, to revolt against the plight under which human beings suffer, the disorder that 'penetrates and poisons and disrupts all human relationships'. This disorder arises, first, because of humanity's transgression of life in fellowship with God and hence one another. It arises, second, because of the destructive rebellion of human abilities against humanity, unleashed as powers seeking to be lordless (such as imperial states, money, ideologies and technologies).[119] (Here the apparently 'magical' conceptuality of the New Testament seems, Barth argues, apt to describe the demonic forces of our times.)[120] Christians are freed to rebel against the oppression and suffering these powers cause. They do so in two related ways. First, they do so by praying for the advent of the kingdom in the coming of the person of Jesus Christ. Second, in so praying, they are projected into going out to meet the kingdom by grasping and actualizing present provisional possibilities for human righteousness, contending in little steps for human rights, human freedom and human peace, and so enacting the responsibility given to them for this world.

Barth's account here also complements and qualifies his earlier exposition from 1946 of the relationship of the Christian Community and the Civic Community.[121] The state, he argues, unwittingly serves God's providential preservation of the not-yet-redeemed world. The church participates in that responsibility and takes responsibility for the civic community, the outer circle within which it is placed. Because Jesus Christ is the hidden centre of both circles, it is possible for the state to exhibit fragile analogies, likenesses, to the kingdom of God which point to it. For this to happen, the state needs the church's participation in its political responsibility, promoting political possibilities that tend towards such analogies, supporting decisions that clarify the lordship of Christ over the whole of life, exemplifying to the state a political community conforming to the kingdom, for the welfare of the human beings who constitute it and above all for those who are socially and economically weaker. Barth's mature theology thus exhibited a developed political theology in striking contrast to what Dorothee Sölle would identify as the apparently apolitical character of Bultmann's theology.[122]

Post-liberal theology after Bultmann

In looking to Barth for inspiration, Frei was out of kilter with the mainstream of German and Anglophone theology in the 1960s, including in the United States, where, if Barth was not ignored, he was widely seen as an example of 'neo-orthodoxy', 'turning theology back towards a sterile dogmatics of repristination' and dividing the gospel from contemporary society.[123] Instead, much of the debate in Frei's context was about how to build on and advance beyond the achievements of Bultmann.

In *Christ without Myth*, Schubert Ogden describes what he calls the contemporary 'post-liberal' situation in Protestant thought, marked by

a near-consensus about the need to surpass the limitations of the constructive work of nineteenth-century liberal theologians while building
on their historical-critical achievements, responding obediently to the
New Testament's message (or *kerygma*, 'proclamation') while embracing
the criticism of the Christian tradition that arises, necessarily, out of the
picture of the world and humanity held by modern people.[124] For Ogden,
Bultmann had clearly articulated that challenge and provided crucial
resources for meeting it (and Barth had not). By the mid-1960s there were
several other thinkers seeking to respond to the post-liberal challenge in
ways that sought to go beyond Bultmann, a diverse group whom John
Cobb labelled 'post-Bultmannians'.[125] As Charles Campbell notes, Frei
was also clearly responding to this group, so we need briefly to outline
some representative positions in order better to situate his Christology in
its immediate academic theological context.[126] Broadly speaking, we can
distinguish two groups with two different concerns about Bultmann's
project.

There were those concerned that the continuity between the historical
Jesus and the present Christ in Bultmann's Christology was too limited
to specify, adequately, who it is who is present in the preaching of the
Christian message. They sought to address this problem by renewing the
quest for the historical Jesus so as to identify a strong continuity, amid
an identifiable difference, between his historical person and ministry,
their expression in the New Testament (especially the Gospels) and their
existential interpretation in the life of the modern-day church. And they
sought to do so in such a way as also to take account of the findings of
the critical analysis of the composition and underlying sources of the
Gospels, to which Bultmann had made such a great contribution in his
History of the Synoptic Tradition, which had problematized the liberal
quest of the nineteenth century.[127]

For example, Günther Bornkamm, Professor of New Testament at
Heidelberg University, Germany, argued that such historical analysis of
the way in which the early church's faith in and expectations of the risen
Christ shaped the presentation of the earthly Jesus in the development
of the literary units of the Synoptic tradition allows us to identify Jesus'
original sayings and understand the church's interpretation of him in the
New Testament as a response to his whole person.[128] While the Gospels'
presentation of Jesus precludes a biographical treatment of his life, they
do present episodes and sayings in which the uniqueness of Jesus' person
and history are present 'in their entirety' with an originality that attests
they are 'brim full of history', despite their unhistorical mode of transmission.[129] A guiding assumption of Bornkamm's analysis seems to be that
while we can often distinguish the accretions of churchly interpretation

of the historical Jesus from authentic material, there is not necessarily so sharp a discontinuity between the two as to require a scrupulous sifting of every last detail before drawing on the overall impression the tradition gives of him. Greater continuity helps make the rise of Christian faith intelligible.[130]

For Bornkamm, the authentic portrait of the historical Jesus that is preserved in the tradition is of a figure of 'astounding sovereignty' and unmediated presence in the way he deals with situations and in his teaching.[131] His words and actions, concerned with the presence of the hidden and coming kingdom and the immediate presence hence of the divine will, focus on the present moment in which decisions of the ultimate future are made.[132] Indeed, he made the reality of God present, which represented the end of the world, in judgement or salvation, and a new present, for those who encountered it.[133] Bornkamm focuses on Jesus' words and actions as the vehicles of his presence in the past and, it seems, to both the historian and the believer. For Bornkamm, Jesus is found and is present in his words and actions, which are a sign pointing to the coming kingdom that is already dawning.[134] In this way the Messianic character of his being was contained in his words and deeds and the unmediated nature of his historical appearance, though he claimed no Messianic title.[135] Whereas for Bultmann the historical Jesus and his message came to be an indispensable part of the background to the present Christ in Christian proclamation in whom God acts, Bornkamm makes the historical Jesus, present in his words and deeds, the medium of God's presence and the focus of Christian faith in the risen Lord.[136] The message and actions of Bornkamm's Jesus are relatively unconcerned with politics in the face of the imminent kingdom, and hence Bornkamm's account of his presence is as apolitical as Bultmann's appears to be.[137]

James M. Robinson synthesized and represented the approaches of Bornkamm and others for a North American readership as 'the new hermeneutic'.[138] This approach, Robinson argued, used historical criticism not to validate the New Testament message but to clarify its understanding of existence in history as that of an actual historical figure, Jesus of Nazareth. In this way it found continuity between the existential meaning of its message and his, and between its explicit Christology and his self-understanding – which is his selfhood – present in his words and actions.

If the 'new hermeneutic' acclaimed by Robinson represented one post-liberal, post-Bultmannian option for US theologians, Schubert Ogden represented the alternative. Bornkamm and others sought to emphasize and better secure the Christocentric character of Bultmann's existentialism. But Ogden thought this Christocentrism, whereby authentic historical existence is only realized through faith in Jesus Christ, was in conflict with Bultmann's claim that Christian faith realizes the existential authenticity that is an original possibility for all human beings.[139] For the latter claim, divorced from traditional notions of a historical fall, presupposes that authentic existence may be realized apart from any particular historical event. This contradiction, moreover, pointed up the tension Ogden saw between Bultmann's Christocentrism and his commitment to doing justice to the unitary selfhood and scientific outlook of modern human beings. Churches in the USA needed a thoroughgoing demythologization of the faith if they were to avoid alienating those whose gifts and cooperation they needed in their life and mission. A consistent demythologization, however, required affirming the universal availability of God's free grace that makes it possible for anyone to live authentically and so makes everyone responsible. The exclusivity in the New Testament's Christological message, he argued, is not about the necessity of the historical Jesus for the realization of authentic existence, but about the decisiveness of the disclosure in Jesus Christ of God's universal saving action. By softening Bultmann's Christocentrism from a condition of authentic existence to a decisive disclosure of God's universal grace, Ogden sought to remove what he saw as a major weakness in Bultmann's otherwise necessary programme. As we shall see, Frei thought both alternatives deeply problematic and sought a way to avoid their shared weaknesses.

Theologians of hope

One more group of theologians will round out our picture of the context to which Frei was responding in his Christology essays of 1966: theologians who in different ways made a future-orientated understanding of New Testament eschatology and Christian hope central to their theological method. In Frei's writings in this period, two of these thinkers feature more prominently: the German Lutheran theologian Wolfhart Pannenberg, and the German Reformed theologian Jürgen Moltmann.

Pannenberg's *Jesus – God and Man*, published in German in 1964, sought objective knowledge of the living, present but exalted Lord Jesus Christ 'from below': in reliable historical knowledge of the events that reveal who he is, the claim he made in his ministry and message and the resurrection which vindicated him.[140] In this way, he parted company with Bultmann but also with Barth, and differed from the post-Bultmannians in affirming Jesus' unity with God not from the authority of his preaching but from its vindication in his resurrection.

In the context of the Jewish apocalyptic expectations of his time, Pannenberg argues, Jesus of Nazareth claimed that the attitude towards him of those who encountered him would determine their fate at the imminent eschatological judgement he proclaimed, for God's coming rule was already anticipated and present in his person.[141] All who acknowledged him would be acknowledged by the Son of Man before God's angels. This claim thus anticipated its future confirmation or verification, which Jesus expected in the judgement of the eschatological figure of the Son of Man at the general resurrection of the dead: it had a 'proleptic structure'.[142] His journey to Jerusalem and his cleansing of the Temple were probably intended to bring about that final verification, even if it involved his own death. In the horizon of those same apocalyptic expectations of the general resurrection – the radical transformation and renewal of a once mortal body – Jesus' disciples could only understand his resurrection appearances and his exaltation to God as the beginning of the general resurrection and the eschatological events, the verification of his claims about himself, his identification with the eschatological judge: the Son of Man.[143] At the same time, in that context they understood it also as the revelation of God in him, since God is fully revealed in his glory and omnipotence only in the eschaton, and thus of his eschatological lordship, which heralded the expected universal salvation of the Gentiles, prompting the Gentile mission to carry that news to them.

Pannenberg argues that Jesus' resurrection is still meaningful to modern human beings, despite our not sharing every aspect of the apocalyptic cosmology of his time, on the basis of what he takes to be a universal truth about human beings. Our humanity, our destiny, cannot be fulfilled in a finite life nor in the society to which we belong, and so the meaningfulness of our lives depends on a hope for existence beyond death.[144] This hope is essential to conscious human existence, as the phenomenon of human openness to the world and freedom in response to our environment confirms. We are always in search of further fulfilment of our destiny beyond every limit. If, on this basis (we may infer), one grants an element of truth to apocalyptic expectations of the general resurrection, then, in the absence of cogent alternative explanations suggested by the New Testament reports of encounters with the exalted, spiritual body of the crucified Jesus, the hope of the resurrection from the dead offers the most likely account – however limited our understanding of it – of several historical realities: the historical events correlating to those reports; the alteration in the inherited apocalyptic expectations of the resurrection in the witnesses to those appearances; and the emergence of primitive Christianity that originated from them.[145] Historical research of Jesus' ministry and historical judgements about the reality behind the

New Testament's resurrection traditions thus provide some certainty, Pannenberg claims, for our knowledge of the resurrection of Jesus. His resurrection, in turn, provides the key to understanding the significance of Jesus, the non-mythological meaning of New Testament Christology and the character of Jesus' presence.

In the horizon of Jewish apocalyptic expectation – and presumably even for modern people as bound to hope (from God?) for life beyond death – God is the author of Jesus' resurrection and this divine action confirms Jesus' claims, in his ministry, to divine authority. And, as the anticipation of God's kingdom, Jesus' resurrection is the direct revelation of God in him. The resurrection thus establishes a revelatory identity, a unity of Jesus and God, which confirms his pre-Easter claims and retro-actively makes them true, determining his essence, just as (Pannenberg asserts) all essences are determined by the future.[146]

So personal is Jesus' claim that this retroactive force reaches back to involve his whole person and history, which, Pannenberg argues, explains the motive for the legends of the virgin birth and allows us to assess their theological significance as a preliminary expression of this valid concern.[147] A similar analysis of the development of primitive Christian tradition in turn explains and interprets the apparently contrary idea of Christ's pre-existence as derived by extrapolating logically to its ultimate conclusion the retroactive effect of Jesus' unity with the eternal God, which is revealed and constituted by his resurrection. 'If God has revealed himself in Jesus, then Jesus' community with God, his Sonship, belongs to eternity.'[148] This logic, furthermore, explains the early Christian adoption of the Hellenistic motifs to express it in the ideas of God's sending the pre-existent Jesus, his descent, incarnation and ascension.

Such ideas are only mythological, Pannenberg argues, if they are under-stood in ways that separate out conceptually a pre-existent divine being, the Son of God, and the earthly, human appearance of Jesus, in order then to reunite them. For mythical thinking is distinguished, he claims, by its separating out the prototypical essence of a reality from its appearance in order to reunite them in some dramatic process. Pannenberg thus offers, in effect, an analysis of the process of mythological objectification that Bultmann found problematic when interpreted at face value, rather than existentially. Pannenberg then uses that analysis in combination with a reconstruction of the logic of the development of primitive Christian tradition from the resurrection appearances and with the meaningfulness of the resurrection appearances for us (given the hopes all humans share with apocalyptic expectation), in order to dismiss Bultmann's claim for the mythological character of the New Testament and thus his proposal for demythologizing interpretation. Understood in that way, Jesus' eternal

Sonship and his humanity are not conceptually separated in mythological fashion. Rather, they are aspects of one single, concrete life in which God comes to humanity. For Jesus' divinity, his unity with the Father as Son of God, established and revealed in the resurrection, is mediated by, given with and dialectically identical to, his personal community with God as one self-consciously related to God in unreserved obedient dedication to his mission, even to the point of self-sacrifice.[149] In this way, Pannenberg could say much more than Bultmann about who the present Christ is, on the basis of his history, while avoiding invoking a pre-incarnate divine hypostasis of the Son that seemed problematically mythological as theology to Bultmann. This procedure, which depends on the retroactive ontological force of the resurrection rather than the eternal triune election of the Son to be God for us as Jesus Christ, also differentiates the way Pannenberg affirms the irreducible historical particularity of Christ from Barth's procedure.

So understood, Jesus' single, historical concrete life bears universal significance for humanity, as it does for Barth and much more clearly and fully than for Bornkamm, let alone Bultmann. However, Pannenberg places a greater emphasis than either on the resurrection as constitutive of that significance, and on its future-orientated eschatological character, as distinct from Barth's view of the resurrection as revealing the accomplishment of salvation that is only to be made publicly manifest in the future. In contrast to Barth (but in some affinity with Bultmann), Pannenberg also correlates this significance with an independent anthropological claim. The destiny of all people, which comes to them as their future, has appeared in advance in him and is accessible to everyone through him, in accordance with his eschatological office.[150] As such, he is universally and savingly relevant because he fulfils humanity's deepest longings. In his message, calling people to live in the light of the imminent kingdom; in God's vindication by resurrection of Jesus' claim to bear eschatological office so that one may participate in eschatological salvation in community with him; and in his resurrection itself: Jesus reveals and makes possible the ultimate destiny and wholeness to which human beings aspire, their essential openness to God and God's future, and the human destiny to community through the forgiveness and love that that openness brings.[151]

God's vindication of Jesus in his resurrection also reveals his accusers as guilty of the crime of blasphemy for which he was executed and thus that he died the death that they were due. This exchange of places extends to all people, Jew and Gentile, as guilty of blasphemy by pridefully identifying some human order with God and in consequence of this self-enclosure, subject to death, as all human beings manifestly are.[152]

This inclusive vicarious death, which means that only Jesus dies God-forsaken and there is hope of resurrection beyond death for everyone, reflects, in its substitutionary character not only Israel's understanding of the power of the sinful deed and the transferability of guilt but the universal reality that social life involves bearing responsibilities representatively on behalf of others, or even the whole. Jesus' divine–human personhood opens up the possibility of personhood in communion with God for all human beings, in fulfilment of their humanity.[153] His resurrection, by vindicating the claim to authority in which his total dedication and openness to God was enacted, determines and reveals that in his earthly existence, in his unity of will with God, he overcame and condemned the self-enclosed, self-centred sinful structure in human existence for us, declaring the sinless righteousness.[154]

Pannenberg's understanding of Jesus Christ's resurrection as the anticipation of God's kingdom, of the vindication of his claims and so of the revelation and determination of his unity with God, also informs his understanding of Christ's presence today. It allows him to affirm the development of primitive Christian tradition as moving logically from the identification of the risen Jesus with the Messianic agent of eschatological lordship of God he had proclaimed in his earthly life, and from his exaltation to participation in that lordship as God's Son, to the conclusion that his personal unity with God means that his future lordship cannot be restricted to the future.[155] Rather, it is already anticipated now, albeit in a hidden mode because in the Son's obedience he preserves its futurity as God's future.[156] The powers that rule the world unwittingly (and unwillingly) serve the coming kingdom. Only Christians recognize Christ's present rule and are incorporated into his kingdom through community and conformity to him and his Sonship by word and sacrament, which is the mode of his rule in the church and in them: a public, precursory form of his kingdom in its form of weakness rather than of glory. That proleptic structure governs the political significance of Christ's presence in Pannenberg's account.

With echoes of Barth's quotation of Barmen, Pannenberg had already argued that Jesus' eschatological message removed the 'glitter of ultimacy from every human political order', so that within its sphere of influence, 'the right of every existing state to bind its subjects to it in the innermost way is contested'.[157] Christian hope for God's kingdom, therefore, can only have a positive relationship to any given political order where that order 'remains conscious of its own provisional character'.[158]

Pannenberg's political theology in *Jesus – God and Man* evinces other similarities to Barth's, qualified by the decisive significance and character of Pannenberg's eschatology. He agrees with Barth that no political order, nor the church, can be identified with Christ's kingdom, but his reasoning stresses the kingdom's futurity and its hidden presence as anticipation of that future. It is present in a preliminary, provisional, anticipatory public form in the church and in a hidden, latent fashion in the political events that serve it.[159] Pannenberg too sees the church's political witness in its proclamation of this hidden reality. As the anticipation and preliminary form of the kingdom, the church proclaims in each social situation the hope of the coming realization of the 'true totality of political life' and the fulfilment of justice, and calls the world to the obedience of sonship in every sphere of life, including the political.[160] Somewhat similarly to Barth, Pannenberg also sees the possibility of partial likenesses between the civic community and the coming kingdom. Before the eschaton, there can be no full political realization of the kingdom of God, only tendencies and closer or more distant provisional approximations of political orders to the kingdom. A plurality of 'Christianly determined' societies and parties are legitimate so long as this provisional character is recalled.[161] But whereas for Barth the church works out its political responsibility in definite decisions between or against possibilities in terms of their relationship to Christ's lordship, for Pannenberg, Christians may serve such societies by offering impartial advice, informed by their eschatological faith, about what may be necessary and possible in them. The separation of the church from the state reflects this situation, even in a society shaped by a Christian ethos, to give people access to the ultimacy of the coming kingdom, to recall the transitoriness of the present political order and to free societies thereby for new possibilities of political formation. The depth of Barth's profound incarnational humanism and the bias towards the vulnerable and oppressed and the note of resistance to the lordless powers and their effects seem to be missing in *Jesus – God and Man*, however.

More radical perhaps than either Barth or Pannenberg, at least in its implied political direction, was Jürgen Moltmann's *The Theology of Hope*, also first published in 1964. Here, Moltmann sought to unfold the promissory character of biblical eschatology as the medium for theology, to give a dynamic eschatological theology of history driven by the promises of God and the hope they engender, and to show 'the disquieting, critical power' of that eschatological hope.[162] Moltmann situated this account by critiquing both Bultmann and Barth for being too preoccupied with the problem of knowledge of God and with the concept of revelation without sufficiently attending to the 'reference and bearing' of revelatory words of God in the Scriptures.[163] Recent work in Old Testament theology had shown that biblical statements about divine revelation are combined with statements about God's promise, and that 'God reveals himself in the form of promise and in the history that is marked by promise.'[164] There-fore, he argued, the key contrast in the context of ancient Israel is not between gods of nature and the God of revelation but between the God of promise and the gods of epiphanies. It is the difference, theologically, between thinking about revelation in terms of the presence of the eternal in time (epiphany) and thinking about it in terms of God's disclosure of his faithfulness to God's promise and himself and his presence in that fulfilment. God and God's self-revelation must be thought about eschato-logically in this sense, rather than primarily in terms of epistemology.[165]

Both Bultmann's account of revelation as the disclosure of authentic selfhood and Barth's understanding of revelation as God's self-revelation were disposed – by the influence of Kant's moral reinterpretation of Christian eschatology – towards a more epiphanic, less hopeful or his-torical, understanding of God's eschatological revelation in Christ.[166] Kant's moral interpretation of the future-orientated 'last things' removed their promissory character and eschatological reference by referring them instead to the eternal, transcendental subjective conditions of moral agency and freedom, removing all teleological movement from history. Barth did the same by referring them to the revelatory presence of the eternal divine Subject in time. So did Bultmann, by referring them to the event of the human subject's self-understanding as existentially related to God and, with it, its knowledge of God in faith, occasioned by revelation in the preached Word. For Moltmann, however, the biblical history of God's promises, culminating in the resurrection of Christ, engenders a very different eschatological understanding of God, and of history, and a more deeply critical, implicitly political, disposition towards present situations.

Moltmann holds that the New Testament's promises of Jesus Christ's future coming announce his crucifixion and resurrection by Israel's God as an event that anticipates the eschaton and so (because the eschaton is universal) has universal significance.[167] The promise of Christ's future in the proclamation of his resurrection issues, Moltmann argues, from the risen Christ's self-identification, indeed self-revelation, as the Crucified. Christ's personal continuity between crucifixion and resurrection unites the total contradiction between the experience of the 'absolute *nihil*' of his Godforsakenness and the total annihilation of that total *nihil* in the nearness of God in his resurrection.[168] The risen Christ is thus revealed as the crucified Jesus in that dialectic of the unity of total opposites.

In the resurrection, God is identified with and differentiated from the God of the Old Testament. The event of cross and resurrection points back to God's promises to Israel, which shaped Israel's experience of history. God's resurrection of the crucified Jesus culminates and transforms the experience of history engendered by God's promises to Israel, which is carried forward by the New Testament.

The memory of the promises of God to Israel's ancestors and in the Exodus, Moltmann argues, conditioned the way they interpreted the settlement of Canaan.[169] They understood it as the fulfilment of those promises, and at the same time experienced in that fulfilment an expansion of the promises and of their desires and hope. In this way, they recognized God's transcendence of that fulfilment: God's inexhaustibility in the overspill of God's promises.[170] In this way, they also experienced reality not as static or cyclical but as historical, where events and facts are provisional and point beyond themselves to something that does not fully exist in them. It conditioned their relationship to time, so that the present is experienced as 'the advancing front line of time as directed purposefully towards its goal in the moving horizon of promise'.[171] With new threats to Israel's existence from Babylon, Assyria and Persia, interpreted as divine judgement, came further expansion of the promises in the classical prophets. God's promise to Israel is renewed as eschatological and universal: the day of the Lord, the new covenant, the coming glory of the Lord as ruler of all the earth and over all its peoples, the overcoming of God's judgement with God's blessing.[172] Then, in Jewish apocalyptic literature, the promise expands to encompass the whole cosmos in history and eschatology, to an end that is greater than the beginning.[173]

With God's resurrection of the crucified Christ, the promise to Israel is born again and made certain.[174] It is born again in the eschatological unconditional certainty of their fulfilment, independent of the keeping of the law, which rests only on God's power to raise the dead, as demonstrated in his raising Jesus Christ. It is born again in the liberation of the promise thereby from the limits of the law and Israel's election. The promise is made universal, Moltmann says, in the creation of a new people composed of Jews and Gentiles, and in the transformation of its content, from promising life and land to promising the resurrection of the dead and a new humanity in which divisions are broken down. In this transformation of the promise, Israel's God is revealed now as the God of all humanity.

God's promise, proclaimed in the gospel, is now also the promise of the future of Christ. By announcing the resurrection of the crucified Christ, it presents him as the coming one. For he appears 'in the foreglow of the coming, promised glory of God'.[175] The resurrection of the crucified Christ actualizes and authenticates God's eschatological faithfulness to God's promise, of whose fulfilment it is the 'dawn and assured promise'.[176] In this way, the Christ event points forward not only to Christ's eschatological, liberating universal lordship, but beyond to that to which it is to be subordinated: the revelation of God's divinity in all things, in which the dialectic between cross and resurrection is resolved into synthesis.[177]

This future can only be stated in promises whose form is illumined by Old Testament prophecy, but determined by Christ's words, suffering and death, which foreshadow and prefigure what is hidden in him.[178] Such statements of promise anticipate Christ's future; in them 'the hidden future already announces itself and exerts its influence on the present through the hope it awakens.'[179] They kindle an anticipatory, provisional, fragmentary, open knowledge of the future, which strains towards it and seeks to gauge the possibilities opened by the Christ event.

This future is one in which God makes human beings right with God, with one another and with the whole creation, and they are thus provided with a new ground for their existence, the revelation of which reveals the groundlessness of sin.[180] This righteousness is present now in faith and baptism as a promise effective now in the life of the believer in a process only completed with Christ's Parousia. That process sets them on a path of obedient seeking of God's righteousness 'in his body, on earth, and in all creatures'.[181] In this way, it brings them to suffer under the contradiction between this godless world and that righteousness, in which suffering the believer gives God God's due in respect of this world and so anticipates God's coming righteousness.[182]

Similarly, the believer recognizes in the resurrection of the Godforsaken Christ the source and beginning of the abolition of Godforsakenness and the deathliness of death, and the latency of eternal life issuing from the negation of that negative.[183] The Spirit, Moltmann asserts, is the power of that overcoming and the opening of the future of life. Its work is the pledge of Christ's future. The Spirit empowers believers to participate in Christ's mission and love and so suffer the passion of the coming possibilities and justice promised in his resurrection: its hidden, urgent latency under the conditions of trial, suffering, death and sorrow, and bodily solidarity with an unredeemed creation.

Just this participation is the form God's coming lordship takes in the present. The eschatological lordship of God has the form of God's raising the crucified Jesus as a new creation. It takes shape in the present in the suffering of Christians who cannot be conformed to the world because of their hope of new creation for all things, 'but are drawn by the mission and love of Christ into discipleship and conformity to his sufferings'.[184] In hope, Christians are drawn into restless contradiction, conflict with and protest against the God-forsakenness of the present, the contradiction of the resurrection to the cross.[185] In this way the kingdom becomes this-worldly as the 'antithesis and contradiction of a godless and god-forsaken world'.[186] Hope thus moves the church, called by the risen Christ in his self-revelation, into motion towards the future.[187] This movement is an exodus from the status quo, which is at the same time a mission of creative, transforming love towards the world and its worthless, lost and dead, empowered by hope in God's promises of new creation; it is a mission of meek solidarity with the suffering humans and the devastated earth, to guide them towards their new being, because it takes its form from Christ's mission.[188]

Moltmann's account of the gospel as the proclamation of the promise of the coming of the risen crucified Christ shares a similar proleptic logic with Pannenberg's understanding of the revelation of God in Jesus Christ, a similarly vicarious interpretation of Jesus' cross and a similarly powerful, politically resonant, note of hope. However, fused with Moltmann's dialectical interpretation of the relationship between Christ's crucified Godforsakenness and his risen glory, it creates an electric, disturbing historical sense of the contingency and wrongness of present oppressive structures, driven by an equally powerful and subversive expectation of their imminent negation and the transformation of all things in God. Moltmann's pneumatology thus gives to faith and hope a far more dynamic, passionate and subversive character than they have in Pannenberg, and suggests more immanent revolutionary possibilities than Barth's account of political responsibility.

Conclusion

This survey of post-liberal Christologies shows the questions current in the theologies to which Frei was responding in his Christological essays and related texts. They concern the meaning of Christocentric faith in a modern, historically conscious age. Who is Jesus Christ and what significance does this particular person have today? What does it mean to believe he is present now? How should we interpret the New Testament texts that portray him, with their ancient cosmology, wonders, miracles and eschatological expectation? What does faith in him mean for Christian existence and how (and how far) does it demand the political engagement of Christian believers in the world? It also shows the range of ways of responding to those questions that were 'live' when Frei wrote.

Frei's Christological essays, I will show, can be read as a rational articulation of his Christological, providential faith, and a complex response to these theological questions and the theological scene I have sought to reconstruct in this chapter. Like Bornkamm, Barth, Pannenberg and Moltmann, Frei sought to understand Christ's presence in the light of his historical identity rather than by way of Bultmann's existential account of the encounter with God's Word. Like them, he offered a theological interpretation of the allegedly mythological features of New Testament Christology that preserved their reference to the concrete figure of Jesus of Nazareth more fully than Bultmann did, though with much less focus on Christ's message compared with Bornkamm. Like Barth, Pannenberg and Moltmann, Frei sought also to explicate the connection between Christ's singular particularity and his universal significance as Saviour. With Barth and in contrast to the others, however, he sought to avoid tying the meaning of the New Testament's Christological stories to a general, philosophical anthropology and sought to understand divine transcendence and action in history, and the universal significance of Christ, through the narratively given meaning of his identity.

Like all three of them, he drew a line from that particularity, through Christ's universal significance and presence, to an ultimately hopeful outlook on human history and human politics. As he later wrote in the Preface to *The Identity of Jesus Christ*, his argument in his Christological essays was that the Christian affirmation of the presence of God in Christ for the world involved 'a doctrine of the Spirit, focused on the Church, the Word, and the Sacrament, and the conviction of a dread yet hopeful cutting edge and providential pattern to mankind's political odyssey'.[189]

Notes

1 Published in *Christian Scholar* 49:4 (1966), pp. 263–306, and republished in Hans W. Frei, *Theology and Narrative: Selected Essays*, ed. W. Placher and G. Hunsinger (New York: Oxford University Press, 1993), pp. 45–93. For this and the reference in the next note, I am indebted to Mike Higton's Annotated Bibliography in *Christ, Providence and History: Hans W. Frei's Public Theology* (London: T & T Clark, 2004), p. 245.

2 Published in *Crossroads: An Adult Education Magazine of the Presbyterian Church* 17:2 (1967), pp. 69–96, and 17:3 (1967), pp. 69–96.

3 I am following Higton's account of the relationship between these texts in *Christ, Providence and History*, p. 245. See also Frei's Greenhoe lectures from 1976, which recapitulated these arguments, now published as 'On interpreting the Christian story' in Mike Higton and M. A. Bowald (eds), *Reading Faithfully: Writings from the Archives, vol. 1, Theology and Hermeneutics* (Eugene, OR: Wipf & Stock, 2015), pp. 68–93, and online in Mike Higton (ed.), *Hans W. Frei Unpublished Pieces: Transcripts from the Yale Divinity School archive* (https://divinity-adhoc. library.yale.edu/HansFreiTranscripts/), accessed 15.11.2023.

4 Higton examines Frei's Christology against the background of Frei's critique of Barth and Bultmann's epistemological monophysitism in his doctorate (*Christ, Providence and History*, pp. 56–118). Paul DeHart does so with less attention to Frei's critique of Bultmann in *The Trial of Witnesses: The Rise and Decline of Postliberal Theology* (Malden: Blackwell Publishing, 2006), pp. 102–47.

5 Hans W. Frei, 'Remarks in connection with a theological proposal', in *Theology and Narrative*, 1993), pp. 26–44.

6 Frei also mentions several other contemporary theologians in these pieces but these are sufficient to grasp the issues at hand. There were, of course, many other important academic theologians active and being debated in North American theology at the time, the best known of whom were probably Reinhold Niebuhr and Paul Tillich, but while Frei wrote a little about Tillich in earlier and contemporary pieces, and would criticize and invoke Niebuhr in later writings and lectures, they are not prominent among the figures to whom Frei was responding or on whom he drew in the Christology essays.

7 This is the way Frei himself had used the term of Barth in his doctorate (see Frei, 'The doctrine of revelation in the thought of Karl Barth, 1909 to 1922: the nature of Barth's break with Liberalism' (Yale University PhD, 1956), pp. 98, 126 n. 173, 133, 136, 173, 362, 384, 412, 431, 437–9, 483, 491–2, 513, 536), and of Barth, Bultmann and Tillich in 'The theology of H. Richard Niebuhr', in Ramsey (ed.), *Faith and Ethics: The Theology of H. Richard Niebuhr* (New York: Harper & Row, 1957), pp. 105–6. A few years later, Schubert Ogden used it in the same way (and to denote a continuing project) in *Christ Without Myth: A Study Based on the Theology of Rudolf Bultmann* (London: Collins, 1962), pp. 18, 170, 183. Later, Frei's colleague George Lindbeck would coin the term 'post liberal' to describe his own (and Frei's) approach to theology, in *The Nature of Doctrine: Religion and Theology in a Postliberal Age* (Philadelphia, PA: The Westminster Press, 1984).

8 James Kay does examine Frei in the context of Bultmann's project in his *Christus Praesens: A Reconsideration of Rudolf Bultmann's Christology* (Grand Rapids, MI: Eerdmans, 1994), pp. 125–42. However, while he offers a detailed and illuminating exposition of Bultmann, his discussion of Frei does not do justice to the latter's argument.

9 As David W. Congdon notes, Bultmann was 'at the center of theological conversation in both Europe and North America' in this period. See *Rudolf Bultmann: A Companion to His Theology* (Eugene, OR: Cascade Books, 2015), p. xiii.

10 See James M. Robinson, *A New Quest of the Historical Jesus* (London: SCM Press, 1959), which notes the 'Bultmannian epoch' in German theology and promoted the work of Bultmann's pupils to an Anglophone audience. For other examples of attempts to build on or go beyond Bultmann, see Ogden, *Christ without Myth*, Paul Van Buren, *The Secular Meaning of the Gospel* (London: SCM Press, 1963) and Carl Michalson, *The Hinge of History: An Existential Approach to the Christian Faith* (New York: Charles Scribner's Sons, 1959), especially from p. 190.

11 See the course outline in Yale Divinity School archive (YDS) 76 IV 13-197.

12 Kay, *Christus Praesens*, p. 125.

13 R. Bultmann, 'New Testament and mythology: the problem of demythologizing the New Testament proclamation (1941)', in R. Bultmann and Schubert M. Ogden (eds), *New Testament and Mythology and other Basic Writings* (Philadelphia, PA: Fortress Press, 1984), pp. 1–44. See also Bultmann's lengthier exposition of his proposal in *Jesus Christ and Mythology* (London: SCM Press, 1960). Some of that response is documented in Hans-Werner Bartsch, *Kerygma and Myth: A Theological Debate*, tr. R. H. Fuller (London: SPCK, 1972). Ogden's *Christ as Myth* is a precedent of using this essay to structure a (more in-depth) exploration of Bultmann's theology.

14 Bultmann, 'New Testament and mythology', pp. 1–8.

15 Bultmann, 'New Testament and mythology', p. 4.

16 Bultmann, 'New Testament and mythology', pp. 9–10.

17 R. Bultmann, 'What does it mean to speak of God?' [1925] in R.W. Funk (ed.), *Faith and Understanding: Collected Essays*, tr. Louise Pettibone Smith (London: SCM Press, 1969), pp. 53–7.

18 Bultmann, 'What does it mean to speak of God?', pp. 58–60; 'Liberal theology and the latest theological movement' [1924], in *Faith and Understanding*, pp. 45–6. For more on the theological and philosophical background to Bultmann's understanding of God as non-objectifiable, see Congdon, *Rudolf Bultmann*, pp. 32–51.

19 Bultmann, 'New Testament and mythology', p. 11.

20 Bultmann, 'New Testament and mythology', p. 15.

21 Ogden, *Christ Without Myth*, pp. 51–6.

22 See 'The significance of "Dialectical Theology" for the scientific study of the New Testament' [1928], in *Faith and Understanding*, pp. 145–64; and 'The problem of hermeneutics', in Bultmann and Ogden (eds and tr.), *New Testament and Mythology*, pp. 69–94. The quotation comes from p. 74. See also Ogden, *Christ Without Myth*, pp. 57–66.

23 Ogden, *Christ Without Myth*, pp. 65–6.

24 R. Bultmann, *Jesus and the Word* [1926], tr. Louise Pettibone Smith, Erminie Huntress (London: Ivor Nicholson & Watson, 1935).

25 Bultmann, *Jesus and the Word*, pp. 8–10.

26 Bultmann, *Jesus and the Word*, p. 11.

27 Bultmann, *Jesus and the Word*, pp. 35–8, 46–8, 68, 103–4. As Congdon observes (*Rudolf Bultmann*, p. 6), Bultmann's thought in this respect reflects the influence of Johannes Weiss' interpretation of the kingdom of God in Jesus' preaching, as Bultmann himself indicates in *Jesus Christ and Mythology* (pp. 11–14).

28 Bultmann, *Jesus and the Word*, pp. 41–2, 48, 51–6, 76–120, 127–32, 151–7, 176–8, 189–90, 195–6.

29 R. Bultmann, *Theology of the New Testament*, vol. 1 (Waco, TX: Baylor University Press), p. 3.

30 Bultmann, 'New Testament and mythology', pp. 15–16.

31 Bultmann, 'New Testament and mythology', p. 17.

32 Bultmann, 'New Testament and mythology', p. 18.

33 Bultmann, 'New Testament and mythology', p. 19.

34 Bultmann, 'New Testament and mythology', pp. 26–30.

35 Bultmann, 'New Testament and mythology', p. 32.

36 Bultmann, 'New Testament and mythology', p. 33.

37 Bultmann, 'New Testament and mythology', pp. 34–5.

38 Congdon, *Rudolf Bultmann*, pp. 7–8.

39 Bultmann, 'New Testament and mythology', pp. 36–7.

40 Bultmann, 'New Testament and mythology', pp. 38–9.

41 Kay draws out this contrast between simultaneity and sequence in Bultmann's understanding of cross and resurrection in *Christus Praesens*, pp. 105–6.

42 Bultmann, 'New Testament and mythology', pp. 39–40.

43 Bultmann, 'New Testament and mythology', p. 40. Bultmann claims that God actualizes faith in 'Liberal theology and the latest theological movement', p. 52.

44 Bultmann, 'New Testament and mythology', pp. 39–40. Kay shows that this theme of the presence of Christ in word and sacraments, whereby his death

and resurrection become present events for recipients, runs through Bultmann's exegesis of the Pauline and Johannine literature of the New Testament (*Christus Praesens*, pp. 38–89). There, Kay also shows that for Bultmann Christ is present and encounters us only in the church's proclamation (so also in Bultmann's theological writings; see *Christus Praesens*, pp. 90–1).

45 Bultmann, 'New Testament and mythology', pp. 41–2.

46 Ogden, *Christ Without Myth*, pp. 106–9.

47 See Bultmann, 'What does it mean to speak of God?', pp. 53–65.

48 J. B. Webster, *Karl Barth* (London: Continuum, 2000), p. 6.

49 Karl Barth, *Church Dogmatics* (hereafter *CD*) (Edinburgh: T & T Clark, 1956), IV/1, p. ix. Timothy Gorringe notes that the rumblings of Barth's debates with Bultmann can be found right through volume IV into the final fragments published as *The Christian Life*. See his *Karl Barth: Against Hegemony* (Oxford: Oxford University Press, 1999), p. 221. See also John Webster, *Barth's Ethics of Reconciliation* (Cambridge: Cambridge University Press, 1995), p. 91.

50 'Bultmann – an attempt to understand him', in H.-W. Bartsch, *Kerygma and Myth: A Theological Debate* (London: SPCK, 1972), pp. 92–101.

51 'Bultmann – an attempt to understand him', p. 108.

52 'Bultmann – an attempt to understand him', pp. 109–11.

53 'Bultmann – an attempt to understand him', pp. 115–16.

54 As reflected in the *Leitsatz* of §57, *CD* IV/1, p. 3.

55 *CD* IV/1, pp. 5, 7.

56 *CD* IV/1, p. 3–4.

57 'Bultmann – an attempt to understand him', pp. 124–7. See also *CD* IV/2, pp. 148–50.

58 *CD* IV/1, pp. 159–62.

59 *CD* IV/1, p. 163.

60 *CD* IV/1, pp. 319–20; IV/2, pp. 159–61.

61 *CD* IV/1, pp. 157–60.

62 *CD* I/2, pp. 46–9.

63 *CD* I/2, pp. 50–3.

64 *CD* I/2, pp. 55–69.

65 *CD* IV/1, pp. 158–60.

66 *CD* IV/1, pp. 159, 164–6.

67 *CD* IV/1, pp. 166–73.

68 *CD* IV/1, pp. 177, 186.

69 *CD* IV/1, pp. 179–80, 186–91.

70 *CD* IV/1, pp. 193–205.

71 *CD* IV/1, p. 163.

72 *CD* IV/1, pp. 216–83.

73 Paul Dafydd Jones, *The Humanity of Christ: Christology in Karl Barth's Church Dogmatics* (London: T & T Clark, 2008), pp. 200–1, referring to *CD* IV/1, pp. 224–8. See also *CD* IV/1, pp. 259–72.

74 *CD* IV/1, p. 188.

75 *CD* II/1, pp. 14–18, 51–6.

76 *CD* II/1, pp. 57–62, 194–202, 210–34. For a more detailed exposition of these ideas, see George Hunsinger, *How to Read Karl Barth: The Shape of His Theology* (New York: Oxford University Press, 1991), pp. 76–102.

77 *CD* IV/1, pp. 299–304.

78 *CD* IV/1, pp. 336–41.

79 *CD* IV/1, pp. 305–8. Barth talks about the 40 days as a temporal event on p. 318.

80 *CD* IV/1, pp. 305–11.

81 *CD* IV/1, pp. 316–17.

82 *CD* IV/1, pp. 349–50.

83 *CD* IV/2, pp. 140–54, 156.

84 *CD* IV/2, pp. 28–30, 73–4.

85 *CD* IV/2, pp. 31–6; II/2, pp. 94–126.

86 *CD* IV/2, pp. 48–92.

87 *CD* IV/2, pp. 96–9.

88 *CD* IV/2, pp. 156–65.

89 *CD* IV/2, pp. 166–232.

90 *CD* IV/2, pp. 266–82, 289–92.

91 So Bruce Marshall, *Christology in Conflict* (Oxford: Blackwell, 1987), pp. 115–60. Hence, Marshall argues, Barth's account of why only Jesus Christ is savingly significant is coherent.

92 *CD* IV/1, pp. 313–14.

93 *CD* IV/1, pp. 313–14.

94 *CD* IV/1, p. 318.

95 *CD* IV/2, pp. 298–313.

96 *CD* IV/2, pp. 511–32.

97 *CD* IV/2, pp. 533–53.

98 *CD* IV/3, pp. 38–48.

99 *CD* IV/3, pp. 72–75, 84–5.

100 *CD* IV/3, pp. 79–81.

101 *CD* IV/3, pp. 76–9, 82–3, 87–134, 160–1.

102 *CD* IV/3, pp. 165–270, 280.

103 *CD* IV/3, pp. 292–314.

104 *CD* IV/3, pp. 303–5, 328–56. See also §71 'The vocation of man', *CD* IV/3, pp. 481–679.

105 *CD* IV/3, p. 504.

106 As Webster puts it in *Barth's Ethics of Reconciliation*, pp. 92–3.

107 *CD* IV/3, pp. 355–65.

108 *CD* IV/1, pp. 644–62 and §67; *CD* IV/2, pp. 614–726.

109 §72 in *CD* IV/3, pp. 681–901.

110 On the political themes of Barth's Christology in *CD* IV/1–3, see Robert E. Hood, *Contemporary Political Orders and Christ: Karl Barth's Christology and Political Praxis* (Allison Park: Pickwick Publications, 1985), pp. 137–94; Gorringe, *Karl Barth: Against Hegemony*, pp. 217–67. On the political character of Barth's theology more broadly, from among a large literature, see also the essays in George Hunsinger (ed.), *Karl Barth and Radical Politics* (2nd edn) (Eugene, OR: Wipf & Stock, 2017 [1976]). And on Barth's own political activism and political views, see Frank Jehle, *Ever Against the Stream: The Politics of Karl Barth* (Grand Rapids, MI: Eerdmans, 2002) and George Hunsinger, 'The political views of Karl Barth', in *Conversational Theology: Essays on Ecumenical, Postliberal, and Political Themes, with Special Reference to Karl Barth* (London: Bloomsbury Publishing, 2015), pp. 179–204.

111 *CD* IV/3, pp. 3, 99–102.

112 *CD* IV/3, pp. 684–701. Barth here alludes to his account, in §§48–9 of *CD* III/3, of God's merciful 'fatherly lordship' of creation, preserving, accompanying and directing creatures in their free activity, in the face of the threat of chaotic non-being, for the sake of and towards their participation in the Kingdom of Jesus Christ.

113 *CD* IV/3, p. 713.

114 *CD* IV/3, p. 717.

115 *CD* IV/3, pp. 718–19.

116 *CD* IV/3, pp. 719–20.

117 *CD* IV/3, pp. 762–95.

118 §78 'The struggle for human righteousness', in Karl Barth, *The Christian Life* (London: Bloomsbury T & T Clark, 2017), pp. 287–379.

119 Barth, 'The struggle for human righteousness', pp. 296, 299–327.

120 Barth, 'The struggle for human righteousness', pp. 303–6, 308, 311, 325.

121 'The Christian community and the civil community', in Karl Barth, *Against the Stream: Shorter Post-War Writings 1946–52* (London: SCM Press, 1954), pp. 15–50.

122 See Dorothee Sölle, *Political Theology* (Philadelphia, PA: Fortress Press, 1974), especially pp. 42–53. For Sölle, the critical impetus towards a political theology is latent in Bultmann's historicism, constrained in the reception of his thought by the absolutizing of his kerygmatic theology and in his own theology by his individualism and focus on the present at the expense of seeing the situation historically. See also Kay, *Christus Praesens*, pp. 126, 171–2. There may, however, be greater political significance to Bultmann's account of eschatological existence than has often been appreciated. See David W. Congdon, 'Deworlded within the world: Bultmann's paradoxical politics in an age of polarization', *Theology Today* 79:1 (2022), pp. 52–66.

123 As Paul Lehmann put it in 1972 in 'Karl Barth: theologian of permanent revolution', *Union Theological Seminary Review* 28:1 (1972), p. 68. A few years later, Joseph Bettis noted that 'American theologians continue to ignore Barth', viewing his influence with suspicion and according his thought only historical interest in the story of modern theology ('Political theology and social ethics: the socialist humanism of Karl Barth', in Hunsinger (ed.), *Karl Barth and Radical Politics*, p. 117).

124 Ogden, *Christ Without Myth*, pp. 14–19.

125 J. Cobb, 'The post-Bultmannian trend', *Journal of Bible and Religion* 30:1 (1962), pp. 3–11.

126 Charles Campbell, *Preaching Jesus: New Directions for Homiletics in Hans Frei's Postliberal Theology* (Grand Rapids, MI: Eerdmans, 1997), pp. 25–7. See, for example, Frei's 1967 'Remarks', pp. 37–9.

127 Ernst Käsemann is usually credited with inaugurating this project with his 1953 lecture on 'The problem of the historical Jesus', in E. Käsemann, *Essays on New Testament Themes* (London: SCM Press, 1964).

128 G. Bornkamm, *Jesus of Nazareth* (London: Hodder & Stoughton, 1960), pp. 20–1. As Leander Keck noted in 1969, this book was the only comprehensive account of Jesus produced by the Bultmannians ('Bornkamm's "Jesus of Nazareth" revisited', *The Journal of Religion* 49:1 (1969), p. 1).

129 Bornkamm, *Jesus of Nazareth*, pp. 25–6.

130 It also helps justify the appeal of faith to the historical Jesus, and Bornkamm

often gives the impression that a concern to assimilate the historical Jesus to the kerygmatic portrait of the evangelists shapes his treatment of the sources. See Keck, 'Bornkamm's "Jesus of Nazareth" revisited', pp. 1–17.

131 Bornkamm, *Jesus of Nazareth*, pp. 58–61, 67, 80.

132 Bornkamm, *Jesus of Nazareth*, pp. 68, 82–3, 87–93, 99–108.

133 Bornkamm, *Jesus of Nazareth*, pp. 62–3.

134 Bornkamm, *Jesus of Nazareth*, pp. 68–9, 108, 169–70.

135 Bornkamm, *Jesus of Nazareth*, pp. 177–8.

136 Although in many respects Bornkamm's Jesus is similar to Bultmann's, as James Robinson noted in his review of the book: '*Jesus von Nazareth*, by Günther Bornkamm', *Journal of Biblical Literature* 76:4 (January 1957), p. 312. As Keck noted, Bornkamm's Jesus is more sharply differentiated from his Jewish background, which Bornkamm distorts ('Bornkamm's "Jesus of Nazareth" revisited', pp. 9–10).

137 See Bornkamm, *Jesus of Nazareth*, pp. 44, 66, 121–2, 153–4.

138 Robinson, *A New Quest for the Historical Jesus*.

139 My account here is drawn from Ogden's *Christ Without Myth*, pp. 111–91.

140 W. Pannenberg, *Jesus – God and Man* (London: SCM Press, 2002), pp. 15–19, 39, 55–64.

141 Pannenberg, *Jesus – God and Man*, pp. 44–55.

142 Pannenberg, *Jesus – God and Man*, p. 48.

143 Pannenberg, *Jesus – God and Man*, pp. 55–74.

144 Pannenberg, *Jesus – God and Man*, pp. 78–80.

145 Pannenberg, *Jesus – God and Man*, pp. 88–105. Pannenberg's case here involves ruling out several alternative explanations – primarily psychological – contesting claims about what is impossible by appeal to the laws of nature and finding in the independent empty grave traditions complementary evidence for the resurrection.

146 For a clear discussion of this counter-intuitive ontological claim, see Christiaan Mostert, *God and the Future: Wolfhart Pannenberg's Eschatological Doctrine of God* (London: Bloomsbury Publishing, 2002), pp. 89–126.

147 Pannenberg, *Jesus – God and Man*, pp. 157–8.

148 Pannenberg, *Jesus – God and Man*, p. 163.

149 They are dialectically identical, Pannenberg explains, in the sense of a dynamic unity of opposites that is synthesized only at the culmination of Jesus' personal history.

150 Pannenberg, *Jesus – God and Man*, pp. 207–30.

151 Pannenberg, *Jesus – God and Man*, pp. 250–62

152 Pannenberg argues that post-exilic Jews of Jesus' time who rejected him did so insofar as they identified the law absolutely with the will of God but that all humanity does something analogous and so comes under the same condemnation when Jesus' opposition to that stance is vindicated in his resurrection. Pannenberg later qualified this interpretation of post-exilic Judaism: see Herbert Neie, *The Doctrine of the Atonement in the Theology of Wolfhart Pannenberg* (Berlin, Boston, MA: De Gruyter, 2012 [1978]), pp. 131–3. Neie offers a helpful critical discussion of Pannenberg's account of the atonement in *Jesus – God and Man* (see especially *The Doctrine of the Atonement*, pp. 129–50).

153 Pannenberg, *Jesus – God and Man*, pp. 394–9.

154 Pannenberg, *Jesus – God and Man*, pp. 416–18.

155 Pannenberg, *Jesus – God and Man*, pp. 419–22.

156 Pannenberg, *Jesus – God and Man*, pp. 425–6.

157 Pannenberg, *Jesus – God and Man*, p. 292.

158 Pannenberg, *Jesus – God and Man*, p. 292.

159 Pannenberg, *Jesus – God and Man*, pp. 428–31.

160 Pannenberg, *Jesus – God and Man*, pp. 431–2.

161 Pannenberg, *Jesus – God and Man*, pp. 432–3.

162 J. Moltmann, *The Theology of Hope* (London: SCM Press, 1993), p. 27.

163 Moltmann, *Theology of Hope*, p. 28.

164 Moltmann, *Theology of Hope*, p. 28.

165 And in this way, he thought, they would also be more faithful to the theology of the Protestant Reformers.

166 Moltmann, *Theology of Hope*, pp. 31–56.

167 Moltmann, *Theology of Hope*, pp. 126–8.

168 Moltmann, *Theology of Hope*, pp. 183–6.

169 Moltmann, *Theology of Hope*, p. 91.

170 Moltmann, *Theology of Hope*, pp. 92–3.

171 Moltmann, *Theology of Hope*, p. 96.

172 Moltmann, *Theology of Hope*, pp. 114–18.

173 Moltmann, *Theology of Hope*, pp. 123–5.

174 Moltmann, *Theology of Hope*, pp. 128–33.

175 Moltmann, *Theology of Hope*, p. 187.

176 Moltmann, *Theology of Hope*, p. 187.

177 Moltmann, *Theology of Hope*, pp. 187, 191.

178 Moltmann, *Theology of Hope*, p. 188.

179 Moltmann, *Theology of Hope*, p. 3.

180 Moltmann, *Theology of Hope*, pp. 189–91.

181 Moltmann, *Theology of Hope*, p. 192.

182 Moltmann, *Theology of Hope*, pp. 192–3.

183 Moltmann, *Theology of Hope*, pp. 196–7.

184 Moltmann, *Theology of Hope*, p. 207.

185 Moltmann, *Theology of Hope*, pp. 4, 7, 75.

186 Moltmann, *Theology of Hope*, p. 207.

187 Moltmann, *Theology of Hope*, pp. 151, 187.

188 Moltmann, *Theology of Hope*, pp. 6–7, 17–20, 169, 187–8, 209–10.

189 Hans W. Frei, *The Identity of Jesus Christ* (Philadelphia, PA: Fortress Press, 1975), p. ix.

3

Jesus Christ, Providence and Political Hope

Frei's Christology essays are the chief source for his political theology. In them, Frei addressed his own concern for a Christological, providential faith, the contemporary theological issues explored in the last chapter and his own political context, in deliberate contrast to the apologetic character of most of the 'post-liberal' theologies of his time. By close conceptual description of the narrative patterns in the Synoptic Gospels that render Jesus Christ to the reader and their elucidation in other New Testament Christologies, Frei offered a description of the singular, concrete and unique figure set forth in those stories. In so doing, he sketched the lines of a Christology at once orthodox and radically revisionary, literary and historical. Drawing on the logic of the identity he had described, Frei interpreted Christian belief in Christ's contemporary presence in a way that yields a non-triumphalist, historical ecclesiology of witness, service and receptivity and a hopeful theology of providence and historical discernment with a marked political character, which sets him apart from those contemporaries. That account has the potential to frame, inspire and orientate Christian political engagement. It also illumines Frei's own political activism.

Against apologetic theology

In part, Frei's Christology essays must be understood in the light of his self-conscious rejection of most of the approaches to Christology explored in the previous chapter (and others). Frei articulated that stance explicitly in a bold lecture about his essays, given in 1967 at Harvard. There he set his proposals in contrast to a broadly sketched, sweeping critique of modern theology and modern theological hermeneutics that anticipates a key theme of his *Eclipse of Biblical Narrative*. It is the story of modern Christian theology as, 'almost exclusively, that of anthropological and Christological apologetics', from the end of the seventeenth century right up to theologians of his own day.[1] Such theology seeks to show, by a variety of procedures, an immanent mutual orientation and coherence between a past event of divine revelation and human faith in the self-consciousness of Jesus Christ and a present unity of the same in the believer.[2] Modern systematic theologies have thus tried to establish 'that the notion of a unique divine revelation in Jesus Christ is one whose meaning and possibility are reflected in general human experience'.[3] The crucial task for systematic theology has been, therefore, 'that of pointing to the potentiality of human existence for Christocentric faith and for Christocentric interpretation'.[4] This approach had run its course, Frei bluntly declared, and theologians now needed to search for alternatives.[5]

Frei was concerned that in such theologies, the meaning of Christology comes to be determined by its correlation with a given anthropology. In such procedures, Frei notes, Christ's person tends to be identified with his work and presence, conceived primarily in terms of self-revelation.[6] The revelatory action of God in Christ, moreover, tends to be thought of in relation to the human reception of it, first in Jesus Christ and subsequently in believers, so that original historical revelation and its contemporary believing appropriation are seen to be orientated towards each other.[7] This account sounds very similar to the analysis of Frei offered in his doctoral dissertation of what he called 'relationism'.

Frei's main concern in his dissertation is to trace Barth's consistent intention through the stages of the development of his doctrine of revelation.[8] For Frei, Barth's basic problem in these writings was pastoral and practical: 'What is normative in Christian faith that one may preach and apply to the changing, concrete issues of history and life, in the midst of which men live?'[9] On Frei's account, Barth had to break with the liberalism of the dominant traditions in nineteenth-century German academic theology because its theological outlook, which Frei calls 'relationism', could not yield the normativity Barth sought. At the heart of relational theology, bequeathed to the tradition by Friedrich Schleiermacher, was the positing of the original and inextricable togetherness of divine presence and human consciousness of God, and of consciousness of God and self-consciousness, which are given directly to us in Christian faith or religious experience in the historical form of the togetherness of Christ's presence with the church's consciousness of sin and grace.[10] Relationism could not provide the objective normativity Barth sought, because the togetherness of Christ's presence and religious experience made Christ an instant or product of that experience, and not something that could stand over against it.[11]

Frei offers a similar analysis on his own account as one part of the background to H. Richard Niebuhr's thought (the other being the Reformed tradition), and again in another article as background to a variety of twentieth-century positions, though the term 'relationism' does not feature in either.[12] The basic similarity of his own analysis indicates that Frei broadly shared Barth's assessment of relationism. With Katherine Sonderegger, we can see Frei himself as in effect belonging to this tradition insofar as he continues to wrestle with its problems.[13] In particular, we may note Frei's sympathy with Barth's critique of the fatalistic character of relationism, that it precluded 'any genuine turning of God toward man and vice versa', and that in such theologies, God crushes humanity in 'Gargantuan, fate-like power' at the very point where 'community between the two, speaking and hearing, command and obedience, should take place'.[14] Frei appears to endorse this criticism in terms that echo his later description of his discovery of an understanding of a gracious God of providence, beyond his own natural inclination to fatalism. Frei's thesis in the dissertation is that Barth's consistent emphasis on God's concrete, objective, eschatological self-revelation in Christ, together with his shift in thought-forms across the two editions, to distinguish his position from relationism, reveal his intention to express God's sovereignty in his self-revelation in Christ 'over the very means and the mode of reception of revelation', founding the doctrine of revelation on the doctrine of God.[15] It is an intention with which Frei seems wholly sympathetic in the dissertation.

The similarity between this account and Frei's polemic in his Harvard lecture suggests that his argument here was motivated by the same concerns about the threat to the freedom, gratuity and objectivity of God in self-revelation that he had seen, with Karl Barth, in the relationist theologies of the nineteenth century. Such a concern explains the force of the point Frei goes on to make, appealing to Barth, that Christian theology should not concern itself with arguing the possibility of Christian truth any more than its actuality. For, 'The possibility follows logically as well as existentially from its actuality.'[16] In the light of Frei's doctoral dissertation, we may take him here to be saying that God's free act of gracious condescension in Christ is not a possibility immanent in human beings and therefore cannot be explained or argued from knowledge otherwise available to us. Its possibility lies with God and can only be affirmed and experienced as God does in fact come close to us in Christ. Indeed, in another piece, written two years later, Frei extended this point to our knowledge of human need for reconciliation. He expressed frank scepticism about the possibility of making the case that human beings are negatively or positively prepared for the gospel or bent towards Jesus Christ, apart from the fact of incarnate reconciliation itself.[17]

Just how far Frei saw himself as taking a stance at odds with the mainstream of modern western theology can be seen in part from the way he attributes such apologetic theology to foundational figures from the German academic tradition such as Immanuel Kant and Friedrich Schleiermacher. It can also be seen from the breadth of contemporary figures he breezily indicts in this passage for using the same basic apologetic procedure in respect of different anthropologies, including several whom we have examined above, such as Bultmann, Ogden, Pannenberg and Moltmann.[18] Although he does not explain what he means in any detail, Frei clearly indicates that each theologian sought to show 'the *possibility* and, hence, the meaning of Christian claims concerning the shape of human existence' in one way or another.[19] Indeed, it is not difficult to see that Frei would have found in Bultmann, for example, a version of the relationism he had criticized in his doctoral dissertation and the Christocentric, anthropological and apologetic theology he had lambasted in his Harvard lecture.[20] For here Jesus Christ is interpreted primarily in terms of a form of revelatory work received in human decision, and the two are connected by way of an existentialist anthropology whereby the human plight of inauthentic existence is relieved by the impetus to authentic decision that comes through the message of Christ. In Bultmann, as Frei understood him, the content of what is believed is shaped by his understanding of the character of faith and of the transition to such faith from the existential condition of modern humans. For Frei, however, the possibility of Christian truth follows logically and existentially from its actuality; that is, from God's free and gracious action in Jesus Christ and not – he implies – from any potential we might identify in human existence. The paths by which people come to believe in Christ are not a fulfilment of such potential and do not, therefore, trace for us the logic of the content of Christian faith. The logic of coming to belief and the logic of belief are 'totally different'.[21]

Even Moltmann's *The Theology of Hope*, of whose critique of Bultmann, recovery of the historical character of human existence, and emphasis on realistic eschatology, history, crucifixion and resurrection and 'the mission of the Church and Christian within a rightly autonomous social world', Frei was quite appreciative, followed the same basic apologetic–anthropological pattern.[22]

> In post-Kantian German theology, there is always some sort of material affirmation concerning human being and its connection with wider reality that forms the necessary presupposition for Christian theology and for making Christian affirmations meaningful. *The Theology of Hope* is no exception.[23]

In Moltmann's case, Frei explains, this anthropology was the claim that the human condition is thoroughly historical in dialectical fashion. Through the interaction of the challenge evoked by a situation of contradiction and the subjective response to it in analysis and action, that situation is transcended in the bringing about of a new situation.[24] Moltmann offered a Christocentric vision of history in that manner, where lines of dialectical transformation converge on and diverge from Jesus Christ's crucifixion and resurrection as the event that anticipates and drives towards its own fulfilment and the fulfilment of God's promises to Israel and the world. Christ's cross and resurrection thus make sense in relation to a dialectical historical vision of human existence. Frei was sceptical of how plausible Moltmann's anthropology would be outside Germany.[25] He thought, moreover, that Moltmann's apologetic–anthropological theological method risked subverting the particularity of Jesus Christ. It was difficult to distinguish, he observed, whether Christ's cross and resurrection determined the dialectical process of history or merely exemplified it.[26]

Against apologetic hermeneutics

In his Harvard lecture, Frei connected the apologetic character of modern theology to modern theological hermeneutics. Here his concern for objectivity is even more apparent and he connects it with the question of the essence of Christianity. The thrust of Frei's analysis is that the hermeneutical strategy adopted by modern theologians tends to replicate the apologetic strategy of their theological method.[27] In these theologians, the question of how to understand the meaning of Christianity, as located in its sacred texts, is shaped by their concern to show the mutual orientation of the historical event of Jesus Christ proclaimed by the New Testament and the perspective of the reader in the present, such that the event of Jesus Christ can be read as potentially meaningful for modern readers. Here too Frei saw himself as dissenting from a breadth of contemporary western theologians.[28] In the lecture, however, he takes issue specifically with the 'post-Bultmannian' theologians whom James M. Robinson had grouped under the label 'the new hermeneutics', including Robinson himself, and Bornkamm.[29] These theologians, Frei notes, sought to grasp the identity of Jesus Christ from his message. They held that Jesus' message expresses his actualized self-understanding in his situation that lay behind his actions and which may be encountered by us today, through a critical analysis of his sayings.[30]

Frei agreed with Schubert Ogden and Van Harvey that to draw conclusions from Jesus' actions and speech to his selfhood depends on chronological historical information about Jesus' life and development as the setting for his sayings, which they (with Robinson) thought we lack.[31] Above all, Frei thought that both the proponents and exponents of the 'new hermeneutics' *and* their critics were too beholden to a common idealist picture of the self, whereby the true self is hidden behind its words and actions, with the consequence that 'the meaning of texts is invariably in part the fruit of the life-perspective with which we approach them.'[32] Frei thought this approach was inappropriate for understanding Jesus as someone depicted in narratives that rendered the theme of his identity through the inextricable interplay of character and circumstances. For such stories involved a very different, more unitary, view of persons in their environment, in which their personal and inner selves cohered with their public actions, and descriptions of the two flowed together, as they do in ordinary language.

He also worried about the perspectivism on which the new hermeneutical procedure depended. The consensus among Bultmannians of different persuasions and their critics was that meaning is, 'at least potentially, life-meaning and, therefore, always a potentially common perspective between past and present, text and interpreter'.[33] This interpretive procedure ensured that the text's meaning is cast as a question of the text's life-meaning relating to a present understanding of life with which it is either in harmony or on conflict. It is the hermeneutical correlate of identifying Christ's person and work, and, as Frei notes, reproduces the anthropological apologetic theological procedure on the hermeneutical level: 'How can we so read the [Christological] text that a life-perspective we find in it can become a significant or genuine possibility for us?'[34] However, Frei argued, if the effect of the story on us is our criterion for determining the meaning of the gospel story then it means whatever the interpreter wants it to mean, depending on their perspective and the apologetic anthropology they wish to see in it. Here again, Frei is evidently concerned with objectivity, this time in the sense of the possibility of the normative interpretation of the Gospels, but in parallel with his concern for gratuity and objectivity of divine self-disclosure.[35]

Dogmatic theology as the conceptual description of the Gospel narratives

In response to this situation, Frei sought to reopen the question of the essence of Christianity first and prioritize that over questions of truth and present-day meaningfulness and to do so in such a way as to enable normative interpretations of the central Christological scriptural texts of the tradition.[36] The only other alternative, he thought, was a metaphysic or ontology to which Christology was peripheral.[37] Frei thus stood in partial continuity with the nineteenth-century liberal tradition and with the Bultmannians insofar as his proposal was Christocentric but sought a Christocentric approach on a non-apologetic or 'dogmatic' basis. In contrast to Bultmann, his followers, Pannenberg and Moltmann, Frei argued that theologians should prioritize understanding the essence of Christianity in a non-perspectival fashion, before raising the question of its truth.[38] Rather than try to explain the possibility of Christian truth and its existential relevance for human beings, they should seek to describe the logic of the content of Christian faith as normatively set forth in the narrative depictions of Christ in the Synoptic Gospels.[39]

We will find this distinction between explanation and description doing important work throughout the Harvard lecture and Frei's Christological articles, and it is therefore worth attending to. Frei had been reading the later work of the philosopher Ludwig Wittgenstein 'in earnest' since 1962 and he remarks in the lecture that Wittgenstein had influenced his understanding of understanding.[40] The distinction between explanation and description also occurs in paragraph 109 of Wittgenstein's *Philosophical Investigations*. In context, Wittgenstein is seeking to dispel several hazy notions. There was the notion of meaning as a strange referential relationship between words and the objects they signify and between propositional sentences and states of affairs; an aura accompanying words in all their uses, which requires exhaustive explanation by burrowing beneath linguistic phenomena to unearth some pure, ideal, essential, definitive form that guarantees this relationship. Then there was the notion of understanding as a mental process or event that could be explained, similarly, by uncovering its pure, essential form. Wittgenstein contends that we can resolve these philosophical conundrums by freeing ourselves from the pictures of language and understanding they involve, and we do that by turning from the attempt to explain, in the sense just summarized, to looking at ordinary linguistic practices, where the meaning of words is a matter of their various uses and what it means to understand them is a matter of different ways of carrying on activities involving language. All these uses and practices can and need to be described, and this description will dispel our illusory quest for essential forms of meaning and understanding.

In part, when Frei talks of describing rather than explaining, he signals a measure of agreement with Wittgenstein. Frei thought there was 'a variety of descriptions for any given linguistic phenomenon, and, hence, above all, no ontological superdescription or explanation for it'.[41] The ruled-use or 'grammar' of such phenomena, moreover, 'is more readily exhibited ... than stated in the abstract'.[42] Frei was, he implied, interested in setting forth or describing the grammar of the Synoptic Gospels as narratives for his theological purpose. But he also extends or stretches (and alters) that distinction theologically, in respect of what is involved in faithful understanding of God's redemptive action in Christ. The possibility of faith in Christ, he argued, lies in God's free action, which transcends our capacities; it is not something we might explain by discovering an underlying human potential for it. That divine action is the meaning of what Christians believe. It is described for us in the form of certain stories that portray Jesus Christ as their chief character, and the understanding available to us is to describe the manner (or 'grammar') of that portrayal, which, Frei thinks, has a peculiar logical character, as we shall see.[43]

Frei was aware that there have been many proposals in modern western theology for how to understand what Christianity is, each of which addressed the question of Christianity's essence only to raise it again, whether in relation to some strand of continuity in Christian history or the Bible or some canon within the biblical canon. He proposed that theologians begin with the Synoptic Gospels, because their nature as narratives or at least partial narratives – texts with at least partially aesthetic characteristics – may make possible normative interpretations, where the meaning of the text remains the same regardless of the interpreter's perspective.[44] By 'aesthetic' Frei seems to have meant a meaning that is given to the interpreter in the structure of the text: 'Normative interpretation is a matter of the structure of the narrative itself and seeing if the text *as given* has a genuine structure.'[45] Answering the question of the essence of Christianity requires starting at a point 'where the meaning is firmly grounded in the text and nowhere else', which unity of text and meaning is the condition of the possibility of authority.[46] This approach would ask about the meaning of the story quite apart from whether it can be meaningful for us.[47] Starting with the narratives of the Synoptics would allow such normative interpretation because their meaning is given to the reader in the way the theme emerges from, and cannot be abstracted from, the direct interaction of character and circumstance, which are inextricably bound together.[48] Frei also indicates a second rationale for beginning here: beginning with the Gospels was the priority of the church's traditional procedure; a minor appeal to traditioned practice that will become more prominent and more developed in his *Eclipse of Biblical Narrative* and even more so in some of his later writings.

This proposed starting point leads to a very different focus and approach to the interpretation of the New Testament from Bultmann's focus on Paul and John, Bornkamm's analysis of Jesus' message and ministry, Pannenberg's reconstruction of Jesus' message and its vindication in the resurrection, or Moltmann's dialectic of cross and resurrection. Although Frei shared with Bornkamm and Pannenberg a concern to grasp the identity of Christ from his history in some sense, Frei took the Gospel narratives *as narratives* to provide at least a literary access to his person, which was identical with the Saviour described in early Christian proclamation, a literary description with the unique force of a historical claim.[49]

Understanding the Gospels in terms of what is given to us in the narrative is a specific kind of understanding, Frei suggested, analogous to understanding the nineteenth-century novel or historical narratives: it involves attending to the structure of the story, to the way in which the theme of the story emerges from the interaction of character and circumstances.[50] To understand those interactions, one needs to work with an understanding of persons as unities of intention and action, of subject and embodiment, which may not be explained but can be described, at least up to a point.[51] In these public interactions, and primarily in embodied intentional action, more than in speech, a character becomes who they are.[52] Because what happens to characters also becomes part of who they are (and not only through their reactions to them), however, the narrative will exceed the descriptive categories of intentional action and embodied subjecthood so that the personal unity of the characters integrating all these things can only be narrated.[53]

In this way, by pointing beyond itself to the story, this aesthetic, formal approach would allow for an unsystematic jumbling of methods – historical-critical and aesthetic – forced by the text itself, and 'in which the text itself is dominant'.[54] Such an approach to understanding the narrative portions of the Synoptics was not 'governed by our perspectives' but described the structure of the story as far as possible.[55] It would thus allow the text to 'force a scramble of our categories of understanding', rather than confirming the pre-understandings we bring to it.[56] In this way, prioritizing the aesthetic in its integrity would also do greater justice to the possibility that we understand stories much better than we can account for the methods and categories by which we understand them than would the 'restrictive and exclusive' methodologies of existentialist interpreters and the new hermeneutics.[57] Prioritizing the aesthetic over the historical, however, would also yield a firm meaning, capable of normativity, in place of a more speculative, inferential and probable character of a historical reconstruction of the history of early Christian tradition and its relationship to the historical Jesus.[58] Nor do we have to choose, on this narrative approach, between prioritizing Christology or eschatology, as Moltmann and Pannenberg would have us do, because Jesus' character is interwoven with the eschatological circumstance of the advent of God's reign, and his completed story belongs to a longer sequence of stories in which it anticipates its eschatological fulfilment.

This approach also offered a more direct access to Jesus as portrayed in the story than either historical-critical reconstruction or understanding his person through his message. For in this kind of story, Frei asserts, character and circumstance belong together so closely that we know the persons portrayed through their story, and such is the case with Jesus in the gospel story.[59] He 'is who he is by what he does and undergoes' and as such is 'indispensable to, and known in, the story'.[60] Indeed, Frei adds, 'Jesus *is* his story.'[61] Frei tends to speak as though the Synoptics told a single story, though he acknowledges that 'one cannot cover even Luke and Mark by the same story analysis'.[62] One would have to proceed 'one narrative at a time'.[63] He seems to assume there would be sufficient affinity or overlap between the portrayals of Jesus in the Synoptics to make it possible to draw some broad conclusion that would cover the differences between them. A high Christology, then, drawn from the Synoptic narratives' accounts of Jesus' life, death and resurrection, would be the 'basic datum' for answering the question of the essence of Christianity, the beginning of an answer to that question.[64] For such was their meaning as stories, rather than the narrative being only 'a mythological or time-conditioned form of the real meaning'.[65]

Frei's narrative procedure could be applied to Johannine and Pauline texts, understood as commentary on the sequence of narratable events of which the Gospel stories are composed. The Gospels might likewise be taken, as per the church's traditional procedure, as an incomplete clue to the significance of the earlier story of the Old Testament.[66] From here, Frei suggests, we might take the Gospels also as an ambiguous clue to the rest of history after Jesus, as we experience it, since his story is (and is part of) the story of God with him and all humanity, rather than (with the theologians of hope) from a wider history with its doubtful unity to the Gospels. This suggestion points forward to his account of the presence of Christ which would yield much of the substance of Frei's political theology. Because that political theology is so deeply rooted in Frei's account of Christ's identity, it is worth explicating that account in some detail here.

The identity of Jesus Christ

In the first of his Christological essays, 'Theological reflections on the accounts of Jesus' death and resurrection', Frei sought to test the main part of this proposal and show that the meaning of the Gospels, 'the cornerstone of the Christian tradition of belief', was indeed a high Christology.[67] In the essay, the more precise style seeking to make clear conceptual distinctions and descriptions that characterizes some passages in the Harvard lecture predominates over the more polemical and informal style of other parts of that lecture.

Here again, Frei tends to talk in the singular of the gospel or New Testament 'story' or 'narrative' of Jesus.[68] He clarifies that he is taking the three Synoptics as one composite account 'with individual variations', sharing a common three-stage pattern of identification of Jesus.[69] His intention, we may infer, is to signal a basic commonality among the various stories told of Jesus in the New Testament, which we might specify in anticipation of his exegesis as commonalities in the identifying force of the stories, such that their different narrative portraits of Jesus render the same unsubstitutable individual. Indeed, Frei states the formal or structural element of that commonality: 'the development of the gospel story is such that Jesus' identity as the singular, unsubstitutable human individual that he is comes to its sharpest focus in the death-and-resurrection sequence taken as one unbroken sequence.'[70] In this way, he argued, the gospel story variously told by the Synoptics is completely and exclusively the story of Jesus of Nazareth, the Saviour, so as to be distinct from other parallel accounts, both in ancient myth and modern fiction. For the narrative form of the Gospels, with its inextricable mutual interaction of specific events and specific individuals, was such that its theme – the pattern of redemptive action, culminating in the passion–resurrection sequence – was so identical to the person of Jesus as to be *his* story, which no one else's story could fully repeat.

Categories for describing Jesus' personal identity

In order to set forth this unsubstitutable individuality, Frei developed a complex way of describing personal identity, drawing upon the analysis of schemes for identity description in the doctoral thesis of his student, Robert H. King, and on some of the philosophical sources King discusses (several of whom took Wittgenstein's approach to philosophy).[71] Frei sought 'low-level' categories for describing, rather than trying to explain the possibility of, the identity given in the narratives. These were tools that would not overwhelm the story but help describe someone whose identity 'is most sharply focused in the passion-resurrection narrative sequence'.[72] Identity, he explains, is something enacted: 'the action and testimony of a personal being by which he lays true claim to himself are the same at an important point in time as well as over a length of time.'[73] And it is public. The concept of identity affirms 'that the singular and true identity of a person is mysteriously and yet significantly manifest and therefore accessible'.[74] Frei sought categories to describe identity so understood, on the premise that, just as with understanding linguistic phenomena, we also need a variety of schemes for describing personal identity but there is no explanatory super-theory available that could unite them.[75]

The first is what he calls an 'intention-action description'.[76] It answers the question, 'What is this person like?' As Frei later wrote, it seeks to pinpoint the person 'in specific actions or in responses to specific occurrences that involve him' and display his or her typical stance.[77] It entails the notion that a person 'is what he does most centrally and most significantly'; that persons are constituted by their most characteristic actions.[78] This description drew on the capacity of the category of intentional action to unite the inner and outer in the self and so understand the self as publicly present and intelligible because intentions are implicit, and so publicly available, in actions.[79] The intentional self is both embodied and social within a public world, so that qualities of the self are knowable to others more directly than by inference or analogy.[80] As we have seen, Frei thought that this mode of description cannot capture the way in which external events enter someone's identity beyond their responses to them. Furthermore, it presupposes – but does not really get at – a persistence or continuity of the person that unites not only someone's various actions but also these actions and the things that happen to someone: what Frei calls the 'ascriptive center' of intentional activity (and, we might add, of passivity).[81] After all, we know ourselves to be prior and subsequent to any of our actions.

What is sought here is not a metaphysical but a logically ultimate descriptive category for that elusive, open-ended persistence in continuity to which predicates, including actions, are ascribed.[82] Because it is elusive, the ascriptive subject may only be described indirectly using a scheme that links it as one pole with another: a scheme that sees the subject as manifest in a public medium, that is different from itself. The sort of scheme of this kind, apt for describing the persistent subject of the narratives that portray Jesus, must be one in which that self is unproblematically public (in contrast to Bultmann's existentialist anthropology in which, Frei thought, the self is ambiguously manifest in distorting objectifications in the world).[83] Frei commends the model found in Karl

Barth's doctrine of revelation, whereby the self is publicly manifest in the medium of speech (for example in naming or performative utterances), and that of the self as manifest in the medium of the body it distinguishes itself from and with which it identifies itself, which he attributes to Merleau-Ponty, Barth and Farrer.[84] Naming, promising and the body all manifest without distortion of a self that is taken to persist across events, actions and situations.[85]

However, the subject-in-manifestation scheme does not allow us to grasp the significance for identity of the temporal events through which the self persists (and to which the New Testament attaches divine agency), which intention–action schemes help us describe. The two schemes are thus complementary to one another. Both identify the self as properly public, embodied and social. Frei's notion of personal identity, then, is not 'intensely individualistic', as David Lee has claimed.[86] Nevertheless, Frei himself acknowledged there are ways he could have enhanced attention to the social context of individual identity, in particular its relationship to social structures.[87]

Although they are categories for the description of human identities, as George Hunsinger points out, their use does not preclude the articulation of a high Christology that Frei intended, as Hunsinger contends.[88] After all, we do not have *any* categories suited for the description of divine identities. Rather, as Frei would later point out, when we speak of God on the basis of the literal reading of the gospel story, we do so analogically, truly referring to the reality but in terms whose meaning does not allow us to say what that reality is.[89] Indeed, Frei is prepared to apply both schemes of identity description analogically to God.[90] As I will show, both schemes are crucial to the description of Jesus' identity as one that combines 'unsubstitutable individuality and universal saving scope', as Frei put it in his second Christological essay.[91] Both descriptions, however, would be exhausted in the face of a subject matter that can only ultimately be narrated, given the irreducibility of narrated portrayals of personal identity. Far from inhibiting an articulation of Christ's divinity, Frei's analysis shows that there is an absolute uniqueness to the irreducible identity of the person of Jesus of Nazareth, an exceptional density to his particularity because of its intrinsic unity with the identity and presence of God, which is also essential to Frei's political theology in his second Christological article.

Jesus' characteristic intentions and his uniqueness as saviour

Frei argues that Jesus' characteristic enacted intentions are crucial to the description of the individualization of the qualities of the Saviour figure in him, a point that will be crucial to his response to Bultmann. In consequence of the Gospels' identification of the pattern of redemptive action with the specific person of Jesus, the early Christians emphasized Jesus as identifying the saviour figure, the cosmic lord and redeemer, rather than emphasizing a hoped-for saviour figure who happened to be exemplified in Jesus.[92] In some New Testament texts, Frei thought, you can still trace the writers' astonishment at having now to think of a pagan or Jewish saviour figure exclusively as Jesus of Nazareth.[93] The strength of this identification of the saviour with the human Jesus of Nazareth precluded the organic transition, found in myths of the dying and rising saviour, between the saviour's need for redemption (because he dies) and his being redeemed (by rising). So completely is the saviour figure identified with Jesus and Jesus with the rest of humanity that this Saviour is as helpless as are other human beings. Hence the saving work of omnipotence he accomplishes is 'mysteriously congruent with [his] all too human helplessness and lack of power in the face of the terrible chain of events leading to his death, once that chain had begun to be wound around him'.[94]

Omnipotence and helplessness are naturally combined in the story, without merger, by hints of his abiding initiative at moments when Jesus is most clearly and genuinely helpless.[95] The key to the way Jesus' power and powerlessness are thus united in the Gospel narratives lies in his characteristic enacted intention. For 'a man's being is the unique and peculiar way in which he himself holds together the qualities which he embodies – or rather, the qualities which he *is*'.[96] And, whatever their relationship to the historical Jesus, the Gospels give us the portrait of a person who holds together his contrasting qualities in virtue of his consistent intention, shared with the God of the universe, to save humanity; an intention of love that is seen precisely, if indirectly, in 'the shaping of all of his personal qualities in conformation to his mission or aspiration in obedience to God'.[97] Jesus was willing, in service and assimilation to the love of God for the world (John 3.16), 'to govern and exercise the power appropriate to it, just as he was willing for its sake to be governed and suffer helplessly when the occasion demanded'.[98] The coexistence and transition between power and powerlessness 'are ordered by the single-minded intention of Jesus to enact the good of men on their behalf in obedience to God'.[99] Jesus is characterized by the way he unites divine power and human helplessness in his obedience and love for humanity through the transitions of his story, a pattern that Frei's second mode of identity description complements.

Frei shows this unity by tracing the transition in Jesus 'from initiative to increasing passivity in the face of circumstances' that begins in Gethsemane.[100] Jesus' arrest enacts outwardly an inner transition that had already taken place in his prayers. Here, as in the Matthean parallel in which Jesus renounces the possibility of angelic salvation, the stories depicts an inner and outer transition from intention to action and the enmeshment of intention into an irreversible chain of circumstances, the unity of all of which pattern is Jesus himself and belongs uniquely to him.[101] This transition, Frei argues, is the point at which we see Jesus being most of all himself, in enacting, in this specific and terrifying way, his intention in obedience to God: the good for human beings on their behalf. Just so he is who he is.

The theme of tension between Jesus' power and powerlessness in the Synoptic narratives reaches a climax, Frei observes, in their testimony to his being raised from the dead. For here, in the narrative sequence, the identity of the crucified Jesus is one and the same as that of the risen Lord; the cosmic redeemer is completely identified with a particular historical human being. To attend to this identification, Frei asks after the persistent, continuous ascriptive focus or subject of Jesus' various, discrete, enacted intentions and the things he undergoes. This persistent, ascriptive subject may be indirectly described through its cumulative manifestation in speech and in the body.[102]

In these terms, there is an ambiguity about who Jesus is that is resolved in the resurrection accounts, especially the Lucan account.[103] In the pre-birth, birth and infancy stories in Matthew and Luke, Jesus is identified entirely 'in terms of the identity of a community, the people of Israel'.[104] He has no individuality; he is 'Israel under the representative form of an infant king figure', symbolically recapitulating and fulfilling Israel's history in miniature.[105] There is no question of his historicity here.

With his baptism, Jesus begins to appear more as an individual in his own right, to a limited extent, performing mighty signs of God's kingdom, proclaiming its advent but also still having a symbolic quality, only now in respect of the kingdom of God he attests and embodies: the kingdom identifies him more than the converse, as his titles indicate. Here Jesus' greater specific individuality in relation to specific situations 'raises the question of historical veracity in acute fashion', since he is generally agreed to have lived, but because Jesus' identity is so tied to the kingdom of God it is very difficult to distinguish actual events from stylized depictions illustrating Jesus' representative character.[106]

From Jesus' passion predictions onwards, Jesus is described with greater specificity in relation to a specific series of events whose meaning is bound up with him as the central character. While he is still identified by the kingdom he enacts, that connection becomes loose and the kingdom more ambiguous. The kingdom and the figure of the Son of Man recede into the background. Jesus emerges increasingly 'as one whose mission it is to enact and suffer a singular destiny', which problematizes his identification with the kingdom, reflected in the increasing tendency to use his titles of authority ironically and pathetically.[107] It requires resolution – the manifestation of Jesus' identity and the specification of his relation to the kingdom and to the Messianic titles – through some train of events.[108]

In the passion–resurrection sequence, the focus is on 'the action by which the destiny of Jesus is accomplished'.[109] Here he is none other than himself, fully focused as a specific individual. His persistent, continuous identity as the subject of all he does and of what happens to it is fully manifest in his resurrection. Here, although Jesus acts, his identity is described less clearly in terms of his own enacted intentions and more clearly and emphatically as 'the manifestation of the presence of God acting'.[110] God's action began to supersede Jesus' with his arrest and now God is 'climactically the agent here' but in a veiled manner.[111] God's preeminent action is in the background, beyond description, its effects 'swathed in confusion and contradiction' between the different accounts.[112] Rather, it is Jesus who is manifest as the presence of God and manifest most fully as an unsubstitutable individual in his own right.[113] This claim of Frei's merges the intention–action and self-manifestation scheme of identity description in their application to God. God is at once hidden and manifest – veiled and unveiled, as Frei implies elsewhere, in echo of Barth – in the specific person of the crucified and risen Jesus.[114]

There is here what Frei will go on to call a pattern of unity in differentiation between God and Jesus.[115] Jesus and God, the one he calls 'Father', are distinct characters. They interact with one another: God sends Jesus on an errand of mercy, declares loving approval of his obedience at his baptism, somehow mysteriously brings about the properly contingent circumstances that lead to his death, and raises him from the dead in vindication of his obedience. Jesus obeys God, and consents to the sequence of events culminating in the cross, exhibiting saving divine power in and through profound human helplessness. His intention is vindicated in the resurrection. Yet the cumulative force of the identification of Jesus in the story is such that their identities are also united. Jesus is the manifestation of the presence of God as agent where God alone acts directly. By this action, God 'makes it impossible any longer to think of God without being drawn to look at Christ', as Higton says.[116] The implication of that analysis is that the identities of God and Jesus are distinct yet inseparable. As with Pannenberg, the resurrection is crucial to Frei's articulation of a high Christology but in a different and less counter-intuitive manner: as the culmination of the cumulative manifestation of the persistent subject of Jesus' story rather than the retroactive determination of his identity.

This difference is pertinent to one of the objections that George Hunsinger has made to the cogency of Frei's argument, which are worth exploring because they go to the heart of what Frei is trying to achieve. Hunsinger finds that Frei's argument borders on problems typical of Antiochene Christologies. In Frei's account, God never seems to be the ascriptive subject of Jesus' intentions and actions, as he needs to be if they are to have universal scope. The union between God and Jesus that emerges from Frei's description of Jesus' enacted intentions is 'much more nearly moral than personal', at least until the resurrection.[117]

It is true that Frei emphasizes such a moral union between Jesus' obedience and God's intentions in sending him, which is both true to the Gospels and an important ingredient in his depiction of Jesus as truly human. Yet Frei's ascription to Jesus of divine power, which seems to be closely congruent with his human obedience and the suffering to which it leads him, suggests something more than a moral union, as we have seen. Moreover, the significance of the resurrection for Frei is not that Jesus begins to be divine from this point but that it manifests who he is throughout the story. This point also tells against Hunsinger's closely related charge of adoptionism, that for Jesus to be the Saviour of all, God needs to be the subject of his actions from the start, yet 'the self-focused presence of God does not seem fully to coincide with that of Jesus until after the resurrection'.[118] However, as Frei puts it in *The Eclipse of Biblical Narrative*, the affirmation that Jesus' self-manifestation is the self-manifestation of God covers the whole story in retrospect (which Hunsinger notes elsewhere).[119] It is true that, as Hunsinger argues, being resurrected in general may not entail divinity. However, as we shall see, Frei's argument is that in the Gospel narratives, Jesus' resurrection means he cannot not be alive, that he shares the divine attribute of essential and absolute livingness. In this way, in Jesus, unsubstitutable individuality coincides 'absolutely' with his manifestation.[120] He has, we might say, an unshakeable identity in which specific individuality is inseparably united with divine presence.

Although at points Frei does observe differences between the ways in which the Synoptic Gospels portray the stages of Jesus' identification in their stories, the overall tendency is to focus mostly on Luke while imply-ing a commonality of structure between all the Synoptics that does not do justice to Frei's remark, in the Harvard lecture, that they would have to be treated individually.[121] I wish too that Frei had also found a way to interpret Jesus' sayings and the deeds of his ministry and the Gospels more broadly, drawing on historical-critical research, under the governing priority of his formal analysis of the story, as the Harvard lecture indicated was possible (though he was not very enthusiastic about it in the first Christological essay).[122] Likewise a fuller coordination of Pauline and Johannine texts with a fuller analysis of the Synoptics in their relative diversity would strengthen his proposal.[123] However, as he later explained in the Preface to *The Identity of Jesus Christ*, he intended only to offer an 'outline of a possible realistic narrative reading of the Gospels' to demonstrate the potential of his approach and by that measure he succeeds.[124] That potential includes a way of responding to Bultmann's argument that the New Testament Christological narrative needs demythologizing in order to uncover the existential meaning in which it speaks to modern human beings.

The resurrection accounts and the demythologization of the Saviour

The literary structure of the Gospels' account pointed, Frei argued, towards the thesis that the passion–resurrection account 'is a demythologization of the dying-rising savior myth'.[125] Frei defines myth, after David Friedrich Strauss's use of the category in *The Life of Jesus Critically Examined*, as 'the unconscious poetizing of a folk consciousness'.[126] However, Frei argued, the unsubstitutable individuality of Jesus, and the strong and exclusive bond between his narrated identity and the redemptive theme he embodies there, distinguishes him and his story from the dying and rising saviours of ancient myth.[127] For, in myths, characters and their actions represent broader psychic or cosmic states that transcend those representing occurrences; characters are not themselves. The passion-resurrection stories, however, concern 'an unsubstitutable series of transpirings concerning an unsubstitutable individual, whose unique identity is, for the description ... directly in and inseparable from the events related in the story'.[128] Hence, the meanings of the saviour figures of contemporary myth are transformed in application to Jesus to conform to his unsubstitutable, unique, historical individuality. In this way, as Mike Higton points out, Frei shows that the Gospels talk about God's self-manifestation in the language not of myth but of history, of 'contingent, finite, complex and messy public actions and interactions'.[129]

There is some similarity here with Pannenberg's non-mythological reading of the Christological titles with reference to the concrete human figure of Jesus of Nazareth in the light of his resurrection, albeit with contrasting understandings of the significance of the resurrection, as we have seen. There is, we might add, no tension for Frei between the full humanity and full divinity of Jesus. For in the resurrection accounts, Jesus' concrete, historical humanity appears there at its most concrete and irreducibly, unrepeatedly singular as the manifestation of God's identity and presence, inseparably united to, yet firmly distinct from, God.

The logic of that claim takes Frei's response further, however. He notes that in Strauss's argument, the identification of myth in a narrative makes questions of historicity redundant: the meaning of the stories is a folk consciousness. The power of myth is its capacity to echo 'a widespread inner experience which cannot be directly or univocally expressed'.[130] They are interpreted by asking about what primordial truths, aspirations or emotions they express, rather than whether they actually happened. By contrast, Frei observes, the resurrection accounts refer exclusively to the figure of Jesus and claim that in his resurrection his human particularity is manifest most truly. In this way, they allow the question of whether his resurrection happened. For narratives that deal with 'specific actions and specific human identities ... the question of factuality is bound to arise precisely at the point where his individuality is most sharply asserted and etched'.[131] In the Gospel stories about Jesus, this point of maximum individuation is the passion–resurrection sequence. But the claim of those stories is stronger; it forces the question of historicity. For the claim, especially in Luke, 'is that the being and identity of Jesus in the resurrection are such that his nonresurrection is inconceivable' (even if his resurrection is beyond conceiving).[132] To grasp who he is, is to believe he has in fact been raised from the dead.

This claim, Frei clarifies, is a claim about the logic of this particular story, not a general claim that maximal lifelikeness in a fictional character entails their historicity. Only in the case of Jesus is his individual identity 'totally identical with his factual existence', because it is fully manifest in his resurrection.[133] The fact-claim 'is involved as part of the very identity that is directly enacted and manifest in the story'.[134] 'Who he was and what he was, did, and underwent are all inseparable for the authors from the fact that he was or is ... that he lives.'[135] Hence the women at the empty tomb are told that they seek the living among the dead (Luke 24.5) as though, against all ordinary expectation, his being alive was self-evidently an implication of his identity, that of the very the one who was, as he prophesied, to be betrayed, crucified and to rise again (Luke 24.7–8).[136] Frei treats the Fourth Gospel as commenting on this idea, albeit in a narrative that is wholly about the manifestation of its subject's abiding identity, rather than events that constitute his being, as in Luke. Here too Jesus is 'the resurrection and the life' (John 11.25): 'He defines life. He is life.'[137] Describing the grammar of the story thus exhibits a unique logical pattern which bridges the gap between literary representation and theological and historical claim, uncovering not the realization of an imminent possibility or a symbol of the historical movement of spirit but the gracious, free coming of God.[138]

Frei's argument then is that the passion–resurrection accounts demythologize any mythical motifs they draw upon by their exclusive reference of them to an irreducibly unique historical figure whose unsubstitutable individuality involves his factual existence. By the same token, their conceptual content is also not reducible to the emergence of the faith of the disciples.[139] Rather, the stories of the resurrection appearances of the once crucified Jesus of Nazareth to his disciples connect the story of the earthly Jesus and his ministry with the early Christian message about him and narrate the transition between them.[140] That analysis, however, also leads Frei to distinguish his understanding of what it means to affirm what the accounts claim – that 'it is more nearly correct to think of Jesus as factually raised, bodily if you will, than not to think of him in this manner' – from the kind of argument for the historicity of the resurrection found in Pannenberg.[141]

For Frei, the transition from literary description to factual, historical and theological judgement is to be made in the passion–resurrection sequence. It cannot be verified. It is, he notes, unlike other facts. The resurrection accounts narrate 'a factual occurrence of a wholly unique kind'.[142] There are no historical facts or natural occurrences to which we can compare it to draw analogies (and hence, we may infer, judgements of probability). Nor can the resurrection appearances be compared with other kinds of occurrences, whether visions or physical miracles, as Pannenberg does.[143] The novel-like quality of the testimony in the resurrection accounts, moreover, seems to mean they do not amount to historical evidence for the resurrection, which is appropriate since Christian faith is not based on factual evidence (on this last point Frei agrees with both Barth and Bultmann).[144] The resurrection is, rather, a logical necessity of Christian faith normed by Jesus' identity as given in these stories.[145] Believing them is less like believing in their historical accuracy and more like believing in their inspiration, a claim vitally important for understanding the nature of the authority Frei ascribes to these stories.[146] It is one that he would in effect clarify in his account of Christ's presence in his second Christological essay in terms that echo Barth's doctrine of the Word: the feeble, often naive scriptural stories become, in Christ's use of them, vehicles of Christ's indirect presence and the testimony by which he testifies who he is (and so normative of Christian faith).[147]

In another way, Frei's account here contrasts with Barth's Christology in the first volume of the *Church Dogmatics*. In his doctoral dissertation, Frei had argued that traces of the relational, liberal theology Barth had sought to break with remained even in the early volumes of the *Church Dogmatics*. One of those traits was a tendency to be overly systematic, assuming a transcendent, synoptic perspective in grounding human knowledge of God in the doctrine of God.[148] Another, closely related, was a tendency to be overly Christocentric, so that all anthropological content may only be understood in the light of Christology, the sole content of divine revelation, so that 'noetically "Jesus Christ alone" is human nature'.[149] This approach, however, emptied Barth's claim that the Spirit grounds the doctrine of human faith *'as a positive human quality'*.[150] In the end, Frei adds, this overly systematic, Christocentric approach makes it difficult to accommodate the particularity of Jesus Christ by negating any historical knowledge of him. This negation amounted to 'a sort of epistemological monophysitism', which in effect eliminated all human knowledge of Jesus' historical humanity in favour of divine revelation, so undermining the very objectivity of God's self-revelation in Christ and the theological realism Barth sought to uphold.[151]

When compared with this evaluation of Barth's 'epistemological monophysitism', Frei's Christology essays can also be seen, as Higton argues, to be offering a more historical account of Jesus' humanity than the one he found in the early volumes of Barth's *Church Dogmatics*, albeit one that works with a rather literary sense of historical knowledge.[152] Yet while Frei was writing his Christological essays he was also revising his view of Barth, especially in respect of volume IV of the *Church Dogmatics*. Frei continued to teach and read Barth when he came to Yale and participated in a panel with him when Barth visited Chicago in 1962.[153] His changing interpretation and evaluation of Barth's *Church Dogmatics*, and especially his appreciation of some of the later volumes, is an index of the direction his own theology was taking, methodologically, substantively and, as we shall see later, politically.[154] As the quip Divinity School students jestingly attributed to Frei and posted under his picture there said, 'This Barth gets better with every volume.'[155]

It is not difficult to see in Frei's essays the strong echoes of several features of Barth's Christology in *Church Dogmatics*, volume IV, in contrast to Bultmann. Frei noted, in an essay first given as a paper in a memorial symposium at Yale Divinity School, held in 1969, that for Barth what the actuality of the incarnation tells us is that while God is and remains transcendent in union with humanity, God is transcendent in God's own way. That is, 'he is not transcendent in such a way that he cannot be related to his creatures'.[156] Here Frei attributes to

Barth what Kathryn Tanner would later call a non-competitive account of transcendence, which is also implied in Frei's theology in these essays.[157] In Frei's account too, God acts in and through the human being, Jesus of Nazareth, and the historical forces that bear upon him, to save humanity, and manifests God's presence in Jesus' risen, embodied person.[158] Frei's literary reading of Jesus' identity also echoes Barth's emphasis on the New Testament soteriological narratives as testimony to God's incarnate action in the history of Jesus. Frei goes further, however, by specifying the realistic narrative structure of the Synoptics as the primary portrayal of that history and the primary objectivity of the textual witness to God's gracious objectivity in self-manifestation in the humanity of Jesus. As Frei noted, Barth's account of the atonement in IV/1 of the *Church Dogmatics* relies on a perceptive close reading of the sequence of the Gospel narratives, especially the passion narratives. That narrative sequence is crucial for Frei too.[159] Indeed, informed by the development of his own theology, Frei would come to pioneer an interpretation of Barth as a narrative theologian in this sense.[160] Yet as Frei himself points out, the way he interprets the cumulative identification of Jesus Christ in the gospel story is, for the most part, quite different from the way Barth does it. Barth divided Jesus' history into his ministry and his passion, understood in the light of his resurrection appearances, as the coming of the eschatological Judge, and the substitution, at the judgement, of that Judge for the guilty. Frei – who also has a substitutionary view of the atonement – focuses more on Jesus' consistent intention and the cumulative manifestation of his identity through the whole story.

Beyond this difference, however, Barth's reading (as with his whole doctrine of reconciliation) is framed by the traditional ascription of the history of Jesus and the narratives that attest to the incarnate Son of God as the subject of that history. Frei relativizes that incarnational frame as commentary upon the prior narrated figure of Jesus Christ, rendered by the Synoptic narratives. For Frei, this figure holds together, in a personal, historical, dramatic fashion, both divine power and human powerlessness and manifests the divine presence in his particular, human, historical, bodily identity. He thus discloses in his own person the inseparability of identity and presence that properly characterizes Israel's God. Incarnation is one scriptural gloss upon that identity. Frei's procedure is not as clear as Barth in articulating the story of Jesus as the story of God's gracious, personal coming to human beings as their Saviour, but it is more effective in addressing the issue of myth and in attending to the particular historical humanity of the specific individual in whom God has drawn close to us.

Frei's Christology, like Barth's, conforms to the grammar of Chalcedonian orthodoxy (affirming the full deity and full, sinless humanity of Christ united in one person without confusion, change, division or separation) while eschewing the idioms of classical metaphysics and embracing a more fully historical understanding of Christ's person. And in his own way he too is as revisionary and radical as his liberal and post-liberal forebears. Just as important, for my purposes, is the significance of Frei's distinctive procedure and its results for his understanding of Christ's significance and presence.

Jesus Christ's presence, providence and political hope

Frei extended his Christological proposals in the pieces published as 'The mystery of the presence of Jesus Christ' in three issues of the journal *Crossroads* in early 1967, which were later republished, very lightly edited and with a new introduction and an epilogue, as *The Identity of Jesus Christ* in 1975. Here Frei asks about Christ's identity in order to address the question, 'What does it mean for Christians to believe that he is present?' What does it mean, that is, to believe he is related to believers and contemporaneous with them now, between his past presence and the future mode of his presence?[161] In answer to that question, Frei explores the claim he had made in his first Christological essay, that Jesus' unsubstitutable individuality coincides absolutely with his manifestation, or, as Frei puts it here, that 'in Jesus Christ identity and presence are so completely one that they are given to us together: We cannot know *who* he is without having him present.'[162] The upshot is what Frei describes as a formal, doxological, rational exercise in ordering the somewhat opaque traditional Christian belief that Jesus Christ 'is a contemporaneous person, here and now, just as he spans the ages'.[163] It is a claim that, Frei notes, is difficult to understand directly of a figure from the past as well as in respect of the utter freedom it ascribes to Christ to share himself without loss of self-presence.[164] This belief becomes clearer, Frei argues, if we begin with the grammar of the identity of its subject.

To that end, Frei undertakes a very similar analysis of Jesus' identity to the one he had offered in 'Theological reflections'. In 'The mystery of the presence of Jesus Christ', Frei expands his analysis of Jesus' characteristic enacted intentions, finding it crystallized in his rejection of Satan and his annunciation of his mission in the synagogue at Nazareth and the story of his prayer in the Garden of Gethsemane.[165] Here he also has more to say about the interaction of Jesus' agency, his circumstances and the agency of God. In the transition from power to powerlessness to which

Jesus consents in Gethsemane, Frei argues, his characteristic obedience and love of human beings meshes savingly with the superseding of his initiative by that of God at work through the historical forces that overwhelm and destroy Jesus.[166] Frei here seems to build on Erich Auerbach's observation that the Gospels portray the unfolding of historical forces in the representation of persons from all classes and occupations who end up in the narrative because historical movements engulf them accidentally and they are forced to respond to them.[167] What Frei emphasizes, however, is the activity of God in and through such forces and responses, including the activity of the central character of Jesus of Nazareth. This understanding of divine agency will also be significant for understanding Frei's account of providence in this piece.

Frei also expands his account of Jesus' atoning work, especially by way of a more extensive contrast with modern Christ figures. Here he notes the cosmic scope of Jesus' redeeming activity signalled by his Messianic titles, but also evident in his miracles, preaching, death and resurrection, along with his personal uniqueness, and adds the pattern of exchange that unites them. This pattern consists in 'the quality that made him an individual who nonetheless incorporated humanity at large into himself'.[168] This quality is the substitution of Jesus in his innocence for the guilty 'by carrying the load of all who suffer with them and even for them'.[169]

Frei's contrast between Jesus and Gnostic redeemer figures serves to underline several features of the pattern of exchange: the innocence of Jesus; the depth of his need of redemption in identification with the helplessness of other humans in the face of death, their sin, and the evil of other God-opposing powers; and the saving efficacy of the vicarious character of this identification in view of the harmony between Jesus' helplessness and his perfect obedience.[170] At this point, then, Frei sketches Jesus Christ as a Saviour whose unsubstitutably individual identity is inclusive of all others in virtue of his cosmic significance and his vicarious exchange of his perfect obedience for their guilt and profound helplessness before death and evil. It is this combination of Jesus' cosmic significance making universally effective the vicarious exchange of conditions that makes Jesus' death and resurrection salvific.

We have already seen how Frei identifies Jesus from the Synoptics in terms of his characteristic quality of obedience towards God and love towards human beings entailed by that same obedience to God in the context of the mission of grace on which God sent him. As we saw, Frei shows that Jesus carries this obedience through the transition from power to powerlessness, in which there is an abiding saving power or efficacy. Christ thus identifies utterly with human helplessness and need of redemption. Indeed, Frei speaks of Jesus being in need of redemption and being redeemed, according to the gospel story and the commentary on it in the sermons of the book of Acts (Acts 2.24–32, 36; 13.35–37).[171] That helplessness, we may infer from Frei's account, has to do with the ways in which human beings lose their liberty of action as finite creatures, through the tightening around them of various webs of circumstances, up to and including death. For it is in these terms that Frei describes Christ's helplessness in the gospel story (recall also Frei's reference to the circumstances that held Jesus 'in thrall').[172] By the implications of the logic of that identification, human helplessness would seem to include especially those ways humans are deprived of that liberty at the hands of others, of earthly powers. In this way we can see grounds in Frei for drawing out a liberatory dimension to the atonement.

The resurrection, we may infer, effects the vicarious redemption of Jesus for us all. Frei indicates the basis for this redemption when he says that the resurrection 'demonstrates Jesus' acceptability to God as being obedient to God's will'.[173] The resurrection is 'the vindication in act of his own intention and God's'.[174] This notion is consistent with Frei's account of the pattern of exchange and it would also be consistent with his account to say that it is because Christ's obedience becomes ours that we may also share in his vindication and redemption. It is this cosmic significance combined with the inclusive character of Jesus' identity, as the obedient one who vicariously identifies with all humanity in our profound guilt and need *and* is vindicated and redeemed on our behalf, that grounds Frei's expressions of the significance of Jesus' irreducibly singular identity for others.

In 'The mystery of the presence of Jesus Christ' (as in his 'Theological reflections'), Frei makes several statements about the significance of Jesus' identity as fully manifest in the resurrection.[175] The first of these concerns the relationship between Jesus and Israel. At the beginning of the gospel story, Frei argues, Jesus is identified by reference to the story of Israel. At the end of the story, they are again fully identified, but the determination of identity is reversed. Now Jesus 'provides the community ... with his identity. He is the Christ of Israel who, in his own singular identity and unsubstitutable history, sums up and identifies the history of the whole people.'[176]

Here David Dawson raises an important question. He argues that Frei secures Jesus' ability to save by his unique relation to God manifest in the resurrection, which separates Jesus from Israel and from history.[177] Now the risen Jesus provides Israel with his identity. 'Is this not full-blown supersessionism', asks Dawson?[178] The force of Dawson's question seems to be that Jesus effectively overwrites the identity of Israel in providing them with his identity. However, in Frei's account, Jesus' unique relation to God does not *separate* him from Israel or indeed from the rest of humanity with whom he has identified himself. He is distinguished from the rest of Israel and all other humans by that relation, but the logic of Frei's analysis is that Jesus is always so related to the Father, and the resurrection makes that relation manifest, that it coexists with his identification with his people and with all humanity. Indeed, it is consistent with Frei's argument to say that it is precisely out of that relation that he identifies himself with Israel and with all humanity. There is not, on Frei's reading of the story, a zero-sum either/or between Jesus' unique relation to God, as the embodiment of God's presence, and his membership of Israel or his full humanity, as Dawson's argument apparently implies. He is fully human and fully divine. Rather, in Jesus we have to do with a transformation of Israel's identity, and of our humanity with Israel.

For Frei, Jesus' passion and resurrection are the culmination of the embodied and verbal manifestation of his identity as the abiding, elusive, continuous subject of the actions and events of his life. Nothing from the earlier stages of that life and its unfolding of his identity is lost thereby. As Dawson brilliantly observes, for Frei, Jesus' resurrection, where God's action fully supersedes his own, is an event of his own life; therefore the spiritual fulfilment of his life effects, rather than subverts, the irreducibility of his embodied identity.[179] The same is true, I suggest, of the way Frei thinks Jesus, in the manifestation of his own identity, sums up the identity of Israel he bears in himself from his infancy and ministry: it is fulfilled without effacement, displacement of focus or loss of its history and meaning. In the earlier episodes of his life, he was identified with Israel as a figure of its stories even as the specificity of his own identity came more into focus. We could and should go further than Frei explicitly does here: Jesus *receives* his identity from Israel before it is transformed in him. In the culmination of his own story and the manifestation of his unsubstitutable identity, he becomes the bearer of Israel's identity on behalf of Israel and recapitulates it in his own singular identity. For, I would suggest Frei might say, in him Israel's faith and redemption and the embodied presence of her Redeemer combine in an everlasting redemption. As Frei says elsewhere, 'his full self-identification with us is perpetual and not temporary'; he maintains his solidarity with us in his eternal rule.[180] The same must, on Frei's terms, apply first and foremost to Israel. Dawson argues that Frei separates the risen Christ from Israel and humanity by an enduring distance, which he represents with the figure of Moses' veil from Exodus 34, for ever blocking the believer's idolatrous confusion of themselves with Christ.[181] Yet on Frei's terms Christ transcends this difference, his lordship embraces both sides of the veil, which does not sever his identification with Israel or humanity.[182] Israel's stories are thus preserved but their meanings are now related to his and are thus extended and intensified in the fullness of the way he bears them; they become figures that speak of his story without loss of their own literal depiction of their subjects.[183]

Frei's second statement about the significance of Jesus' identity concerns the possibility of others having identities. Since Jesus in his resurrection is manifest as himself, and he is so on behalf of everyone else (by virtue of his vicarious identification with them in dying and rising for them and his cosmic significance) 'as the first of many brothers', the rest of us also have identities.[184] Dawson is helpful here in understanding Frei's position. It is because Jesus' identity is enhanced in being raised by God from death, and because the resurrection is incorporated into his embodied identity, that it is irreducible and that he is able to secure identities for others, even though we are sinners in need of his redemptive power.[185] Hence no one can be rightly understood as alienated from themselves.

We may adduce here a point Frei makes when dismissing schemes of identity description in which the subject is manifest in a world that alienates them from themselves to some degree, that objectifies and distorts them. Frei argues that the Fourth Gospel in effect rejects such a scheme to describe Jesus' identity: he is truly manifest in the medium of speech and embodiment there. But it would be applicable, he adds, to the Johannine non-believers' conception of themselves and the human situation, thinking of themselves as having an identity in themselves that is finally no true identity. This view amounts to a 'sinful error', a product of the non-believer's alienation from Jesus and from their true self, 'because Jesus does have an identity, and we have our identities in him'.[186] The vicarious character of Jesus' identity in bearing and overcoming human guilt and subjection to powerful forces that reduce them to helplessness and death, in his absolute livingness, means that all human beings have authentic identities in him. Through this relationship he forges in himself, each of them in the historical pattern of their lives, their interaction with one another and their circumstances, is united to him and is real, authentic and meaningful in the social, historical public world. This claim that seems to imply that all human beings really participate and will participate in Jesus' resurrection, is a point we will return to when considering Frei's eschatology.

We could take Frei's thinking a step further, however, if we consider that one prevalent sense of self as alienated in its social embodiment is a product precisely of the subjugation of human beings to powerful forces that Christ shared on Frei's account. In other words, we might see selfhood-in-alienation in terms of the double consciousness that

W. E. B. DuBois described, and which Frei himself experienced as a Jew in Nazi Germany: being socialized in a world that only lets you see yourself through the eyes of the groups that dominate and oppress your own.[187] In that case, Frei's claim that the identity of Jesus secures all human identities in him could be extended not to deny the experience of double consciousness but to radically denaturalize it, indeed to cast it as an effect of social sin that Christ has overcome in his person for everyone.

Third, Frei also renders this claim about Jesus' identities and ours with imperative force. Jesus' unsubstitutable identity is such that it not only identifies the community of Israel but all human beings, who are called to identify themselves by relation to Jesus of Nazareth 'who has identified himself with them and for them'.[188] Human beings are to live out of this reality and authenticity of their particular identities as secured in Christ. Like Barth and Pannenberg, then, Frei finds cosmic, saving significance in the particularity of the concrete figure of Jesus of Nazareth in virtue of his particular, historical and vicarious divine–human identity. Frei's brief exposition lacks the richness and dynamism especially of Barth's account of the sanctification of humanity, but it has similar dignifying, humanizing force. Indeed, to pick up the argument of the last paragraph, it seems to license resistance to dehumanizing social structures and cultural stereotypes and the self-perceptions they impose on subjugated peoples.

Frei explicates this significance in a manner that is, in a loose sense, profoundly existential, not through its dependence on an existential account of the alienated human situation but precisely in refutation of it and in virtue of the same identifying force that demythologizes mythic themes in the Synoptic Gospels. The ascription to Jesus of those soteriological tropes around his unique, irreducible and public, social and historical identity makes them serve this articulation of his significance in such a way that, in contrast to Bultmann, his pupils and interpreters, Jesus can be understood to redeem and humanize human beings in their embodied, social, historical situatedness. These claims too will bear on the political character of Frei's doctrine of providence.

Jesus Christ's presence, providence and political hope

Frei's account of Christ's presence is, as we have seen, grounded in his analysis of Jesus' identity as one who cannot not be thought to be alive.[189] Jesus Christ is manifest in his resurrection as the one who is Life.[190] Frei's key assertion here is that the unity of identity and life manifest in the risen Christ means that he is lord of his own life such that he can communicate it to us, a claim framed in the language of presence. One of the main arguments of 'The mystery of the presence of Jesus Christ', then, is that 'Jesus, raised from the dead, is present to himself and therefore can and does share his *real* presence with us.'[191] His unity with God explains the freedom and self-focus with which he, as a unique and living individual, shares his presence with us. He does so from a 'location of his own'.[192] As such, his life is so at his disposal that he can turn and share it with us, he can be our contemporary across the ages.

It is worth noting that Frei talks interchangeably of the risen Christ being present, being alive and being contemporaneous.[193] He also combines them. Jesus is manifest in his resurrection, Frei writes, as one whose identity 'involves his actual living presence'.[194] There is a shift to talking mainly of Christ's presence in Frei's pneumatology at the end of the book, when Frei wants to talk about Christ communicating his presence and its effects in the world. Frei worried about the idealist connotations of a notion of the self as constituted by its unique perspective in the moment on itself, others and the universe and its performance of itself, but in the context of his argument about Christ's embodied, social identity, those connotations are difficult to hear.[195] As he claims, it 'involves nothing philosophically more high-flown than a doctrine of the Spirit'.[196] The category of presence does not overpower the work, as Hunsinger worries it does. Rather Frei successfully accentuates the 'living Christ in his concrete presence to faith ... as a presence that [is] active, independent and self-communicating'.[197]

Frei's analysis of Christ's identity, then, clarifies the strangeness of Christian talk and experience of his presence. Frei goes on to apply that clarification to different aspects of Christian belief in the presence of Christ – in word and sacrament, in the church and in the world – under the rubric of pneumatology.[198] He takes those beliefs for granted and clarifies them, rather than seeking to provide a hermeneutical warrant for them and the connection between affirming Christ's presence on the basis of his identity and affirming these modes of his presence.[199]

Frei interprets Christian talk of the Spirit as denoting a number of facets of the 'pattern' of Christ's presence now, as distinct from during his earthly life, death and resurrection or his eschatological appearance: the complex unity of Jesus of Nazareth and the presence and action of God; the indirectness of the presence of Jesus as the presence of God now; the unity of factual affirmation with commitment and love in response to this presence (that we have already seen); and the church as witness to, and public communal form of, that presence.[200] The indirectness of that presence is important here. It is the presence of one who cannot be thought not to be present, but whose mode of presence cannot be 'directly grasped or conceived'.[201] The emphasis in Luke-Acts and the Fourth Gospel on Jesus' withdrawal in order to bestow his presence, Frei adds, expresses both this indirectness and the reality of this self-gift, which we may grasp as something mysterious and 'self-focused'; that is, a presence that is at Christ's free disposal.[202] There is a 'distance' between the life Christ lives to God, veiled to our understanding, and our time and existence in which he died.[203] Yet as one who can freely share his presence because of who he is, and who is the one who underwent his passion out of love for humanity, he reaches across the distance to share his life with us with and under creaturely realities. It is in this context that Frei's political theology begins to emerge as he articulates how the living, gracious presence of Christ constitutes the church.

Frei explains that the forms in, with and under which Christ shares his life with us are word and sacrament, and the church. Word and sacrament are the spatial and temporal bases of Christ's presence. Here, presence 'means something like physical proximity and verbal communication' on the basis of self-presence, yet without being subject to the confinements of these spatial and temporal bases 'in such a way as to be trammelled in its freedom'.[204] For Frei, the closing lines of George Herbert's poem 'The Agonie' convey best the reality and indirectness of Christ's self-gift, the veiledness of what he shares and how he shares it and his free, efficacious (and affectively potent) sharing of it: 'Love is that liquor sweet and most divine/ Which my God feels as blood, and I as wine.'[205]

Christ's presence in word and sacrament, Frei continues, is what make possible the 'relatively permanent institutional structure' Christian community needs.[206] As such, the church is the communal form of Christ's presence. But Christ is also the 'ultimate presence in and to the world in its mysterious passage from event to event in public history'.[207] Talk of the Spirit denotes the unity of Christ's presence in word and sacrament and his presence 'in and to the shape of public events of the world and of human history'.[208] The church is constituted by this unity as a communal disciple with its own narrative.

What Frei means by this striking claim becomes clearer as his exposition develops. The heart of his proposal seems to be the claim that the church should be thought of historically, on analogy with the twofold identity description that Frei applied to the New Testament rendering of Jesus of Nazareth. On the one hand, the church's identity can be thought of on analogy with the continuous but elusive subject of a life across all its changes. In the case of the church, this centredness to which the church's story is ascribed is constituted by Christ's presence to it by word and sacrament (across all the changing ways in which these are celebrated, we may presume). On the other hand, like the people of Israel, the church also needs to be described on analogy with something like an intention–action identity description, in terms of the interaction of the church with other characters and circumstances, namely, 'humanity at large through history'.[209] In this sense, the church '*is* nothing other than its as yet unfinished history, transpiring from event to event.'[210]

The church is not another saviour: that role has been fulfilled by Jesus Christ. Rather, the church's calling in this history is to follow Christ's pattern 'at a distance' – echoing, not repeating it – in its interaction with its neighbour, humanity at large, whom it is to love and serve. Because Christ's identity and presence are uniquely inseparable, we cannot conceive of the believer's affirmation of Christ's risen presence except as united with both their love of Christ and their love of the neighbour for whom Christ gave up himself and in whom Christ is present.[211] As Christ's disciple, unlike its Lord, the church also accepts 'the enrichment given to [it] by [its] neighbor ... the human world at large, to which the church must be open in gratitude without forsaking its own mission and testimony'.[212] I will return to this note of receptivity below.

The church does not exclusively or triumphantly embody Christ's presence in the world. As a witness, it is distinct from Christ and points away from itself to his mysterious presence in the history of the world. As a creaturely witness, indeed, the church is a 'frail human instrument', which struggles to hold together its commitment to the integrity of word and sacrament, on the one hand, and the passionate concern for the world, on the other, which both derive from the pattern of Christ's identity and presence.[213] Indeed, these things cohere only by the presence of Jesus Christ, on whom the church depends entirely. Christ's presence to the church by word and sacrament and public history means that its frail, often compromised, communal life becomes a form of his presence, embodying that to which it bears witness, 'the public and communal form the indirect presence of Christ now takes', foreshadowing, not embodying, the reign of God, as he put it in a later lecture on this theme.[214]

Eschatology, providence and politics

The pattern of the church's interaction with humanity in their history is unfinished. The church awaits its eschatological consummation together with the rest of the human world, an ultimate summing up of all history in Christ's future presence. Just as Jesus in his irreducible identity summed up, incorporated and identified 'the history which is the people of Israel', so also the church 'moves toward an as yet undisclosed historical summing up' that cannot yet be narrated because it is unfinished and hidden.[215] The church thus has an unfinished, and to that extent somewhat ambiguous or only partially resolved, identity, and a sense of dynamic orientation under the 'determining impulse' of God's providential rule to an end it does not determine and cannot predict.[216]

The interaction of church and world, Frei writes, is 'public history – the intention-action pattern formed by the interaction of the church with mankind at large'.[217] It forms a 'mysterious pattern of meaning to be disclosed by the presence of God in Jesus Christ in the future mode'.[218] (One aspect of the mystery is presumably, as Frei indicated in a later lecture from 1981 on 'History, salvation-history, and typology', the hidden manner of the cohesion of the histories of church and world, salvation history and universal history.)[219] It has such a pattern because Christ's presence to history means it is 'providentially ordered in the life, death, and resurrection of Jesus Christ, who is Lord of the past, the present, and the future'.[220]

This terse but striking claim follows from Frei's analysis of Jesus Christ's identity. God's action and God's presence is manifest in the bodily risen person of Jesus Christ. Thus, Christ is 'the very presence of the God of providence'.[221] As Frei later put it in 'History, salvation-history, and typology', God 'has focused his providence in the person of Jesus Christ in whom the reign of God has come near'.[222] Because of the way Frei understands Christ's presence in terms of the complex pattern of his historical identity, we may infer that he thinks that that pattern, marked by his obedient intention to save humanity and the way it shapes the pattern of exchange and the confluence of events, and the inseparable unity-in-distinction with God manifest in his resurrection, is the form of God's rule in history now.

Frei distinguishes God's providential ordering of history in Christ from the action 'of a mechanical fate'.[223] It is not deterministic, but 'mysteriously, abiding mysteriously, coexistent with the contingency of events'.[224] This claim is consistent with Frei's Christology, in which, as we have seen, contingent historical forces and actors 'coincide' with God's work, and Jesus Christ's own characteristic salvific, obedient intention is one with God's purpose in them and in him.

This congruence of divine shaping with historical contingency, and the eschatological reserve Frei believes believers should apply to the future mode of Christ's presence, means that God's providential action cannot be read off a single event (not even the history of Jesus Christ) or described by a scientific rule.[225] It cannot be captured by any universal theory of history, either. Christians, therefore, 'precisely because they believe in providence, know far less than certain ideological groups about the shape of the future'.[226] They share with Marxists, for example, an interest in 'the future shape of public history' and so have a basis for conversation with them, but because they cannot claim to know the future to anything like the same extent as the predictions of Marxists' ideology, they will find agreement with them difficult.[227]

Nevertheless, Frei insists, Christians do not know nothing about God's providence. Applying Paul's words in 1 Corinthians 13.8–12 about the partial knowledge of God's mysteries before the coming of eschatological fulfilment, he affirms that it is possible to discern something, albeit 'in a glass darkly'.[228] The history of God's providence may be narrated, after a fashion, by reaching for 'parables that might serve to set forth a kind of pattern', though no one parable will give us a definitive clue to the pattern of history, so varied and unexpected are historical events, so mysterious is God's providential work.[229]

Frei's concept of the parable here seems to denote an event or sequence of events taken up into a chastened form of analogical thinking. Their meaning is 'symbolic', by which I take Frei to mean that they are tokens whose pattern stands for and gives limited access to the meaning of a fuller reality, insofar as one can trace a limited likeness of a partially evident pattern between different sets of events, like the family resemblances between extant fragments of different stories, perhaps.[230]

The first parable is the pattern the apostle Paul finds in the intertwined destinies of Jews and Gentiles in God's purposes, and expounds in Romans 9—11. Frei quotes the final part of Paul's argument to the effect that God's gifts to and call of Israel are irrevocable, and that just as by Israel's disobedience the disobedient Gentiles have received God's mercy, so Israel's disobedience is for the purpose that they may receive mercy by way of the mercy shown the Gentiles (Rom. 11.29–32). 'For God has imprisoned all in disobedience so that he may be merciful to all' (Rom. 11.32). Frei then applies the interaction pattern Paul describes of Israel and the Gentile as a parable for the 'providential presence of God in Jesus Christ to the history that takes place in the interaction of the church with humanity at large'.[231] He suggests an analogy between the interaction between the destinies of Israel and the Gentiles in God's purposes and between the church and humanity at large, the church's neighbour 'through whom Christ is present to the church' and from whom it receives enrichment.[232]

In effect, Frei is proposing that God's providential ordering of the history of church and world is patterned in a way that shares something of the reciprocity of its constituent collectives that Paul identifies in God's dealings with Israel and the Gentiles. Frei implies that the church may receive God's blessing, may indeed encounter Christ, through this collective human neighbour, even as that neighbour also finds blessing in and through its encounter with the church. Therefore, Frei argues, other events in human history may be even more significant parabolic signs of the presence of Christ than moves towards ecumenical unity. This parable in effect serves to underline the importance of the interaction of Christian community and wider history for Frei's ecclesiology and theology of history. Though Frei's account makes the church integral to his theology of history as one of two collective agents, it also decisively precludes any triumphalism or sectarian separation or inward preoccupation.

It does so by appealing to what is in effect an 'Israel-like' view of the church, as George Lindbeck would put it, by drawing on Romans 9—11 as a parable of Christ's presence to church and world. Lindbeck's biblical motif of the church as belonging to the continuing existence and mission of Israel, the people of God, of which Frei was probably well aware, is only implicit in Frei's account here.[233] Making it explicit would have strengthened his ecclesiology in several ways. It might have allowed him clearly to repudiate supersessionism. It would resource his understanding of its identity through figural reading of stories of biblical Israel. In that way, it would underline the church's historical character, visible concreteness and communal nature and would frame his remarks both about its frailty and the Spirit's enabling of its integrity, through that biblical figure. Similarly, Lindbeck's motif of the church as a *pilgrim* people, journeying towards the inaugurated but unconsummated eschatological kingdom, would also underline the eschatological telos of Frei's ecclesiology. It would lend a sense of direction to the agency implied in the image of the collective disciple without inscribing any immanent teleology to history: a movement towards the future presence of Christ, accompanied, motivated and enabled by his indirect presence now (which does come through in one of Frei's later pneumatological writings).[234]

The orientation of the church to the service of the world is one that Frei shares with contemporary writings by Lindbeck (whose allusion to the suffering servant motif of second Isaiah as an ecclesiological motif nicely supplements Frei's logic of discipleship).[235] At the same time, however, Frei's use of Romans 9—11 contrasts with Lindbeck's ecclesiology, and that of Stanley Hauerwas (for whom the church is parallel to Israel as two interdependent people walking God's way), in another respect.[236] Lindbeck and Hauerwas advocate a church orientated constructively to wider society in its distinctive witness and service.[237] Frei shares their concern for that distinctive witness, including by the very life of Christian communities. Yet even when they emphasize such a role, Lindbeck and Hauerwas often cast wider society, beyond the church, in contrast to it, in largely negative terms and never as a resource for the life of the church, despite affirming Christ's gracious, providential presence in the world.[238]

Frei's doctrine of providence in this text, as we shall see, was likewise cognizant of the presence of violence and oppression in the history of the wider world. However, his analysis of Christ's providential presence, and his characterization of the church as disciple, following the pattern of Christ's identity only 'at a distance', enabled him to strike this complementary note of receptivity, openness and enrichment.[239]

The second parable is the pattern of the exchange of opposites that is central to Jesus' identity.[240] Frei observes that 'Hints of the pattern of union through the agonized exchange of radical opposites do break forth in history.'[241] He speaks of 'terrible sacrifices' that dimly set forth this pattern, and share the same final and ineradicable 'thereness' that pertains to Jesus' death in his story.[242] Jesus' story ends in resurrection, as we have seen, but this pattern as glimpsed in other historical events only anticipates such an ending.

These are events which retain a significant element of ambiguity and which, one suspects, are capable of being read as tragedy without the parabolic clue Christ's identity supplies. Frei is not proposing that that clue resolves all their ambiguities. The function of his account of providence in offering partial, tentative interpretations of such events is to give grounds for hope that even such events are not without the configuring action of God in Christ. Rather, they may exhibit traces of an ordering that echoes Christ's redemptive, reconciling history in ours. For Frei it is not the sacrifices in themselves, and the slaughters they involve, but the pattern they are part of, which 'looks towards reconciliation, redemption, and resurrection', even though there is as yet no full realization of those goods for the creatures of history, only hope of it.[243]

Frei's meaning is brought out more fully by the examples he brings forward, in which he sketches elements of a providential interpretation of key moments in the history of the United States of America. He begins with the Civil War, which he describes as 'a nation of brothers fighting a civil war to purge itself of the curse of slavery and so achieve concretely a union previously little more than a contractual arrangement'.[244] In the context of his argument about Christ's presence in history, Frei's pithy providential interpretation of the Civil War alludes to the awful slaughter of its battlefields as 'terrible sacrifices' that hint at or dimly evince the Christological pattern of union through the 'agonized exchange of opposites'.

Frei here is not assimilating the dead of the Civil War to Christ's sacrifice, in the way, for example, much British commemoration of their First World War dead does. Frei has already argued that no one can reproduce the combination of irreducible individuality and universal saving scope we find in Jesus Christ's story, and there is no attempt here to align the motives and intentions of the combatants with the intention of Jesus Christ; they are not Christ figures. We can quickly rule out the idea that Frei was proposing any ennobling of Northern or Southern sacrifice. There is, moreover, considerable difference implied in the logic of analogy as qualified by the language of hints and dimness, and restricted to finding some measure of reconciliation, or progress towards it, eventuating from an 'agonised exchange of radical opposites'. In the case of the American Civil War, the limited reconciliation Frei has primarily in mind is presumably between the dominant white population and their African American neighbours, hence the reference to purging the nation of 'the curse of slavery'. The language of expiation here, and the echoes of Abraham Lincoln's providential interpretation of the war in his Second Inaugural, suggest an element, in this partial historical anticipation of eschatological reconciliation, of divine judgement on a society that enslaved people.[245] The 'agonised exchange of opposites' in this case would presumably be the sacrifices made on the two sides, opposed over the question of slavery. That may be what Frei meant by referring to 'the conviction of a *dread* ... cutting edge and providential pattern to mankind's political odyssey'.[246]

That Frei thinks the Civil War amounts to a limited figure of reconciliation between white people and African Americans is clear from his description, which follows, of the Civil Rights struggle as the 'unfinished task of reconciliation of those who have lived in estrangement from each other because of racial discrimination'.[247] The unfinished reconciliation, we may suppose, denotes what was not completed following the conclusion of the Civil War: the limited gains of emancipation, the failure of reconstruction, the forms of segregation (legal and de facto) that followed, the disenfranchisement of African Americans and profound racial inequalities in housing, education and employment.

It is significant that, as the example of the Civil War illustrates, Frei's proposal for the figural reading of history focuses on political communities, for it is in this way that it offers a framing of the gestures towards a political ethics. That focus of the working of providence in the history of human polities is borne out in two further applications which Frei offers of the parable of Christ's pattern of exchange.

The first, as I have already indicated, is to the Civil Rights struggle, where perhaps Frei had in mind an exchange of power and relative lack of power between whites and African Americans through the struggles and sacrifices of activists and victims. The second is prospective, with respect to the war in Vietnam, which was dividing campuses when Frei first published these essays and against which he, like so many others, protested. He asked:

> Dare we hope that the terrible suffering inflicted on a small East Asian people by the defensive provincialism of a large power may someday in retrospect exhibit the same pattern of reconciliation of extreme opposites, instead of mere aimless and terrible futility?[248]

In other words, Frei held out the hope that it might one day be possible, in a manner as yet unclear, to read the story of the Vietnam War in the sort of way he was proposing to read the Civil War and the Civil Rights struggle, in terms of another expiation, perhaps, another instance of the formation of national unity, reconciliation and redemption in the aftermath of European colonialism and Cold War imperialism. In these three examples, then, Frei seems to point to the possibility of the partial, provisional discernment, by way of figures, of traces of providential patterns in episodes in the history of political communities on the scale of the nation state, and of the possibility of fragmentary ways of narrating the history of those communities in the light of that discernment.

That consummation is the import of the third and final parable, that of Christ's passion and resurrection. Its significance is not really parabolic but a clue, in its summing up of Israel's history, to a final 'summing up of history ... of the history of the church together with the world'.[249] The scope of this summation is not limited to the events illumined by the application of parables, but universal, even cosmic, encompassing a great range of projects, problems, practices, cultural endeavours and political struggles:

> the technological revolution with its present hopes *and* fears, the marvellous secular integrity of the sciences, the fight against poverty and discrimination, the agony of the Vietnamese people, the reunion of the church, the gift of literature and the arts, the horror of overpopulation as well as the fight against it and the despoliation of nature, the search for humaneness and for the care of people's souls – in short, a summing up of the story of humanity within the vast world of nature.[250]

Christ's eschatological presence will be an event that brings history to fulfilment and so makes it fully narratable and intelligible, securing its meaningfulness. Frei thus seems to fill out, in an indication of expansive scope, the consequences of the claim that human identities are redeemed in Jesus Christ, but much more than that. His brief list indicates a profound affirmation of God's world along with the church, and of a range of human projects, forms of flourishing and struggles against all that threatens the well-being and dignity of creatures and the creaturely environment. All these are comprehended in the providential governance of

God in Jesus Christ, and what we can discern of that governance gives us cause to hope that none will ultimately be aimless and futile. Frei affirms that all these things will 'find their place' in the eventual summation of the human story and its natural setting in Christ.[251] In this way, Frei offers an ultimately comic eschatological vision of history, one that implicitly affirms God's goodness and governing presence in history without tipping over into the perils of a classic theodicy or speculative passibilist or kenotic alternatives.[252]

As he would later argue in 'History, salvation-history, and typology', Frei thus sees a universal scope to God's 'encompassing mercy'.[253] God endows '*all* his human creatures with freedom and preserves his *full* creation from ultimate loss or absurdity'.[254] Here Frei amplifies the hints in the passage just quoted that the non-human creation is fully included in this universal scope and in God's providence in Jesus Christ. The Christian belief in providence is that God 'sustains his creatures, non-human as well as human, whom he has called into being, one creation in two realms, cosmos and history'.[255] This sustaining work is not directly evident in any natural process or process of consciousness but revealed in Jesus Christ 'as the all-governing providence of God' in whom the unity of cosmos and history, non-human and human creatures is also revealed.[256] He also adds an element of preservation to the understanding of providence, which would become more important in his political theology towards the end of his life.

A post-Christendom secular sensibility

This ecclesiological sketch amounts to what Frei later called for, following the disappointments of hopes for the modern missionary movement and the surprises of the twentieth century: a reconsideration of Christians' relationship with their neighbours 'in a way that calls for candor, a sense of equality, a grace that we have not often mustered in the past'.[257] The lecture in which he made that call encourages us to see his ecclesiology in 'The mystery of the presence of Jesus Christ' as a modulation of the tradition of Christian accounts of the relationship of sacred and profane history and of the relationship of the passing, temporal world to something permanent that transcends it, from Irenaeus and Augustine onwards. For it involves a powerful affirmation of the presence of Christ to and ultimate redemption of humanizing cultural, social and political projects and activities, alongside ecclesial ones, whether or not that presence may be indirectly discerned in the particular figures of reconciliation and redemption which attest that presence. There is perhaps an echo here of Frei's appreciation, in his piece on 'Niebuhr's theological background' and on Niebuhr's theology, of Ernst Troeltsch's aesthetic, intensive vision of the Spirit at work in the particularity of diverse cultures for their own sake, rather than for their value for any apologetic agenda.[258] However, the logic of Frei's position more closely resonates with features he affirmed in Karl Barth's Christocentric figural imagination in his paper at the memorial symposium at Yale in 1969.[259]

There Frei draws his understanding of figural fulfilment from Erich Auerbach's essay, 'Figura'.[260] A figure is a 'description of personal, earthly existence ... which is itself and yet points beyond itself to something else that it prefigures'.[261] That 'something else' fulfils the figure: it is more real and more significant than it. The figure signifies that fulfilment precisely in the figure's historical, literal character, without detraction from that character. Indeed, its historical reality is confirmed by the deeper meaning of its fulfilment; it is understood more fully in its historical meaning by being interpreted as a figure of its fulfilment. Such is the relationship between Jesus Christ, the personal enactment of reconciliation between God and humanity, and every creaturely reality, on Barth's account, Frei argues.

This outlook shaped Barth's secular, sceptical sensibility, evident in his appreciation of the secular element in America in his visit in 1962. Alluding to Barth's Foreword to the American edition of his *Evangelical Theology*, some of which he delivered as lectures in Chicago and Princeton in 1962, Frei describes how Barth delighted in and affirmed every part of 'the vast variety of this indefinitely expansive human experience in this vast natural context [and] affirmed every part of it, at once in and for itself and for its potentiality as a *figura* of God's fulfilling work'.[262] At the same time, he regarded it all sceptically because 'he believed that none of it shows that figural potentiality by any inherent qualities or signs of its own – either positive or negative'.[263] For Frei, Barth was a welcome theological witness in an era in which there is not 'any discernible transition from secular, sceptical sensibility to a "Christian" sensibility or to Christian faith'.[264] Yet at the same time, because of God's reconciling work in Christ, there is a transition from Christian faith to a secular sensibility. In virtue of the comprehensive difference God makes in Christ to the world, all creaturely realities may be figures of that work. That sensibility had, in Barth's appreciation of America, a political dimension, to which Frei draws our attention:

And therefore, no matter how sceptical one's native tendency, one works with pleasure and hope on behalf of his fellow-men in the very contexts of secular life in which we are all set. One is grateful for the rise of black self-consciousness, one battles for nuclear disarmament, and one pleads with fellow-theologians to make their theology in this time of 'nearly apocalyptic seriousness' a theology of (human) freedom.[265]

Frei's way of summing up Barth's words implicitly identifies his own perspective with Barth's. As we have seen, Frei had arrived at a similarly secular (and sceptical) sensibility, albeit one with a more explicitly providential character and, in a way, more focused figural outlook. His affirmation of Barth's stance in this passage, all the more significant in a context where progress in Civil Rights was stalling and Black Power was emerging as a mode of black self-consciousness, also helps us see how his account of church and world in terms of an eschatologically orientated providence goes together with – indeed makes sense of – his participation in efforts to transform Yale, to oppose the war in Vietnam and in human relations activism on desegregating schools and housing in Greater New Haven.

A political theology

Frei's eschatologically orientated account of providence also completes the trajectory in Frei's thought from his 'low-level' conceptual description of the pattern of identity of the narrated, historical figure of Jesus Christ in the Synoptics, through his living presence in the church and in history, to a political understanding of the church's responsibility to and reciprocity with its human neighbour-at-large. It also points to a kind of theology of hope. Frei's account of the discernment in episodes of political history of figures of the providential ordering of history in Christ's life, death and resurrection in anticipation of eschatological redemption and reconciliation in him seems to warrant hope not only for that final redemption but also for further figural anticipations of it in the conflictual history of humanity in its natural context. Such hope, in turn, should, we may infer, guide, orientate, inspire and inform the ways and the spirit in which Christians and Christian communities enact the loving service and passionate concern for the world that should characterize followers of Jesus Christ, according to Frei.[266]

In following a trajectory from the particularity of Jesus Christ to a political theology, Frei's account differs from Bultmann, as did those of Barth, Pannenberg and Moltmann, though much briefer and less developed. In comparison with these peers, Frei's account also stands out for his fulsome articulation of the providential dimension of Christ's presence, grounded in his Christology.

In the *Church Dogmatics* III/3, Barth offers a fully developed, Christo-centric account of providence in his doctrine of creation in which the history of creatures, preserved and governed by God, is conditioned, determined by and serves the history of Jesus Christ, as the medium of its revelation. The special history of the covenant is woven into the creaturely history, so that they condition one another. God coordinates creaturely history with the history of the covenant, making it serve it and integrating it with the advent of his kingdom, working through creaturely agency and contingent events. Creaturely history is thus by God's grace the theatre and instrument of God's action in covenantal history and mirrors it in certain respects (the contrast between heaven and earth, the fellowship of men and women in marriage and various antitheses), which allows for some measure of provisional contemplation of God's activity in 'world occurrence'.

Barth's account of Christ's prophetic ministry in the form of his Spirit conditions the times and events of all people as it progresses through them and has more of an eschatological orientation than his doctrine of providence, insofar as it precedes and anticipates Christ's final appearance. Barth also thinks that, in virtue of Gods' coordination of creaturely history with Christ's history, Christ as prophet can be recognized, in the light of the revelation of reconciliation attested in Scripture, to speak beyond Scripture and outside the Christian community, in secular 'parables of the kingdom'.[267] These are true words pointing to Jesus Christ, spoken by extraordinary witnesses raised up and empowered by him, in which he speaks. They are recognized by their agreement with the witness of Scripture; by the way they take the church deeper into the communion of saints by extending and supplementing the church's dogmas and confessions; by their fruitfulness in their context and their character of affirmation and criticism; and by their call to faith and repentance, within that alignment.[268] They thus lead the church more deeply into the witness of Scripture and speak correctively as well as comfortingly to its life in particular situations.

Frei's account resembles Barth's in the close relationship of the history of church and of world and the possibility of provisional discernment of divine action in history. But in contrast to the static figural contrasts of Barth's providence and the revelatory focus of the parables of the kingdom, Frei's figures of Christ's providential presence echo the pattern of his identity in ways that anticipate reconciliation and redemption in historical events, though they are similarly recognized by this measure of similarity to Christ's identity attested in Scripture.

In the same way, Frei's understanding of Christ's providential presence goes further than Pannenberg's account of Christ's hidden lordship.

Here worldly powers unwittingly serve the coming kingdom (as in Barth), and the church, ruled through word and sacrament, is a precursor of that kingdom without any wider anticipation in history. Barth and Pannenberg both have more to say about the possibility of some assimilation or approximation of the state to the kingdom and Barth has more to say about political resistance. But Frei's account seems to offer a greater scope for a sombre, realistic hope in respect of the conflicts and challenges of the contemporary world and the church's responsibility among them.

Finally, Frei's account of providential figures has a similar note of promise – without the accompanying systematic dialectic theological architecture – to Moltmann's *Theology of Hope*. Indeed, one could extend Frei's account of their hopeful import by inferring something more of that disturbing character of promise of which Moltmann writes (and to which Frei was, as we know, sympathetic). Thus the promissory character of the figure of reconciliation and redemption in a historical event, like the Civil War, might, by its incompleteness and limited fulfilment, evoke hopeful action and drive and shape critique of the status quo.

Moltmann thinks about the church's responsibility in more (vaguely) revolutionary terms than Frei, and with greater emphasis on solidarity in suffering. Yet in Moltmann, the work of the Spirit and the lordship of Christ appear to be limited to the empowerment of the church and the leading of believers into participation in the Christ event and contradiction with the present, moving towards the future in love for the world and the Godforsaken, and so into suffering solidarity with their fellow creatures. It does not directly configure wider history.

Conclusion

Frei's Christology charts a path in contrast to many of his contemporaries, even Barth to some extent. Here Christ's narratively rendered identity entails and interprets his living presence of Christ to the church and to history, the saving efficacy of his identification with humanity and his redemptive inclusion of all human beings, securing the meaningfulness of their particular identities in himself. Frei's account of the providential configuration of the historical interaction of church and world, and of the discernment of figures of that ordering which anticipate his eschatological fulfilment of the reconciliation and redemption of all humanistic projects and labours, amounts to a political theology. It offers a way of understanding and orientating the church's political responsibility to and reciprocity with the wider world in particular situations, normed and guided by the identity of Christ. In the next chapter, I read Frei's best-known work, *The Eclipse of Biblical Narrative*, as filling out further the conditions for this kind of theo-political imagination and the understanding of Christian responsibility that goes with it.

Notes

1 Hans W. Frei, 'Remarks in connection with a theological proposal', in Hans W. Frei, *Theology and Narrative*, ed. G. Hunsinger and W. Placher (New York: Oxford University Press, 1993), pp. 27–8, 30.

2 Frei, 'Remarks', pp. 28–9.

3 Frei, 'Remarks', p. 29.

4 Frei, 'Remarks', p. 30.

5 Frei, 'Remarks', p. 27.

6 Frei, 'Remarks', p. 28.

7 Frei, 'Remarks', p. 29.

8 Hans W. Frei, 'The doctrine of revelation in the thought of Karl Barth, 1909 to 1922: the nature of Barth's break with Liberalism' (Yale University PhD, 1956), p. 92. For a fuller analysis of the argument of the dissertation, see Ben Fulford, 'Barth and Hans W. Frei', in G. Hunsinger and K. L. Johnson (eds), *The Wiley Blackwell Companion to Karl Barth*, vol. 2 (Oxford: Wiley Blackwell, 2020), pp. 645–56, and Mike Higton, *Christ, Providence and History: Hans W. Frei's Public Theology* (London: T & T Clark, 2004), pp. 39–66. For an introduction to Barth's theology, see J. B. Webster, *Karl Barth* (London: Continuum, 2004).

9 Frei, 'The doctrine of revelation', p. 108.

10 Frei, 'The doctrine of revelation', pp. 251–3.

11 Frei, 'The doctrine of revelation', pp. ii, 72–3, 79, 84–5.

12 Hans W. Frei, 'Niebuhr's theological background', in *Faith and Ethics: The Theology of H. Richard Niebuhr*, ed. Paul Ramsey (New York: Harper & Row, 1957), pp. 36–40; Frei, 'Religion (natural and revealed)', in M. Halverson and A. Cohen (eds), *A Handbook of Christian Theology* (New York: Fontana Books, 1962), pp. 316–17.

13 K. Sonderegger, 'Epistemological monophysitism in Karl Barth and Hans Frei', *Pro Ecclesia* 22:3 (2013), p. 259.

14 'Niebuhr's theological background', pp. 46–7, quoting K. Barth, *The Word of God and the Word of Man*, tr. D. Horton (Cleveland, OH: Pilgrim Press, 1928), pp. 216–17.

15 Frei, 'The doctrine of revelation', pp. iv, vii–viii, 135.

16 Frei, 'Remarks', p. 30.

17 Frei, 'Karl Barth: theologian', in Frei, *Theology and Narrative*, p. 171.

18 Frei also mentions the Swiss theologian Fritz Buri, the German theologians Emil Brunner and Paul Althaus, and the Roman Catholic theologian Karl Rahner (Frei, 'Remarks', p. 30).

19 Frei, 'Remarks', p. 30; his emphasis.

20 Frei offered a non-polemical (and reasonably fair) summary of Bultmann's 'New Testament and mythology' a few years later in an article on 'German theology:

Transcendence and secularity', in Charles E. McClelland and Steven P. Scher (eds), *Postwar German Culture: An Anthology* (New York: E. P. Dutton & Co., 1974), pp. 98–112.

21 Frei, 'Remarks', p. 30. It is clear in context that by the logic of coming to believe Frei means more precisely 'the possibility of believing immanent in human existence' ('Remarks', p. 30) and that this phrase denotes the various accounts of human existence theologians have been correlating with their Christologies, rather than an actual immanent possibility, which Frei is at pains to deny here.

22 For Frei's interpretation and appreciation of Moltmann, see Frei, 'German theology', p. 109; 'Remarks', p. 30; and 'Review of Jürgen Moltmann, *The Theology of Hope* (New York: Harper & Row, 1967)', *Union Seminary Quarterly Review* 23:3 (Spring 1968), pp. 267–72. The quotation is from p. 269 of this review.

23 Frei, 'Review of Jürgen Moltmann, *The Theology of Hope*', p. 270.

24 Frei, 'Review of Jürgen Moltmann, *The Theology of Hope*', p. 269.

25 Frei, 'Review of Jürgen Moltmann, *The Theology of Hope*', pp. 269–72.

26 Frei, 'Review of Jürgen Moltmann, *The Theology of Hope*', p. 269.

27 Frei, 'Remarks', p. 31: 'the same problems and attitudes I referred to will arise again over the notion of what it is to understand Christianity.'

28 Frei, 'Remarks', pp. 30–1.

29 Frei, 'Remarks', pp. 37–40.

30 Reading Frei's summary here in the light of that of Schubert Ogden and Van Harvey, with which he agreed. See Schubert Ogden and Van Harvey, 'How new is the "New Quest of the Historical Jesus"?' in C. E. Braaten and R. A. Harrisville (eds), *The Historical Jesus and the Kerygmatic Christ* (Nashville, TN: Abingdon Press, 1964), p. 221, and Frei, 'Remarks', p. 38.

31 Frei, 'Remarks', p. 38; Ogden and Harvey, 'How new', pp. 239–41.

32 Frei, 'Remarks', pp. 38–9. Frei has in mind the German Idealist tradition, which he summarized in his essay on 'Niebuhr's theological background', pp. 17–18.

33 Frei, 'Remarks', p. 39.

34 Frei, 'Remarks', pp. 39–40.

35 Frei, 'Remarks', p. 33.

36 Frei, 'Remarks', p. 31.

37 Frei, 'Remarks', p. 27.

38 Frei, 'Remarks', p. 31.

39 Frei, 'Remarks', pp. 30–2.

40 See John Woolverton, 'Hans W. Frei in context: a theological and historical memoir', *Anglican Theological Review* 79:3 (1997), p. 385. The description of the lessons Frei took from his reading of 'common language' philosophy indicate that he has in mind the approach of Wittgenstein's later period, when he employed close attention to the uses of ordinary language to solve philosophical problems, as he puts it in *Philosophical Investigations* §109 (tr. G. E. M. Anscombe, P. M. S Hacker and J. Schulte, rev. 4th edn, Chichester: Wiley-Blackwell, 2009), p. 51.

41 Frei, 'Remarks', p. 33.

42 Frei, 'Remarks', p. 33.

43 Frei certainly drew on Wittgenstein's insights and there is a family resemblance between Wittgenstein's mode of philosophy and Frei's theological method, but to describe him as basically a Wittgensteinian thinker, as John Allen Knight does, is to miss the determinative priority of the story of Jesus Christ in Frei's thinking and the strange things that priority does to Wittgenstein's categories at the heart

of Frei's theological method. See J. A. Knight, *Liberalism Versus Postliberalism: The Great Divide in Twentieth-Century Theology* (New York: Oxford University Press, 2013), and my review in *The Journal of Theological Studies* 65:1 (2014), pp. 363–7. As Mike Higton points out, 'Frei's work has repeatedly been misread by those who prematurely turn his comments into general theories' (*Christ, Providence and History: Hans W. Frei's Public Theology* (London: T & T Clark, 2004), p. 99).

44 Frei, 'Remarks', p. 32.

45 Frei, 'Remarks', p. 33; his emphasis.

46 Frei, 'Remarks', p. 42.

47 Frei, 'Remarks', p. 40.

48 Frei, 'Remarks', p. 34.

49 Hans W. Frei, 'Theological reflections on the accounts of Jesus' death and resurrection', in Frei, *Theology and Narrative*, pp. 74–5, 82–5.

50 Frei, 'Remarks', pp. 32–4. James Kay is right that Frei might have looked for narrative analogues closer in historical context to the Gospels, though in itself that does not negate the point of Frei's analogy with the nineteenth-century novel, which has to do with the rendering of a theme through the inseparable interaction of character and circumstances (see James Kay, *Christus Praesens: A Reconsideration of Rudolf Bultmann's Christology* (Grand Rapids, MI: Eerdmans, 1994), p. 129).

51 Frei, 'Remarks', p. 35.

52 Frei, 'Remarks', p. 36.

53 Frei, 'Remarks', pp. 36–7.

54 Frei, 'Remarks', pp. 40–1.

55 Frei, 'Remarks', p. 32.

56 Frei, 'Remarks', p. 32.

57 Frei, 'Remarks', p. 41.

58 Frei, 'Remarks', p. 42.

59 Frei, 'Remarks', p. 37.

60 Frei, 'Remarks', p. 37.

61 Frei, 'Remarks', p. 42; his emphasis.

62 Frei, 'Remarks', p. 43.

63 Frei, 'Remarks', p. 43.

64 Frei, 'Remarks', pp. 31–2, 42.

65 Frei, 'Remarks', p. 40.

66 Frei, 'Remarks', pp. 42–3.

67 Frei, 'Theological reflections', p. 46.

68 See, for example, 'Theological reflections', pp. 46–8, 73–83.

69 Frei, 'Theological reflections', p. 77.

70 Frei, 'Theological reflection', p. 59.

71 Frei, 'Theological reflections', p. 91 n. 6. The dissertation is published as R. H. King, *The Meaning of God* (London: SCM Press, 1974). His analysis of identity can be found in chapter 2.

72 Frei, 'Theological reflections', p. 59.

73 Frei, 'Theological reflections', p. 60.

74 Frei, 'Theological reflections', p. 60.

75 Frei, 'Theological reflections', p. 61.

76 Frei, 'Theological reflections', p. 62.

77 Hans W. Frei, *The Identity of Jesus Christ* (Philadelphia, PA: Fortress Press, 1975), p. 91.

78 Frei, *The Identity of Jesus Christ*, p. 92.

79 Frei, 'Theological reflections', pp. 61–3. King points out this advantage of 'action' as a category in *The Meaning of God*, pp. 37–40 (and goes on to discuss intentional action in more depth on pp. 49–63). Frei cites the philosopher Gilbert Ryle here but King's influence is also apparent. Ryle's argument that explanations of intelligent action that appeal to mental causation erroneously think of minds in disjunction from, but analogous to, mechanical physical processes, whereas intelligent action is a single action without prior purely intellectual antecedent, distinguished (as intelligent) by the manner or skill of the performance, which the competent person can recognize (see chapters 1–2 of Gilbert Ryle, *The Concept of Mind*, Harmondsworth: Penguin, 1973). King, however, emphasizes the significance of agency and intention, which are also to the fore in Frei's account.

80 Frei, 'Theological reflections', p. 63.

81 Frei, 'Theological reflections', pp. 64–5; Frei, *The Identity of Jesus Christ*, p. 93. King discusses the importance of ascription of actions to agents alongside considering implied intention in talking about intentional agency, in *The Meaning of God*, pp. 57–9.

82 Frei, 'Theological reflections', p. 65. Frei draws on Ryle's account of the elusiveness of the 'eternal penultimacy' of the self in commenting on its own activities: the commenting self always eludes its own grasp (*The Concept of Mind*, pp. 186–9).

83 Frei, 'Theological reflections', pp. 68–70 and 91 n. 12.

84 Frei, 'Theological reflections', pp. 67–8. On promising, Frei notes, the 'person himself stands surety for his utterance'. With respect to the subject–body relationship, he observes that we talk both of keeping ourselves fit and of getting our bodies in shape.

85 Frei singles out promising as an example of performative utterance.

86 See D. Lee, *Luke's Stories of Jesus: Theological Reading and the Legacy of Hans Frei* (Sheffield: Sheffield Academic Press, 1999), p. 69. Lee also underestimates the importance of the subject-in-manifestation scheme to Frei's Christology in these essays when he claims Frei basically considers the self only as enacted intentions (p. 65).

87 In the Preface to *The Identity of Jesus Christ* (p. x), Frei gestures to further supplementation of these categories with analytical devices, drawn from Marxist literary criticism and the sociology of knowledge, which identify the relations between 'individual personhood and the contextual social structures'.

88 G. Hunsinger, 'Frei's early Christology: the Book of Detours', in G. Hunsinger, *Conversational Theology: Essays on Ecumenical, Postliberal, and Political Themes, with Special Reference to Karl Barth* (London: Bloomsbury Publishing, 2015), pp. 138–9. Hunsinger says that Frei's two identity description schemes 'militate against' a high Christology, as they are ill equipped to portray him as anything more than fully human.

89 See Frei's 'Response to "Narrative Theology"', and 'Conflict in interpretation', in Frei, *Theology and Narrative*, pp. 209 and 166.

90 See Frei, 'Theological reflections', p. 70 and *The Identity of Jesus Christ*, pp. 117–18.

91 Frei, *The Identity of Jesus Christ*, p. 74.

92 Frei, 'Theological reflections', p. 48.

93 Frei, 'Theological reflections', p. 49.

94 Frei, 'Theological reflections', p. 49.

95 Frei, 'Theological reflections', pp. 49–50.

96 Frei, 'Theological reflections', p. 50; his emphasis.

97 Frei, 'Theological reflections', pp. 50–1.

98 Frei, 'Theological reflections', p. 51.

99 Frei, 'Theological reflections', p. 51.

100 Frei, 'Theological reflections', p. 56.

101 Frei, 'Theological reflections', pp. 56–7.

102 Frei, 'Theological reflections', pp. 64–5, 67–68, 70.

103 Frei, 'Theological reflections', p. 74.

104 Frei, 'Theological reflections', p. 77.

105 Frei, 'Theological reflections', p. 77.

106 Frei, 'Theological reflections', p. 78.

107 Frei, 'Theological reflections', p. 79.

108 Frei, 'Theological reflections', p. 80.

109 Frei, 'Theological reflections', p. 80.

110 Frei, 'Theological reflections', pp. 74–5.

111 Frei, 'Theological reflections', pp. 74–5.

112 Frei, 'Theological reflections', pp. 75–6.

113 Frei, 'Theological reflections', pp. 74, 76, 80–1.

114 Frei, *The Identity of Jesus Christ*, p. 120.

115 Frei, *The Identity of Jesus Christ*, pp. 124–5.

116 Higton, *Christ, Providence and History*, p. 80.

117 G. Hunsinger, 'Hans Frei as theologian: the quest for a generous orthodoxy', *Modern Theology* 8:2 (1992), p. 116. Hunsinger makes similar points in 'Frei's early Christology', pp. 137–9.

118 Hunsinger, 'Hans Frei as theologian', p. 116.

119 Hans Frei, *The Eclipse of Biblical Narrative: Study of Eighteenth and Nineteenth Century Hermeneutics* (New Haven, CT: Yale University Press, 1974), p. 315, as noted by Hunsinger, 'Hans Frei as theologian', p. 127 n. 21. Hunsinger says that this point is not made in *The Identity of Jesus Christ*, which is true, but it is clearly implied there by the terms of Frei's analysis.

120 Frei, 'Theological reflections', p. 81.

121 See Lee, *Luke's Stories of Jesus*, pp. 64–7. Lee also cites Maurice Wiles, whose sharp criticism of the book is a little more qualified on this matter: Frei, if faithful to his own method, would have taken 'far more account of the differing forms of narration within the New Testament'. See Lee, *Luke's Stories of Jesus*, p. 66, and Wiles' original review in *Journal of Theological Studies* 27:1 (1976), pp. 261–2, which also anticipates Lee's point on historical inquiry. See also Kay's less nuanced criticism that Frei's 'Gospel narrative' is merely a literary-critical construct imposed by him on the Synoptics (*Christus Praesens*, p. 133), and his correct observation that Frei neglects the *Sitz-im-Leben* of the Synoptics (pp. 141–2). However, Kay does not consider the terms on which Frei claims to read these Gospels 'synoptically' or the commonality he claimed to find there, which do not obviate the criticism altogether but do invite some qualification of it.

122 Frei could admit the possibility of some success in reconstructing 'the setting of Jesus' preaching and acts in his own life and in the cultural matrix of his time', which could only (he agreed with Nils Dahl) be absolutely uninteresting to faith at the risk of Docetism ('Theological reflections', pp. 92–3, citing Dahl, 'Der historische Jesus als geschichtswissenschaftliches und theologisches Problem', *Kerygma*

und Dogma 1 (1955), pp. 104–32; translation in C. Braaten and R. A. Harrisville (eds), *Kerygma and History* (Nashville, TN: Abingdon Press, 1962), pp. 138–71.)

123 Several works have shown the importance of narrative for Pauline Christology, and Frei's work has, among others, informed some of this scholarship. See, for example, Richard B. Hays, *The Faith of Jesus Christ: The Narrative Substructure of Galatians 3:1 – 4:11* (Grand Rapids, MI: Eerdmans, 2002), p. xxv. Richard Longenecker credits Hays' book with generating much of the impetus for this line of inquiry ('Narrative interest in the study of Paul', in B. W. Longenecker (ed.), *Narrative Dynamics in Paul: A Critical Assessment* (Louisville, KY: Westminster John Knox Press, 2009), pp. 5–6.

124 Frei, *The Identity of Jesus Christ*, p. xv. As Frei's colleague Leander Keck noted in his review of the second essay, republished as *The Identity of Jesus Christ*, Frei's argument and exegesis are a sketch (L. E. Keck, 'The Identity of Jesus Christ: The Hermeneutical Basis of Dogmatic Theology: by Hans W. Frei, Philadelphia, Fortress Press, 1975', *Theology Today* 32:3 (1975), pp. 312–20, at p. 314).

125 Frei, 'Theological reflections', p. 82.

126 Frei, 'Theological reflections', p. 82.

127 Frei, 'Theological reflections', p. 46.

128 Frei, 'Theological reflections', p. 82; see also p. 59.

129 Higton, *Christ, Providence and History*, p. 76.

130 Frei, 'Theological reflections', p. 82.

131 Frei, 'Theological reflections', p. 83.

132 Frei, 'Theological reflections', p. 83.

133 Frei, 'Theological reflections', p. 83; his emphasis.

134 Frei, 'Theological reflections', p. 84.

135 Frei, 'Theological reflections', p. 84; his emphasis.

136 Frei, 'Theological reflections', pp. 83–4.

137 Frei, 'Theological reflections', p. 85.

138 Frei points out the resemblance to Anselm's 'ontological argument' in 'On interpreting the Christian story', in Mike Higton and M. A. Bowald (eds), *Reading Faithfully: Writings from the Archives, vol. 1, Theology and Hermeneutics* (Eugene, OR: Wipf & Stock, 2015), p. 83. Frei's conclusion also distinguishes his theology further from the legacies of German idealism in modern theology as traced in his dissertation.

139 Frei, 'Theological reflections', p. 47.

140 Frei, 'Theological reflections', p. 47.

141 Frei, 'Theological reflections', p. 86.

142 Frei, 'Theological reflections', p. 47.

143 Frei, 'Theological reflections', p. 47.

144 Frei, 'Theological reflections', pp. 86–7. It is not clear what Frei would do with the testimony Paul gives and summarizes in 1 Corinthians 15.3–8, to which Pannenberg appeals.

145 Frei, 'Theological reflections', p. 87. For a more extended treatment of Frei on faith and history, see Higton, *Christ, Providence and History*, pp. 93–176, and my *Divine Eloquence and Human Transformation: Rethinking Scripture and History Through Gregory of Nazianzus and Hans Frei* (Minneapolis, MN: Fortress Press, 2013), pp. 191–230.

146 Frei, 'Theological reflections', p. 86.

147 Frei, *The Identity of Jesus Christ*, pp. 164–5. Higton noted this likeness

to Barth's account in his 'Hans Frei', in J. Holcomb (ed.), *Christian Theologies of Scripture: A Comparative Introduction* (New York: New York University Press, 2006), p. 231. See his chapter there and my *Divine Eloquence and Human Transformation*, pp. 231–72, for a fuller account of Frei's theology of Scripture.

148 Frei, 'The doctrine of revelation', pp. 566–7.

149 Frei, 'The doctrine of revelation', p. 570.

150 Frei, 'The doctrine of revelation', p. 570; his emphasis.

151 Frei, 'The doctrine of revelation', p. 576; Frei, 'The theology of H. Richard Niebuhr', in Paul Ramsey (ed.), *Faith and Ethics: The Theology of H. Richard Niebuhr* (New York: Harper & Row, 1957), pp. 106, 111. In this way I am essentially agree with Katherine Sonderegger in seeing this term as denoting a fault in Barth's Christocentric epistemology and not simply his Christology, as Higton seems to say. See Sonderegger, 'Epistemological monophysitism', pp. 258–9, and Higton, *Christ, Providence and History*, p. 55.

152 Higton, *Christ, Providence and History*, pp. 54–75.

153 In an interview with me (20 February 2015), one of his former students recalled a seminar on Barth that Frei taught early in his career at Yale in which the class read all the published volumes of the *Church Dogmatics*! The panel met on 25 and 26 April. It was moderated by Chicago's Jaroslav Pelikan and also included Edward Carnell of Fuller Seminar, Jakob Petuchowski of Hebrew Union College, Bernard Cooke of Marquette University, Schubert Ogden of Southern Methodist University, and William Stringfellow. See *Criterion: A Publication of the University of Chicago Divinity School* 2:1 (1963), p. 3.

154 See Frei, 'Remarks', pp. 28, 30, 35, 42–3; Frei, 'Theological reflections', pp. 67–8, 70–1; Frei, *The Identity of Jesus Christ*, pp. 128 n. 1, 137 n. 2; *The Eclipse of Biblical Narrative*, p. viii. Michael Root recalls Frei making the case to him in the early 1970s that there was a kind of drift in which, in volume IV of the *Church Dogmatics*, the doctrine of reconciliation, Barth became less constrained by the vision of election laid out in volume II/2, less tightly systematic in his theological construction (transcript of phone interview with Professor Michael Root, Catholic University of America, former doctoral student of Hans Frei, 23 October 2015, 2 p.m. GMT). I explore this shift in Frei's reading of Barth in more depth in 'Barth and Hans W. Frei', pp. 649–51.

155 Transcript of phone interview with Gene Outka, 27 February 2015, 3.24 p.m. GMT.

156 Frei, 'Karl Barth: theologian', pp. 170–1.

157 See Kathryn Tanner, *God and Creation in Christian Theology: Tyranny or Empowerment?* (Minneapolis, MN: Fortress Press, 1988).

158 Although Frei does not appeal to an eternal triune relationality as the condition of possibility of this divine freedom, as he notes Barth does.

159 Frei, *The Identity of Jesus Christ*, p. 128 n. 1.

160 See, for example, 'Scripture as realistic narrative: Karl Barth as critic of historical criticism', in Hans W. Frei, *Reading Faithfully: Writings from the Archives, vol. 1, Theology and Hermeneutics*, ed., M. Higton and M. Bowald (Eugene, OR: Wipf & Stock, 2015), pp. 49–63.

161 Frei, *The Identity of Jesus Christ*, pp. 2–3.

162 Frei, *The Identity of Jesus Christ*, p. 4; his emphasis.

163 Frei, *The Identity of Jesus Christ*, pp. 5, 12–13.

164 Frei, *The Identity of Jesus Christ*, pp. 12–13, 24–5.

165 Frei, *The Identity of Jesus Christ*, pp. 108–19.

166 Frei, *The Identity of Jesus Christ*, pp. 109–19.

167 See E. Auerbach, *Mimesis: The Representation of Reality in Western Litera-ture* (Princeton, NJ: Princeton University Press, 1953), pp. 43–4.

168 Frei, *The Identity of Jesus Christ*, p. 64.

169 Frei, *The Identity of Jesus Christ*, p. 64. Hunsinger claims that Frei fails to derive the pattern of exchange from the Gospel stories but has to import it from Isaiah 53 and Philippians 2 ('Frei's early Christology', p. 141). Frei comes close, however, when he identifies 'the complex relation of efficacy and helplessness and of ironic reversal between them' in the rulers' testimony to Christ's saving power on the cross (Mark 15.31; Matt. 27.42; cf. Luke 23.35) in *The Identity of Jesus Christ*, p. 113. He could also have noted Jesus' quotation of Isaiah 52.12 ('he was numbered with the transgressors') during the Last Supper narrative in Luke 22.37, with reference to his arrest, trial and death, and linked this to Christ's condemna-tion by Pilate, as Calvin does with Isaiah 53.5 (*Institutes* II.16.5., Philadelphia, PA: Westminster Press, 1960, p. 509).

170 Frei, *The Identity of Jesus Christ*, pp. 57–8. Frei also underlines the integrity and finality of Jesus' need of redemption, especially in death (pp. 57–8). In this way also the resurrection cannot be said to be narratively necessary for Frei. Each step of the story is contingently linked to those before and after.

171 Frei, *The Identity of Jesus Christ*, p. 121.

172 Frei, *The Identity of Jesus Christ*, pp. 112ff.

173 Frei, *The Identity of Jesus Christ*, p. 103.

174 Frei, *The Identity of Jesus Christ*, p. 121.

175 For the references in 'Theological reflections', see pp. 71, 86.

176 Frei, *The Identity of Jesus Christ*, p. 170. Frei references 'similar interpre-tation of Jesus as the sum and climax of the history of God's "covenant" with Israel', in Karl Barth, *Church Dogmatics* (hereafter CD) (Edinburgh: T & T Clark, 1956), IV/1, §57 (*The Identity of Jesus Christ*, p. 170 n. 2).

177 D. Dawson, *Christian Figural Reading and the Fashioning of Identity* (Berkeley, CA: University of California Press, 2002), pp. 13, 181, 185.

178 Dawson, *Christian Figural Reading*, p. 177; see also p. 12.

179 Dawson, *Christian Figural Reading*, pp. 142, 159, 163.

180 Frei, 'Of the resurrection of Christ', in *Theology and Narrative*, pp. 205–6.

181 Dawson, *Christian Figural Reading*, pp. 13, 188, 192.

182 On Christ's lordship embracing both sides of the veil, see Frei, *The Identity of Jesus Christ*, p. 173.

183 I am borrowing here from the categories Frei will draw from Erich Auer-bach in *The Eclipse of Biblical Narrative* (see next chapter), and from Dawson's gloss upon them in *Christian Figural Reading*, p. 141.

184 Frei, *The Identity of Jesus Christ*, p. 138.

185 Dawson, *Christian Figural Reading*, pp. 159, 180, 185.

186 Frei, 'Theological reflections', p. 71.

187 W. E. B. DuBois, *The Souls of Black Folk* (New York: Dover Publications, 1994), p. 2. In thinking about selfhood in alienation in this way I am indebted to Vincent Lloyd's contribution to the panel on Politics and Theology at the 'Gener-ous Orthodoxy: Hans Frei and the Future of Theology' conference at Yale Divinity School, 28 October 2022, which can be found on the school's YouTube channel. See also his forthcoming chapter in D. Collins and B. Fulford (eds), *Hans Frei and*

the Future of Theology (Eugene, OR: Wipf & Stock). I am also grateful to a participant in a research seminar at King's College, London, in 2015, who first asked me what Frei's account of identity had to say to DuBois' account of double consciousness, which I have been thinking about ever since.

188 Frei, *The Identity of Jesus Christ*, p. 149; 'Theological reflections', p. 86.

189 Frei, *The Identity of Jesus Christ*, p. 149.

190 Frei, *The Identity of Jesus Christ*, p. 148.

191 Frei, *The Identity of Jesus Christ*, p. 33; his emphasis.

192 Frei, *The Identity of Jesus Christ*, pp. 33, 49, 154–6, 172.

193 Frei, *The Identity of Jesus Christ*, pp. 32, 143–52. On these pages Frei variously claims a unity in respect of the narrated identity of Jesus Christ in the Gospels of his identity and his presence (pp. 143, 146–7), of his identity and his existence or being (pp. 145, 146, 148–9), of the inconceivability of his resurrection not having taken place, or of his being resurrected or existing in fact (pp. 145–6), and of the inconceivability of his not being alive and the unity of his identity and his life (pp. 147–9). The claims use different concepts to make more or less the same affirmation.

194 Frei, *The Identity of Jesus Christ*, p. 147; 'Theological reflections', pp. 84–5.

195 Frei, *The Identity of Jesus Christ*, pp. viii–ix. Higton describes them as dangers in his work rather than actual failures, which sounds about right (*Christ, Providence and History*, p. 88).

196 Frei, *The Identity of Jesus Christ*, p. ix.

197 As Hunsinger argues it should in 'Frei's early Christology', p. 131.

198 As Higton says, Frei uses his account of Christ's presence and identity 'to criticize existing claims about the Church: in part confirming them, in part calling them into question' (*Christ, Providence and History*, p. 84).

199 David Demson notes this omission with respect to Frei's doctrine of Scripture. See D. Demson, *Hans Frei and Karl Barth: Different Ways of Reading Scripture* (Grand Rapids, MI: Eerdmans, 1997), pp. 43–8. Demson's analysis of the way Barth connects the risen Christ and the production of the scriptural witnesses through his analysis of the appearance narratives offers one hermeneutical supplement here. See also my analysis of the connection in the book of Acts, in 'Thinking about marriage with Scripture', in J. Bradbury and S. Cornwall (eds), *Thinking Again about Marriage: Key Theological Questions* (London: SCM Press, 2016), pp. 44–61. Such arguments could be extended to baptism and the Eucharist, I would suggest.

200 'The pattern of Christ's presence' is the title of chapter 14 of *The Identity of Jesus Christ*.

201 Frei, *The Identity of Jesus Christ*, pp. 155–6.

202 Frei, *The Identity of Jesus Christ*, pp. 155–6.

203 Frei, *The Identity of Jesus Christ*, pp. 172–3.

204 Frei, *The Identity of Jesus Christ*, p. 155.

205 Frei, *The Identity of Jesus Christ*, p. 173.

206 Frei, *The Identity of Jesus Christ*, p. 158.

207 Frei, *The Identity of Jesus Christ*, pp. 158–9.

208 Frei, *The Identity of Jesus Christ*, p. 157.

209 Frei, *The Identity of Jesus Christ*, p. 160.

210 Frei, *The Identity of Jesus Christ*, p. 159; his emphasis.

211 Frei, *The Identity of Jesus Christ*, pp. 156–7.

212 Frei, *The Identity of Jesus Christ*, p. 160. Gene Outka notes that Barth had made a similar point about Christ in *CD* III/2, p. 262 ('Following at a distance: ethics and the identity of Jesus', in Garrett Green (ed.), *Scriptural Authority and Narrative Interpretation* (Philadelphia, PA: Fortress Press, 1987), p. 153).

213 Frei, *The Identity of Jesus Christ*, pp. 158–9.

214 Frei, *The Identity of Jesus Christ*, p. 157; Frei, 'History, salvation-history, and typology' from 1981, in *Reading Faithfully, vol. 1*, p. 151.

215 Frei, *The Identity of Jesus Christ*, pp. 159–60.

216 The phrase 'determining impulse' is from Frei, *The Identity of Jesus Christ*, p. 155.

217 Frei, *The Identity of Jesus Christ*, p. 161.

218 Frei, *The Identity of Jesus Christ*, p. 161.

219 Frei, 'History, salvation-history, and typology', p. 151.

220 Frei, *The Identity of Jesus Christ*, p. 161.

221 Frei, *The Identity of Jesus Christ*, p. 165.

222 Frei, 'History, salvation-history, and typology', p. 151.

223 Frei, *The Identity of Jesus Christ*, p. 163; see also p. 161.

224 Frei, *The Identity of Jesus Christ*, p. 163.

225 Frei, *The Identity of Jesus Christ*, pp. 163–4.

226 Frei, *The Identity of Jesus Christ*, p. 163.

227 Frei, *The Identity of Jesus Christ*, pp. 163–4.

228 Frei, *The Identity of Jesus Christ*, p. 161.

229 Frei, *The Identity of Jesus Christ*, p. 161.

230 Frei, *The Identity of Jesus Christ*, p. 161.

231 Frei, *The Identity of Jesus Christ*, p. 162.

232 Frei, *The Identity of Jesus Christ*, p. 162.

233 Lindbeck first championed this motif in his writings on the Second Vatican Council, where it featured in the Constitution on the Church, *Lumen Gentium* (1965). This affirmative treatment is a notable feature of his analysis of the likely direction of Roman Catholic ecclesiology as indicated in the Council's documents, in *The Future of Roman Catholic Theology* (London: SPCK, 1970), see pp. 27–38. Lindbeck, however, had already argued in 1965 that the Church's Declaration on the Relation of the Church to Non-Christian Religions, *Nostra Aetate*, that Christianity's Messianic faith made no sense apart from its Jewishness, for awaiting a Messiah is to be part of the one enduring, elect people of God, and the health of the church depended on recovering this perspective ('The Jews, renewal and ecumenism', *Journal of Ecumenical Studies* 2:3 (1965), pp. 471–3). Notably, Lindbeck emphasizes the appeal to Romans 9—11 in *Nostra Aetate* – the same text to which Frei would appeal. Frei's calendar books from this period show he was meeting (and socializing) with Lindbeck throughout the 1960s (Yale Divinity School archive (YDS) 76 VI 27). This motif is a theme of Lindbeck's ecclesiology throughout his career.

234 In Frei's piece 'Of the Holy Ghost', from 1987 (in Frei, *Reading Faithfully, vol. 1*, pp. 193–4), he writes of the appropriation to the Holy Spirit of the work 'of being God's living and sustaining presence to his people as they make their way through the world in living testimony to God's grace and goodness'.

235 Lindbeck, 'Ecumenism and the future of belief' (1968), republished in *The Church in a Postliberal Age* (London: SCM Press, 2002), pp. 102–3. This theme had already appeared in the Second Vatican Council's 'Pastoral Constitution on

the Church in the Modern World', *Gaudium et Spes* (1965), and Lindbeck reflects positively on its significance when framed in a realistic eschatology in *The Future of Roman Catholic Theology*, pp. 48–9.

236 For Stanley Hauerwas on the church and Israel, see *The Peaceable Kingdom: A Primer in Christian Ethics* (Notre Dame, IN: University of Notre Dame Press, 1991), p. 107.

237 For Lindbeck, see note 235 and also his 'Confession and community' (1990) in *The Church in a Postliberal Age*, pp. 7–9. For Hauerwas see, for example, *Resident Aliens*, with William H. Willimon (Nashville, TN: Abingdon Press, 2014), pp. 46–7, 51–2, 80–3; *The Peaceable Kingdom*, pp. 99–102; *Christian Existence Today: Essays on Church, World, and Living in Between* (Eugene, OR: Wipf & Stock, 2010), pp. 15–16.

238 See references in note 237. Lindbeck affirms that the strands in the Second Vatican Council's documents reflect a view of God's providential preparation of history for the full inbreaking of God's kingdom in *The Future of Roman Catholic Theology*, pp. 18–23, but strikes a more ambiguous note on pp. 44–7. Hauerwas affirms Christ's extra-ecclesial presence in *The Peaceable Kingdom* and appeals to God's redemption of the world and the breadth of God's kingdom to explain why non-Christians may manifest God's peace better than Christians do (see pp. 97, 101). See also *Christian Existence Today*, p. 17 and *With the Grain of the Universe: The Church's Witness and Natural Theology* (Grand Rapids, MI: Baker Academic, 2013), pp. 201–2, for similar affirmations. In the latter, he also strikes a balanced note ruling out both negation of the world and positive acceptance of its worldliness by assimilation to its attitudes and idioms. Hauerwas' dialogue with Romand Coles in *Christianity, Radical Democracy and the Radical Ordinary: Conversations between a Radical Democrat and a Christian* (Cambridge: The Lutterworth Press, 2008) offers incisive, generous interrogation of Hauerwas' resistance to go further and articulate a note of receptivity on the part of the church.

239 Here Frei echoes *Gaudium et Spes*, 44.

240 A little later Frei corrects himself: Christ's passion and resurrection is not a parable but 'an event climactically summing up a long series of events', *The Identity of Jesus Christ*, p. 163.

241 Frei, *The Identity of Jesus Christ*, p. 162.

242 Frei, *The Identity of Jesus Christ*, p. 162.

243 Frei, *The Identity of Jesus Christ*, p. 162.

244 Frei, *The Identity of Jesus Christ*, p. 162.

245 Frei quotes the Second Inaugural later in his life in 'Reinhold Niebuhr, where are you now that we need you?', in *Reading Faithfully, vol. 1*, p. 180. Lincoln quotes Christ's pronunciation of woe upon the world because of stumbling blocks, and especially upon those through whom they come, even though they are bound to come. Supposing American slavery to be one of those offences that must come in God's providence, and which now God wills to remove, Lincoln suggests that the Civil War might be 'the woe due to those by whom the offence came'. He affirms the righteous character of these judgements of God even should the war continue until the point where 'all the wealth piled by the bond-man's two hundred and fifty years of unrequited toil shall be sunk, and until every drop of blood drawn with the lash, shall be paid by another drawn with the sword'. There is a logic of retributive justice in Lincoln's providential reading of the Civil War, which Frei himself does not embrace in *The Identity of Jesus Christ*.

246 Frei, *The Identity of Jesus Christ*, p. ix; my emphasis.

247 Frei, *The Identity of Jesus Christ*, p. 162.

248 Frei, *The Identity of Jesus Christ*, pp. 162–3.

249 Frei, *The Identity of Jesus Christ*, p. 163.

250 Frei, *The Identity of Jesus Christ*, p. 163; his emphasis.

251 Barth made a similar claim: 'Everything that happened in the course of that history [of creation] will then take place together as a recapitulation of all individual events' (*CD* III/3, pp. 87–8). For Barth this preservation did not involve a continued existence of creatures, but their presence in their limited temporal durations to the eternal God. It is not clear whether Frei has a similar notion in mind.

252 Frei avoids theodicy in the classical sense defined by Kenneth Surin of an attempt to reconcile 'the existence of an omnipotent, omniscient and morally perfect God with the existence of evil', by offering a teleology of evil and suffering in the providential scheme of things (*The Turnings of Darkness and Light: Essays in Philosophical and Systematic Theology* (Cambridge: Cambridge University Press, 1989), pp. 73, 78). Frei seems close here to the way he describes H. R. Niebuhr's 'bold and agnostic' approach to theodicy in 'H. Richard Niebuhr on history, church and nation', *Theology and Narrative*, p. 223, where he contrasts him with process theodicies and inner-trinitarian equivalents, which I take to be a reference to Moltmann's trinitarian theology. Frei described Karl Barth's figural imagination as comic, echoing a remark by David Kelsey. See Hans W. Frei, 'Scripture as realistic narrative: Karl Barth as critic of historical criticism', in *Reading Faithfully, vol. 1*, pp. 50–1; John Woolverton, Notes of Frei Oral History RG M73, John Frederick Woolverton Papers, box 5, folder 4, Virginia Theological Seminary Archives, Alexandria, Virginia (1973), 30.8.73, p. 3; and 'The encounter of Jesus with the German academy', in *Types of Christian Theology* (New Haven, CT: Yale University Press, 1992), p. 135.

253 Frei, 'History, salvation-history, and typology', p. 151.

254 Frei, 'History, salvation-history, and typology', p. 151; his emphasis. This universalism, he stresses, in no way detracts from a Christocentric understanding of providence or understanding the church as the foreshadowing of God's reign in Christ, which is clear from his argument in *The Identity of Jesus Christ*.

255 Frei, 'History, salvation-history, and typology', p. 153.

256 Frei, 'History, salvation-history, and typology', p. 153.

257 Frei, 'History, salvation-history, and typology', pp. 150–51.

258 Frei, 'Niebuhr's theological background', pp. 59–61; 'The theology of H. Richard Niebuhr', p. 94.

259 For another, excellent account of Frei's figural reading of history and his appropriation of Barth in this connection, with which I am in substantive agreement, see Higton, *Christ, Providence and History*, pp. 163–74.

260 From E. Auerbach's *Scenes from the Drama of European Literature* (New York: Meridian Books, 1959), pp. 11–76.

261 'Karl Barth: theologian', pp. 168–9.

262 Frei, 'Karl Barth: theologian', p. 172. See Barth's *Evangelical Theology* (Grand Rapids, MI: Eerdmans, 1979 [1963]), pp. v–xiii. Barth describes his 'fantastic' impressions of America and his 'intense pleasure' at being there on pp. vi–ix.

263 Frei, 'Karl Barth: theologian', p. 172.

264 Frei, 'Karl Barth: theologian', p. 172.

265 Frei, 'Karl Barth: theologian', pp. 172–3. See Barth, *Evangelical Theology*,

pp. xi–xii, where Barth refers to the 'self-consciously rising American Negro population', championed by Dr Anna Hedgeman (p. ix), and urges the need for a theology of freedom in a time of 'nearly apocalyptic seriousness' (p. xii).

266 As Higton notes, Frei advocates hope here because he seeks 'a robust theological vision which funds and shapes action' (*Christ, Providence and History*, p. 86).

267 *CD* IV/3.1, pp. 114–34.

268 *CD* IV/3.1, pp. 126–30.

PART II

Towards a Generous Orthodoxy

4

The Figural Imagination and the
Ethics of Responsibility

The work for which Frei is best known is his *The Eclipse of Biblical Narrative*, published in 1974. The book is an offshoot of a research project on Christology in modern theology that would occupy Frei throughout his career at Yale. It is a widely influential account of the development of modern biblical and theological hermeneutics whose constructive significance in those areas has been much discussed. It also develops in extensive detail Frei's critique of modern western theological hermeneutics, articulated in his Harvard lecture from 1967. Despite widespread discussion of its hermeneutical significance, however, its importance as a work of theology has been largely overlooked and it plays a relatively minor role in most detailed treatments of Frei's theology, mainly as the critical-historical complement and backdrop to his constructive work in *The Identity of Jesus Christ*.[1] Yet in *The Eclipse of Biblical Narrative*, Frei takes forward several constructive aspects of the Christology essays in ways that are important for my argument.[2]

First, Frei develops there his account of the essence of Christianity. He identified in western Christianity a traditional practice of attending to the narrative meaning of biblical stories, centred on those concerning Jesus Christ and a practice of understanding situations and lives as figures within the world as seen through those stories. Second, while the book mainly documents how developments in biblical and theological hermeneutics obscured that meaning while still prioritizing those stories, it also indicated the conditions for the recovery of that 'essence' and that practice. Third, in that way Frei outlined in *The Eclipse of Biblical Narrative* the conditions for the kind of theological imagination needed to frame Christian ethical and political engagement that he had written about in the essay on Christ's presence. Indeed, Frei's argument in *The Eclipse of Biblical Narrative* gestured to an understanding of Christian ethics as responsibility that resonates with and combines aspects of the accounts of human responsibility in Karl Barth and H. Richard Niebuhr.

Frei's Christological project

Frei's teaching at Yale gives us some further orientation to his mature theological project. According to Julian Hartt's 1957 announcement to the Yale community, when Frei was appointed at Yale, he was to teach a half-term module on the history of religious thought in the West up to the Reformation and two term-length courses dealing with major developments in western religious thought after the Reformation, in 1957–58.[3] The subject of the history of modern western religious thought would, in various forms, remain a constant in Frei's well-regarded teaching at Yale over the course of his career.[4] In his 'Autobiographical notes' from 1983, Frei describes taking a social and religious-psychological approach to the history of ideas, exploring what it was like to live at the time these ideas were articulated, and to have the kind of sensibility expressed in them, and using the history of ideas as a way of getting into systematic issues. From the evidence of his lecture notes, Frei seems to have used the history of ideas as a way into systematic questions about the Christian religion and its relationship with philosophy and culture in the modern West, a topic that would also preoccupy him in the latter part of his life.[5] This approach, as we shall see, is also reflected in *The Eclipse of Biblical Narrative*.

The scope of Frei's undergraduate teaching reflected not only his expertise gained through his doctoral studies but also the emerging focus of what would be a lifelong research project, one that set him at odds with many of his contemporaries. In May 1959, Frei was awarded a Morse Fellowship and Fulbright Scholarship for the academic year 1959–60, which would allow him to conduct research on 'the place of Jesus Christ in the intellectual history of Germany and England' in those countries.[6] Frei's calendar book from 1960 places him in Germany, Paris and London during the early part of that year.[7] Frei made a further research trip to Germany and England during a sabbatical in 1966–67.[8] He was still describing 'The history of Christology from 1700–1950' as his 'long-range project' in an undated CV in the Yale Divinity School Archives, which is probably from 1976.[9] It was the same project, though its scope had now expanded to 'Britain, Germany and the U.S.'. Frei's research project was never completed or published in definitive form but many of his writings in the 1960s and early to mid-70s belong to its first phase, distinguished from its later products by the reliance on the category of realistic or history-like narrative. *The Eclipse of Biblical Narrative*, published in 1974, is the main publication arising directly from the project. It is a complex work with several interwoven strands of argument that are historical but also polemical.[10] It also exhibits profound theological concerns, in continuity with his earlier writings, which we need to appreciate in order to understand its significance for his political theology and ethics. The most overt argument Frei makes is the historical one alluded to in the title of the book.

Pre-modern western Christian reading of biblical narrative

Frei's main argument begins with an account of western Christian reading of the Bible before historical criticism rose to prominence in the eighteenth century. Western Christian reading of the Bible before the rise of historical criticism, Frei claims, tended to be realistic: at once literal and historical.[11] Augustine exemplified this approach, which 'was never wholly lost in western Christendom' and was renewed in the Renaissance and Reformation.[12] Indeed, Frei takes the Protestant Reformers, chiefly Martin Luther and especially John Calvin, to exemplify this reading practice on the eve of its fragmentation in modernity. On Frei's account, that practice had three key features, which enabled it to attend to the realistic character of realistic biblical narratives: three congruent, connected unities, each more effectively exhibited in practice than grounded in general theory.

First, for such readers, parts of the Bible – many of its narratives – demanded a reading in which what the words appeared to describe was taken to be their meaning, rather than being the allegorical vehicle for some other meaning besides the characters and action depicted. Allegorical or spiritual interpretations of some texts were allowed in subordination to this literal reading. The literal sense, the Reformers affirmed, was the true sense and the surest guide to the obscurer passages of Scripture.[13]

Second, where these readers understood the meaning of biblical stories to be literal, they also assumed the story to be historical: to describe real events in the right terms. Literal reading involved the coherence or even logical identity between the literal-grammatical explication of the stories and the judgement that the events they described actually happened.[14] 'The true historical reference of a story was a direct and natural concomitant of its making literal sense.'[15]

Third, western Christian readers joined some of these stories into a single overarching story read as the history of the temporal world, from creation to future eschatological consummation, covering the natural and historical and cultural realms. The chief means for joining stories in this way was figural or typological interpretation, which Frei understood from Erich Auerbach's account of it.[16] Events, persons, prophecies and rites in earlier stories with their own semantic integrity and temporal specificity were, without loss of their literal meaning, recognized as figures fulfilled by later persons or events. This figural relation was a connection in God's providential design which, as Mike Higton points out, was thus exhibited rather than explained (for example, by some account of historical development).[17] Frei thus describes figural reading as a 'natural extension' of literal reading: it finds a coherence between two passages, literally read for their narrative shape, as exemplified in Calvin's restrained Christological reading of the Old Testament.[18] Yet Frei also recognized that it was a delicate and risk-laden procedure with respect to the earlier story in a figural relation. It placed greater strain on that earlier event to see it as both real in its own right and yet standing for another, equally real, later event that fulfils it.[19] Without firm rooting in literal reading and the temporal sequence of events, therefore, figural reading could result in the depreciation of the earlier event in favour of the later. Likewise, there was the danger identified by Auerbach that where a figural reading rested on a structure of meaning removed from the story's sensuous, temporal depiction of events, that sensory base might be dissolved in favour of its figural application to a later temporal occurrence, as in allegorical exegesis.[20] Clearly implied here, in both authors, is a worry about Christian readings in which figural reference to Christ not only fulfils but supersedes and evacuates Jewish sacred history. Nevertheless, in principle, where carefully practised, figural reading allowed an extension of the literal reading of individual stories into an overarching story uniting both Testaments in a single canon.[21] Both Luther and Calvin used figural reading in this way, such that Christ was the subject matter of the whole, prefigured in much of the Old Testament as well as in the fulfilment of those figures depicted in the New.[22]

Finally, this whole biblical story, composed of individual stories linked by figural reading, rendered to readers the real world of which they were a part, and demanded that they interpret their circumstances and experiences in its terms.[23] Frei quotes Auerbach's observation that these biblical narratives offer a universal history that, in Erich Auerbach's memorable (and perhaps ambivalent) phrase, 'seeks to overcome our reality' and incorporate us into its structure.[24] In part, the realistic character of the stories helped make this possible. Frei notes that by depicting lifelike individuals interacting with ordinary events that together constitute powerful historical forces, these ordinary individuals can become realistic 'types' without loss to their random individuality.[25] That is, they become figures in whose particular destinies and circumstances others can come to understand their own.

Pre-modern western Christian reading, on Frei's account at least, thus treated realistic biblical narratives in terms of a series of unities: the identity of the shape of these narratives with their meaning and subject matter; the identity of literal meaning with the historicity of the events and persons they portray; the delicate cohesion of the literal meaning of individual stories and their figural connection with other stories; the unity of the whole biblical story composed of figurally connected units; the identity of the world rendered through biblical narrative and the real world; and the conformity of readers to that world in their understanding of their circumstances, in their affective dispositions and in their actions. It was a practice of reading which was flexible enough to allow the production of a great variety of ways of construing the composite, overarching story and of the world, rather than a single, dominant and seamless metanarrative.[26] 'In the process of interpretation,' Frei notes, 'the story itself, constantly adapted to new situations and ways of thinking, underwent ceaseless revision', through which it continued to depict, adequately, the 'common and inclusive world' until the advent of modernity.[27]

Frei's focus, he tells us, was not on the Reformers' theologies of Scripture, but upon their procedures for attending to realistic biblical narrative.[28] Nevertheless, it is important to note that Frei understood that for pre-modern western Christian readers these things just enumerated held together not only on account of the realistic quality of the narratives, but also because of the unity between God's providential governance of the world, God's speech in Scripture, and the work of the Spirit in the reader. As Higton observes, the story Frei tells in *The Eclipse of Biblical Narrative* is a story about 'profound theological alterations' underlying the changes in hermeneutical concepts and procedures he traces, which begins with his account of pre-modern biblical interpretation.[29]

The primacy of the literal-grammatical meaning of Scripture, as practised by the Protestant Reformers, was bound up with their belief that God speaks in Scripture. Although Frei is not very clear on the matter, he implies that the convergence of story, history and doctrine is a matter of their inclusion in the 'storied word' in which God speaks and which is his Word.[30] Likewise, the coherence of figure and fulfilment is a matter of the unity in the divine plan.[31] The story's rendering of the real world ordered by the divine plan belongs to this coherence within the comprehension of the scriptural story and so also, we may infer, to that story's being God's Word.[32] In a similar way, the coherence of that 'storied word' and the conformity of readers' understanding, affections and actions through the internal testimony of the Holy Spirit is of a piece with this cohesion.[33] It is God who made the narrative; the real world it rendered and the religious appropriation of that world cohere: 'for He who moves the world in particular ways moves the human heart also.'[34] It is God whose action makes the biblical narrative render the real world effectually to its readers. The testimony of the Spirit is 'the effective rendering of God and his real world to the reader by way of the text's appropriate depiction of the intercourse of that God and that world, engaging the reader's mind, heart, and activity'.[35] In this way, as Higton observes, densely particular, contingent public history, as rendered by the stories, was understood as the idiom in which God graciously speaks.[36]

The burden of Frei's analysis is to detail the breakdown of this way of reading, and the consistent failure of exegetes and theorists of hermeneutics thereafter to find a way to value the realistic meaning of biblical stories. Frei's argument thus involves a claim that certain biblical stories, valued in western Christianity, have a realistic or 'history-like' quality, in addition to their other qualities and their status as documents of their culture and context, a claim he took to be a matter of consensus among modern commentators.[37] By the term 'realistic' Frei meant to denote a number of features of certain biblical stories in virtue of which they render to the reader a world that resembles, in significant degree, the way historians relate and explain historical events.[38] These are stories whose meaning is a function of the way they depict the events they relate: their narrative 'shape', including the use of chronological sequence.[39] They are stories whose theme or subject matter is rendered cumulatively through the narrated unfolding of a pattern of events in continuous chronological sequence, and cannot be set forth apart from that shape.

In 'Theological reflections on the accounts of Jesus' death and resurrection' of 1966 and in his Harvard lecture of 1967, Frei had argued that the Synoptic Gospels include narrative sequences with this quality, in virtue of which they bore resemblance to historical narratives and novels.[40] In *The Eclipse of Biblical Narrative*, he formally categorizes those stories within a genre, that of realistic narrative, which the Synoptics illustrate, alongside other stories in the biblical canon. In *The Eclipse of Biblical Narrative*, Frei also amplifies his discussion of one feature of these stories to which he had drawn attention in those Christological writings from the mid-1960s. He asserts that it is distinctive of realistic stories that they depict their character in their relationship to their natural environment and especially their social settings.[41] Characters are set forth by way of their involvement in their circumstances, and events are set forth by way of the involvement of characters in them.[42] This interaction of characters and circumstances is the subject matter of the story. It is in respect of all these qualities that biblical narratives bear some significant resemblance to the way modern historians relate and explain events, notwithstanding the presence of supernatural agency and miracle in the former and the absence of recourse to these features in modern historiography.[43] In this respect, Frei holds, realistic biblical narratives may be called 'history-like' in the sense that the action portrayed 'is indispensable to the rendering of a particular character ... or a particular story'.[44]

Finally, Frei adds one more characteristic to his account of realistic narratives, which was implied in his analysis of the Synoptics in his earlier Christological essays and which echoes Auerbach's account of Old Testament narrative in *Mimesis*. Realistic narratives, he claims, are also characterized by rendering the serious effects of powerful historical forces in and through accounts of believable individuals and ordinary events described in ordinary language.[45] In this way, he notes elsewhere, they are a little like the modern realistic novel.[46] Realism in this case means the portrayal of the 'fateful depth' in the interaction of 'powerful, shifting historical forces and their infrastructures ... and the "random" individuals whom they engulf "as it were accidentally" and force to react one way or another'.[47] It meant 'depicting the relation of society and the individual and of people within the conventions set by given social structures'.[48]

Some of Frei's critics have leaped on this point, accusing him of claiming, anachronistically, that modern biblical interpreters failed to interpret the Bible like a nineteenth-century novel, and that in effect pre-modern readers read it as though it were one.[49] In fact, Frei is careful to observe the differences between these two forms of literary realism: 'In the ancient day it was the intersection between God and man, in the later era the impact of constant and changing historical movements and social infra- and superstructures on individuals.'[50] Nevertheless, there is a certain affinity. Both share:

> the description of random and ordinary human beings caught up in a 'real' world which defines them, in which they are at home, but which can also pin them down by the sweep of majestic forces of a moral or a morally neutral sort.[51]

Hence one might have seen that biblical narratives might make sense 'most nearly as realistic narratives' (note the careful qualification) regardless of their religious applicability or factual status.[52]

The eclipse of the narrative meaning of biblical stories

Frei's main argument describes a shift in biblical hermeneutics that begins with the breakdown of pre-modern reading practices which fostered a certain kind of attention to this narrative meaning. This breakdown Frei describes as a cultural development, and a shift in thought and sensibility.[53] He does not dwell extensively on the causes of this shift, though he does describe various contributory factors to its development. He instances several of these: the impact of empirical philosophy, specifically John Locke's philosophy of language; the sense of the imagination being under attack in English literature in the late seventeenth and eighteenth centuries; and the shift in English thought and style to follow 'the precision and sobriety ... of scientific discourse divorced from immediate appeal to sensibility'.[54] However, he was more concerned with the development and the effects of the shift. At its heart, this change involved the dissolution of the multifaceted cohesion between textual meaning and history that pertained before modernity and its reintegration on terms that obscured the narrative character of that meaning.

Frei's account of the eclipse of the realistic meaning of biblical narratives involves several stages. The first identifies precursors to the shift, in whose work signs of the coming cultural change can already be detected. Frei finds such evidence in both radical figures such as Baruch Spinoza, on the one hand, and conservatives like Johannes Cocceius, on the other.[55] In both figures, in quite different ways, the realistic meaning of biblical narratives and the historicity of the events they describe no longer coincide *in principle* but are separable, whether their historicity was conceived as something doubtful and incidental to the religious significance of the stories (in Spinoza) or in terms of a scheme of covenantal history that was the true subject matter of the stories. Cocceius' hermeneutic put the figural connections between biblical stories that he sought to uphold under strain to conform to the unity and uniformity of the temporal world set forth in his scheme. It likewise strained his attempts to read events of post-biblical history as figures of the biblical stories.

The second stage is constituted by controversies in English and German theology in the eighteenth century, in which the split and reintegration of narrative and history is clearly observable. The English debate will suffice here to illustrate Frei's argument. It was about whether the Old Testament prophecies that the New Testament claimed were fulfilled in Jesus Christ actually referred to him. Here the Deist thinker, Anthony Collins, was central. Collins argued that the New Testament claims must either be literally false or meaningless. His stance rested on the assumption that the only way to make a link between passages so far separated in time was to show the 'identity between the predictive description and the features of the later event to which it was (later) claimed the description referred'.[56] Collins' implied criterion for the meaningfulness of the New Testament claims was similar to that of early logical positivists in the twentieth century: 'If one can state the conditions under which a statement could be seen to be true (or false) it is meaningful or, the same thing, literally descriptive.'[57] Thus, whereas for pre-modern Protestant readers historicity followed logically from the judgement that the meaning of a biblical story was literal, Collins subsumed literal meaning 'under the dominance of an independent criterion for deciding whether or not a statement is historical', namely whether the statement describes a state of affairs whose factuality can be independently established.[58]

Yet this move was implicitly theological too. Frei brings out the theological character of Collins' position by contrasting it with those defenders of figural interpretation and the figural fulfilment of prophecy who operated, residually, on the grounds of the Protestant Reformers 'and those of the Western Christian tradition at large'.[59] For these thinkers, it was the divine author who mattered most, who 'could easily supplement if not supplant with a second, greater, and more inclusive meaning the sense intended by a limited human author and appropriate to his finite understanding'.[60] For them, the unity of literal meaning and the historical truth of Scripture involved 'a cognate unity on the part of God: the divine author of the book is the same as the governor of the history narrated in it. Being both author of the text's meaning and governor of actuality he unites meaning and fact.'[61] Hence, for these thinkers, there was no separation between meaning and reference such that they were logically independent of one another. God's literal statements naturally refer to the states of affairs they describe, the description doing duty for the reference because of the identity of the divine author with the One who governs history.

On that same identity rested the possibility of the figural extension of literal meaning, of a statement describing two events simultaneously, one literally and the other by prefiguration. Thus, God may providentially intend a description to refer also to a future event beyond what its human author intends, so expanding the original pattern of meaning by this extension of its temporal reference. Figural interpretation thus depended on assuming adequate access to the providential design through which meaning and reality, 'God's truth and history', cohere.[62] By contrast, Deists like Collins restricted authorial intention and meaning to the immanent level of the human authors of Old Testament texts and so, we might infer, severed the unity of authorial intention and verbal meaning with the providential governance of the real world.

Collins also drastically reconfigured verbal meaning. For him, words were at once clues to authorial intentions, when studied in their historical contexts, and empirical propositions (unless they reflected on cognition). As such, the meaning of words was bound up with their reference or failure to refer to a single spatio-temporal occurrence or state of affairs.

The result when applied to biblical stories was the loss of the immediacy of the world rendered by the story, and 'the rich but orderly and inter-connected variety of levels of meaning' presented by the words.[63] The unity of story and world and the wealth of meaning involved in that close connection was replaced by a different kind of relationship, one of language to authors and external states of affairs in which the role of language is much diminished compared with the divinely authored rendering of a complex, contingent and divinely governed world. Things came to 'dominate' words as mere clues to authors' intentions and mere signs representing known states of affairs.[64]

This change is what Frei means by 'the eclipse of biblical narrative'. It is a shift he traces in several other figures of different theological persuasions in England and Germany. Under the impact of the Deist controversy, supernaturalists, liberals, historical critics and hermen-eutical theorists alike came to identify the meaning of the narratives with their reference to rational ideas or historical events, assessed by general, rational criteria of meaning and probability, whether they defended or doubted their historicity.[65] A third stage of German debate, in the late eighteenth and early nineteenth centuries, clarified four alternatives on these terms, all of which understood the subject matter of the text as something other than what they depicted. That subject matter was vari-ously: the miraculous events intended by the authors, whose possibility could be independently established in the court of natural reason; his-torically reconstructed non-miraculous events; ideal truths allegorically conveyed, whether intended by the author or not; or the historical group consciousness underlying the author's intended meaning and expressed in the form of myth.[66] In each case, the narrative meaning of the stories as a focus of hermeneutical interest in its own right was overlooked.

Factors in the eclipse of biblical narrative

The second part of Frei's main argument is his explanation of the failure of modern biblical exegetes and theologians to attend to the narrative meaning of realistic biblical stories, even when cultural or philosophical developments favoured such attention. Here he elaborated on the critique of apologetic hermeneutics he had given in his 1967 Harvard lecture. In response to the reversal of the direction of interpretation of biblical narratives, theologians sought to show the religious meaningfulness of biblical narratives by appeal to general moral experience and general religious principles, which concern led them away from the narrative meaning of the texts.

Such was the case theologians like Conyers Middleton and John Locke made for Christocentric revealed religion, for example. Here:

> Redemption in history becomes intelligible from its natural context in our moral and religious experience, so that the wise man readily appreciates that rational, natural religion and morality need to be perfected from beyond themselves by a revealed religion which is above rather than against them.[67]

Even where the argument admitted some contradiction between revealed and natural religion, the meaningfulness of revealed religion still depended on an antecedent awareness of morality and religion, for a felt need to which Jesus was the answer.

The same basic apologetic logic would be repeated in different terms by later theologians, including conservatives, right up to Frei's time of writing.[68] This stance amounted to a general principle of the religious application of biblical texts, or 'applicative hermeneutics': 'the full or partial pertinence of mankind's general religious and moral experience to the biblical narratives at issue'.[69] This welding of hermeneutics and apologetics was not inevitable. In Frei's account, the sceptical writer Reimarus stands for the possibility, in modernity, of not attaching the interpretation of the Gospel narratives to a project of religious apologetics.[70] He alone, in this period, said '*both* that the texts mean what they say *and* that they are religiously meaningless, misleading, or anachronistic'.[71]

The apologetic concern that governed both conservative and liberal theological writing in the modern period had significant consequences for the interpretation of realistic biblical narratives. Theologians might differ sharply over the subject matter of New Testament Christological narratives. Some contended the stories made a factually true claim about Jesus that was essential and religiously meaningful. Others denied both these assertions and maintained that the narratives had a sense that was religiously meaningful but non-literal. Still others wavered on whether the religious meaningfulness of these literal stories was bound up with their historicity or not. In each case, however, their concerns precluded them from attending to the narrative meaning of the texts quite apart from the questions of its truth and meaningfulness. Historical critics contributed to the elision of this option because they were apt not to recognize the logical distinction between historical criticism and narrative interpretation. Thus, neither religious apologists nor historical critics were able to 'take proper and serious account of the narrative feature of the biblical stories', despite noting it and thinking it significant in one way or another.[72]

This same apologetic concern meant that English and German theologians failed to exploit favourable conditions for attending to the narrative meaning of realistic biblical stories (the advent of literary realism in England, and in Germany the rise of critical scholarship which focused on realistic narratives).[73] In Germany, the lack of a culture of literary realism contributed to this failure. So too did the hermeneutical focus, in German idealist thinkers like Johann Gottfried Herder, on the interpreter's empathy with the cultural spirit 'behind' the story, and the idealist tendency to spiritualize history as the development of a collective human self-consciousness. Schleiermacher's focus on reproducing the process of understanding that generated the text had the same effect.[74] All illustrated the problems for interpreting this kind of text that arose from relying on idealistic conceptual schemes. Indeed, as Higton points out, Frei espied in Herder 'the emergence of a subject-alienation framework for understanding history' antagonistic to the irreducible interaction of character and circumstances, which replaces the providence that orders such public history with an immanent providence, 'brooding beneath the surface of the chaotic external world'.[75]

All these problems came together, Frei argued, in the hermeneutics of David Friedrich Strauss, the key figure in the development of the analysis of the Gospel narratives as myths, in his *The Life of Jesus Critically Examined*. Strauss thought the supernatural elements in the Gospel accounts of Jesus were improbable, and therefore there was no historical basis for the doctrine of the incarnation, which, he argued, is a philosophical truth that needs no historical basis.[76] The best explanation for those stories lay not in a deliberate deception, as Reimarus had argued, but in the consciousness of their authors, 'which was historically conditioned to the level of their cultural and religious context'.[77] This remote, historically conditioned consciousness, the authors' mythical outlook, which the stories express, is their meaning, even where the stories have realistic elements.[78] For Strauss, as for the mythical school in general, the meaning of stories of miraculous events must lie either in the reference they make to miraculous events or in the expression of a mythical consciousness that gave rise to them.[79] If, on grounds of probability, they could not be judged reliable reports of factual occurrence, their meaning must lie in the mythical consciousness that produced them.

It is at this point in Frei's analysis that he emphasizes the contingency of the eclipse of the narrative meaning of the Bible. For, he argues, the disjunction between seeing the meaning of the stories as their reference to miraculous historical events or as the expression of an ancient mythical consciousness is a false one, eliding a third option, namely that the narrative itself is the meaning of the text. The mistake Strauss and others made was to try and encompass biblical narratives within the general category of myth, and the difficulty they faced was in accommodating the category of myth to the history-like form of some of those stories. Frei traces the adjustments that Strauss had to make to the definition of myth to make it applicable to those stories.[80] Myth as the history of the gods did not fit much of the Bible. The direct intercourse of the divine with men of heroic, near-divine, stature did not really fit biblical heroes. Strauss then identified myth with miracle, the unmediated presentation of an embodied form of a general idea, and finally with the representation of matters that cannot be experienced in history-like form.

The challenge Strauss and other mythophiles faced was in attending to history-like characteristic they acknowledged in these stories. The nature of that challenge had to do with the specific literary form of these stories, and with making a distinction between different kinds of narrative writing in terms of their history-likeness and the relative unity of their form and subject matter. However, they had no category for making this distinction other than the disjunction between stories that referred ostensively and myths. Yet 'myth' as they understood it is not a literary category, but a 'genetic-psychological one', concerned not with genre but with explaining the origins of miraculous stories in terms of their authors' time-conditioned consciousness.[81] Likewise, treating history-like meaning in terms of the question of historicity, fact or fiction, is reductive. Hence Strauss, while noting the greater history-likeness of biblical narratives as compared with pagan myths, ended up eliding that difference by reducing the question to the issue of fact or fiction: since the biblical stories were fictional, they were mythical.[82]

The mythophiles' false disjunction of mythical versus ostensive meaning, Frei concludes, is only a symptom of a number of underlying issues already rehearsed in his argument.[83] It illustrates a wider tendency to privilege subject matter over the specific usage of verbal forms, and interpret the latter in the light of a pre-conceived notion of the former.[84] It was also driven by the theological preoccupation with 'positivity' (whether the doctrine of the incarnation has a basis in historical fact) and the alignment of hermeneutics with apologetics (even Strauss was 'apologetically inclined' when he wrote *The Life of Jesus*). And, finally, it was influenced by the tendency to identify the theory of meaning with epistemology. In *The Eclipse of Biblical Narrative*, then, Frei in effect amplifies the critique of the application of myth to biblical narrative that he had made in his earlier Christological essays.

It is beyond the scope of this chapter to evaluate Frei's main argument in *The Eclipse of Biblical Narrative* as a historical argument, though it is relevant to observe some obvious limitations, beyond its self-imposed focus on English and German Protestant biblical hermeneutics. George Schner notes that the roots of the eclipse Frei describes go back at least to the period of the Protestant Reformations and may lie in the longer tendency in Christian spirituality for charismatic endowment with the Spirit to lead to claims to supersede the letter of the text.[85] The causes of the eclipse may also, he argues, be illuminated by a broader consideration of the context of reading practices, for example in parallel developments in eucharistic theology, liturgical practice and ecclesial politics.

Equally, as Frei himself acknowledged a few years later, his account concentrates on practices and developments in biblical interpretation and culture among a small highly educated elite group of authors.[86] It does not attend to how biblical narrative was interpreted and used for and by the ordinary people, the settings of whose lives, Frei thought, resonated with its manner of storytelling. Nor does it consider to any great extent the socio-political functions of the figural reading of biblical narrative in the period, including by ordinary people as well as the powerful, by members of minoritized populations at the margins of European societies and by members of subjugated groups within their empires. Frei's scope rules out consideration of the use of biblical narrative to legitimate or contest the system of transatlantic trade in enslaved humans or the institution of chattel slavery as a vital component of the economic systems whose wealth helped fuel the socio-economic transformations whose impact on high culture he observes in *The Eclipse of Biblical Narrative*. Ironically, Frei's concern to trace the hermeneutical impact of modern theology's apologetic agenda may have contributed to that delimiting of his subject matter.

Frei's account of realistic biblical narrative in *The Eclipse of Biblical Narrative* also has some limitations. It underplays the interpretive agency of readers, something he would correct in later writings, even if he would not concede the radical indeterminacy of textual interpretation that Cornel West claimed follows from focusing on writing and from Auerbach's analysis of realistic literature in *Mimesis*.[87] From what we have seen, Frei may have been more attentive to biblical writers' use of narrative art to make all-encompassing historical truth claims and the way their own assumed divine inspiration was integral to this communicative purpose ('history telling') than Meir Steinberg credits him with.[88] Nevertheless, Frei's analysis of the eclipse of biblical narrative would be much clearer had he used Steinberg's category of 'history telling', considered more overtly and fully the communicative dimension that Steinberg advocates, and distinguished inspiration as a tenet of the reader from inspiration as a convention of the narratives.[89] He could still, in this way, have identified the failure to attend to biblical narrative on its own terms by attempting to force it into the parameters of other writing conventions while acknowledging the usefulness of historical critical inquiry for making sense of ancient texts, as Steinberg does. Such attention to communicative purpose would be a step towards attending to the presence of ideology in biblical narratives, which David Kamitsuka notes is missing in post-liberal theology.[90] These limitations, however, do not seem fatal to the constructive argument Frei advances in and through his historical arguments.

The recovery of biblical narrative

Frei's analysis also implies a constructive direction by the way in which he identifies a logical option ignored by most biblical interpreters in this period, for the reasons examined above. Before I turn to his exploration of that possibility, it is important to note the secularity and realistic historical tenor of Frei's understanding of the societies in which the eclipse of biblical narrative took place. Those features of that understanding are evident, for example, in his account of how contextual historical forces fostered or inhibited the development of literary realism in eighteenth-century England and Germany.

Frei explains the extent to which literature attained a realistic character in these contexts in terms of the degree to which authors and readers in those societies had been exposed to revolutionary political, economic and social change. Thus religious, political, scientific and economic revolutions in England, for example, 'created a climate favourable' to realistic literature, which endured through the agrarian and industrial revolutions and the massive changes in terms of population movement and social structure they entailed, despite the advent of Romanticism, and 'enhanced the novelist's sense of the appropriateness of mundane reality for imaginative representation and scrutiny'.[91] Conversely, the cultural conditions for the intellectual and literary movements of late eighteenth-century Germany were not conducive to the development of literary realism. There 'a thoroughly fragmented political situation and a backward economy, each tending to paralyze the other'.[92] The literary and intellectual movement began from a 'fragmented, narrow and provincial ... political base, and in [a] stagnant ... social and political climate'.[93] Hence even younger intellectuals like Goethe and Schiller, when faced with the French Revolution's reality, drew back 'from depicting human nature and destiny through the interaction of human beings with the upheaval of the large-scale social and historical forces generally characteristic of their own era'.[94] It is similarly noteworthy that Frei saw an element of realistic literature in this period in its treatment of money as 'one significant social element entering into individual character, molding personal relations in a social context'.[95]

Frei's secular appraisal of modernity in *The Eclipse of Biblical Narrative* can also be seen in his exegesis and apparent endorsement of Marx's claim from 1844 that the criticism of religion in Germany was 'in the main complete'.[96] Marx understood, Frei explains, that the completion of the criticism of religion in the historical criticism of the Gospels, culminating in Strauss, was not the cause of the secularization of society but its product. It was the result of the secularizing force of industrialization and the socio-economic changes it drove upon society and its ideological superstructure, an index of the obsolescence of religion as a historical force. Indeed, Frei notes, it signalled the full extent of the eclipse of biblical narrative as a power shaping western culture. It was 'an admission of the discernment that the real world in which we ineluctably exist is not the biblical stories' world' and of the cultural decline of the notion of Christological salvation in history.[97] Frei seems to endorse Marx's analysis when he praises the shrewdness of his appraisal of 'the long-range cultural significance' of the tradition of inquiry into the historical Jesus.[98]

Thus we may infer that Frei did not think that modernity is simply the product of the history of ideas nor that we should or could unwind its course in order to re-enchant the world. But he did think there was a missed possibility in these developments. For he argues that the realistic biblical narratives, while not rendering a historical understanding of modernity as modern realistic novels do, nevertheless have a certain affinity with a historical understanding of the modern world. When describing realistic literature in the eighteenth century, Frei argues that it has the capacity to deal with changing societies, and to portray the lives of those caught up in those changes and their moral existence in that context, with intimacy and ambiguity, embodying in this way a certain kind of historical sensibility or consciousness (which Frei contrasts to the universalizing and spiritualizing tendencies of German historicism in this period).[99] It is especially striking, then, that in that context Frei moves from considering the realism of the English novel in the late eighteenth century to reminding us of the realistic, history-like characteristics of biblical narratives, inviting us to consider their potential to help to shape an imagination that combines such a historical consciousness with a providential outlook.[100] The biblical narratives, he seems to imply, may still shape Christians' understanding of themselves and their circumstances as public actors in a turbulent modern world, with the contingent historical forces that shape it, and understand it to be governed by God. For one necessary condition of such an imagination – the literal interpretation of biblical narrative – remains available. Successive generations of theologians and interpreters failed to find a way to attend to the narrative meaning of the stories they recognized to be history-like, but the logical option of doing so was there all along and certain historical circumstances were favourable to its pursuit. None of the factors that inhibited scholars from pursuing this logical option, moreover, were inevitable consequences of the social and cultural shift to modernity. Perhaps, Frei implies, we might be able to incorporate the modern world figurally into the biblical world if we could learn again to attend to the latter.

As Higton notes, Frei is not very clear in *The Eclipse of Biblical Narrative* about what such a recovery of the narrative meaning of biblical stories would look like, except that he points to Karl Barth's figural exegesis in his treatment of election in *Church Dogmatics* II/2, his 'narrative treatment of the Gospel story' in *Church Dogmatics* IV/1 and to his own work in *The Identity of Jesus Christ*.[101] In *The Eclipse of Biblical Narrative*, however, Frei identifies other modern theologians from the past who performed this function and who amplify his account of the other conditions necessary for a renewal of western Christian reading practices with respect to biblical narratives and to the modern world.

Two of these conditions are the connected ideas of divine authorship and providence. In Frei's account of the eighteenth-century English debate about the fulfilment of Old Testament prophecy in New Testament events, Thomas Sherlock features as someone who offered a defence of figural reading. His defence offered a possibility not covered by the disjunctive alternatives offered by Anthony Collins: that either New Testament claims to the fulfilment of prophecy are false because the events they describe do not fit the terms of the prophecy read literally, or that they are meaningless ways of reading since they are non-literal. In *The Use and Intent of Prophecy in the Several Ages of the World* (1728), Sherlock argued that New Testament claims to fulfilment were retrospective claims made from the standpoint of the event depicted in the New Testament. They discerned 'a connected, providential scheme in the general bearing of the Old Testament texts, so that what was said and recounted there is now seen to have foreshadowed and led to the climax or fulfilment claimed by the New Testament writers'.[102] Indeed, Sherlock's account was a good fit for Collins' own definition of a type as a pattern or mould of something that is a sign or symbol designed by God to signify a future thing.[103] Sherlock's account, and Collins' own definition, escaped the terms of Collins' critique of the fulfilment of prophecy, as they did not demand that 'the intentional description of a later event by the earlier text, with a one-to-one correspondence between their features, is the only meaningful basis for recognizing similarity and possibly some form of providential connection between the two'.[104] Collins, however, never argued against his own definition nor with Sherlock's argument, though he engaged with his essay.

The example of Sherlock is significant for understanding the nature of the constructive possibilities that Frei indicates with cases like his. Frei identifies an ambiguity in Sherlock's position, and that of other defenders of typological interpretation. All appealed to a pattern of providential design partly manifest in the history of sacred covenants, which connected the Testaments with one another and with the rest of history. However, it was never clear whether the typological interpretations offered the basis for this assumption, or whether the doctrinal assumption was necessary 'for making typological interpretation operative and cogent'.[105] In any case, the doctrine of providence functioned in their arguments as a substitute for their opponents' assumption that the meaning of every rational statement lies in the intention of its human author to give it that meaning, especially for its original audience. For the defenders of typological interpretation, this assumption was superfluous: there was a divine author 'who could supplement if not supplant with a second, greater, and more inclusive meaning the sense intended by a limited human author and appropriate to his finite understanding … through the text's literal words'.[106]

This assumption about divine authorship went hand in hand with another about divine providence. As for the Protestant Reformers, so for these thinkers: the unity of the literal and historical senses of Scripture involved the unity of the divine author of the book with the divine governor of the history it narrates.[107] Thus meaning and fact are united, and there is no distance between words and referents 'of such a sort that each has a status logically independent of the other'.[108] What God intends literally, naturally also refers to the events so described; the linguistic description does duty for the reference. And 'in view of God's providential governance there is no reason why a statement he makes should not describe two events at the same time, the one literally and the other by prefiguration'.[109] Figural interpretation thus did not supplant literal interpretation; it followed the way God extended temporally the reference of the literal description by way of divine providence (whereby one event foreshadowed another), and it followed the concomitant extension of the literal meaning pattern in its application to the event in which the type was fulfilled.[110] Moreover, this argument suggests that the unity of God as author and governor of history could perhaps replace the need for recourse to a cumbersome, ill-fitting general theory of meaning and reference. And, in turn, the practice of figural reading exhibited and explicated the content of the doctrine without recourse to theoretical explanation or demonstration of (immanent) temporal causal links, neither of which would have been apt to the implicit logic of divine transcendence and immanence involved in this outlook.[111]

Here, then, Frei indicates an alternative possibility, escaping disjunctive options for thinking about the meaning and figural interpretation of biblical narratives, on account of its theological character. It does so, implicitly, by appeal to the providential and discursive agency of God, which is conceived as being in non-competitive transcendence of other agencies so as to work through them without prejudice to their finite integrity.[112] This kind of approach, by relying on the intimate connections between figural reading and this kind of doctrine of divine speech and providential action, supplies an alternative model of theological rationality. That model involves exhibiting a historical pattern set forth in biblical narratives read literally and linked figurally, a design with a particular logic, whose conditions of possibility are rooted in transcendent-immanent action of God. It describes this pattern and logic but does not seek to account for its mysterious conditions of possibility by a general theory. And it does these things to sustain in modernity a mode of reading of both the text and of the world of the readers that makes possible the indwelling of the world as governed by God, similar in function to that which Frei found in pre-modern Christian reading.

A third condition for the recovery of the literal reading of biblical narrative and the figural procedures predicated upon it, which harks back to some of Frei's hermeneutical remarks in his Harvard lecture of 1967, is a modest theory of textual meaning. Here the key figure is Johann August Ernesti, whom Frei contrasts with most of the figures he discusses in the history of modern biblical hermeneutics. Ernesti exemplifies the possibility in this period of restricting general hermeneutics to the grammatical meaning of the text and of locating textual meaning in an author's intentional use of words as governed by the conventions of their time, and of making inquiry into the subject matter of those words a secondary matter to the explication of their sense. Later, Frei goes on to say explicitly that it ought to be possible, with respect to realistic narratives, that 'the function of general hermeneutics should be formal rather than material; it should be confined to identifying a piece of literature as belonging to that particular genre rather than some other, rather than claim to interpret its meaning or subject matter.'[113]

It is worth noting that Frei also sees in Ernesti's emphasis on the conventional use of words as constituting authorial intention a qualified similarity with the view of present-day 'philosophical analysts', by which he means the later philosophy of Ludwig Wittgenstein and ordinary language philosophy.[114] Like them, Ernesti did not think of authorial intention 'as a privileged realm beyond his words, to which either he or we, the exegetes, have special access'.[115] Earlier in the argument Frei cites Wittgenstein in similar vein, in order to criticize the view of language he finds in J. S. Semler's hermeneutics, where the use of words was assumed to be univocal across contexts. Semler saw words as the basic units of stable, lexically determined meaning, and meaning 'as a kind of unvarying subsistent medium in which words flourish or, to change the figure, a kind of conveyor belt onto which words are dropped for transportation to their proper reference or destiny'.[116] Semler's view of language, he argues, is much like that which Wittgenstein critiques as imagining verbal sense as '"an atmosphere accompanying the word, which it carried with it into every kind of application"'.[117] As in his Christological essays, however, Frei's recourse to Wittgenstein is limited and more in service of critiquing certain notions of linguistic meaning than articulating a full-blown 'Wittgensteinian' general theory of meaning and truth.[118]

In these respects, Frei's multi-stranded argument in *The Eclipse of Biblical Narrative* represents a development of the theology he had outlined in his Christology essays, not least his theology of Scripture. He also offered a fuller account of the essence of Christianity as a reading tradition.

The essence of Christianity

Frei does not directly make a claim about the essence of Christianity, as he had done in his Harvard lecture in 1967 and in the Christological essays of 1966–67. However, his argument effectively rests on something approaching one, and one that moves his earlier proposal in a more historical, practical direction.[119] In *The Eclipse of Biblical Narrative*, he does not identify Christianity with the narrative meaning of the realistic portions of the Synoptics. Rather, he describes a history of interpretation, pre-modern and modern, characterized by a consistent focus on certain biblical narratives, the Gospel stories pre-eminent among them, and on the central figure of the Gospel stories, Jesus Christ.

As we have seen, he narrates a complex history, marked not only by the influence of philosophical ideas, whether empiricist or idealist, but more so of cultural developments and the socio-economic changes that shaped them. Frei thus ends up describing historically contextual continuities and discontinuities of practice, haunted by a logical option largely ignored or eschewed for the contingent, circumstantial reasons just enumerated. It was also a tradition that might be retrieved and renewed, as in Barth's exegesis and the energetic and consistent, figural Christocentrism of his mature theology.[120] For Frei, the *Church Dogmatics* was a necessarily prolix exercise in re-creating a Christian discourse with its own integrity, rooted in Scripture, instructing Barthe's readers in the use of this language as much by showing as by stating its rule and by indicating that the discursive world of biblical narrative is 'the one common world in which we all live and move and have our being'.[121]

Frei's account amounts to a more historical and practical understanding of the essence of Christianity, compared with his Harvard lecture of 1967. Here the essence is not simply located in certain narratives but in a practice of reading them, a practice that varies historically but has a consistent focus and certain characteristics that may be more robustly instantiated or may be subverted in their capacity to attend to the central features of the narratives they privilege.

We can assess this revised position against the criticisms of historical claims about the essence which Frei rehearsed in his earlier essay on H. Richard Niebuhr's theological background. Thus, in *The Eclipse of Biblical Narrative*, Frei does not conceive of the essence of Christianity in quasi-idealistic terms as an inner, identical reality variously manifest in historical forms, as did Adolf von Harnack and Alfred Loisy. Like the writers of the *religionsgeschichtliche Schule*, Frei's way of thinking is too historicist and particularistic for that.[122] Nor did he repeat the attempt of nineteenth-century liberal theologians and their twentieth-century heirs to rescue the notion of a unique, unitary historical essence to Christianity in terms of the unique effects of that history recognized in the believing historian's normative evaluation of their relationship to it. Frei's understanding of history was too firmly attached to the social, public location of historical agents as well as opposed to this implicit relationism.[123]

In *The Eclipse of Biblical Narrative*, however, Frei also gestures to something more than the effective erasure of historical identity to Christianity involved in pursuing a historicist perspective to its logical conclusion. As he argued in 'Niebuhr's theological background', the *religionsgeschichte Schule* held that 'the essence of a historical manifestation *is* its development' and is not distinguishable from it.[124] However, once one has identified essences with the development of particular manifestations of Christianity, all one is left with is the evolution of those manifestations and no real underlying continuity across forms. In that case one cannot draw boundaries around a unique, unified historical essence. 'All one may see is the particular process of particular forms developing within a network of universal interconnections. Christianity becomes one continuing, shifting series of religio-cultural syncretisms in the context of others.'[125] The logical consequence of this view would be 'the denial of any real identity ... between Christianity in its origin and the Western cultural religion of our day which bears the same name'.[126] And the same would be true to some degree between intermediate forms of Christianity and its origin (and presumably among them also). Such historical relativism would preclude making normative judgements of any manifestation of Christianity in terms of its Christianity. Frei's argument in *The Eclipse of Biblical Narrative*, however, seems to be that there are meaningful basic continuities to the highly variable interpretation of realistic biblical narrative in western Christianity's interpretation of biblical narrative, which persist to some degree but come under significant strain (at least in certain strands of interpretive practice) in the modern period. Implicitly, for Frei, it is in the basic focus of that discourse on the narrative texture of biblical stories, and especially on the irreducible narrative depiction of Jesus Christ, that gives it its identity (albeit contingent and vulnerable) across so much historical change. In large part, the significance of that argument and that vulnerability for Frei rested on its pastoral and ethical implications, to which I turn next.

The figural imagination and the responsible reader

As George Schner observes, Frei's historical argument, by identifying what I am calling the essence of Christianity in the practice of reading for the storied meaning of realistic biblical narrative, advances an agenda for the retrieval of that practice as essential for Christians theologically and pastorally. Only by construing the biblical texts as realistic narrative can Christians 'come to a knowledge of Jesus as Lord and Saviour into whose world we are all to be taken up'.[127] I want to argue that for Frei, it is also essential ethically and politically. To see how, we need to return to his account of pre-modern Christian reading of biblical narrative.

As we have seen, Frei's account picked out five characteristic features of those practices that rested on some basic theological assumptions. First, where Christian readers determined that a biblical story was to be read literally, they took what it narrated to be its meaning, and, second, they took it thus to depict real historical events. Next, they joined such stories into a single story, a unified pattern of stories constituting an overarching, comprehensive history, chiefly through figural interpretation. Third, because they took this story to be authored by the God who is also the one who governs history, they took it to depict the actual history of the world in which they lived: a universal history that seeks to incorporate us into its structure. Fourth, the story therefore functioned as a guide to life, especially by way of its realistic depictions of lifelike individuals

interacting with ordinary events combining to constitute powerful historical forces, to offer without loss to their 'random individuality' figures in
whose destinies and circumstances readers could understand their own.
And this rendering of the real world to the reader was effectual and the
reader's religious appropriation of that world cohered with it, because of
the unity between the God who speaks in Scripture and governs history
and the Spirit who moves the human heart.[128]

In his Introduction, Frei presents these last aspects of pre-modern
Christian reading in the form of a demand, an imperative:

> since the world truly rendered by combining biblical narratives into one
> was indeed the one and only real world, it must in principle embrace the
> experience of any present age and reader. Not only was it possible for
> him, it was also his duty to fit himself into that world in which he was
> in any case a member, and he too did so in part by figural interpretation
> and in part of course by his mode of life. He was to see his disposition,
> his actions and passions, the shape of his own life as well as that of his
> era's events as figures of that storied world.[129]

Christian readers were to see themselves as figures of the world as
depicted in biblical stories, finding illumination in its characters' stories
for understanding their own circumstances and destinies, without
prejudice to their 'random individuality' or temporal specificity as part of
the same world, in which the design of the same God was, in some measure, legible. Specific experiences and general categories for interpreting
experience were all drawn into the terms of that story and took shape
from that incorporation. Those readers were to shape their lives in the
light of this understanding of themselves and their circumstances. In the
rest of this section, I will argue that, in the context of the constructive
argument of the book, Frei's description here amounts to advancing an
account of Christian responsibility.

Ethics and responsibility

Albert Jonsen's overview of *Responsibility in Modern Religious Ethics*,
published in 1968, sought to clarify the uses of 'responsibility' in contemporary Christian moral literature.[130] The salience of the concept of
responsibility in academic theological ethics in North America at that
time – when Frei was working on what would become *The Eclipse of
Biblical Narrative* – can also be seen from the publication of a selection
of texts on responsibility, co-edited by Frei's then Yale colleague, James
Gustafson, the following year.[131]

For Jonsen, such uses seemed to draw on notions from moral philosophy of the accountability of agents for their actions in two senses. The first is others' attribution of voluntary intentional actions and their foreseeable consequences to agents, and their evaluation of those actions against the standard of goods and the rules for how they should be attained.[132] The second is the agent's own habit, developed through a process of maturation, of appropriation of their actions, carrying them out with consideration of alternatives and consequences, with conscientious and consistent adoption of norms of action and with public commitment to a course of action, a way of life.[133] These meet in the agent giving a rational account of themselves to others of the moral principles to which they are committed.[134] Contemporary Christian ethicists, Jonsen argued, incorporated this sense of the agent's specific responsibility within a theological understanding of the total, inescapable accountability of human beings in relation to God as supreme lawgiver and final, omniscient judge. The ethics of Karl Barth, Bernard Häring, Dietrich Bonhoeffer and H. Richard Niebuhr all illustrate this combination, he argued. It is also fair to say that for each of these thinkers, such an integration of moral and theological responsibility allowed them to articulate understandings of ethics with several further characteristics. They recentred God, not the self, as the source and final arbiter of moral norms; they understood the human good to be determined by God's gracious action. They saw the space and character of human moral agency to be shaped by and responsive to that action within the context of particular historical situations, in a way that cannot be comprehensively anticipated by rule-based reasoning. And they situated human moral accountability in personal relation to this God. In respect of Frei, the most pertinent and illuminating of these accounts are those of Barth and Niebuhr.

Karl Barth's ethics of responsibility

In volume II/2 of the *Church Dogmatics*, Barth makes the concept of responsibility central to the treatment of ethics he offers in the context of his doctrine of God and of divine election of God and humanity in Christ. According to that doctrine, the God who is known in Jesus Christ elects himself to be God for us in Jesus Christ, freely binding himself to humanity. He also elects humanity to be persons who are partners in this covenant and witnesses to his glory in Jesus Christ.[135] In Christ, God thus takes responsibility for humanity but also determines human beings to be responsible, self-determining agents, answering and accountable to God within this covenant, by requiring their obedience to his rule.[136] The gospel thus also has the form of law or command. It claims, regulates and judges how humans use their freedom, disposing and impelling them to conform to God's being and to enjoy fellowship with God in eternal life.[137] It raises the ethical question of how human beings will respond to this determination of their being, to the demand for their obedience as covenant partners. This is a question of their attitude towards that determination and of what they will do with the agency bestowed on them in this way.

Consistent with his Christocentric doctrine of God's Word, Barth understands Jesus Christ to be the command of God as Creator, Reconciler and Redeemer, since reconciliation takes place in him and he is the presupposition and epitome of creation and redemption.[138] God's command is thus one and yet internally diverse, just as God is triune. Jesus Christ also obediently fulfils God's command and so is also the answer to the question God puts to human beings.[139] He is the determined, created image of God; the One beloved and preserved in bearing human sin; and the glorified realization and revelation of the divine image in his resurrection. He fulfils God's determination of human self-determination to obedience and does the good. He answers the ethical question put to human beings. Right conduct for them is determined in him, in whom God acts rightly towards us, judging and restoring us and in whom we have conformed to the divine image.[140] In him, says Barth, we recognize ourselves as in a mirror as God's creatures, as pardoned sinners and as expectant heirs of God's coming kingdom: the subjects of theological ethics.[141] Christ is thus both the good for human beings and the norm for their lives, the embodiment of right action and the revelatory paradigm of human beings as responsible beings.

In this way, Barth insists, God in Christ precludes (and condemns) ethical reflection from any general anthropological starting point.[142] All that is left for human beings to do is to endorse and glorify his realization of the good by corresponding to it, an obligation deriving from God's transformative self-gift to us in Jesus Christ.[143] Barth understands this obligation as liberation to embrace the good. By the Spirit, God's command in Christ sets us free, gives us permission for the freedom and obedience realized in him.[144] Where it is performed consciously, that obedience attests the universal lordship and claim of Christ, which are also fulfilled unconsciously by people outside the church.[145] Humans are those responsible in answering this claim upon them, but also in being always accountable to the divine command in Jesus Christ in our being, willing and activity.[146] 'The seriousness of the human situation consists in the fact that it is always lived in responsibility, both as a whole and in detail, and whether we understand it or not. The whole of our life ... is one long responsibility.'[147] Good human action thus consists in acting in and from our responsibility to this divine address in Christ.[148] Its goodness derives from the goodness of that address and of God.

Such responsibility, Barth explains, involves repeated self-examination and preparation, in each moment, to ask what we are to do.[149] Christians are to ask this question, genuinely, openly and humbly, without relying on but repentant for their previous answers, which are at best 'a refraction of the divine command in the dim and fallacious prism of our own life and understanding'.[150] This principle of repetition, repentance and renewal constitutes 'the law of the spiritual growth and continuity in our life', and its observance is the practice of perseverance in correspondence to God's steadfast use of his freedom.[151]

This question, what are we to do, seriously asked, expresses desire for knowledge of God's command and recognition of God's sovereignty in it.[152] It expresses acknowledgement of its unconditioned, objective and intrinsic validity, authority and goodness for us in Christ's saving work on our behalf, over against our willing and desiring.[153] It attests to knowledge of its having been revealed to us and that we have received it. It is a question about our own personal responsibility, collective then individual, as those elected in Jesus Christ to covenant partnership, to God's will in his command in their situation.[154] It involves interpreting our whole life, recapitulating the past, anticipating the future, 'as a closed circle of responsible being, willing, doing and not doing', normed by the sovereign covenant God has established, sealed and embodied in Jesus Christ's person, work and lordship.[155]

Christ's presence to the world ensures that God's command in Christ is close at hand to everyone. God in Christ 'is present to the world and each individual and confronts him in the smallest of his steps and thoughts as his Commander and Judge'.[156] The question is not whether we can hear it but whether we will, whether we will obey or disobey. There is no latitude here for human judgement about what to do in response to it. God's command, as a single, integral whole, is a definite decision. Hence God's command, as attested in Scripture, never meets us in the form of general rules to be applied by us.[157] Rather, it always encounters us with 'a specific meaning and intention, with a will which has foreseen everything and each thing in particular', in which nothing is left to chance or our caprice.[158] We are responsible to it as given in this concrete way, with only the choice of obedience and correspondence to the command or disobedience, faith or unbelief.[159]

The historical contingency of divine commanding as it meets us, however, does not make it random or accidental. For what characterizes and inspires all divine commanding, and is its true *ratio*, is the reconciling work of God in Jesus Christ. The meaning and content of the covenant of grace and divine commanding happens within its history, that of the twofold people (Israel and the church) who bear witness to it.[160] Indeed, God himself, 'the Lord in the fulfillment of His work is Himself the divine command ... rich over all and for all, abounding in counsels and purposes for all, and working in all things, in the whole space-time multiplicity of their existence'.[161] Christ as God's command is, Barth implies, not so much a universal maxim, uniformly imposed, as a living, abundant wisdom, specific and entirely apt in the direction it gives to each of its addressees in every different circumstance they face.

There is then a definite specificity to the command of God in Christ as it is given to us in each circumstance, which Barth conveys here with the idea that Christ issues concrete commands, and in his special ethics by talking of the concentration of the command in concrete, particular forms.[162] These are given to human beings 'in concrete fulness and with definiteness of content ... an individual command for the conduct of this man, at this moment and in this situation'.[163] They are comprehensive, leaving nothing to our interpretation and judgement, only the choice of whether to obey. They are thus an appeal to human freedom, to our voluntary and genuine agreement with the command in the realization of real freedom in the good enacted by obedience to God; to become God's confidants.[164]

The medium of those commands is the scriptural witness to Christ, through which he speaks.[165] God thus commands Christians by way of the historically concrete, specific, singular commands given to the people in the Bible for their time and situation. We are to act:

> as those who then and there were addressed by God, allowing the command given to them to be again, in our very different time and situation, the command given here and now to us, and therefore ranking ourselves with them, and in their divinely addressed person taking our place in the history and sequel of the covenant of grace, accepting and fulfilling our mission ... as the renewal and confirmation of the task laid upon them ...[166]

We do so as their contemporaries and fellow members of this people of God in its history, says Barth. Yet this specific definiteness for different people is not a disparate diversity. God's command is united, and unites its addressees, together and as individuals, in its rich goodness.[167] If we are willing to be addressed by it as they were, and accept it, we will hear it in its concreteness and definiteness for us. What God wills is that human beings should correspond to this history, should be called and gathered to this people to share its office of witnessing.[168] Like Moses, David, Peter and Paul, the centurion of Capernaum or the rich young ruler, Christians are moved by hope, gratitude, or expectant or fulfilled joy in performing specific commissions integrally connected with the establishment and proclamation of God's covenant and coming kingdom.[169]

This alignment of Christians with biblical recipients of divine commands and their correspondence to the history of God's covenant assumes and implies what Barth articulates in his treatment of special ethics: the constancy and unity of the divine command in God's faithfulness to himself across 'all the infinite diversity in which He gives and reveals His command'; and the constancy of human action, of human subjects determined by the order of God's creative, reconciling and redeeming action.[170] For the individual moments in which God encounters and commands individuals are moments in the history of God's action, 'in the commencement, continuation and completion of His guidance of the whole history of salvation and of the world'.[171] They owe their particular concreteness to the purpose and disposition of God, which are connected with God's other dispositions in this history. Similarly, there is a hidden connection between human actions in encounter with God. For who and what the human recipient of these commands is 'is determined by the creation and providence, by the reconciling and redeeming action, of the God to whose command, to whose claim, decision and judgment, man is subject in all these individual cases'.[172]

In this history, which connects individual ethical events of encounter between them, both the identity and nature of the God who encounters us in the ethical event, and the common identity of human beings in that event, have an outline form, a character that is revealed by God's word.[173] In this history, God's action and human beings in relation to God are both sequentially articulated and differentiated so that the event of their encounter is likewise articulated and differentiated in three distinct spheres, namely: creation, reconciliation and redemption. In each of these spheres of their history, God's action and human response have distinct forms, wherein we may describe their character by narrating that history.[174] By describing these forms by tracing their historical outline, we cannot anticipate God's command for anyone at any given moment but we may approximate the ethical event by a generally valid description (what Barth calls a 'formed reference') and give guidance through directives which approximate to a knowledge of the divine command and of right human action in response to it, deferring always to the authority, guidance and judgement of the Holy Spirit.[175] Special ethics can thus give 'instructional preparation' for the ethical event and for what Barth calls 'practical casuistry': the venture 'of understanding God's concrete specific command here and now in this particular way, of making a corresponding decision in this particular way, and of summoning others to such a concrete and specific decision'.[176]

Frei's account of the duty of pre-modern western Christian readers to fit themselves, by figural interpretation and mode of life, into the real world cumulatively rendered by history-like biblical narratives does not use the concepts of divine command and responsibility. Nor does it have anything like the depth and range of conceptual explication of Barth's account. Nevertheless, we can recognize in it the lineaments of something like Barth's concept of responsibility, especially when we bear in mind how, for Frei, this figural reading went together with an understanding of the coherence of God speaking in the biblical stories, providentially ordering the world of the reader and moving them to act.

The note of duty in Frei's account recalls Barth's understanding of the human obligation to obey the divine command. Similarly, Barth's account of what it means to align oneself with biblical characters in their reception of the divine command, to make oneself their contemporary, resonates closely with Frei's description of the urgent imperative on pre-modern western Christians to see themselves as figures of the biblical world and act accordingly. In this same way, Frei's account here strongly echoes Barth's understanding of the possibility of describing, even narrating, the general form of the ethical encounter and of the outline form or character of God and human beings in that encounter, within the differentiated spheres of their encounter in the history of the covenant. And where Barth considers human beings as ethical agents, Frei similarly describes Christian readers learning to see themselves, through figural reading, as characters defined in their interaction with one another and their circumstances, and to align themselves with biblical characters in those interactions; that is, as agents.

One can also read Barth's account here as one way of renewing the sense of responsibility Frei ascribes to pre-modern western Christian readers of biblical narrative. It must have done so for Frei himself, especially in the light of his view of Barth's figural imagination in those latter parts of the *Church Dogmatics* and his commending of volume II/2 as an example of a model of the kind of narrative reading that could be done in the wake of the eclipse Frei described.[177] Indeed, a few years later, commenting on the increasingly evident temporal character of the world of Christian discourse Barth sought to reconstruct and describe, through the retelling of biblical narrative, as in volume II/2, Frei says that Barth sought to indicate in his ethics that 'this narrated, narratable world is at the same time the ordinary world in which we are responsible for our actions'.[178] While Frei here gives no hint of Barth's sense of the divine command as something that ultimately lies beyond our ability to anticipate and that might enjoin exceptions to the general forms we might describe from the history of the covenant, it is consistent with his emphasis on the contingency of events in realistic biblical narrative and in the historical world of its Christian readers and his commitments elsewhere to divine freedom.[179] If anything, however, Frei is more explicit and emphatic that practices of literal and figural narrative reading of history-like biblical stories, and their extension to the historical world of the reader, are basic to the practice of Christian moral responsibility. In that way, he brings out the importance of those practices to several features of Barth's ethics of responsibility, features that can also be attributed to Frei's implicit ethics of responsibility here.

The first of these has to do with the way divine action establishes and shapes real moral agency on the part of human beings, as it does in Barth's ethics in the *Church Dogmatics*.[180] On Frei's account, the literal and figural reading of biblical narrative is essential to the shaping of that human moral agency. For those stories, so read, render the real world to the imagination as a historical world of contingent events produced by interacting forces and agencies, yet mysteriously governed by God. As it depicts them, those truly contingent interactions are constituted into patterns of providential design in which human beings' characters and actions have meaning and reality. As such, it is a world in which God's providential presence underwrites, situates and gives specific form to the finite, mutually conditioned reality of human moral agency, rather than subverts it.[181]

Second, Frei indicates the importance of those reading practices and their focus on realistic biblical narratives to moral realism in a Barth-like ethics of responsibility.[182] We may infer that for Frei, as he thought for Barth, the composite, overarching story the narratives relate, when read literally and figurally as a sequence, sets forth the consistency of God's ways with human moral agents and the continuity of the being of those moral agents, with which divine commanding in our present is likewise consistent.

Third, in this way these reading practices are also essential to the way in which the history of God's dealings with creation and with human creatures provides a framework for understanding instances of the concretization of divine commanding for individuals or communities, after the fact. Werpehowski likens this *post facto* understanding of the command by the moral agent in Barth's account to that gained in following a story, where one is pulled along towards an open conclusion, across surprising, contingent events, where what happens has a context which makes it intelligible.[183] Such a framework, he explains, also enables moral agents to give reasons for their actions in response to divine commanding, in terms of their understanding of how their circumstances are implicated and intelligible in the light of the pattern of God's history rendered in those stories, and how their response in that context correlates analogically with God's characteristic action depicted there. Frei's account of the role of biblical narrative in Christian responsibility, and his pointing to Barth as a renewal of this tradition, strengthens such a defence of Barth's ethics against the charge that his concept of the divine command seems to transcend rational assessment and to preclude the moral agent's self-criticism or the possibility of moral dialogue between Christians and non-Christians.[184] The same intelligibility of what God requires in any situation, and the scope for Christians offering reasons for obedient actions, would also seem to hold for Frei's implied ethics of responsibility in *The Eclipse of Biblical Narrative*.

Fourth, in virtue of all these features, the literal and figural reading of biblical narrative would seem to support the practice of discernment, or practical casuistry, that is integral to ethical responsibility for Barth in the sense of a manner of asking as to the divine command, in a particular situation.[185] Such asking seeks to apprehend God's gracious command as it encounters us in relation to the issue at hand, following faithfully the indications of the history of the covenant and the scriptural summaries of particular commands issued within it, while open to being directed in unforeseen ways. Something similar seems to be indicated by Frei's description of the responsibility of the western Christian reader to see themselves within the biblical world and act accordingly. In Frei's account, however, God's providence features more prominently in the historical sensibility fostered by the literal and figural reading of biblical narrative and so in the responsibility of readers and their practices of discernment in and with the figural reading of themselves and their circumstances.

Barth's account certainly acknowledges that part of the character of the God who commands is not only to create human beings and the world as an external basis for the history of the covenant, but also to govern the historical world. Providence likewise factors into his exposition of the general forms of God's command as creator and of the good action of human beings determined by God's action, especially in his description of vocation in terms of a summons to a path of life in respect of the particular, orientating limitations of a person's 'place of responsibility' with their possibilities.[186] Nevertheless, Frei can be read as placing greater and more central emphasis on providence in his implied account of responsibility in *The Eclipse of Biblical Narrative* in the broader context of his account of pre-modern western Christian reading and the constructive implications of his analysis of the eclipse of biblical narrative.

As we have seen, Frei gestures towards the recovering of some kind of view of the providential configuration of human history, together with something like a doctrine of the divine inspiration of the realistic meaning of biblical narrative, and implies the possibility thereby of recovering a kind of responsibility, which we have been exploring. Taking all those together, one can infer that fitting oneself, in one's interactive relations with others and with one's circumstances, into the biblical world, and altering one's mode of life accordingly, involves seeing one's contingent circumstances and relationships as subject to divine providence. Frei's account invites us to connect the imperative to fit oneself, our circumstances, our social context and our interactions with all of them, to the providential ordering of our world and to the true rendering of it in the biblical stories, such that we come to see our responsibility as responding not only to God's word but to God's action in our history. In that respect, his account invites comparison with H. Richard Niebuhr's account of the responsible self.

Responsibility in H. Richard Niebuhr

Niebuhr's account of the responsible self, in his Robertson Lectures of 1960, offers responsibility as an additional way to conceive of human existence, beyond the limitations of the teleological symbol of humans as makers and the deontological picture of humans under law.[187] He seeks to take seriously the human situation of acting in response to actions upon us, as we interact with natural and social forces. Humans are 'responsive beings, who in all our actions answer to action upon us in accordance with our interpretation of such action'.[188] Who we are as national communities emerges 'from response to challenge rather than from the pursuit of an ideal or from adherence to some ultimate laws'.[189] The same is true of individuals, especially with regard to suffering. Anyone with experience of life 'is aware of the extent to which the characters of people he has known have been given their particular forms' not only by their sufferings, but by their responses to those sufferings, which are shaped by their interpretations of what they suffered.[190]

Where there is response to action upon us as interpreted by the agent, there is moral action, Niebuhr argues.[191] The interpretation of situations, of actions upon us, therefore, is crucial to the moral character of that action. This interpretation involves us seeing events 'as parts of wholes, as related and as symbolic of larger meanings'.[192] Those interpretations shape our responses. Thus, responsibility is responsive action 'in accordance with our *interpretation* of the question to which answer is being given'.[193] Responsibility is about asking, at every moment, 'What is going on?' and seeking 'the *fitting* action, the one that fits into a total inter-action as response and as anticipation of further response'.[194]

Personal responsibility involves continuity of self and so presupposes a relatively consistent scheme of interpretations.[195] This interpretive activity includes our reinterpretations of the past and expectations of the future, which frame our sense of what response would be fitting, within a larger, more stable sense of the ultimate context of our histories, which Niebuhr calls the 'interpretive pattern of the metahistory, within which all our histories and biographies are enacted.'[196] Further, our actions are respon-sible where they also anticipate answers to our responses, and accept accountability in this way, like a participant in a dialogue. Responsible action in this way participates in an ongoing dialogue among humans in a 'continuing society'.[197] Finally, our interpretations of actions upon us refer also to an ultimate context and community of interaction, that on which our finite interactions are completely contingent, indeed on which they depend absolutely. To that ultimate we attribute the 'radical action' by which each of us is the particular individual we are, the 'fated' character of our particularity in this time and place, with this specific body, situations, thoughts, emotions and religious formation.[198] All our interpretations of events, and all our responses, are conditioned by our response to this ultimate context, whether in trust or distrust.[199] Our unity as selves obtains in this way, that in all our responses we respond to this One.[200] Where that response is in trust, we call the referent of that trust 'God'.[201] Hence the ethics of responsibility 'affirms: "God is acting in all actions upon you. So respond to all actions upon you as to respond to his action."'[202]

Our predicament as human beings, Niebuhr continues, is one of being conflicted through our unreconciled, diverse responses to the diverse agencies and systems acting upon us (natural, political, social, biological, emotional), leaving us with only 'a small seed of integrity, a haunting sense of unity and of universal responsibility'.[203] From the perspective of the Christian doctrine of reconciliation, our outlook in sin is to interpret our predicament as the enmity of the One who acts on us in all that acts upon us, and so to respond accordingly in all our responses.[204] Salvation delivers us from this deep distrust. Redemption is the liberty to interpret in trust everything that happens 'as contained within an intention and a total activity that includes death within the domain of life, that destroys only to re-establish and renew'.[205] For Christians, the possibility of this change is bound up with Jesus Christ's trusting response to God in his life and death and God's response to him in his resurrection, by which we and God are reconciled. 'Through Jesus Christ, through his life, death, resurrection, and reign in power, we have been led and are being led to metanoia, to the reinterpretation of all our interpretations of life and death.'[206] It is an as yet incomplete process of reconciliation, and, to the extent that we are reconciled, it reshapes our interpretations and actions (and not only those of Christians) so that they are informed by trust, love of all being, hope in the open future. The responsible self we see in Christ is:

> a universally and eternally responsive I, answering in universal society and in time without end, in all actions upon it, to the action of the One who heals all our diseases, forgives all our iniquities, saves our lives from destruction, and crowns us with everlasting mercy.[207]

The action we see in such a life is 'action fitted into the context of universal, eternal, life-giving action by the One'.[208]

Frei's account of pre-modern Christian readers in *The Eclipse of Biblical Narrative* does not have the dialogical and existential aspects of Niebuhr's account of the responsible self, nor does he appeal to a general account of selfhood in order to frame a particular Christian one, as Niebuhr does. Nevertheless, there are important similarities in other respects. Frei's readers, like Niebuhr's responsible self, are temporally and socially situated in particular contexts. They too interact with others and their circumstances, and are subject to wider forces in and through the events to which they respond. Frei's readers, like Niebuhr's responsible self, are called to interpret themselves, the forces that act upon them, and their situations, in terms of the action of God in and through finite creaturely agencies, and to make their response fitting to that interpreted context, furnished by literally read and figurally connected biblical narratives. For them also, the event of divine–human reconciliation in Jesus Christ is central to their interpretive schema, and they too attribute the efficacy with which they see the world in this way, and to act accordingly, to divine grace. Frei's readers are in this sense responsive beings, responding according to their construal of actions upon them and to the divine action in and through those actions, by the grace of God.

Conclusion: the political character of responsibility in Frei's *The Eclipse of Biblical Narrative*

I have argued, then, that Frei's *The Eclipse of Biblical Narrative*, in addition to its historical argument, takes forward his theological project and its ethical dimensions in several respects. It develops a more historical, practice-orientated and robust account of the essence of Christianity than the one offered in the Harvard lecture of 1967 in its description of pre-modern western literal and figural reading of realistic biblical narrative. It indicates conditions for the renewal of those practices and so for the renewal too of an ethics of responsibility framed by the figural reading of the reader's circumstances in history.

There is also a political character to the critical and constructive dimensions of Frei's thesis and his implicit account of responsibility. Frei's implicit sketch of Christian responsibility in *The Eclipse of Biblical Narrative* has a political character in the sense that the responsible Christian reader he depicts interprets and enacts faithful response to God in a public, natural and social setting that embraces the whole world. The public social character of responsibility is underwritten by the unity of God as governor of history and speaker in Scripture that underlies figural reading.

In this way Frei's account contrasts sharply with some forms of modern Christian political thought that seek to limit the public character of religious identity to spiritual matters separate from political matters, such as the preservation of self, others and property, our rights and obligations and our relationship to the state, such as John Locke's *Letter Concerning Toleration*.[209] The story of Jesus Christ and its narrative shape makes no substantive difference to Locke's understanding of Christianity as toleration, respectful of individual rights grounded in natural law, and of religion as personal preference and public persuasion.[210] Indeed, we can find in Locke's *Letter* another form of the shift Frei traces in the seventeenth century, whereby, rather than viewing the political duties of Christian citizens in the light of the central story of Jesus of Nazareth, Locke reads Christ as merely exemplifying the independently established political virtue of toleration in his refusal to use coercion; a Christology in which the shape of Christ's story is insignificant. The eclipse of his narrative in Locke's argument goes hand in hand with the relegation of religion to the private realm. Frei's implied constructive argument implicitly seeks to affirm Christian responsibility and its figural practices in the public realm, together with the narrative meaning of history-like biblical stories. In its valorization of the realism of biblical narratives, and especially of their depiction of the realization of God's will in humble and everyday circumstances, moreover, Frei's account has a further political implication. It is that the lives and interactions of ordinary people, shaped by the changing historical forces of modernity, matter to God and therefore to the responsible Christian.

Frei's intimation of an ethics of responsibility in *The Eclipse of Biblical Narrative* is brief and implicit. Understandably, it does not address a host of questions we might ask about what it might mean to have one's awareness and exercise of responsibility framed by the world of biblical narratives. Nor does it tell us how to distinguish between good and bad ways of inhabiting the world rendered by biblical narratives, or how to inhabit stories that seem to jar with Frei's own affirmation of the dignity of all human beings in virtue of Christ's vicarious identification with them and his death and resurrection for them. It does, however, suggest we may read Frei's earlier Christological essays as sketching a mode of renewal of the figural ethics of responsibility whose possibility he indicated in *The Eclipse of Biblical Narrative*.

Frei's *The Eclipse of Biblical Narrative* remains the fullest expression of his characteristic combination of historical and theological argument but it is not the terminus of his theological-historical thought, which continued to develop in the 1970s and 80s. Its later articulation, in his lectures on his typology of modern Christian theologies and related writings, addressed challenges to his project but also look forward to some of the ways the constructive argument of *The Eclipse of Biblical Narrative* framed his political ethics.

Notes

1 For example, Charles Campbell's *Preaching Jesus: New Directions for Homiletics in Hans Frei's Postliberal Theology* (Grand Rapids, MI: Eerdmans, 1997); Paul DeHart's *The Trial of Witnesses: The Rise and Decline of Postliberal Theology* (Malden: Blackwell Publishing, 2006); and Jason Springs, *Toward a Generous Orthodoxy: Prospects for Hans Frei's Postliberal Theology* (New York: Oxford University Press, 2010).

2 George P. Schner rightly observes that what Frei's historical thesis uncovers in *The Eclipse of Biblical Narrative* 'functions as an agenda for both a refusal and a retrieval within Christian theology' ('The Eclipse of Biblical Narrative: analysis and critique', *Modern Theology* 8:2 (April 1992), p. 151).

3 'Standard major program introduced in expanded religion curriculum', *Yale Daily News* 110 (15 March 1957), p. 8.

4 Higton's Annotated Bibliography includes lecture notes for 'Modern Christian thought, 1650–1830' and 'Modern Christian thought, 1830–1950' in Frei's papers at Yale Divinity School archive (YDS 76 IV 14-211), which seem to correspond broadly to the latter two courses announced by Hartt in 1957, and which Higton tentatively dates to 1978 and 1985 (Mike Higton, *Christ, Providence and History: Hans W. Frei's Public Theology* (London: T & T Clark, 2004), pp. 253, 264). Frei's papers in YDS also include notes, a bibliography and an exam paper for 'The formation of German religious thought in the passage from Enlightenment to Romanticism' (RS 371b 771b), dating (at least in parts) from 1981 (YDS 76 IV 13-198).

5 Frei, 'Autobiographical notes', p. 2 (YDS 76 VI 27-336). See, for example,

his note for his lectures on Herder (YDS 76 IV 18-271) and 'The formation of German religious thought in the passage from Enlightenment to Romanticism' (YDS 76 IV 13-199), as well as the closely related but more polished text he used for his Rockwell lectures (YDS 76 III 10-168/9 and 76 IV 13-198), all available here: https://divinity-adhoc.library.yale.edu/HansFreiTranscripts/. The Rockwell lectures have also been published in Hans W. Frei, *Reading Faithfully: Frei's Theological Background, Vol. 2*, ed. M. Higton and M. Bowald (Eugene, OR: Wipf & Stock, 2016), pp. 1–59.

6 Franklin B. Weinstein, '12 faculty members selected to receive Morse fellowships. Fellows to get year's leave of absence for research; most to travel abroad', *Yale Daily News* 150 (15 May 1959), p. 1.

7 1960 Calendar Book from YDS 76 VI 27.

8 See 'Yale Dean and three professors to study and travel next year', *Yale Daily News* 69 (7 January 1966), pp. 1, 9. Frei was to spend the year 'studying the history of nineteenth-century theology', reading German romantic and English periodical literature and comparing the problems faced by the two groups of authors. He was to travel to Germany and England and then return to Yale for the rest of the year.

9 YDS 76 VI 27-335. Mike Higton in his annotated bibliography dates the CV to February 1976 (Higton, *Christ, Providence and History*, p. 251).

10 Schner likens *The Eclipse of Biblical Narrative* to 'an immense set of brightly coloured counterbalancing weights suspended ultimately from one pivot and in constant motion, often passing through the same trajectory, the whole not being available to appreciation unless one considers the skill it takes to keep the parts in balance and motion' ('The Eclipse of Biblical Narrative: analysis and critique', p. 149).

11 Hans W. Frei, *The Eclipse of Biblical Narrative: A Study in Eighteenth and Nineteenth Century Hermeneutics* (New Haven, CT: Yale University Press, 1974), p. 1 (hereafter, *Eclipse*).

12 Frei, *Eclipse*, p. 1. Frei contrasts what he describes as Luther's drastic simplification of Scripture being self-interpreting with the traditional theory of the fourfold sense on p. 19.

13 Frei, *Eclipse*, pp. 18–19.

14 *Eclipse*, p. 2. Frei speaks of 'the logical identification of the explicative interpretation of biblical narratives with their historical factuality' (*Eclipse*, p. 40), and the subsequent split between their 'explicative meaning and ... historical estimation' (p. 41). In this way the Reformers were consistent with 'a large consensus of western Christendom from earliest times' (p. 40).

15 Frei, *Eclipse*, p. 2.

16 He cites Erich Auerbach, *Mimesis: The Representation of Reality in Western Literature* (Princeton: Princeton University Press, 1968), pp. 48f., 73ff., 194ff., 555, along with his essay 'Figura', from his *Scenes from the Drama of European Literature* (New York: Meridian Books, 1959), pp. 11–76.

17 Higton, *Christ, Providence and History*, p. 139, citing *Eclipse*, p. 174.

18 *Eclipse*, pp. 2, 24–37.

19 *Eclipse*, p. 29.

20 *Eclipse*, pp. 29–30, citing Auerbach, *Mimesis*, p. 48.

21 Frei notes that the more the earlier event prefigured the later by way of a symbolism that was not rooted in the earlier occasion, the more it put the cohesion between the earlier occasion's visual content (that is, the scene or action it presents

to the imagination) and its meaning under strain. He gives the example of interpreting God's provision of manna in Exodus 16 as a figure of Christ's saving work by
way of seeing the former as a symbol of divine succour to the spiritually starving.
Here the line between figure and allegory could be very thin. See *Eclipse*, pp. 29–30.

22 Frei, *Eclipse*, pp. 19–20.

23 Frei, *Eclipse*, p. 3.

24 Frei, *Eclipse*, p. 3, quoting Auerbach, *Mimesis*, p. 15.

25 Frei, *Eclipse*, p. 15.

26 As Higton notes in *Christ, Providence and History*, pp. 140–2.

27 Frei, *Eclipse*, pp. 3–4.

28 Frei, *Eclipse*, p. 20.

29 Higton, *Christ, Providence and History*, pp. 137–8.

30 Frei, *Eclipse*, pp. 21–2.

31 Frei, *Eclipse*, p. 29.

32 Frei, *Eclipse*, p. 24. On the story setting forth the world ordered by the divine
plan, see Frei, *Eclipse*, p. 3, quoting Auerbach, *Mimesis*, p. 15.

33 Frei, *Eclipse*, pp. 21–5.

34 Frei, *Eclipse*, p. 24.

35 Frei, *Eclipse*, pp. 24–5.

36 Higton, *Christ, Providence and History*, pp. 143–4. Higton takes the idea of
history as the idiom of divine speech from John David Dawson's 'Figural reading
and the fashioning of Christian identity in Boyarin, Auerbach and Frei', *Modern
Theology* 14:2 (1998), p. 187.

37 Frei, *Eclipse*, pp. 10–11, 12–13, 15–16.

38 Frei, *Eclipse*, pp. 13–15.

39 Frei, *Eclipse*, p. 13.

40 Hans W. Frei, 'Theological reflections on the accounts of Jesus' death and
resurrection', in Hans W. Frei, *Theology and Narrative: Selected Essays*, ed. G.
Hunsinger and W. Placher (New York: Oxford University Press, 1993), p. 76; Hans
W. Frei, 'Remarks in connection with a theological proposal', in Frei, *Theology and
Narrative*, pp. 32–4.

41 Frei, *Eclipse*, p. 13.

42 Here Frei quotes the novelist Henry James: '"What is character but the
determination of incident? What is incident but the illustration of character?"',
Eclipse, p. 14, citing James, 'The art of fiction', in *The Future of the Novel* (New
York: Vintage Books, 1956), pp. 15f. His account here also recalls Auerbach's
observation of the way that Old Testament characters are bearers of the divine will
yet fallible and subject to misfortune and humiliation, in which their words and
acts reveal God's transcendent majesty, so that their circumstances give them 'a
personal stamp which is recognised as the product of a rich existence, a rich development', which gives to Old Testament stories 'a historical character, even when
the subject is purely legendary and traditional' (Auerbach, *Mimesis*, p. 18).

43 Frei, *Eclipse*, p. 14.

44 Frei, *Eclipse*, p. 14.

45 Frei, *Eclipse*, pp. 14–15. Auerbach emphasizes the way in which Old Testament narratives, while incorporating legend, tend to avoid the simplification,
smoothing down and harmonization of events and the simplification of motives
and static definition of characters found in legend. Characters like Abraham, Jacob
and Moses produce 'a more concrete, direct, and historical impression than the

figures of the Homeric world ... because the confused, contradictory multiplicity of events, the psychological and factual cross-purposes, which true history reveals ... still remain clearly perceptible' (*Mimesis*, p. 20). He also notes how the social picture of the early patriarchal narratives give a less stable impression than do the Homeric poems because the characters are nomadic or half-nomadic tribal leaders and, after the Exodus, the activity of the people is often discernible as a whole and in separate groups and through individuals. He notes too the way the sublime and tragic events and conflicts of Old Testament stories take place in domestic settings and daily life. See *Mimesis*, pp. 19–23. For Auerbach's view that realistic literature, including biblical narrative, depicts the dynamic play of historical forces in every-day life, see *Mimesis*, pp. 32–33, 40, 43–4.

46 Frei, *Eclipse*, p. 136.

47 Frei, *Eclipse*, p. 147.

48 Frei, *Eclipse*, p. 148.

49 So Nicholas Boyle in *Sacred and Secular Scriptures: A Catholic Approach to Literature* (London: Darton, Longman & Todd, 2004), p. 60.

50 Frei, *Eclipse*, p. 136.

51 Frei, *Eclipse*, p. 136.

52 Frei, *Eclipse*, p. 137.

53 Frei, *Eclipse*, p. 5.

54 Frei, *Eclipse*, pp. 11, 51–2.

55 Frei, *Eclipse*, pp. 42–50.

56 Frei, *Eclipse*, p. 72.

57 Frei, *Eclipse*, p. 77.

58 Frei, *Eclipse*, pp. 76–7.

59 Frei, *Eclipse*, p. 73.

60 Frei, *Eclipse*, p. 73.

61 Frei, *Eclipse*, p. 74.

62 Frei, *Eclipse*, pp. 77–8.

63 Frei, *Eclipse*, p. 79.

64 Frei, *Eclipse*, p. 81.

65 Frei, *Eclipse*, pp. 86–102, 134–6.

66 Frei summarizes these options in *Eclipse*, pp. 255–66.

67 Frei, *Eclipse*, p. 126.

68 Frei, *Eclipse*, p. 128. Of his contemporaries, Frei lists Emil Brunner, Rudolf Bultmann, Karl Rahner, Gerhard Ebeling, Wolfhart Pannenberg and Jürgen Molt-mann: a list with significant overlap with those criticized in his Harvard lecture of 1967.

69 Frei, *Eclipse*, p. 128.

70 Frei, *Eclipse*, pp. 114, 133.

71 Frei, *Eclipse*, p. 119; his emphases.

72 Frei, *Eclipse*, p. 136.

73 Frei, *Eclipse*, pp. 136–54, 183–232. Frei's analysis of these developments is far more nuanced and subtle than I have space to explore here, however.

74 Frei, *Eclipse*, pp. 307–24. Again, Frei's analysis of Schleiermacher's hermen-eutics is more subtle and nuanced than this brief summary.

75 Higton, *Christ, Providence and History*, p. 150.

76 Frei, *Eclipse*, pp. 233, 235.

77 Frei, *Eclipse*, p. 233.

78 Frei, *Eclipse*, pp. 235, 237, 243.

79 Frei, *Eclipse*, p. 244.

80 Frei, *Eclipse*, pp. 271–2.

81 Frei, *Eclipse*, p. 274.

82 Frei, *Eclipse*, pp. 275–7.

83 Frei, *Eclipse*, pp. 277–9.

84 Frei seems to give much greater emphasis to this issue in the latter sections of *Eclipse*, compared with the prominence of the reduction of meaning to possible reference earlier in the book. The longest discussion, focused on a contrast between Johann August Ernesti and Johann Salomo Semler, and the controversy between Ernesti and Johann Philip Gabler, is on pp. 247–55.

85 Schner, 'The Eclipse of Biblical Narrative: analysis and critique', pp. 160–1, citing Henning Graf Reventlow, *The Authority of the Bible and the Rise of the Modern World* (Philadelphia, PA: Fortress Press, 1985), and Michael Buckley, *At the Origins of Modern Atheism* (New Haven, CT: Yale University Press, 1987). Schner also thinks Frei's position has more common ground with Kant and especially with Hegel than Frei's reading of either acknowledges.

86 In an untitled paper with the pencilled date '1979–80' but probably from 1979, Frei talks of wanting to get a feel for a period's low culture (p. 3) and adds, on p. 4, 'Stephen Crites hit me right amidship when he asked me gently, in a review of *The Eclipse of Biblical Narrative*, where the non-high culture users of the Bible were, and what had happened to narrative among them?' (YDS 76 III 11-182). As Higton notes (*Christ, Providence and History*, p. 256), Frei may be referring to this paper in a letter to William Placher from December 1979 (YDS 76 I 4-78), which would date it to earlier that year.

87 In a review of *Eclipse*, Cornel West argued that, in *Eclipse*, the anti-Hegelian Frei had reduced biblical texts to a surface history-like realism, ignoring the interplay between surface and hidden depths of meaning which the Hegelian Auerbach had identified ('On Hans Frei's *Eclipse of Biblical Narrative*', in Cornel West, *Prophetic Fragments* (Grand Rapids, MI: Eerdmans, 1988), pp. 236–9). In this way, and in his nostalgia for figural reading, Frei had shunned the radical indeterminacy in textual interpretation that follows from acknowledging that interplay. Frei is more interested in Auerbach's account of the partial representation of otherwise hidden historical forces in biblical narratives than West credits him, though he 'had none of Auerbach's residual Hegelianism', as Higton puts it (*Christ, Providence and History*, p. 136). I would also suggest that the kind of figural interpretation Frei celebrates in *Eclipse* is not as totalizing as West claims, involving the recognition of providential connections between persons and events that are mysterious and made without loss to their sensuous rendering in the stories.

88 Meir Steinberg, *The Poetics of Biblical Narrative: Ideological Literature and the Drama of Reading* (Bloomington, IN: Indiana University Press, 1987), pp. 81–2.

89 Steinberg, *The Poetics of Biblical Narrative*, pp. 1–57.

90 David G. Kamitsuka, *Theology and Contemporary Culture: Liberation, Postliberal and Revisionary Perspectives* (Cambridge: Cambridge University Press, 1999), p.143.

91 Frei, *Eclipse*, pp. 148–9.

92 Frei, *Eclipse*, pp. 214–15.

93 Frei, *Eclipse*, p. 215.

94 Frei, *Eclipse*, p. 215.

95 Frei, *Eclipse*, p. 210 (concerning the symbolism of money in Lessing's *Minna von Barnhelm*).

96 Frei cites Marx's Introduction to 'Contribution to the critique of Hegel's Philosophy of Right' in *Deutsch-Französische Jahrbücher*, 1844, in *Marx and Engels in Religion* (New York: Schocken Books, 1964), p. 41. See Frei, *Eclipse*, p. 224.

97 Frei, *Eclipse*, p. 227.

98 Frei, *Eclipse*, p. 232.

99 On English novels linking moral existence to social experience in an intimate and ambiguous way, see Frei, *Eclipse*, p. 148. On the contrast with German historicism in the late eighteenth and early nineteenth centuries, see *Eclipse*, pp. 212–14.

100 Frei, *Eclipse*, pp. 149–52. For example: 'Like history and the novel, much biblical narrative in explicative interpretation is not "system" or pure factual description but the cumulative rendering of a temporal framework through realistic depiction and chronological continuity' (p. 152).

101 Higton, *Christ, Providence and History*, p. 137; Frei, *Eclipse*, pp. vii–viii. On Barth's figural exegesis in the *Church Dogmatics* II/2 (hereafter *CD*) (Edinburgh: T & T Clark, 1957), see Higton, 'The fulfilment of history in Barth, Frei, Auerbach and Dante', in John C. McDowell and Mike Higton (eds), *Conversing with Barth* (Aldershot: Ashgate, 2004), pp. 120–41.

102 Frei, *Eclipse*, p. 70.

103 Frei, *Eclipse*, p. 71, citing Anthony Collins, *The Scheme of Literal Prophecy Considered* (London: 1727), p. 358.

104 Frei, *Eclipse*, pp. 71–2.

105 Frei, *Eclipse*, p. 73.

106 Frei, *Eclipse*, p. 73.

107 Frei, *Eclipse*, pp. 73–4.

108 Frei, *Eclipse*, p. 74.

109 Frei, *Eclipse*, p. 74.

110 Frei, *Eclipse*, p. 74.

111 Frei, *Eclipse*, p. 174.

112 See again Kathryn Tanner's exposition of non-competitive accounts of divine and human agency in *God and Creation: Tyranny and Empowerment?* (Minneapolis, MN: Fortress Press, 1988).

113 Frei, *Eclipse*, p. 273.

114 Frei, *Eclipse*, p. 252. In note 11 (p. 340), he is explicit about the comparison, though careful to qualify it considerably: 'A modern reader may be startled by the apparent similarities between Ernesti and the later work of Ludwig Wittgenstein on matters of use, rules, and language as a "form of life."' However, he notes, the comparison would be difficult since Ernesti was an eighteenth-century rationalist who thought 'sense' was generally invariant within a historical period, and that the chief use of words is to signify.

115 Frei, *Eclipse*, p. 252, citing J. A. Ernesti, *Elements of Interpretation*, tr. Moses Stuart (1824), introduction and part 1, chapter 1.

116 Frei, *Eclipse*, p. 109.

117 Frei, *Eclipse*, pp. 109–10, citing L. Wittgenstein, *Philosophical Investigations*, tr. G. E. M. Anscombe (Oxford: Blackwell, 1963), §117.

118 Here again I disagree with John Allen Knight's reading of Frei. See J. A. Knight, *Liberalism versus Postliberalism: The Great Divide in Twentieth-Century*

Theology (New York: Oxford University Press, 2013), pp. 161–2, and Ben Fulford, '*Liberalism versus Postliberalism: The Great Divide in Twentieth-Century Theology. By John Allen Knight*', *The Journal of Theological Studies* 65:1 (April 2014), pp. 365–6.

119 See also George Schner, who wonders if the category of realistic narrative was for Frei a way not only of restating the problem of the scandal of particularity in Christian theology but also of naming the uniqueness of Christianity ("The Eclipse of Biblical Narrative: analysis and critique', pp. 159–60). However, that way of putting it overemphasizes the category of realistic narratives where Frei seeks to emphasize the narrative meaning of certain Christological stories.

120 Frei, *Eclipse*, p. viii; 'Karl Barth: theologian', in Frei, *Theology and Narrative*; and 'Eberhard Busch's biography of Karl Barth', in Hans W. Frei, *Types of Christian Theology*, ed. G. Hunsinger and W. C. Placher (New Haven, CT: Yale University Press, 1992), pp. 158–61.

121 Frei, 'Eberhard Busch's biography of Karl Barth', p. 161.

122 For Frei, Harnack's thesis, that the essence of Christianity lay in Jesus' original teachings, repr₋ ₋ents the notion that 'the essence of a historical manifestation is present in unique and normative fashion' in its original form ('Niebuhr's theological background', in *Faith and Ethics: The Theology of H. Richard Niebuhr*, ed. Paul Ramsey (New York: Harper & Row, 1957), p. 26). Loisy's counter-thesis, influenced by Cardinal Newman's *Essay on the Development of Christian Doctrine*, was that the essence of Christianity lies in the unity of its development in successive external forms, which are only normative in their unity (Frei, 'Niebuhr's theological background', pp. 26–7). Both these proposals shared the assumption that some distinction between essence and particular shapes or forms was inevitable, whether in Harnack's distinction of the kernel of Jesus' teaching and the husk of its cultural expression or Loisy's vaguer distinction between the essence and changing dogmatic expressions (which of them develops and how they are related was unclear, Frei noted).

123 Frei, 'Niebuhr's theological background', p. 59.

124 Frei, 'Niebuhr's theological background', p. 28; his emphasis.

125 Frei, 'Niebuhr's theological background', p. 28.

126 Frei, 'Niebuhr's theological background', p. 28.

127 Schner, 'The Eclipse of Biblical Narrative: analysis and critique', p. 152.

128 Frei, *Eclipse*, p. 24.

129 Frei, *Eclipse*, p. 3.

130 Albert R. Jonsen, *Responsibility in Modern Religious Ethics* (Washington/Cleveland, OH: Corpus Books, 1968).

131 James M. Gustafson and James T. Laney (eds), *On Being Responsible: Issues in Personal Ethics* (London: SCM Press, 1969).

132 Jonsen, *Responsibility*, pp. 36–59.

133 Jonsen, *Responsibility*, pp. 61–70.

134 Jonsen, *Responsibility*, pp. 71–2.

135 *CD* II/2, p. 510. I discovered Barth on responsibility through co-supervising Michael J. Leyden's excellent doctoral thesis, 'Responsible before God: human responsibility in Karl Barth's moral theology' (University of Chester, 2014).

136 *CD* II/2, p. 511.

137 *CD* II/2, pp. 511–12, 566.

138 *CD* II/2, p. 549.

139 *CD* II/2, p. 517.
140 *CD* II/2, pp. 538–9, 567.
141 *CD* II/2, pp. 549–50.
142 *CD* II/2, pp. 517–20, 543.
143 *CD* II/2, pp. 539–40, 557–8.
144 *CD* II/2, pp. 587–8, 593–4, 603–6.
145 *CD* II/2, pp. 569–71.
146 *CD* II/2, p. 641.
147 *CD* II/2, p. 642.
148 *CD* II/2, pp. 546–7.
149 *CD* II/2, pp. 634–6, 643–4.
150 *CD* II/2, pp. 646–7.
151 *CD* II/2, p. 647.
152 *CD* II/2, p. 648.
153 *CD* II/2, pp. 651–3.
154 *CD* II/2, pp. 653–7.
155 *CD* II/2, p. 660.
156 *CD* II/2, p. 669.
157 Even where it looks like general rules, taken out of context. Such passages are best understood as summaries of particular commands, qualifying their character as divine command, Barth argues (*CD* II/2, pp. 679–704).
158 *CD* II/2, pp. 663–4, 672–6.
159 *CD* II/2, p. 669.
160 *CD* II/2, pp. 676–8.
161 *CD* II/2, p. 705.
162 See *CD* III/4, p. 9.
163 *CD* III/4, p. 11.
164 *CD* III/4, pp. 11–14.
165 *CD* II/2, pp. 704–6.
166 *CD* II/2, p. 706.
167 *CD* II/2, pp. 710–32.
168 *CD* II/2, p. 678.
169 *CD* II/2, pp. 703–4. Lamentably, Barth's list includes none of the women commanded by God in Scripture.
170 *CD* III/4, pp. 16–17.
171 *CD* III/4, p. 16.
172 *CD* III/4, p. 17.
173 *CD* III/4, pp. 18–26.
174 *CD* III/4, pp. 25–29.
175 *CD* III/4, pp. 15–16, 29–31.
176 *CD* III/4, pp. 9, 18.
177 Frei, *Eclipse*, p. x.
178 'Eberhard Busch's biography of Barth', in Frei, *Types of Christian Theology*, p. 161.
179 Most clearly in his doctoral dissertation but also evidently implied in his Christological essays.
180 See George Hunsinger, 'Double agency as a test case', in *How to Read Karl Barth: The Shape of His Theology* (New York: Oxford University Press, 1991), pp. 185–224; John Webster, 'Freedom in limitation', in *Barth's Moral Theology*

(Edinburgh; T & T Clark, 2004), pp. 99–123; Paul T. Nimmo, *Being in Action: The Theological Shape of Barth's Ethical Vision* (London: T & T Clark, 2011), pp. 87–135.

181 'Situated freedom' is how Webster characterizes Barth's understanding of human freedom in the *Church Dogmatics*, borrowing the term from Charles Taylor (Webster, *Barth's Moral Theology*, pp. 122–3). It seems apt to describe Frei's anthropology in *Eclipse* too.

182 William Werpehowski follows Frei in making this connection in respect of Barth, in *Karl Barth and Christian Ethics: Living in Truth* (Farnham: Taylor Francis Group, 2014), pp. 57–63.

183 Werpehowski, *Karl Barth and Christian Ethics*, p. 28.

184 This is the criticism made by Robin Lovin as summarized by Nigel Biggar in *The Hastening that Waits: Karl Barth's Ethics* (Oxford, Clarendon Press, 1993), pp. 24–5, and by James Gustafson as summarized by Werpehowski in *Karl Barth and Christian Ethics*, p. 15. Both Biggar and Werpehowski emphasize this importance of biblical narrative to Barth's ethics in this way. See Biggar, *The Hastening that Waits*, pp. 104–5, 109, and Werpehowski (with explicit appeal to Frei), *Karl Barth and Christian Ethics*, pp. 21–2, 49.

185 Here again following Werpehowski, *Karl Barth and Christian Ethics*, pp. 29–32, 64–9.

186 See CD III/4, §56.2.

187 H. R. Niebuhr, *The Responsible Self: An Essay in Christian Moral Philosophy* (Louisville, KY: Westminster John Knox Press, 1999).

188 Niebuhr, *The Responsible Self*, p. 57.

189 Niebuhr, *The Responsible Self*, p. 58.

190 Niebuhr, *The Responsible Self*, p. 58.

191 Niebuhr, *The Responsible Self*, p. 61.

192 Niebuhr, *The Responsible Self*, p. 62.

193 Niebuhr, *The Responsible Self*, p. 63; his emphasis.

194 Niebuhr, *The Responsible Self*, pp. 60–1; his emphasis.

195 Niebuhr, *The Responsible Self*, p. 65.

196 Niebuhr, *The Responsible Self*, p. 106.

197 Niebuhr, *The Responsible Self*, p. 65. Niebuhr goes on to develop a triadic account of responsible selfhood as social, encountering the other in the context of society, and communicative, in dialogue about something to which they are responding, such as natural events (pp. 69–84).

198 Niebuhr, *The Responsible Self*, pp. 108–15.

199 Niebuhr, *The Responsible Self*, pp. 115–21.

200 Niebuhr, *The Responsible Self*, pp. 121–6.

201 Niebuhr, *The Responsible Self*, p. 119.

202 Niebuhr, *The Responsible Self*, p. 126.

203 Niebuhr, *The Responsible Self*, p. 139.

204 Niebuhr, *The Responsible Self*, pp. 137–42. The quotation comes from p. 139.

205 Niebuhr, *The Responsible Self*, p. 142.

206 Niebuhr, *The Responsible Self*, p. 143.

207 Niebuhr, *The Responsible Self*, pp. 144–5.

208 Niebuhr, *The Responsible Self*, p. 145.

209 J. Locke and J. Tully (eds), *A Letter Concerning Toleration* (Indianapolis,

IN: Hackett Publishing Company, 1983). See Elizabeth Pritchard, *Religion in Public: Locke's Political Theology* (Stanford, CA: Stanford University Press, 2013). See also Judd J. Owens' account of Locke in *Making Religion Safe for Democracy: Transformation from Hobbes to Tocqueville* (New York: Cambridge University Press, 2014), pp. 57–112.

210 See J. Locke and P. Laslett (eds), *Two Treatises of Government* (Cambridge: Cambridge University Press, 1988), pp. 271–92, and Locke and Tully, *A Letter Concerning Toleration*, pp. 23–5. I make this case at greater length and use it to interrogate the moderate/radical binary in contemporary British political discourse in 'Moderating religious identity and the eclipse of religious wisdoms: lessons from Hans Frei', *The Review of Faith and International Affairs* 15:2 (2017), pp. 24–33.

5

A Generous Orthodoxy:
The Literal Sense and Christian Liberal
Humanism after Christendom

Frei's project on modern Christology continued to develop after the publication of *The Eclipse of Biblical Narrative* in ways that are significant for understanding its political and ethical implications. In the years after he stepped down as Master of Ezra Stiles College in 1980, and during and after his time as Chair of the Department of Religious Studies at Yale (1983–86), he produced a series of lectures and papers in which he reconceived his project. He did so in response to criticisms that his kind of theology was not properly public, especially on the question of faith and history, and out of a desire to reconnect academic theology and Christian practices. This rethinking took the form, primarily, of a typology of the ways modern theologians negotiate the demands of the ecclesial and academic contexts of Christian theology and of the consequences of their approaches for their treatment of the narrated scriptural figure of Jesus Christ in the Christian reading practice called 'the literal sense'.[1]

Frei's typology at once carries forward the historical and constructive theological concerns and focus of his Christological project and develops it in significant ways. It represents a sophisticated answer to the question of the publicness of Christian theology but also a far more subtle, complex, social, practical and historical account of the essence of Christianity and its normativity, compared with his Christology essays and *The Eclipse of Biblical Narrative*.[2] In this way it reframes his ethics of responsibility and strengthens his account of its publicness. Indeed, as I will show, for Frei, a theology hospitable to the literal sense, and learning from the example of Judaism, would foster a practice that would make possible a social and political vocation for Christianity in post-Christian societies. It also lays the basis for a Christian liberal humanism that would uphold human dignity and practise a generous love of neighbour, by appeal to the identity of Jesus Christ. These are the components of his quest for a generous orthodoxy.

Rethinking the project (1974–81)

The roots of the later development of Frei's thought lie in problems he was ruminating over during the 1970s even as his reputation was growing following the publication of *The Eclipse of Biblical Narrative*.[3] During this period, Frei's administrative responsibilities significantly curtailed his ability to pursue his project on modern Christology, which was still his main focus.[4] He spent eight years as Master of Stiles, despite approaches from other institutions for posts that might have given him more time for research, primarily because his family were settled in New Haven.[5] After four years in the Master's Office, he confessed in 1976 to his friend Van Harvey that he felt rusty and had written little.[6] Frei would spend four more years at Ezra Stiles and in 1979, with the end finally in sight, he was still worrying about returning to writing 'after years of administration'.[7] This anxiety was coupled with uncertainty as to his proper disciplinary location, a sense of doubt and marginality about his faith and theological vocation, and a sense of the culmination of a gradual estrangement from the Episcopal Church, all articulated in correspondence with several academic friends and former students.[8] Indeed, he had returned to attending Quaker meetings, which he found 'glorious' but which had little to do with his theological convictions and would not suffice as a church setting for his theology.[9] In his Holocaust Testimony, recorded in April 1980, he traced this remoteness towards the church to a tendency to mistrust strong communal ties and his inability to form strong attachments, going back to his experience as a refugee with minimal identity except for what he could gain from his immediate family and his own inquiry through life. He described this disposition as the social or political wound he carried from his refugee experience.[10] It may also be linked to his lonely identity as a Christian Jew, an insider and outsider to Judaism.[11] This estrangement was one of the reasons he doubted his credentials as a theologian, given the importance he attached to having 'a firm contextual reference to the religious community' in which his writing was located.[12]

This worry foreshadows the emphasis Frei would place on the socio-linguistic location of Christian theology in his later writings. That emphasis in turn intersects with a related concern he articulates in the late 1970s: to make his writing less purely theoretical, and to address the question of the relationship between theory and ecclesial praxis, though he did not specify which sense of 'praxis' he had in mind.[13] Frei took an active interest in Latin American liberation theology in the 1970s and 80s (in addition to feminist and black liberation theology), and his preoccupation with theory and praxis in theology may well stem from that engagement.[14]

Frei initially developed this concern by advocating that the intellectual history of modern Christianity be studied in connection with what he called sensibility, in ordinary social, economic and institutional contexts.[15] By sensibility, Frei meant: what it felt like to experience the world, including its religious aspects, in a particular time and place.[16] He also sought to correct the elite focus of his historiography in *The Eclipse of Biblical Narrative* by essaying a more social historical approach to his modern Christology project, researching the social function of popular religion in eighteenth-century England, to get a feel for 'a period's low culture as well as its high'.[17] By the time of his death, he had not found a way of incorporating it into his lectures or writing for publication, although he did integrate social and popular religious history in his teaching of intellectual religious history at Yale.[18] Nevertheless, the shift is significant: it began to bring the focus of Frei's scholarly attention in line with the implicit politics of his analysis about the world of ordinary life rendered to the reader by realistic biblical narrative. It also went together with a concern for a non-reductive, descriptive approach to the study of religion that would not treat human action, institutions, and linguistic and social structures as secondary to consciousness: a concern that is also reflected in his later writings.[19]

The liberation theologies Frei was reading by the early 1970s contributed to a turbulent scene for Christian theology in the United States of 'powerful counter-cultural movements, a search for new life styles, serious dissatisfactions with traditional modes of religious expression, and widespread questioning of long-accepted views on the church, the university, and the state' that contrasted with 'the postwar period of affluence and religious revival'.[20] It also followed the death of Karl Barth in 1968 and saw the passing of the hegemony in the academy of 'neo-orthodox' theologians like Paul Tillich and Reinhold Niebuhr and the emergence of theological voices advocating the radical reconstruction of Christianity.[21] In that polarizing context, as Paul DeHart comments, Frei, like his friend George Lindbeck, sought to combine sympathy to progressive change with the retrieval of the generative classic Christian tradition to which they had been introduced at Yale.[22]

We can trace this concern to the period before the publication of *The Eclipse of Biblical Narrative*. Frei's lecture notes for his course on Contemporary Christian Thought in the autumn of 1972 show that he was analysing different theological responses to what he saw as a secularizing 'revolution' in religion and moral attitudes in the United States in the 1960s.[23] By 'secularizing', Frei meant the dwindling authority in society of Christian sources and norms and the questioning of received views and institutions referred to above. Frei distinguished theologies in which secular culture sets the agenda, those for which it partly supplies the meaning of Christian concepts (and so secures their relevance) and those who, like his colleague Lindbeck, distinguished Christian self-understanding from secular culture in order to reassert a distinct, ecumenical Christian identity as a minority religion, embodying this-worldly suffering service as exemplified by Martin Luther King Jr.[24] In this way, an exclusivist, sectarian stance (in a sociological sense) might have a constructive relationship to culture: a view that resonates with Frei's position in later writings and indicates the constructive practical and political concerns behind them.

Finally, and most decisively, there were unfinished questions relating to the arguments and reception of *The Eclipse of Biblical Narrative* and *The Identity of Jesus Christ*. Van Harvey's essay 'Christology for Barabbases' was one key prompt. There Harvey articulated a Christology for sceptical followers of Jesus Christ who find it impossible that much of the New Testament portrait of Jesus can be true given the findings of modern biblical criticism, yet find it compelling because it portrays life as graced and summoned to responsibility.[25] It was a view with which Frei felt a certain kinship yet disagreed hermeneutically. It challenged him to re-engage with the question of faith and history, as originally posed by David Friedrich Strauss.[26] He felt pressed by questions of how to relate his hermeneutic to historical criticism systematically and about what understanding of truth lay behind his claim that the Gospel narratives are true, questions that would be raised again forcefully in the mid-1980s, coupled with the charge of fideism.[27] He hoped to address such questions through his project on modern theology. As he confessed to Placher, 'the only way I can make a systematic statement is by way of history.'[28]

Several of the resulting writings took shape in the context of further administrative duties. Frei served as a very active chair of the Religious Studies department from 1983 to 1986, furthering its diversification, begun under Wayne Meeks, from a narrow concentration on Christianity 'with an occasional nod to Judaism as an important ancillary discipline' to something that would represent the changing contemporary world.[29] He wanted to shape a department that would examine multiple religious traditions, repair the strained relations with the Divinity School and make some 'affirmative action' appointments, and he had some success in all three respects.[30] Despite these duties, in the eight years between leaving Ezra Stiles and his untimely death in September 1988, Frei seemed to make up for the stagnation and doubt of the latter half of the 1970s with a flurry of writing.

The types of modern theology

Frei's main research project remained the work on modern Christology, whose subject he described in 1986 as 'the figure of Jesus of Nazareth in England and Germany – in high culture, ecclesiastical and otherwise, as well as popular culture – since 1700'.[31] Within that project, however, he began to develop a typology of modern theologians, which was to be published as a book with Yale University Press.[32] The typology would at once advance an analysis of modern Christology and address the question of faith and history and the charge of fideism. This motive for the typology seems to have gone curiously unnoticed by many of those who have studied Frei's later thought.[33]

Frei first identified the problematic of the typology in an essay on David Friedrich Strauss for the three-volume survey of *Nineteenth-Century Religious Thought in the West*, which was completed by the summer of 1981, though not published until 1985.[34] Frei used the essay to explore what he took to be the issue underlying the modern question of faith and history in Christology, which Strauss had clarified: the question of the relationship of Christian faith to the formal methods of inquiry for a given field of study (*Wissenschaft*).[35] Strauss clarified this question, Frei argued, by making the meaning of the different options for relating faith and *Wissenschaft* depend on how they are deployed to answer two questions: whether the canonical Gospels' portrait of Jesus of Nazareth is historically accurate; and whether its accuracy was critical to the truth of Christianity's claim that he is the absolutely unique embodiment of salvation and religious truth.[36] Strauss did so by asserting that the historical-critical reconstruction of the figure of Jesus in the Gospels could and did settle the question of whether Jesus is the absolutely unique embodiment of religious truth, the Messiah.[37] In his typology, Frei set out to trouble that assertion and that positioning of historical criticism as arbiter of theological claims about Jesus. In doing so, however, he also rethought his approach to the essence of Christianity, its normativity and publicness and hence the framework of his ethics of responsibility, to which the whole typology was orientated, as I shall show.

Frei first expounded his typology in his 1983 Schaffer Lectures, delivered at Yale Divinity School in 1983.[38] There Frei picks up the way that Strauss framed the question of the relationship between theology and *Wissenschaft* around the question of the relationship between the historian's reconstruction of Jesus and the Christological faith of the church.[39] Historical inquiry into Jesus will never produce a unique figure, because of the assumptions of historical method, 'which arranges events into a naturally explicable sequence of similar occurrences'.[40] However, neither can theologians refuse historical inquiry into someone they claim is a historical figure. It was this methodological claim by Strauss (and Van Harvey) to the prioritization of historical criticism over theology in the reading of Scripture that Frei wanted to question.

To that end, in the Schaffer lectures and other extant material on the typology, Frei framed his analysis of modern Christology within the exploration of the relationship between the nature of Christian theology and the interpretation of Christian Scripture. The former involved the relationship between two understandings of Christian theology.[41] First, there is the western academic inquiry into the concept of God and whether and how it refers, and Christian theology as an instance of this endeavour, linked to Christianity's privileged institutional status as the increasingly tenuous, residual religion of western culture, of which culture universities are higher educational representatives.[42] For this approach, the religious symbol system of Christianity is merely the external sign of that religion; indeed, specific religions are no more than 'positive, historically specific expressions of beliefs and morals based on universal reason'.[43] On this account, the condition for the entrance of theology to the university is that it abide by the rules for academic disciplines in higher education in that culture: freedom from external authorities; and adherence to public, generally valid modes of explanation and to whatever theory exercises jurisdiction over those modes of explanation. Christian theology here is a species of a generic type, theology, which in turn must conform to general criteria of validity as dictated by some general theory of valid explanation.[44] On this conception of theology, therefore, the academic discipline to which it is closest is some kind of transcendental philosophy that claims to provide theoretical justification for all explanation, and gives to theology its criteria of meaning and truth, and also provides it with its academic organization.[45] This kind of theology is 'vocationally the profession of an intellectual, a theorist'.[46]

Second, there is Christian theology as an inquiry undertaken by a specific religion, identified after the central claim made on behalf of its founding figure, Jesus of Nazareth.[47] It is an activity of Christian communities, an exercise in their self-description. It may not even belong to a general class: one would have to work out on a case-by-case basis whether other religions have theologies or another activity with a function analogous to that of theology in Christianity.[48] Christianity here is not a system of beliefs or something experienced, primarily, but 'a complex, various, loosely held, and yet really discernible community', with features common to religions, such as a sacred story fixed in a sacred text.[49] Like other religions, he wrote elsewhere, it is held together both by 'constantly changing yet enduring structures, practices, and institutions', such as the regulated relations between an elite and the rest, and by a set of rituals and common beliefs and attitudes, all linked to the sacred stories as interpreted in the community's tradition.[50]

There is a danger here of reifying Christianity as a structure abstracted from the lived practice, but in another contemporary paper, Frei mitigates that danger by describing Christianity, as a religion, as both a semiotic system composed of beliefs, rituals and patterns of behaviour and 'the community which is that system in use', an acted document.[51] These features include, he noted in his Princeton lectures, a 'communal memory of Jesus of Nazareth as its founder and the image of God, [and] a set of cultural attitudes in which compassion is prominent, and so on'.[52] Here, Christian theology is primarily 'the first-level statements or proclamations made in the course of Christian practice and belief', such as creeds.[53] But there is also a second order of Christian-specific theology, in which a given Christian community describes the rules of correct use implicit in its first-level statements (their logic or grammar) and evaluates them against an internal norm, such as Scripture.[54] There is also a third-level exercise in trying to articulate to others how these rules compare to their ruled discourses, which shows an orientation towards an extra-ecclesial public internal to Christian self-description.[55] Such theology is a practical discipline, undertaken by a skilled participant in the culture of a Christian community and belongs to the ruled practice of its social tradition.[56]

In practice, the two kinds of theology often overlap because of Christianity's 'problematic penchant for making universal truth claims, establishing normative guidelines for interpretation, etc.', while being a particular social phenomenon.[57] Frei's focus was on the way they overlapped in modern western academic theology, in a particular, contingent form of theological education with its roots in the German academic tradition that began with the inclusion of theology in the founding of the University of Berlin in 1810. He explores this story in the Cadbury lectures he gave at the University of Birmingham, in the UK, and at Princeton, both delivered in 1987.[58]

The case of the University of Berlin

Berlin was 'the prototypical German university and the model for many others on both sides of the Atlantic ... [and] nowhere more so than in American higher education'.[59] The inclusion of theology in the new university was controversial. The University of Berlin was to be a secular institution organized around a rational ideal encompassing all knowledge, so that the philosophical faculty 'became, in effect, the cement and the most important faculty in the university'.[60] It was to be *wissenschaftlich* not only in the sense that it was neutral with regard to religion, and would set the pace for other universities abandoning religious qualifications for teachers and students, but also in the sense that academics were to be free of any 'institutional or intellectual allegiance' that might inhibit free, critical inquiry.[61] Although the university was state-owned, the state accepted this ideal and the consequent need for the university to enjoy a relatively high degree of autonomy in self-government. However, the church also came under the bureaucratic oversight of the Prussian, Christian state, which entrusted the monopoly for training candidates for ordained ministry to the university, the very institution whose ideal of *Wissenschaft* involved freedom from allegiance to the church. In the intellectual planning for the new university, then, the central questions for modern western academic theology were at stake. Is theology 'a suitable subject for a university whose ideal is the dissemination of Wissenschaft'?[62] And conversely, can such a university 'provide training appropriate to the exercise of ministry in the Christian Church'?[63]

For Frei, the case of Berlin illustrates, paradigmatically, the question of the relationship between Christian theology and its academic context and the tension between the practical orientation of Christian theology in its ecclesial context and the academic demand for some distance between theory and practice.[64] In 1809 Friedrich Schleiermacher argued, successfully, for the inclusion of theology in the university as one of several professional faculties required by society and the state, which bring together praxis with a low-level kind of theory without the need for a theoretical explanation of how they may be brought together.[65] Here theology amounts to the transmission, by way of critical conceptual re-description, of the customs and language, the tradition, of ecclesiastical culture, as a practical skill needed for church government. Under Schleiermacher's proposal, theology with this practical aim and descriptive character was correlated with non-reductive explanatory academic approaches to the study of culture and history, without being systematically subordinated to them. Three generations later, Adolf von Harnack resisted transforming Berlin's theology faculty into a faculty of the science of religion in large part because he believed that education for clergy belonged in the university. However, Harnack saw Christianity more as an intellectual or moral–spiritual essence than a 'social and cultural artefact, a continuous and constantly re-created structure in its own right'.[66] It should be studied objectively by means of historical study, and its practical aims were subordinate to this academic ideal. The difference between Schleiermacher and Harnack thus opens the possibility of a typology of theological schools of thought in this tradition in terms of the way they resolved the tension between *Wissenschaft* and theology.[67]

The typology explores five different ways in which modern, mostly Protestant theologians negotiated the demands of theology's academic and ecclesial contexts, of practice and publicness, through their construal of its relationship to other academic disciplines. At stake was what kind of relationship Christian theology should have with other academic disciplines and their standards of public inquiry and argumentation, and thereby also how Christianity should be studied as a religion. For each type, Frei examined whether it prioritized theology as academic discipline or Christian self-description, and how it related Christian self-description to external descriptions of Christianity and to an account of the general criteria for meaningful description. He then evaluated them primarily in terms of how hospitable each was to what he called 'the literal sense' or *sensus literalis*.[68]

The literal sense

The literal sense, Frei explains, is an integral component of the life of the church as a religious community, with something like a culture with its sacred text.[69] Here, as in other religious communities, informal, flexible rules and conventions govern the way Scripture is used and understood within the community as an enacted semiotic system. These rules cover both the Jewish Scripture Christians came to read as the Old Testament and the new Scriptures they united to it as the New.

In western Christianity, the priority of the literal sense over other meanings or ways of reading the texts – whether allegorical, moral, spiritual or critical – came to be basic and coordinated with other guidelines like Augustine's rule that interpretations must promote the love of God and neighbour.[70] The content of the literal sense has varied over its history, but Frei thought that we can trace some significant continuities that run into modernity, even into the most liberal of modern discussions of the relationship between the historical Jesus and the Christ of faith. This continuity can be stated in terms of some 'rough rules' of practice, rather than in terms of stable hermeneutical concepts.[71] First, literal reading is a matter of the meaning of the text about which there is the greatest consensus in the use of the text in the Christian community. That maximal consensus identifies Jesus as the subject matter, in one way or another, of the stories told about him in the New Testament, whether as chief character in the plot, as a historical person, or in ontological terms; it does not cover how we are to understand his reality.[72] That consensus is basic to all the meanings of 'literal sense' in this tradition and the root of its hermeneutical priority over other ways of reading.

Elsewhere, Frei explains that the primacy of the literal sense in the western interpretive tradition of Christianity emerged from the centrality of the sacred story of Jesus Christ's life, teachings, death and resurrection in the way early Christians took over Jewish Scripture in its figural interpretations of narrative, law, prophecy and wisdom literature and in the way it made sense of cultic and moral regulations.[73] Despite the possibility in the context of spiritualizing its meaning, the consensus or plain reading of that central story was a literal one, in the sense of taking the fact that Jesus is the subject of those stories 'to be their crucial point' so that descriptions of events, sayings and characteristics are 'literal' by being ascribed to him.[74] The literal sense is thus 'very specifically focused on him as the specific, unsubstitutable personal subject of the stories'.[75] It focuses on him as the central character identified by his actions and sufferings, the point of their coherence and the subject of his titles, preaching and ministry:

> [He] is what he does and undergoes; he is the Kingdom he proclaims, the self-enacted parable of God which he speaks; he is himself as the crucified and resurrected Jesus ... He is the subject of his personal predicates and doings and sufferings, and holds them together.[76]

The priority of this rule of reading the stories of Jesus led to them being treated as the centre of the canon of Scripture from which literal reading was extended to other scriptural texts as relating back to it in some way, however loosely.[77]

Second, the literal sense is understood to be a fit enactment of the author's communicative intention so that intention and enactment are one continuous process; authorial meaning is enacted in the text, you do not need to reach behind it as an interpreter. Third, in the literal sense, there is a fit or harmony between the semantic sense and its subject matter, to the point where a sharp distinction between them is called into question.

Frei presents this basic, complex, flexible consensus as one that frames, indeed enables, particular interpretive disagreements, even different ideologies at work in exegesis, within Christian tradition.[78] In relation to his typology, Frei did not propose to identify one type as offering the right interpretation of the Bible; he took that achievement to be an eschatological hope. Rather, he sought to assess their hospitality to the literal sense understood in this way.

Types One and Five represent the two logical extreme ways of resolving the tension between Christian practicality and academic publicness, so that the typology maps points on a spectrum. In Type One, theology 'is a philosophical discipline within the academy, and its character as such takes complete priority over communal self-description'; indeed, the distinction between the two collapses.[79] In Gordon Kaufman's *An Essay on Theological Method*, for example, the theologian examines the uses of the concept of 'God' as the focus for a whole vocabulary in the ordinary language of western culture, rather than in any specific religious community. It is the focus of a potentially universal quest for ultimate meaning.[80] Theology is thus a practical discipline yet makes a theoretical case in accordance with general philosophical criteria of meaningfulness and universality. Here Christianity is meaningful as part of a larger cultural heritage, included in external description and accountable to it. Specific religions are in effect 'as old as creation', republishing 'the natural and universal quest', as the eighteenth-century Deist Matthew Tindal put it.[81] Christian self-description (and the study of it as a religion) is subsumed into general intellectual-cultural inquiry.

There are no prospects for the integrity of the literal sense here: a general meaning is substituted for Jesus as the subject matter for the stories.[82] Kant's *Religion within the Limits of Reason* illustrates this hermeneutical consequence well, Frei observes. For Kant, the Bible must be interpreted, and discriminations made among its materials, on the basis of a 'rational moral understanding of our duties, freely imposed by ourselves upon ourselves – but in the Bible set forth as divine commands'.[83] Still conditioned by the Christian tradition to see the Bible as one story in which the New Testament fulfils the Old, Kant interpreted this story and its characters as an allegory for 'the stages in the self-understanding and self-improvement of the moral reasoner'.[84] In his interpretation, Jesus Christ is a personification of the archetype of humanity well-pleasing to God, as well as of the split between radical evil and the new disposition for good within the reader, and of the unity in transition between them: of 'reconciliation' in this sense. He is not the focus of meaning of the stories as he is in the literal sense.

Type One is thus inhospitable to the literal sense. The place, function, meanings of Scripture as the sacred text of a religious community are interesting but ultimately not important.[85] However, at least one of its proponents, J. G. Fichte, claimed this was the only way a faculty of theology could be included in the modern university.[86] Its presence in the typology functions to interrogate all the others on that issue while making clear that it is not a viable option for a theology that wants to describe Christianity as practised by Christian communities.

Type Five is unique among the types in eschewing any relation to general theories in the practice of Christian self-description. Frei held D. Z.

Phillips and similar thinkers to exemplify this position (rather unfairly in Phillips' case at least).[87] Theologies of this type describe the grammar, the internal logic, of the faith that is learnt through the acquisition of the appropriate conceptual skills, guided by normative instances, as much dispositional as linguistic. For the meaningfulness of religious language can only be seen in relation to its context of use, and the criteria for judging its meaningfulness and questions as to what it is about or whether it refers are entirely internal to religious traditions.[88] Nothing more is needed or possible, for there 'is no formal, context-independent or independently describable set of transcendental conditions governing that internal logic'.[89] To apply putatively universal philosophical criteria to religious languages is to be confused about the nature of religious language and in error about the generality of your criteria.[90] The same goes for all philosophical schemes whether anthropological or metaphysical: terms found in both contexts, like 'God' and 'knowledge', denote diverse concepts.[91]

Type Five theology thus rejects the options for Christian self-description represented by the other types on the basis, ironically, of a philosophical argument as to the absence of universal rules for meaningful, coherent knowledge.[92] In this negative way, it comes close to the first type in its essentially philosophical character.[93] More importantly, for Frei, by ruling out the use of external categories, it makes it very difficult to describe the beliefs that are 'part of the ruled language of Christian self-description', and distinct from the logic of coming to belief, such as beliefs about God, Jesus Christ, creation and redemption, the nature of the church, grace and works, and so on.[94] It also makes it very difficult to discriminate between different conceptual uses within a religious tradition, to identify normative instances, or what is more than attitudinal in communal self-description, or decide what are appropriate ways to describe them or how they may be authorized, or evaluate them.[95] For the same reason, Type Five also obviates any description of the meaning of biblical texts as Christian Scripture or of creedal formulae, or any discrimination among interpretations of them. Understanding biblical statements amounts merely to acquiring the skill of their appropriate use.[96] The literal sense is reduced to the repetition of the texts, which is not its function in Christian tradition.[97] As a form of Christian self-description, then, Type Five falls into incoherence in the face of the demands of Christian practice for more descriptive capacity. Its function in the typology is to make clear the need for theology to have some relationship to general theory. The heart of the argument of the typology concerns the remaining options for that relationship.

Type Two theology prioritizes theology as an academic discipline yet seeks to take seriously the specificity of Christian religion.[98] David Tracy's *Blessed Rage for Order* is Frei's main example here, though Frei finds this type crossing divides between liberals and conservatives.[99] Type Two seeks to hold together theology as an academic discipline and Christianity's religious specificity and integrity by using a general foundational philosophy to interpret the latter. It also articulates the compatibility of Christianity, so interpreted, with meanings in human experience, to explain the possibility of their correlation with one another and so of the demonstration of Christianity's meaningfulness.[100] In Tracy's book, Frei contends, he does all this by means of a general phenomenological description of religious experience.[101] Such a description analyses the internal structures of an extreme kind of experience of the world ('limit experience'), either in despair or ecstasy, which is also the way in which the experiencing self inhabits the world (a 'mode-of-being-in-the-world'). These are generic, constant kinds of experiences and modes of being, which amount to essences of the self. Religious language ('limit language'), separable as text from authorial intention, has a correspondingly extreme semantic structure that has a similarly stable, constant meaning. Its intensifying and transgressive metaphorical character transcends the ordinary world of experience to disclose an experience of an extreme limit of our lives and a possible mode-of-being-in-the-world.[102] Applied to the New Testament, this procedure discovers such metaphorical language in the proverbs, eschatological sayings and parables, where the interaction between eccentric modes of behaviour in everyday settings discloses an authentic possible mode of being marked by wholeness, total commitment, honesty and agapic love in the presence of the God of Jesus Christ.[103]

Tracy's procedure, Frei notes, merges together internal and external description of Christianity by means of a common context of the structure of meaning of the self as consciousness and by means of the common procedure of phenomenological analysis. In this way, like Type One theologies, those of Type Two, as exemplified by *Blessed Rage*, subsume Christian self-description under a general philosophical anthropology. In contrast to Type One, they may afford a way of distinguishing culturally conditioned forms of religious consciousness. However, this approach also takes no account of the church as the social-linguistic context for Christian language and use of concepts, replacing it with generic experience, and in that way is at some distance from Christian self-description for which that context is essential.

In consequence, Frei argues, Type Two theology has 'little use for any form of the literal sense'.[104] In Tracy's case, the view of language in general and religious language given by his choice of general theory interprets much of Jesus' language through its paradigm of disclosive metaphor. It also casts the Gospels' stories about Jesus in the same mould, as extended parables with the same disclosive function, to 're-present the possibility of the agapic mode-of-being-in-the-world as an existential possibility now'.[105] The story is not about Jesus Christ as a character cumulatively identified in his own story but 'a successful or unsuccessful evocation of a mode of present consciousness', of which Jesus himself is a powerful symbol.[106] Such is the outcome, Frei argues, when theology owes nothing to 'Christian self-description as normed by the religious community with its traditional linguistic forms'.[107] For the name and title of Jesus Christ function very differently in that ecclesial context.[108]

Frei examines Type Three chiefly by a revised appraisal of the theological method of Friedrich Schleiermacher. In his earlier work, Frei is usually careful and nuanced in analysing Schleiermacher's thought-world, but, following Barth, is implicitly or explicitly critical of Schleiermacher's tying together of divine presence and human selfhood. However, a rather different Schleiermacher appears through the prism of the typology, as we have already begun to see, and affords Frei a fresh critical perspective on Barth, as I shall show. To reprise: in his *Brief Outline of Theology* and the prolegomena of *The Christian Faith*, Frei argues, Schleiermacher presents theology as at once a practical discipline training people in the conceptual skills needed for ministry and an academic discipline, grounded in 'a unitary theory of explanation for all disciplines'.[109] In this dual discipline, academic method and Christian self-description 'are correlated as two autonomous yet reciprocally related factors'.[110] In just this way, in answer to Fichte, Schleiermacher successfully argued for the inclusion of theology in the University of Berlin as a professional school alongside law and medicine, fulfilling its purpose of uniting teaching and research but in their own way rather than in strict subordination to the formal strictures of *Wissenschaft*.[111]

In contrast to Types One and Two, philosophy is not the natural context for theology in Type Three. Rather, theology is the Christian church's second-order description of its first-order religious language. Christian language expresses a combination of the feeling of absolute dependence – a universal religious human condition never encountered except in specific cultural forms – with a specific cultural form, whereby that feeling is referred to the redemption accomplished by Jesus Christ. To describe that language, Frei argues, Schleiermacher borrows propositions – non-reductive phenomenological descriptions – from other disciplines, with increasingly specific focus: from the study of culture to the comparative study of religion, to the study of the essence of Christianity.[112] He does so to guide the reader to the point where they can replicate internally, or by an act of empathetic placement of oneself in the religious context of Christianity, what Schleiermacher describes in the didactic language of dogmatics. Schleiermacher's prolegomena were thus 'mobile connected thoughts helping to transport the reader's mind, mayhap her heart, into the communal context in which dogmatics is done'.[113] Frei implies that Schleiermacher thought this maieutic work possible because Christian language expresses a consciousness that is already a fusion of an always culturally mediated universal condition with a specific cultural form. No grand philosophical theory is necessary for this kind of correlation; all you need is 'a little introspection' to see how Christian statements make sense as expressing Christian modifications of human religious experience (most basically the antithesis represented by the terms 'sin' and 'redemption').[114] The experiential correlate for this antithesis – pain and pleasure in the feeling of absolute dependence – was, Frei suggests, 'simply a kind of evocative analogue to the Christian concept'.[115]

Schleiermacher's Christian self-description is phenomenological, like Tracy's, describing Christian self-consciousness. However, in contrast to Tracy, Schleiermacher locates Christian self-consciousness within a broader experience structure that is the church, rather than meaning or religion in general. It gives rise to a first-order use of language that 'always remains distinct and irreducible to any other' in Schleiermacher's analysis.[116] His method is restrained and indirect, compared to Tracy's, 'allowing your internal experience to make the important moves'.[117] Yet Christian dogmatic descriptive statements remain something distinct from and irreducible to the discourse that moves us from outside to inside, even while both are concerned with describing modifications of the immediate self-consciousness.[118] It is this irreducibility of Christian discourse to another conceptual language which, as DeHart rightly argues, separates Type Three from Type Two.[119] In the former, then, theology is not founded on transcendental philosophy, nor is it at odds with it. For theology describes a way we are related to a transcendent ground to which moral philosophy and metaphysical thought lead, but of which they do not provide real knowledge, allowing theology and philosophy to be autonomous yet reciprocally related.[120]

Hermeneutically, Schleiermacher extended this strategy to the literal sense. He locates Scripture within his ecclesiology, among the sociolinguistic and institutional features of the church. And he correlates that Christian self-description of Scripture with Christian religious experience: Scripture normatively expresses 'the pious Christian self-consciousness of the first Christians' and thereby the self-communication of Jesus Christ's perfect God-consciousness.[121] He thus understood the literal sense as an interpretive tradition based on the historical consensus that the New Testament's Christological texts 'refer literally to Jesus as the originator of our experience ... as redeemed sinners within the Church'.[122] The essence of Christianity, for Schleiermacher, was therefore not 'a permanent ideal or a gradual development in the history of human-kind' but the God-consciousness 'unequivocally realized in the historical individual Jesus Christ', to whom Schleiermacher traces the transformation in self-consciousness in the church.[123] For Schleiermacher, then, the incarnation of this divine archetype in this historical individual is what the Christological stories of the New Testament were about. The Word incarnate 'was the Redeemer experienced in Christian consciousness and church, *and* the person described in the Gospels taken as a source of historical information'.[124]

Literal meaning, therefore, meant reading these texts historically, to show that Jesus of Nazareth is the Redeemer, and that entailed extending his strategy of the correlation of theology with academic disciplines to history. Schleiermacher needed to demonstrate that 'a modern, purely historical interpretation of the story of the historical Jesus depicted in the New Testament and an equally modern theological reading of Jesus as the unique, fully incarnate archetypal and unsurpassable originator of the Christian God-consciousness would be compatible with each other.'[125]

Frei notes the 'astute and devastating criticism' of this venture by critics like David Friedrich Strauss, not least in respect of the claim, on which Schleiermacher's procedure depended, that the portrait of Jesus in the Gospel of John is historically reliable.[126] Strauss argued that Schleiermacher had in fact shown that theology and historical method could not be coherently correlated as autonomous disciplines in their integrity. For historical criticism generalizes for every period 'our present uniform experience of the natural cause-effect connections between natural events' and excludes any divine interruption of those connections.[127] It is, he argued, impossible to think 'of any person as being at one and the same time fully ingredient in the natural chain of causal history and qualitatively, absolutely unique'.[128] Thus, in order to make that case from the Gospels by means of historical argument, you have to force historical exegesis. Schleiermacher's theology governed and distorted his efforts at historical critical exegesis, skewing his evaluation and interpretation of his sources as a historian.[129] For Strauss, Schleiermacher's failure showed that there could be no mediation between historical-critical *Wissenschaft* and Christian faith.[130]

Nevertheless, though entirely unsuccessful in his case, Schleiermacher's procedure illustrates for Frei a logical option contrasting with Type Two: a correlation between theology and principles of biblical exegesis that does not involve subsuming them under a foundational philosophical scheme and that preserves a form of the literal sense. For Jesus 'in his uniqueness and finality for Christian faith' remains the subject of the stories and, unlike an allegorical figure, he governs his predicates.[131]

Type Four theology also argues for a non-systematic combination of Christian self-description and method founded on general theory. However, rather than correlate them as 'heterogenous equals' it mirrors Type Two in reverse, subordinating general theory to practical Christian self-description so that the latter 'governs and limits the applicability of general criteria of meaning in theology'.[132] Barth is the main representative of this type. For Frei, Barth insists 'even more unequivocally than does Schleiermacher that Christianity has its own distinctive language, which is not to be interpreted without residue into other ways of thinking and speaking'.[133] Christian theology uses the semiotic system of the Christian socio-linguistic community. It exhibits and critically examines that community's implicit rules of practice (sometimes fragmentary) against the scripturally attested norm of God's presence to the church in Jesus Christ.[134]

In contrast to Type Five, Barth's Type Four theology recognizes that to describe the ruled use of Christian language, Christian theology needs formal categories and categorical distinctions and rules and criteria for coherence, meaning and truth.[135] However, instead of founding theology on a general theory that would determine what these categories and criteria mean and how they are applied, Barth seeks to use an eclectic combination of formal rules, categories and criteria descriptively, in context-dependent ways, governed by the specific theological issue to be described and the absolute priority of Christian self-description in the context of Christian community.[136] He does so consistently but unsystematically, Frei maintains, without a systematic explanation of the possibility of his procedure or how Christian meanings relate or belong to a general context. The application of external categories, borrowed from other systems of thought, must therefore be an ad hoc performance rather than a correlation with another discipline in its integrity.[137] Nor do they replicate in their theological use the explanatory function they may perform in their original contexts.[138]

Barth recognizes, Frei notes, that Christians also use their language practically, in self-involving and existential ways, which are meaningless without the appropriate attitude and enactment, whether in gratitude to God or in love of God and neighbour.[139] In view of the theological situation of his day, Barth had to prioritize the internal logic of Christian faith over its practical enactment and insist on the 'integrity or irreducibility of Christian language as a form of description'.[140] But he did not confuse them or seek to integrate them under one theory. For Barth, Frei argues, the formal rules, criteria and categories for describing what Christians do with language must be subordinate to that usage and may be left fragmentary 'if that is what the proper and consistent use of the language seems to imply'.[141] These different kinds of use do belong together, do cohere, but the fullness of that coherence, the rationale of faith, is hidden to us.

Rather than interpreting Christian language-use through a general theory, as Tracy did, Barth's procedure reverses the direction, interpreting concepts from various general theories in Christian terms without seeking to offer a comprehensive account or mastery of their meaning and rationality so understood. Ultimately, for Barth, general theory and Christian self-description are not in conflict but under the conditions of finitude, where the fullness of the rationale of faith is hidden; we cannot know, or prescribe in the abstract, how they cohere in principle.[142]

Barth's eschatological epistemic reserve about the coherence of Christian theology and other academic disciplines also meant he respected the autonomy of each but could not exclude the possibility that they might overlap – and even contradict each other – at specific points. Equally, he could not rule out the possibility, on some matters, of delimiting the respective spheres of competence of theology and more exact sciences like biology. This reserve meant that Barth had to see the absence of universal criteria as provisional: 'there might be enough overlap among contexts to allow limited overlap between logics or criteria', which might mean that those criteria are in fact universal from God's perspective, though not ours.[143]

While seeking coherence and clarity, then, this kind of theologian understands that there may be 'something incomplete and fragmentary' about their reasoning, that they will be able to describe but not explain a subject that is not irrational but a mystery 'indefinitely penetrable by reason'.[144] Under the limitations of our knowledge in this life, therefore, doctrines function rather like grammatical rules, guiding faithful speech (and practice), whereas in the life to come we will be able to see their coherence and that they are grounded in reality. Thus, says Frei, for Barth, the incarnation is not an instance of a general class nor a logical contradiction. For someone to be both human and divine 'is not intrinsically irrational, but the condition of its possibility, or rationality, is one we cannot know in this present finite state'.[145]

The analogy with grammatical rules is meant to indicate both the way doctrines display the indefinite rationality of the mystery in a partial, fragmentary fashion and the practical, formative function of such discourse. Frei gives a fuller example of the descriptive and practical character of doctrines as rules in Christology in 'The "literal reading" of biblical narrative'. The Chalcedonian affirmation prescribes rules for the use of concepts of human and divine nature as predicates of Jesus Christ's unitary person. These rules have a 'reserved or negative cast'.[146] They articulate a requirement that, when making this affirmation in these philosophical terms, ascribing their coherence with one another to the person of Jesus must not come at the expense of their integrity. However, they do not make affirming the unity of divine and human natures as predicated of Jesus logically dependent on the conceivability of uniting these categories, and any attempt to do so will break down or remain incomplete. For, again, 'the full, *positive explanation* of the rule's rational status ... will have to await another condition than our present finitude'.[147] The dogma thus exhibits the logic of faith in a manner that is 'rational yet fragmentary'.[148] By displaying this rationality in this limited rule-form, Frei implies, the dogma helps Christians shape their speech and action in conformity with the transcendent reality that is at the heart of all things.

It follows from this theological epistemology that for this kind of theology, by means of the ad hoc use of external concepts in the description of the logic of Christian practices, 'we can understand more and communicate better ... than we'll ever be able to understand *how* we understand, or what the conditions of the possibility of our understanding might be'.[149] Such a theology involves, Frei thought, a sort of theological realism about Christian discourse and practice, whereby God's reality is given (by God) 'in, with and under' the concept 'God' in its Christian usage in the context of the Christian semiotic system as used in actual Christian communities, and in a manner adequate for us. But the logic of that realism theology can only describe, not explain.[150]

Hermeneutically, Frei argues, Barth's Type Four theology is the most robust of all the types in upholding the integrity of the literal sense and the unity of Jesus as the subject of the New Testament stories. For this kind of theology prioritizes the description of Christian practices and their rules in their socio-linguistic and institutional context in Christian communities, including the description of the meanings of scriptural texts so used in that context. The practical goal of such description is to 'shape and constrain the reader' to discover their capacity to subordinate themselves and the pre-understandings and interests they bring, to the text as Scripture.[151] It disposes them so that they may discover its 'richness and complexity' and the way it acts upon and resists the reader, at once precluding comprehensive interpretations of texts and meaning that our readings must be checked against their features.[152]

Type Four theologians, like Barth, follow the literal sense in prioritizing certain more perspicacious texts, more conducive to hermeneutical

consensus, and the story of Jesus chief among them as 'loose organizing center of the whole'.[153] With him, they also follow the literal sense
carefully in focusing on the way this story answers the question, 'Who
is Jesus in this text?'[154] As commentators, they seek to re-describe those
identifying narrative descriptions of him. When they do so, then, they
find the coherence of these descriptions in their focus on him and they
take the meaning of the terms used to describe him, his predicates, to
depend on their connection to him. These are *his* predicates, governed
by the personal identity rendered by his specific story.[155] Type Four
theologians recognize the need for concepts from general theory, from
philosophy, to re-describe or interpret and reflect upon that meaning.[156]
However, rather than do so by means of some form of correlation with
a hermeneutical philosophy and method, they borrow and use external
philosophical tools in an ad hoc manner, and subordinate them to this
descriptive task in its Christian communal context.[157] Frei thought Barth's
Type Four approach involved a mode of theological exegesis of Scripture
where theological description converges, unsystematically, with an external discipline, namely the literary study of realistic biblical narrative, for
Barth treated the Gospels 'like a loosely organized nonfictional novel', as
David Kelsey had put it.[158]

   That approach precludes the attempt, typical of mediating theologians
since the eighteenth century, to commend the meaningfulness of Jesus
by fitting his specific identity to 'the criteria of the world of our general
experience'.[159] Instead, theologians like Barth saw the literal reading of
scriptural texts as a way by which readers can incorporate themselves
into 'the world of discourse he shared with us'.[160] There is an echo here
of Frei's account of Jesus' presence as something he turns and shares in
virtue of his specific identity, as given in the Gospel stories. His meaning
seems to be that Jesus himself provides, in his person, the centre of the
true meaning of the world we inhabit, and, in the literal sense, an orientation to that meaning. Rather than relate him to our understanding of
that world, we discover ourselves and our world in relation to him. As
Frei goes on to say, his saving significance for us is determined by and
inseparable from his particularity in the actions and events of his story
and can only be articulated from a description of him as a particular
person.[161] In consequence, this kind of theology avoids making Jesus the
mere cipher, symbol or embodiment of qualities or meanings whose real
focus lies elsewhere, as in Types One and Two.

   Barth's Type Four approach contrasts with attempts to correlate the
theological description of the meaning of Jesus Christ for Christian communities with a historical reconstruction of his person. On Frei's account,
Type Four theologians insist on a logical distinction between the literal

reading of the Gospel narratives and the question of how we refer to the reality of their subject beyond the text. To read the stories according to the literal sense is not to be confused with insisting in principle on their historical reliability (with fundamentalists) nor with the task of the historical reconstruction of his person (with liberals).[162] For this kind of theologian, any discipline's general criteria for meaning and explanation, if applied to the description of the literal sense and the meaning of the Gospel stories in that practice, must be subordinated to the logic of the practice and its focus on the identity of Jesus given in the story. Here too we are dealing with a mystery indefinitely penetrable by reason. In this life, theologians can only describe what Christians mean when they read their sacred texts according to the literal sense and refer by means of it to Jesus beyond the text or claim that the way the texts render the identity of Jesus is true. But they cannot explain the nature of truth in this sense or how such reference is possible. Here too, under the epistemological limitations of this life, we can only speak of the logic of faith in terms of grammatical rules for faithful speech, rather than testable propositions, and only exhibit their coherence and rationality in fragmentary fashion.[163]

In the material from the Cadbury lectures in *Types of Christian Theology*, Frei talks about Barth's interpretation of Anselm's ontological argument to illustrate his point that in Barth's kind of theology, the reality of God is given adequately 'in, with, and under the concept' and not separately from it, where the right conceptual description logically implies God's reality.[164] As he once wrote to a doctoral student working on Barth and Wittgenstein, for Barth, 'the real object fits itself to our concepts and words'.[165] But they will not be able to explain how this reference is possible, or the nature of this truth, beyond describing how, according to the logic of the story, it depends on God's self-identification with Christ and Christ's self-identification with his identity as rendered in this story. In that context, we may reasonably infer that he would have seen his own analysis, in the earlier Christological essays, as an example of a Type Four theological description of the literal sense of the Synoptic Gospels.

From this perspective, the categories and assumptions of the historical method are not a good fit for talking about the reality of the person specified by the narrative descriptions of the Gospels.[166] As a descriptive category, 'fact' is closer than 'fiction' for this purpose, yet the stories finally identify Jesus most specifically by his relation to God in the resurrection. 'Factuality' (and the criteria for assessing the probable factuality of an account) is therefore an inadequate way of talking about God or about one identified by his (unique) relation to God. A Christian theology that prioritizes Christian self-description must thus eschew subordinating exegesis to the criteria and procedures of historical criticism and tend, instead, to a more literary approach to the literal sense.

The limits and applicability of the typology

The problematic of Frei's typology and the examples of his types all stem from one tradition and its Anglo-American heirs. Frei was certainly aware of the provincial character of his typology. It was, he acknowledged, neither the only nor an exhaustive way to organize the field of theology 'in the modern West, to say nothing of the South or the Third World, or of churches as different as the Roman Catholic and the Pentecostal'.[167] He acknowledged also that for some forms of theology the tension between theology and *Wissenschaft* might not arise, where theology's practical aims predominate.[168] The story he told was the institutional as well as intellectual history of a particular tradition in its socio-political context, which evinces both contingency and some ambiguity.[169] The settlement of theology's inclusion in this kind of university secured for it (and the church) the benefits of the academic freedom and public status afforded such institutions but involved the professionalization of the discipline, its practitioners and those it trains.[170] This professionalization, he implies, together with the influence of the ideal of *Wissenschaft*, have contributed to the degree of alienation between academic theology and practice, theology and worship, and between theology and 'the advocacy of and commitment to social and moral change', of which its conservative and liberationist critics complain.[171]

Frei could also conceive of an alternative institutional model, in which remnants of academic theology and the training of professional ministers were fused with 'communal nurture in something like basic communities' in such a way that retained features of the old model but did not define the enterprise.[172] Such a transformation might even bring in its train what the old model with its academic hegemony had never attempted: 'the successful laicizing of theology'.[173] Nevertheless, the question faced by the German academic tradition, of the correlation or coordination between theology and other forms of knowledge, would recur, he believed, wherever theologians appealed to the public character of the theory informing theology, as it did when liberation theologians appeal to hermeneutical theories.[174] Wherever that happens, the insistence that theology be public in some way would inhibit or modify any attempt to shift theological education towards a greater emphasis on formation for action.[175] Frei, thus, was just beginning, at the end of his career, to give critical attention to the structuring of power in theological institutions.

Public theology and ethics

Frei's typology is thus complex, sophisticated and fascinating, with potentially wide relevance, but what is its significance for his ethics? Frei thought of his typology as a revision of the arguments of both *The Identity of Jesus Christ* and *The Eclipse of Biblical Narrative*.[176] Scholars have parsed this remark in various ways when analysing Frei's later writings. For Charles Campbell, they show a turn away from even his own general hermeneutical theory to a more fully communal hermeneutic, the cultural-linguistic description of concrete Christian interpretive practices, to supplement his unchanged Christology.[177] For Mike Higton, the shift amounts to a theoretical simplification of the scaffolding around that unchanged Christology, towards a more historical and social view of Christianity, a 'continuation and clarification of his earlier work'.[178] For Jason Springs, there is more continuity than shift: Frei's later thought is the refined development of his application of Wittgensteinian cultural-linguistic insights.[179] There is truth in all these observations.[180] Yet the remark also invites us to consider its significance for the kind of ethics he had indicated in those texts.[181] Indeed, Frei's ethics of responsibility are not far away from its argument. For the theme of responsibility that Frei articulates as part of his account of pre-modern western literal reading in *The Eclipse of Biblical Narrative* seems to be implicit in his later descriptions of the literal sense.

In effect, he reworks the idea that the history-likeness of realistic biblical narrative enables Christians to orientate their action within the world as a feature of the literal sense. As a mode of reading, the literal sense privileges and focuses on a discursive world rendered by the narratives, which is like our own, in which 'persons and circumstances shape each other and their stories cannot be told without that interaction'.[182] In literal reading, this narrative world functions to govern and orientate readers' understanding of their circumstances. It 'reaches into the mode of our reading', shaping our understanding of ourselves as embodied agents and our actions and sufferings within the contexts with which we interact.[183] Indeed, it is the necessary and sufficient basis 'for our orientation within the real world'.[184] The hermeneutical telos of social embodiment that Campbell thought underdeveloped in Frei is clearly present and integral in Frei's later thought, as it was in *The Eclipse of Biblical Narrative*.[185]

The practical, ethical dimension of the literal sense, shaping Christians' orientation to the world they share with others of various different persuasions, raises the question of how public Frei's ethics is and on what terms. One of the principal contributions of the typology to Frei's theology and ethics is that it offers a greatly developed answer to that question. To understand how, we need to comprehend the centrality and significance of his account of Types Three and Four, and his own position in relationship to them.

As representatives of Types Three and Four, Schleiermacher and Barth stand at the centre of Frei's typology.[186] They exemplify two alternatives for the practice of Christian theology as an exercise in the internal description of the Christian community as an enacted semiotic system, while making use of external categories of description to that end and thus two ways of upholding the literal sense. Frei argues that they represent a choice of priorities in the face of the challenges of faith and history and the publicness of theology. He spells out that choice in terms of the question of the publicness of theology in a paper he gave in 1986 at a celebration of the centenary of Barth's birth, entitled 'Barth and Schleiermacher: divergence and convergence', where he argued for the possibility of a convergence between Schleiermacher's theology and Barth's mature theological outlook in the later volumes of the *Church Dogmatics*.[187] Here he rehearses in more detail the reading of Schleiermacher and Barth advanced in the typology and draws out implications from their close juxtaposition.

On Frei's reading, Barth and Schleiermacher converge on a view of theology as a practical discipline concerned with the tradition of the Christian community's self-critical inquiry into its use of language, premised on 'the irreducible specificity of [the church's] communal language'.[188] They differ in how to relate that practical discipline to other academic disciplines. As we have seen, on Frei's account, Schleiermacher correlated as independent equals the traditional conceptual skill of Christian inquiry into Christian language with propositions borrowed from the contemporary equivalents of social scientific descriptions of the church as a cultural phenomenon, by means of the common phenomenon of immediate self-consciousness disclosed by the common-sense instrument of introspection. Barth, however, used philosophical categories but subordinated them to the rules implicit in the church's linguistic practices.

Frei draws out what is at stake in that difference by articulating the worries each would have about the other's procedure. Barth would worry that correlating theology with an independent academic discipline governed by philosophically founded general rules already concedes the independence and practical purpose of theology. In particular, he would worry that the feeling of absolute dependence might end up being a more comprehensive integrative factor between them and a stronger systematic focus for interpreting dogmatic statements. Schleiermacher, however, would worry that by subordinating the concepts of an academic discipline to Christian self-description, their meanings would be so different as to be incompatible with their sense in their original context, so forfeiting the possibility of meaningful discourse with those outside the community.[189]

Both options, then, offer ways of describing Christianity in its cultural-linguistic specificity in ways that make it publicly intelligible. Schleiermacher represents the prioritizing of the greater public intelligibility at the risk that correlation will compromise the independence of theology in describing Christian meanings. Barth represents the prioritizing of that independence at the risk of compromising public intelligibility. In the end, Frei argues, theologians must cut their philosophical losses and decide what matters most and which set of risks they are willing to bear. Doing so need not be disastrous, so long as you are not choosing between cutting yourself off from philosophy, on the one hand, or subordinating theology to philosophy and so precluding the possibility of Christian theology, on the other.

In his lectures on the typology, Frei presents a similar choice between Types Three and Four about the literal sense and the question of faith and history. As we have seen, he agrees with Strauss that Schleiermacher's attempt to correlate a description of the Jesus of history with one of the Christ of faith fails. There is hermeneutical consistency insofar as both theological and historical methods seek to describe the same person, but the correlational procedure risks contradiction 'or sheer confusion'.[190] Frei wondered whether the problem is fatal or whether it is possible here, also, to talk of cutting losses 'because this correlation does not rest on a tight method but always remains an experiment and an imperfect one'.[191]

By contrast, Barth's approach was more consistent than Schleiermacher's; he had gone 'as far as one can in articulating the largely implicit logic governing' the literal sense; his theology was the type 'most nearly congruent' with it; and he had articulated the unity and centrality of Jesus as the subject of the Gospel narratives more consistently and successfully than any other modern theologian.[192] He did so, however, at the price of not being able to specify in what sense the text's claims about him are historical, as he claims they are, or how, in general, textual exegesis and historical claim are related.[193] At best, Frei argued, Barth's use of the category of history might be said to be analogical, by which I take him to mean that it fitly describes something of the adequacy of the textual rendering of Jesus' identity but that we are unable, in this life, to account for how it signifies the reality so rendered (and hence is difficult to understand). Here again, Barth's approach, like Schleiermacher's, involves a cutting of philosophical losses. He more successfully upholds the specificity of Christian self-description at the risk of compromising the public intelligibility of the description of the truth claims that emerge in this core Christian reading practice.

In what way, then, is the typology a response to the question Frei sought to address about whether theology and ethics of his kind could be genuinely public, and to the challenge presented by Strauss and his intellectual heirs about faith and history? In the published lecture materials, Frei does not seem to bring the typology to bear conclusively on those questions, though he is addressing them all through the material. However, we can infer such a conclusion. As Frei saw it, critics of his and similar projects held that Christian theologians are faced with a choice between ensuring the public character of theology by demonstrating its adherence or correlation to the procedures and criteria of a general theory of religious meaning and truth, and fideism: forswearing the making of publicly intelligible, responsible truth claims.[194] In respect of historical claims about Jesus of Nazareth, and especially his uniqueness and resurrection, Strauss and others present theologians with a choice between such fideism and adhering consistently to the procedures and criteria of historical critical inquiry.

The force of Frei's typology in both respects is to show that the matter is more complex than those binary options allow.[195] Indeed, those options are forced and arbitrary when we consider that Christian theology involves description of the literal sense as a central feature of Christian religion. Here, general criteria for religious or historical meaning and truth assumed by historical criticism or explained by some general theory turn out to be a poor fit for the kinds of meanings and truth-claims that emerge from the ways Christians read their sacred texts. There are other, better options for how Christian theology can draw upon philosophical and hermeneutical categories and procedures to describe and evaluate those meanings and truth-claims, those represented by Schleiermacher and Barth. Neither is perfect but imperfection in the rational description of the literal sense and its products, Frei indicates, is a consequence of the limits of our reason in this life before the divine mystery, which demands an intellectual humility or modesty on our part.

That important theological note is developed in remarks made by Frei that help us place him in relation to the dynamics and alternatives presented by his typology. David Ford relates that in discussions after one of the Cadbury lectures, Frei said he would probably place himself between Types Three and Four but that 'aesthetically' he participated in all five, which I take to mean he was appreciative and receptive of the basic concerns and intentions that animate each of them.[196] That appreciative receptivity is reflected in Frei's central placement of Types Three and Four, in which the concerns at stake in Types One, Two and Five all meet.

Frei's placement of himself between Types Three and Four reflects his sharing of Schleiermacher and Barth's commitment to the broad, flexible cultural-linguistic specificity of Christianity and their common refusal to pursue theology in subordination to a foundational or material philosophical scheme or apart from any philosophical resources. There was, he put it to Carl F. H. Henry, 'more continuity in the language of the church and the Scripture than there is in philosophical languages' and their use of categories like truth and factuality.[197] Christians' basic trust in that language, he thought, is warranted not by appeal to a philosophical foundation but by their experience of 'the actual, fruitful use religious people make of it in ways that enhance their own and other people's lives'.[198] The visibility, suppleness and vitality of the literal sense would depend on how far it was rooted in its practical religious context, not a foundational scheme.[199] Likewise hermeneutically, coherence with the rules of practice was, rather than conformity to a general hermeneutics, the only sustainably plausible way to warrant plain readings of the Scriptures.[200]

But Frei is also between Schleiermacher and Barth because he combines elements of both, taking Schleiermacher's maieutic borrowing from the social sciences towards a more Barth-like use of philosophy in theological and hermeneutical description.[201] In one way, Frei leant towards Type Three by advocating for borrowing from a kind of social anthropology, in a maieutic role similar to that which he attributes to Schleiermacher's use of propositions borrowed from the social scientific equivalents of his time. The external discipline most useful for theology were forms of social scientific description that are rich and complex, use theoretical resources sensitively and eclectically, and are non-reductive and cautious about resorting to explanatory hypotheses.[202] Max Weber's focus on 'intentional personal agency in a social context' resembled the way Christians describe divine action, for example, allowing for continuity and overlap between internal and external descriptions of participants' behaviour. By keeping his use of theoretical resources unsystematic, he allowed that intentional agency priority over explanatory and descriptive devices.[203] In a similar way, Frei found Clifford Geertz's focus on understanding symbolic actions in terms of participants' complex frames of interpretation, which shape their action and options, and his low-level theorization of these interpretations, to be congruent with how Christians might describe their religion, theologically.[204] Geertz's analogy between social scientific interpretation and textual interpretation, moreover, had particular affinities with the theological description of a religious tradition for which the plain reading of Scripture is both an integral component of its cultural-linguistic matrix and normative for evaluating the use of its language.[205] Frei thus seems to suggest the possibility of ad hoc correlation between Christian theology and this kind of social scientific description. It is an approach that allows for the possibility of shared understanding of religious belief and practice between outsiders and insiders and so for public intelligibility, without the need of grounding in a general explanatory theory.

However, although he had identified a precedent for this kind of maieutic procedure in Schleiermacher, Frei thought that its use of this kind of social scientific description would lead to a dogmatic theology more like Barth's.[206] In this sort of social scientific approach, he explains in his second Princeton lecture, concepts are means by which people trying to live together in groups seek to solve the problems involved in that endeavour. They are 'socially embodied rational acts, to be understood through the uses to which they are put in determinate contexts', according to shared conventions following common rules.[207] These rules illustrate proper usage and are largely implicit because they vary according to the context-dependent uses they illustrate. It follows, he argues in his piece on 'The "literal reading" of biblical narrative', that general categories, like 'meaning' and 'truth', may need to be adapted or bent to be fit to describe such ruled uses.[208] Such is the case with the way these concepts apply to the description of literal sense. For here, the history-likeness of Jesus of Nazareth, when understood to be the subject of the Gospels' Christological stories, is 'taken to be itself the ground, guarantee, and conveyance of the truth of the depicted enactment, its *historicity*, if you will'.[209]

In context, Frei means that this extraordinary claim to the embodiment of truth in meaning is not an instance of a general category but is grounded in the Christian doctrine of the incarnation, as a description of the literal meaning of the Gospels. It is, we may infer from the wider argument there, a derivative analogue of the identity of the divine Word 'with the bodied person it assumes'.[210] Elsewhere, Frei spelt out this position, borrowing from Karl Barth. The fourfold gospel story of Jesus Christ is a human witness to the Word of God, the truth 'ontologically transcendent and historically incarnate'.[211] Yet by the condescension of that truth to it, by the Spirit's grace, its witness is made sufficient. In virtue of the gift of Christ's presence, there is an indirect coherence of meaning and truth by which the text is adequate as a witness to him, he explained in a letter to William Placher, in terms closer to his own pneumatology in *The Identity of Jesus Christ*.[212] In another letter, to Gary Comstock, Frei argued that it is this instance of the perfect, fully public coherence of meaning and truth that allows us to reason analogously to other, imperfect, semi-public instances of that coherence, which the incarnation makes possible.[213] The Scriptures' graced attestation of the incarnate Word affirmed in the literal sense warrants affirmations of the possibility of all public truths and points to him as their ground.

This remarkable account, however, does not amount to an explanatory theory of the coherence of truth and meaning in Christ, or in Scripture, or more generally. Here Frei articulates the position he attributes to Barth in his lectures on his typology. In the case of the incarnation, the conceivability of that identity of divine Word and embodied person, and the implicit rules under which it is described, are dependent on the fact of their unity in Jesus Christ. Those rules have a reserved or negative cast, because a full, positive statement of their rational status 'will have to await another condition than our present finitude'.[214] For now, under that condition, that rationality is in the mode of faith seeking understanding; it is 'rational yet fragmentary' and the statement of its logic is 'modestly transcendental', by which I take Frei to mean that it describes in this reserved fashion the rational conditions of possibility for faithful interpretation of the doctrine.[215]

It follows that a similar reserve will apply to the rationality of belief in the sufficiency of the Gospel portraits to convey their truth. Frei thought his position involved something like a correspondence claim about the truth of the Gospels and of Christian talk of God and the Word incarnate but did not allow for a theory to back up and explain that claim. Rather, the claim follows, strangely, from a coherence argument, namely the argument Frei had made in his Christology essays, that the meaning of the Synoptic Gospels' identification of Jesus is such that he cannot be thought not to be risen, living and present.[216]

In respect of the correspondence claim, however, the notion of truth or reference 'must be re-shaped extravagantly' to allow for this 'condescension of truth to the depiction in the text', for the self-identification of the truth, the transcendent, historically incarnate Word, with 'the fourfold story of Jesus of Nazareth', such that it is adequate 'by the Spirit's grace'.[217] A full explanation of the possibility of the sufficiency and truth of the text, or of referring to the divine Word by use of it, however, is not possible, he explained to Carl F. H. Henry. For God is 'beyond genus and species'.[218] Therefore, when we speak of God creating the world, or Jesus Christ as the Word made flesh, we are talking of events without analogy in our ordinary experience.[219] Our referring, in such cases, 'is simply not ordinary referencing'.[220] To articulate what we mean by referencing in this case, we can only talk about divine condescension, or a 'miracle of grace', but we cannot explain how God's action is possible.[221] At the heart of Frei's position is the rational mystery of the presence of the incarnate Word to the story that identifies him and to the discourse that names him accordingly, which invites understanding but requires the transformation of our concepts and transcends explanation.

This stance explains Frei's greater sympathy with Barth's more literary procedure for reading the Gospels. For it allows us to attend to the specificity by which the Gospels' 'fragmentary, diverse fourfold description' renders him to us, which Frei was sceptical about the historian's capacity to reproduce by relating Jesus to a generalization about his context.[222] Yet Frei also seems to have been open to an approach that could draw on historical criticism among other kinds of description of Christ. In his final Princeton lecture, he returned to H. Richard Niebuhr's moral Christology at the end of *Christ and Culture*.[223] What he seems to commend here is that Niebuhr's commitment to the priority of the literal sense, of the ascription to Jesus of the stories about him, permitted him to incorporate, unsystematically, elements of historical critical descriptions of Jesus' character drawn from his liberal forebears. Niebuhr, Frei argues, did not correlate a theological reading of the Christ of faith with a historical reconstruction of Jesus of Nazareth. It is not possible, Frei thought, to do so. But the literal sense can accommodate, in an ad hoc manner, historical critical ways of describing Jesus.

This complex analogical appropriation and transformation of coherence and correspondence notions in effect articulates what it means to talk of the truth to which Christian practitioners of the literal sense conform their lives as that mode of reading reaches into their mode of living, drawing them into responsible action. But to describe what truth means in relation to the literal sense, Frei thought you also need a way of describing that pragmatic, lived responsibility as truth. For, he wrote to Placher, Christian discourse is also true in Christians' enactment in their lives of what they depict and assert when they use scriptural stories; it is true in the way they are true to the grace of God.[224] And for this truthfulness, they depend on the Holy Spirit. Thus, he claimed in his response to Carl F. H. Henry, alluding to John 16, the truth of Christian God-talk is also a matter of 'being true to the way it works in one's life, and by holding the world, including the political, economic and social world, to account by the gauge of its truthfulness'.[225] Christians' speech is truthful when they live out the meaning of the way they identify God by being those through whom the Spirit convicts the world of what we might broadly label 'social sin'.[226] Some kind of trinitarian rules, Frei thought, would be required to describe God as the eternal transcendental ground of the rationality and unity of these appropriations of correspondence, coherence and pragmatic notions of truth in Christian theology.[227]

In these ways, Frei articulates the terms on which he thought Christian theology must pursue the intelligibility of Christian practice, including its existential, ethical and political dimensions, both for the sake of its own critical understanding of Christian faith and for a wider public. It makes Christian discourse and practice accountable primarily to the narrative

patterns in which God and Jesus Christ and the creaturely world are identified when Scripture is read according to the literal sense. It facilitates
evaluations of how far aspects of Christian discourse and performance
are either directly warranted by the central features of the text picked
out in literal reading, or by other scriptures read in accordance with it,
or are coherent with a given instance of Christianity as a whole cultural
system, insofar as it in turn is consistent with that basic norm. It is a
kind of use of the text that, as Higton notes, 'hands itself over to the
texts, and which allows ... those texts to stand over against Christian use
and understanding'.[228] It also permits (and encourages) secondary kinds
of evaluation, subordinate to this one, such as the dialogue with other
thinkers in the Christian tradition that Frei himself practised, or comparisons with widely accepted examples of faithful Christian practice and
living. These are forms of accountability that are specifically Christian
but publicly intelligible; indeed, they open Christians to public challenges
in terms of their own modes of reasoning.

These kinds of accountability may be furthered and enhanced by
another. As we have seen, the internal character of Christian discourse
requires theologians to borrow criteria and categories from philosophical
and, we may add, ethical schemes, using them analogically on the warrant
that there is an underlying, transcendent coherence between Christian
truth and the truth of the latter, albeit one that cannot yet be conceived
or articulated. In so doing, theologians make possible comparisons with
their uses in other rational discourses and of the relative capacities of
different accounts across traditions to make sense of similar practical
commitments, modes of interpretation and judgement, as William
Werpehowski has argued.[229]

Rethinking the essence of Christianity

This public accountability depends on another significant feature of Frei's
lectures on his typology and related pieces, which is the development
of his account of the essence of Christianity as a basis for normative
theological and ethical assertions, in a manner that takes much fuller
account of the social and historical character of Christian community
and Christian tradition. For Frei, the literal sense was now the answer to
the question, 'What is the essence of Christianity?'[230] This claim amounts
to a revision of Frei's argument in his Harvard lecture of 1967 and *The
Eclipse of Biblical Narrative*, one that pushes it further still in a practical,
historical and contextual direction and makes it yet more flexible and
capacious. Whereas in *The Eclipse of Biblical Narrative*, literal reading

was a practice that recognized the realistic narrative meaning of certain biblical stories, here it is a consensus that takes the story told by way of those formal features of the text to be the adequate rendering of their subject matter. The formal literary generic categories of narrative realism and history-likeness are now less central, more clearly borrowed for descriptive rather than explanatory use, as analogues of the coherence of meaning and truth ascribed to the texts in this Christian reading practice.[231] It is a more historically conceived tradition, beginning with choices made in early Christianity about how to read Christological stories and other sacred texts in relation to them. It is also a more comprehensive and accommodating conception of Christian scriptural reading practices.

First, such minimal regularities of practice may be plausibly identified as continuous across considerable historical change and variation in different forms of Christianity. As Frei puts it, 'Few will doubt that Jesus of Nazareth has in all ages been at the center of Christian living, Christian devotion, and Christian thought.'[232] Its minimal and flexible yet concrete specificity with reference to the primacy accorded to the narrated figure of Jesus of Nazareth allows for continuity, indeed for a very minimal yet meaningful identity, across considerable change and variations of practice, content and institutional and socio-political context. It is, he says in the second Princeton lecture, a matter of continuity of form.[233] Furthermore, as a practice, it also extends beyond the western tradition in which the formal conception of the *sensus literalis* developed.[234] Nor is it difficult to imagine its extension to popular culture, as Frei had intended.[235]

Frei's claim is 'daring', as David Ford observes.[236] There is an expansive catholicity to Frei's later account of the essence of Christianity in terms of the literal sense. For it encompasses virtually any group whose claim to Christian identity is predicated in some way on the unsubstitutable identity of Jesus of Nazareth. On Frei's account, the Christian tradition includes unambiguously a whole host of groups and figures often consigned either to its shadows or to its margins, including many deemed heretical by powerful Christian constituencies and ecclesial polities. In the Princeton lectures in particular, Frei also began to see Christianity in more global terms, with the potential to decentre western Christianity, on which his account tended to focus.

That catholicity is also what Frei's Christocentric account of the essence of Christianity has to recommend it over 'the other main candidate for Christian distinctiveness … the trinitarian God'.[237] Ford is right that the two proposals are not antithetical. Nevertheless, Frei's option does seem to get at a basic condition underlying trinitarian formulations. It does not depend on being able to identify a common content or consistent grammar among them. It envisages Christianity more expansively

by encompassing parties who have divided and remain divided over trinitarian questions while sharing a common focus on Jesus Christ. It helps
explain why they have been able to have such intense, detailed arguments
about the doctrine, and identifies a shared basis on which they might
continue to do so, constructively. Indeed, it is the basis on which Frei
himself makes a case for a high Christology leading towards a trinitarian
understanding of God, as we have seen.

Second, because he understands that the consensus constituting the literal sense concerned the meaning of the texts and not the manner of their
reference to reality, Frei was now better able to recognize the continuation
of the literal sense into modernity, even to the various forms of mediating
theology of the eighteenth, nineteenth and twentieth centuries, which he
had criticized in *The Eclipse of Biblical Narrative* and his Harvard lecture
of 1967.[238] He could even envisage it extending before and beyond the
European–North American frame of his writings. As he says in his third
Princeton lecture, it is a 'consensus [that is] tenuous and yet constantly
re-emerging from the earliest days through the Enlightenment period into
the twentieth century, East and West, North and South'.[239]

Third, literal reading in this sense permits a greater plurality of modes
of reading than Frei had entertained in *The Eclipse of Biblical Narrative*,
so long as they are congruent with the other rules it prescribes.[240] These
include allegory in ancient and modern equivalents, but also historical
criticism.[241] Indeed, elsewhere Frei argued that historical criticism, insofar
as it continued literal ascriptive reading, was not so much a secularizing
emancipation of interpretation from ecclesiastical tradition as 'a kind of
loose-jointed extension of the ecclesiastical tradition of interpretation
into an Enlightenment and post-Enlightenment conceptual mode'.[242]

This pluralism and catholicity is not relativistic, however. For Frei's
account involves a rethinking of normativity in Christianity. In his earlier
writings, Frei had relied heavily on the narrative structures of Christological stories as allowing them to bear a normative function as the iconic
vehicle of Christ's self-disclosure. In the typology and related pieces, it is
a combination of the qualities of those textual features and the hermeneutical consensus as to their fundamental, basic priority for Christian
readers, given (we may infer, from what we have seen above of Frei's
doctrine of the Word) that the Word incarnate graciously self-identifies
to Christian communities by way of them. From the regularities of communal reading practice (responding to the presence of the Word) emerge
norms to which readers socialized into the practice are accountable, as
Springs observes.[243]

These norms bind readers to texts with 'a richness and complexity
that act on the reader', that exert their own pressure over against read-

erly pre-understandings and interests, and which allow us to check one another's interpretations against its features and which mean that there can be no complete interpretation of a text.[244] The force of the plain-sense hermeneutical consensus is thus 'object-directed', as Springs puts it, focusing attention on something being investigated.[245] It focuses attention on the narrated figure of Jesus as the most basic object of Christian reading of its most central texts and to make Christian readings of those texts accountable to how well they read the textual features that identify him.[246] What Frei calls the literal ascription of the Christological stories to Jesus of Nazareth is at the heart of this normativity. The gospel story cannot be understood in this tradition apart from its being 'the literal identification of someone identified as Jesus of Nazareth'.[247] In this way, as Higton says, Frei in his later writings is concerned for the way Christian reading practices allow Christians 'to make stable reference to and identification of Jesus by means of the Gospels'.[248]

The literal sense makes coherence with his identity, as given in this way, central and fundamental to any assessment of the faithfulness of Christian practices in each context. It is a prioritization that at once secures the accountability of Christian practice and theology to a norm internal to the life of Christian communities while relativizing confessional formulas and traditions to it and underscoring the provisionality and corrigibility of different interpretations of Christian sacred texts, including those that render this identity. There is thus a certain possibility of ecumenical generosity inherent in Frei's approach to the essence of Christianity and to orthodoxy, which goes together with its flexible robustness. As William Young III argues, it enjoins a hospitality among Christians towards one another, embodying a 'contingent, pluralistic unity' in reading, which enables a contingent, pluralistic unity in the church.[249]

More than that, Frei makes useful distinctions between the object of scriptural witness and the graced witness of the scriptural narrative rendering of the identity of Jesus; between that witness and the basic rules of the literal sense that orientate readers to its rendering of that object; between those rules and their varied instantiation in practice and formal codification; between the narrative depiction and various conceptual descriptions of its logic from resources in one's cultural context; and between different strategies for using those conceptual resources, with their respective merits, in response to contextual pressures. Taking account of them could help disagreeing parties de-naturalize and de-absolutize their own formulations and arguments. In some cases, at least, they might help us recognize in one another's positions a response to the person of Christ more or less analogous, from its own positionality, to our own, while still allowing for identifying problems and infelicities in those responses and their uses of the texts in their ecclesial and socio-political contexts today.

The literal sense and Christian hybridity

At this point we need to consider a potent objection to Frei's understanding of Christianity in these later texts, which raises questions about it as a basis for his ethics. As Kathryn Tanner has argued, accounts like Frei's tend to reproduce problems found in cultural anthropological accounts of cultures in theorists like Clifford Geertz, as identified in postmodern theories of culture.[250] She criticizes postliberal theologians for securing the Christian identity of Christian social practices in their mingling with cultural elements from their social settings by appealing to a stable, underlying framework of rules that precedes, and whose meaning is self-contained and intelligible on its own terms, independent of those contextual interactions.[251]

This picture of Christian identity, she argues, is unrealistic, ignoring the way cultural identities are formed from the outset through varied borrowings and transformations of cultural elements from their context and as Christian identities have been in the history of Christianity. It also excepts rules of practice from the historical processes that produce, shape and change them, overestimates their sufficiency to determine proper action in a situation, and underestimates their diversity and contestation across and within historical contexts.[252] The search for a consistent logic underlying the messiness of Christian practices involves projecting onto them the coherent whole required by that procedure. It privileges the perspective of the academic theologian, disqualifies ordinary Christians from having a say about their meaning. It tends to reify those practices, lifting them out of the social processes that form them, giving them a fixity and absoluteness that they do not possess and obscuring the theologian's responsibility for constructing proposals from their selection and interpretation of Christian cultural materials in response to problems arising from changing contexts and practices.[253] And it leads postliberal theologians to 'try to guarantee Christianity's dominance in contacts with the wider world and other religions by nullifying theological claims that might put these others on a more equal footing with Christianity'.[254] In all these ways, she adds, postliberal theologians tend to limit the grace and freedom of God's action in the world and in the lives of Christians and to substitute some feature of Christian practice for God's Word as the guarantor of Christian identity.[255]

None of these criticisms undermines Frei's move to locate the literal sense and Christian theology within the social-cultural setting of relevant religious communities in whose practices it is found. Indeed, Tanner shares this concern.[256] These criticisms do raise questions about the way he characterizes both that setting and the literal sense as a consensus, ruled-governed practice, however. For, when drawing on Geertz to identify the context of the literal sense, he does tend to talk about Christianity as a community that is an enacted symbolic text, a unified whole, a self-contained, internally consistent culture. His talk of the figural incorporation of extratextual concepts so that the scriptural stories 'provide the interpretive pattern in terms of which *all* of reality is experienced and read', absorbing the world in Lindbeck's much criticized metaphor, also seems vulnerable to Tanner's critique.[257] Still, there are several things that may be said in mitigation of Frei on this score.

A first step would be for Frei to acknowledge more explicitly the plurality and diversity of empirical Christian communities and the practices that make up their life and interactions with their context. Nothing key to his account of the literal sense as the essence of Christianity would be lost thereby, and his emphasis on the variability of the literal sense in history already envisages considerable diversity across time.

Second, Frei's formulation of the literal sense as a minimal practical consensus about certain basic, flexible hermeneutical rules explicitly envisages it co-existing with internal and intra-communal conflict over interpretations. Far from occluding conflict, that coherence is said to make conflicts over meaning possible. For the literal sense does not determine one way of interpreting what the New Testament's Christological narratives say about their central character. Rather, as Springs argues, as a set of normative constraints, it enables Christian readers to refuse interpretations and dissent from majority readings by invoking those norms and appealing to the Christological object towards which they orientate the practice.[258] There is a certain pressure, on Frei's account, towards coherence in the following of the literal sense but no necessary assumption that it be actually attained in any historical or living Christian community.

Third, Frei's understanding of rules in this context does not seem especially vulnerable to the charge of reification and abstraction from historical contingency. For Frei frames the rules constituting the literal sense as loose, vague regularities in Christian practice, variously conceptualized in formal rules. The regularity consists in a common orientation of ordinary Christian practice to the narrated figure, Jesus of Nazareth, and a common trust in the adequacy of the portrayal of him to render him and to orientate Christian life. These are regularities he finds in ordinary Christian practice and western theological hermeneutics that happen to persist, contingently, in widely varying ways across historical contexts:

a contingent, wobbling continuity.[259] They do not determine a tightly bounded cultural identity but delimit a common focus to a diversity of practices and understandings.

They are, moreover, a graced response to the faithfulness of God in Christ in graciously making the narrated identity of Jesus Christ in the New Testament a consistent vehicle of his turning and making himself present as Word in Christian communities. Far from limiting the freedom and grace of God, Frei's account seeks to acknowledge how Christian practices have been drawn, by the persistent work of God's Spirit, towards this figure as the personal embodiment of God's gracious, free condescension to humanity. For Frei, indeed, it is this constancy that *discloses* the primacy of God's Word and the freedom and grace of God, to which Tanner's theological arguments appeal.

Finally, Frei's account already allows for and acknowledges that Christianity and Christian theology are intrinsically and variously hybrid all the way down. We may recall that, in contradistinction to some post-liberal theologians, Frei has a positive understanding of the presence of Christ in the world beyond the church and of the church's need of enrichment by this neighbour, which includes its cultural resources and projects.[260] And as we shall see shortly, Frei thought we have not met the Jesus identified by the New Testament until we have met him incognito in a crowd, a claim that points in a similar direction, as Paul DeHart observes.[261]

Those observations should give us pause in making too much of Frei's single invocation of Lindbeck's metaphor of the Scriptures absorbing the world.[262] Indeed, his commendation of theologians' ad hoc borrowing of conceptual resources as required by the character of Christian practices implies an understanding of Christian identity as always hybrid, centred not on the illusory stability of some homogenous, ahistorical cultural core but on the irreducible singularity of Jesus of Nazareth as a unique person in a particular story. What diverse instantiations of Christianity share is the common stories they turn towards, but the stories alone do not constitute Christianity; it only exists in a plurality of fusions of the self-same story with various world views.[263] If we understand every Christian practice as theological, we could say that for Frei, as for Tanner, Christian communities build the cultures by which they live in responsibility before God by borrowing and adapting elements of culture from their surroundings in this way, turning and transforming them to articulate meanings orientated around the figure of Christ. To ascribe such cultural agency to members of Christian communities, moreover, would be consistent with Frei's own theological anthropology. The extent to which Frei thought Christians were dependent on their neighbours for the integrity and vitality of their own distinct identities is most power-fully evident in the case that he makes (as we shall see) for Christians to renew the literal sense and their own vocation in a post-Christian society by learning from Judaism and the practice of Midrash, as William Young III implies.[264]

Our understanding of Frei's account of the figural interpretation of cultural resources can be rethought by these lights. One can construe him, generously, as understanding the borrowing and transformation of cultural elements as figures of a Christ-centred set of stories to be intrinsic to the way Christians have built and continue to build their beliefs, values, practices and institutions, right back to the origins of Christian-ity. For on Frei's own terms, nothing can be said or done or built without them.[265] In the light of Frei's earlier understanding of the figural reading of history and culture, we can say that in this borrowing, in one way or another, their sense and function is reorientated by treating their patterns of meaning as having their fulfilment and basis in the one to whom the Christological stories of the New Testament bear witness.

We may wonder, however, whether Frei has fully explored the theo-logical possibilities of the interplay between the Christocentric and pluralistic, contextualizing elements in his early and later thought. For Frei, in both periods, the identity of Christ is finished, objective, graciously given and abundantly rich in meaning, while the vast plurality of human beings, their identities, projects and cultural artefacts, have their own distinct patterns of meaning which are fulfilled in relationship to Christ, not absorption by him. It would be tempting to think of Christ as con-taining that teeming diversity pre-eminently in himself so that the whole dynamic is grounded in him alone and our faltering efforts to shape our thinking and practice after him would be but an echo of his fullness. Frei does not make that move, however. Moreover, he gestures towards people finding their own particular figural interpretations of their lives, contexts, experiences and elements of their culture in connection with Christ. What I want to suggest constrains this vision is its still overly Christocentric character or, rather, its underdeveloped pneumatology. Christ's free sharing of presence is what makes the scriptural witness to him the vehicle of his self-disclosure and the conforming of history and culture to him in Christian living and thinking: it seems at times to be encompassing both poles of the relation. One might ask with Colin Gunton whether Frei, that fine observer of modern theology's excessive Christocentric preoccupations, had a way out of them?[266]

Yet there are some counter-indications.[267] One is Frei's sympathy, in his earlier published writings, for Ernst Troeltsch's pneumatological vision of a plurality of direct, independent relations of creatures to God with its deep appreciation of the mysteries of history, and for what is admirable in each culture, resisting their assimilation to a preconceived theological framework.[268] It is too diffuse for Frei but it suggests his openness to a pneumatological supplementation to his reaching towards a more Christocentric version of this kind of vision. The other is Frei's later sketches towards a more explicit trinitarian theology of truth to encompass the truth of the scriptural witness as graced correspondence (by the condescension of Christ as God's Word) and the enabled living out of this truth by human beings. Might not a fuller articulation of the identity of the Spirit in relation-and-distinction with Christ allow Frei more fully to explore and affirm the contextual breadth of the ways in which Christian practice and experience are related to Christ as figures? Indeed, it might allow him to go further, first to allow that the diversity of these relations might contribute to the interpretive plurality in respect of the Christological stories he recognized in the tradition of the literal sense. Second, it might enable him to see that, insofar as they do, they might offer complementary, corrigible and partial perspectives on the contours, abundance and inclusivity and presence of Christ given in and with his irreducible, unique and objective identity. Taken with Frei's later emphasis on the importance of recognizing Christ incognito in the crowd, among the marginalized, in order for us to know him, we might take a further step and imagine that Frei could acknowledge the possibility of particularly important, transformative or revolutionary insights into his identity and presence being afforded from marginalized perspectives.[269] Perhaps it is among those in whom Christ's identity funds resistance to double consciousness that it comes most clearly into focus.

The literal sense and Christian humanism

This argument begins to indicate the practical import of Frei's use of hospitality to the literal sense to evaluate his types, given its significance for Christian practices and Christian identity. In his lectures, however, Frei develops that significance in a particular direction relevant for our understanding of his ethics. For him, the future viability of the literal sense was important for the cultural and political vocation of Christian communities in post-Christendom western societies, as making possible arguments for a Christian humanism centred on the generous love of neighbour.

This theme emerges first in Frei's piece on 'The "literal reading" of biblical narrative in the Christian tradition'. Here, he argues that Christianity has much to learn from Judaism in two respects. First, renewed relations with Judaism might be indispensable to recovering and prioritizing Christian theology as Christian self-description.[270] Frei's point is striking. He implies that it is only in a relationship of learning from Judaism and its interpretive practices (such as Midrash) that Christians will be able to properly grasp again the means for understanding themselves and critically examining their discourse and practices.[271] This recovery matters for Christianity, Frei adds, since 'the most fateful issue for Christian self-description is that of regaining its autonomous vocation as a religion, after its defeat in its secondary vocation of providing ideological coherence, foundation, and stability to Western culture.'[272]

As we have seen, Frei had long thought that Christianity was better suited to being a minority religion. In western contexts, Christian communities now needed to rediscover how to do that, which involved renewing how to describe their particularity. But that renewal also concerned the constructive purpose of Christian communities in post-Christian societies, and here also 'the example of Judaism in the modern Western world might be a beacon to a reconstituted Christian community'.[273] Should Christianity recover its autonomous vocation and learn from the example of Judaism, one never knows, Frei wrote, 'what this community might then contribute once again to that culture or its residues, including its political life, its quest for justice and freedom – and even its literature'.[274] In this enterprise, Frei believed that 'the literal sense may be counted on to play a significant part' in the context of theology understood primarily as Christian self-description.[275]

It is a remarkable argument from a Christian coming from a secular, assimilated Jewish family. It is also in keeping with what, as a much younger man, he had sought in Christianity: the kind of religious tradition that could resist the sort of pressure to self-hatred he had experienced in Berlin in the 1930s. Above all, for my purposes, and as William Young III also notes, it brings out the political implications of the literal sense as a form of Christian discipleship.[276]

Frei's interpretation of Lindbeck's *The Nature of Doctrine* sharpens his point against the background of Frei's own biography. In his epilogue to a volume of essays on Lindbeck's theology, Frei describes the poignancy of Troeltsch's liberal humanism in the Germany of his time. There were not enough people like Troeltsch, Frei says, who 'saw barbarism, cruel and enslaving intolerance, and a steadily increasing loss of humanity in human intercourse looming ahead among his fellow Germans, and … detested polarization as inhuman from the bottom of their hearts'.[277] Yet for Troeltsch, the church's tradition of unvarying normative belief gave way under his feet, and he came instead to a more relativistic view of cultures 'as the location of proximity to the unknown divine, each in its own distinct way, and the better ones with that high ideal of humanity and that respect for persons which comes with the sense of a hidden purpose to all things historical'.[278] There was thus for Troeltsch no effective norm to 'authorize restraint and humaneness in the chaos', in the flux of normative cultural symbols for the divine.[279] For him, cultural change was 'real ... basic and permanent: the language of the church was various, changing, and not basic'.[280] That judgement is the one that Lindbeck's book had 'simply, so gently, and almost imperceptibly' turned on its head, Frei suggested.[281]

Lindbeck's argument meant there was a basic identity to Christianity in its central narrative by which Christians might reinterpret changing world views by fusing them with the self-same story of Jesus.[282] Here Frei reads Lindbeck on Frei's terms, for the identity he ascribes to Christianity amounts to the most basic rule of the literal sense as he describes it: the rule of literal ascriptive reading of the Gospel stories and its primacy in Christian hermeneutics.[283] He detects, 'almost imperceptibly' present in *The Nature of Doctrine*, a case for the literal sense as the basis for Christians, as a religious minority in post-Christian societies, to practise a liberal humanism to check polarization, intolerance and inhumanity.[284] In this way, in keeping with the bent of his own thought, he describes here 'the orthodox Christian as liberal humanist'.[285] Such Christians might be 'a reconciling presence wherever bitter enmity threatens to pit human individuals and groups against each other'.[286] In so doing they would be authorized by the reconciling work of One whose identity is picked out and prioritized in literal reading, 'Jesus of Nazareth, whose community is the community founded on that reconciliation'.[287]

That connection between Christocentric literal reading and a Christian liberal humanism of reconciliation is further amplified in a passage from Frei's third Princeton lecture. Here, as in the epilogue to *The Identity of Jesus Christ*, he recalls Albert Schweitzer's invocation of Christ as one who comes to us 'as One unknown', who commands us, as he did his first disciples, to follow him, and sets us 'to the tasks which He has to fulfill for our time'.[288] Schweitzer's words convey Christ's demand with 'authentic force'.[289] Yet, Frei urged, we should not appeal to Christ's compelling call to difficult discipleship without also recalling his 'profound humanness' and his equally great compassion exhibited in the Gospels, and his hidden presence among the marginalized.[290]

One aspect of that compassion is Christ's self-identification with the poor, which Frei, in common with several other theologians, grounds in Jesus' saying in Matthew 25.40, that what his disciples do to the least of his brethren, they do to him.[291] That saying describes Jesus as identified (not identical) with 'the poor, the undeserving, the spiritual and economic underclass', and it gives a clue to his living, risen presence: he walks incognito among them.[292] Frei suggests we have not met the textual Jesus until we have also met him 'in forgetfulness of himself or incognito in a crowd', and in particular among 'these least of the underclass' with whom he identified.[293] Christ's humane, compassionate, inclusive identification with all humanity was reflected, he observed, in the love of neighbour 'with simple delight and generosity' shown by some disciples.[294]

At the beginning of his Schaffer lectures, Frei notes that for many Protestant and probably many Roman Catholic theologians, 'the central persuasion of Christian theology ... is that Jesus Christ is the presence of God in the Church to the world.'[295] It is not difficult to see how the typology essays effectively rework the theological method of Frei's Christological essays to serve the same end of clarifying the grammar of that central persuasion in the light of Christ's identity. Here, however, Frei allows Christological sayings, read in their narrative context, to contribute to our understanding of Christ's presence and its practical force for Christian disciples. As in those earlier essays and in *The Eclipse of Biblical Narrative*, Frei's Christology flows into an ethics of responsibility and discipleship. We find here the central orientation of that responsibility in the love of neighbour normed by the identity of Christ but now in the context of a much fuller, more sophisticated account of how the theological framework and practical setting of that responsibility may be publicly and faithfully articulated.

Conclusion: the literal sense and generous orthodoxy

Here, then, is the culmination of Frei's arguments in the typology lectures. His careful analysis of options for negotiating and holding together the demands upon theology of its practical function in the life of Christian communities and its public role in the academy and wider society, after Christendom; and his commendation of a way of upholding the literal sense while making Christian meanings and their rationality public – both are intended to promote the conditions for the articulation of this sort of vision of Christian responsibility and discipleship.

Frei's articulation of a broad, flexible essence to Christianity as the basis for a compassionate humanism and a generous love of neighbour, is, moreover, what I suggest he meant when he said he was searching for a generous orthodoxy. Generous in its identification of orthodoxy and orthodox in grounding its generosity in the narrated rendering of the person and presence of Christ, it begins to fill out Frei's gestures towards an ethics of responsibility and discipleship in ways that are both interpersonal and political. It is to those political dimensions and their significance that I turn in the next and final chapter.

Notes

1 As Higton notes, Frei's account in this period thus integrates history and dogmatic theology more fully than in *The Identity of Jesus Christ* and *The Eclipse of Biblical Narrative* (Mike Higton, *Christ, Providence and History* (Edinburgh: T & T Clark, 2004), p. 188).

2 Higton describes the shift as a simplification of the scaffolding around Frei's unchanged Christology, towards a more historical and social view of Christianity, a 'continuation and clarification of his earlier work' (*Christ, Providence and History*, pp. 177–213). It is a hard-won simplification in terms of becoming less encumbered with theory but conceiving Christianity as more historical and social brings its own kind of descriptive complexity. Springs is right to note the continuity in the fact that insights from Wittgenstein and those who build on his thought inform Frei's thinking before and during this period but underplays the significance of his later application of those ways of thinking to Christian readers (Jason A. Springs, 'Between Barth and Wittgenstein: on the availability of Hans Frei's later theology', *Modern Theology* 23:3 (2007), pp. 393–413).

3 For another, insightful account of this background, with which mine overlaps, see Higton, *Christ, Providence and History*, pp. 178–88.

4 On a CV from 1976, Frei listed 'The history of Christology from 1700 to 1950' in Britain, Germany and the USA as his 'long-range' project: the same project he had been engaged upon for the past decade or more, with the addition of the USA to its scope (Yale Divinity School archive (YDS) 76 VI 27-335).

5 Frei was offered a post at Stanford, California, sounded out about others at Union Theological Seminary in New York and at the University of Virginia, and approached about another at the Candler School of Theology. See Frei's letters to Clebsch of 1 and 19 April 1976, and Clebsch to Frei on 7 April (all in YDS 76 I 1-15); Robert King's letter to Frei of 12 September 1977, and Frei's reply of 6 January 1978 (YDS 76 I 2-51); Frei's letter to Gerald Sheppard, 19 June 1977 (summarized in Higton, *Christ, Providence and History*, p. 253); Jim L. Waita to Frei, 16 February 1979 (YDS 76 I 5-102); Leander Keck's letter to Frei, 22 March 1979, and Frei's reply on 30 August (YDS 76 I 3-52); Hartt to Frei, n.d. (YDS 76 I 2-36). In an oral history interview for Stanford University, Van Harvey relates that Frei told him he had been offered the chair at Stanford and gave this reason for having turned it down. Harvey relates this episode from about 9 minutes into the interview, which can be found here: https://exhibits.stanford.edu/oral-history/catalog/jp140pm6824 (accessed 14.12.2022).

6 Frei to Van Harvey, 22 June 1976 (YDS 76 I 2-39), reproduced in Hans W. Frei, *Reading Faithfully: Writings from the Archive, vol. 1, Theology and Hermeneutics* (Eugene, OR: Wipf & Stock, 2015), pp. 24–6. Frei and Van Harvey must have met when they were students at Yale in the late 1940s and 1950s. See Stanford's obituary for Harvey: https://humsci.stanford.edu/feature/stanford-professor-religious-studies-van-harvey-has-died (accessed 14.12.2022).

7 Letter to Bill Clebsch on 27 August 1979 (YDS 76 I 1-15). On 25 March

1976, the *Yale Daily News* reported that Frei was to step down from the Master's Office at Ezra Stiles and take two terms' research leave ('Seven masters, deans to leave their colleges before autumn', p. 3).

8 See Frei to Van Harvey, 22 June 1976; his letter to his former doctoral student Charles Wood, 21 March 1978 (YDS 76 I 5-104); a letter to another former student, William Placher, 19 December 1979 (YDS 76 I 4-75); and correspondence with his former Austin colleague and close friend John Woolverton of 26 January 1978 and 23 January 1980 (YDS 76 I 5-98), quoted in J. Woolverton, 'Hans W. Frei in context: a theological and historical memoir', *Anglican Theological Review* 79:3 (1997), pp. 378–9. As Frei told Woolverton, the estrangement began during their time in Austin. In his 'Autobiographical notes' from this period, Frei records how, in Austin, the middle-class narcissism of treating church as a therapeutic community, together with his experience of liturgical worship, 'drove me to the periphery'.

9 See also Frei, 'Autobiographical notes', pp. 2 and 3 (YDS 76 VI 27-336), where he wonders how his Quaker religious practice could be combined coherently with his Enlightenment scepticism and Barthian theology.

10 Hans F. Holocaust Testimony HV 170, Fortunoff Video Archive for Holocaust Testimonies, Yale University, 1980, from 1 hour 21 minutes.

11 How lonely this identity may have been for Frei may be gauged from a letter to him from the Jewish philosopher Michael Diamond, recalling a moment of understanding and deep, silent mutual affirmation he felt they had shared between them at a recent meeting of 'the group', perhaps the New Haven Theological Discussion Group, of which they were both members (YDS 83 I 75-111). Both Diamond and Frei are on membership lists for the Discussion Group for 1969 and 1974 among Sidney Ahlstrom's papers in YDS 83 I 9-121. Diamond had spoken of Jewish self-hatred, a phenomenon that 'generates the most violent hatred of others when they opt out of the tribe in one way or another'. Nothing, he added, 'is so loaded as opting out via Christianity'.

12 Frei to Placher, 19 December 1979, see also his letter to Woolverton of 23 January 1980. In his letter to Placher, Frei also lists a lack of a clear view and well-developed theological method applied across several loci among his shortcomings. The limited application is perhaps the fairest observation here.

13 Frei to Placher, 24 March 1976; Frei to Green 2 January 1977 (YDS 76 I 2-31). The letter is addressed to 'Gary'. Frei has written at the top 'Garrett Green?' The reference to a Cambridge University Press edition of a work by Fichte confirms this identification: Green's translation of Fichte's *Attempt at a Critique of All Revelation* was published by Cambridge University Press in 1978.

14 Interview with Margaret Farley, 13 March 2015, who discussed some of the major texts in Latin American liberation theology with Frei from time to time.

15 See Terry Foreman's letter to Brooks Holifield, 3 September 1979, a copy of which Foreman forwarded to Frei on 18 September, and Frei's annotation in the margins of that copy (YDS 76 I 2-23); and Frei's letter to William Placher, 19 December 1979 (YDS 76 I 4-78). It is not clear whether this was delivered at the envisaged AAR panel discussed with Foreman. Clebsch's brand-new book, which Frei had endorsed, *Christianity in European History* (Oxford: Oxford University Press, 1979), seems to have been the main inspiration for Frei's interest in sensibility. See Frei's letters to Clebsch of 27 August 1979 and 4 December 1979 (YDS 76 I 1-15).

16 This section of the lecture is reproduced as 'Is religious sensibility accessible to study?' in Frei, *Reading Faithfully, vol. 1*, pp. 141–8.

17 Frei to Clebsch, 15 July 1981. Frei wrote to Henry Chadwick on 8 May 1981 asking for advice on researching parish records for this purpose (YDS 76 I 1-10 Ca-Cl) and spent June in England reading visitation returns and other primary sources (Frei to Clebsch 15 July 1981; Frei to Julian Hartt, 19 August 1981 (YDS 76 I 2-36 Ha)). For the quotation, see Frei's untitled paper, dated in his own annotation to '1979–80', in which he discusses his changing approach to writing theology in a Religious Studies department (YDS 76 III 11-82). This may be the paper referred to in his letter to Placher of 19 December 1979, as Higton suggests (*Christ, Providence and History*, p. 256).

18 On this aspect of Frei's teaching at Yale, see Higton, *Christ, Providence and History*, p. 184 and nn. 14 and 18 on pp. 214–15. Higton also notes that Frei did bring 'increasing amounts of material on popular religion into his undergraduate lecturing', n. 26 on p. 215.

19 'Is religious sensibility accessible to study?', pp. 147–8.

20 Sidney Ahlstrom, 'The radical turn in theology and ethics: why it occurred in the 1960's', *The Annals of the American Academy of Political and Social Science* 387:1 (1970), p. 1.

21 Paul DeHart, *The Trial of the Witnesses: The Rise and Decline of Postliberal Theology* (Oxford: Wiley-Blackwell, 2006), pp. 13–20. In 1978, Frei commented to Paul Ramsey that 'in the wake of the bloody demise of neoorthodoxy all of us find ourselves regrouping, if not retooling' (Letter of 21 March 1978, in The Paul Ramsey Papers, David M. Rubenstein Rare Book & Manuscript Library, Duke University).

22 DeHart, *The Trial of the Witnesses*, p. 14.

23 Notes for Contemporary Christian Thought 1972 (Religious Studies 23a) (YDS 76 IV 13-197).

24 Frei's take on George Lindbeck's article, 'Ecumenism and the future of belief', *Una Sancta* 25:3 (1968), pp. 3–18.

25 'A Christology for Barabbases', *Perkins Journal* 29:3 (Spring 1976), pp. 1–13.

26 Frei to Harvey, 22 June 1976. He also mentions Paul Meyer's recently delivered Schaffer lectures that year as another such challenge, which is reflected in Frei's annotations on a typescript of those lectures (see Higton, *Christ, Providence and History*, pp. 252–3).

27 Letter to Wood, 2 June 1978 (YDS RG 76 I 5-108). See also Gary Comstock, 'Truth or meaning: Ricoeur versus Frei on biblical narrative', *Journal of Religion* 66:2 (1986), pp. 117–40; Letter from James Gustafson to Outka, 30 July 1984, enclosed with Frei's letter to Outka of 8 August 1984 (YDS 76 I 4-74); and Carl F. H. Henry, as 'Narrative theology: an Evangelical appraisal', *Trinity Journal* NS 8:1 (1987), pp. 3–19.

28 Frei to Placher, 19 December 1979 (YDS 76 I 4-78).

29 Interview with Professor Meeks, 6 November 2015.

30 Letter to Maurice Wiles, 10 October 1983 (YDS 76 I 5-107). He obtained funding to make an affirmative action appointment to mitigate the lack of women in the department (see letters to Ellen Ryerson, Yale's Associate Provost (YDS 76 I 5-11), and to Peter Hodgson, 19 June 1984 (YDS 76 I 2-43)). He made an appointment in Islamic studies (Frei to Wiles, 10 October 1983 (YDS 76 I 5-107); see also correspondence with Peter Demetz, 12 October 1983 and 24 April 1984). In April

1984 he announced the creation of an endowed chair in Judaic studies ('In brief. Moses gives $1 million to establish professorship', *Yale Daily News*, 25 April 1984, p. 1). And he repaired relations with the Divinity School (letter to Hodgson, 19 June 1984 (YDS 76 I 2-43); Memo from Frei and Keck to Yale's Provost and Associate Provosts, 29 May 1984 (YDS 76 II 7-137)).

31 See his National Endowment for the Humanities Proposal in Hans W. Frei, *Types of Christian Theology*, ed. G. Hunsinger and W. C. Placher (New Haven, CT: Yale University Press, 1992), p. 1.

32 Higton (*Christ, Providence and History*, p. 267) also notes a CV from 1987, which again lists 'A book on Christology in Germany and England from 1700 to 1950' alongside 'A book on theological typology and sensus literalis in modern theology', based on Frei's Schaffer and Cadbury lectures.

33 For example, Charles Campbell, *Preaching Jesus: New Directions for Homiletics in Hans Frei's Postliberal Theology* (Eugene, OR: Wipf & Stock, 2005), pp. 63–82; Higton, *Christ, Providence and History*, pp. 177–213; Jason Springs, *Toward a Generous Orthodoxy: Prospects for Hans Frei's Postliberal Theology* (Eugene, OR: Wipf & Stock, 2016), pp. 41–62; Daniel Shin, *Theology and the Public: Reflections on Hans W. Frei on Hermeneutics, Christology, and Theological Method* (Lanham, MD: Lexington Books, 2019), pp. 99–112. DeHart is an exception here, see *The Trial of the Witnesses*, pp. 193–7. I am less convinced by the more speculative case that Barth's interrogation of Schleiermacher was equally important in the genesis of the typology. The questions for Schleiermacher that DeHart thinks Frei took from Barth were already present in a contrast Frei drew between Schleiermacher and Harnack, as we shall see.

34 As DeHart also notes (*The Trial of the Witnesses*, p. 195). See Frei to Clebsch, 15 July 1981 (YDS 76 I 1-16). Frei sent the completed manuscript to his friends William Clebsch and Maurice Wiles. See his letters to Clebsch, 15 July 1981, and to Wiles, 2 March 1982 (YDS 76 I 5-107). It was published as 'David Friedrich Strauss', in N. Smart, P. Clayton, P. Sherry and S. T. Katz (eds), *Nineteenth Century Religious Thought in the West*, vol. 1 (Cambridge: Cambridge University Press, 1985), p. 215.

35 Frei, 'David Friedrich Strauss', pp. 218–21.

36 Frei, 'David Friedrich Strauss', pp. 223–4.

37 Frei, 'David Friedrich Strauss', pp. 232–3.

38 Published posthumously in *Types of Christian Theology*. See the Foreword, p. vii.

39 Frei, *Types of Christian Theology*, pp. 8–11.

40 Frei, *Types of Christian Theology*, p. 10.

41 Frei first introduced this distinction in a paper delivered at Haverford College in 1982, entitled 'Theology and the interpretation of narrative: some hermeneutical considerations', published in Hans W. Frei, ed. G. Hunsinger and W. Placher, *Theology and Narrative: Selected Essays* (Oxford: Oxford University Press, 1993), pp. 95–116.

42 Frei, *Types of Christian Theology*, pp. 19–20; 121, 'Theology and the interpretation of narrative', p. 95.

43 Frei, *Types of Christian Theology*, p. 131.

44 Frei, *Types of Christian Theology*, p. 122.

45 Frei, *Types of Christian Theology*, p. 126.

46 Frei, *Types of Christian Theology*, p. 126.

47 Frei, *Types of Christian Theology*, p. 20.

48 Frei ventures that Midrash, though very different from Christian theology, may have a similar function in Judaism in showing the community how to use its sacred text. See *Types of Christian Theology*, p. 124.

49 Frei, *Types of Christian Theology*, p. 12.

50 Frei, 'Theology and the interpretation of narrative', p. 96.

51 'The "literal reading" of biblical narrative in the Christian tradition: does it stretch or will it break?', *Theology and Narrative*, pp. 143–4, 146.

52 Frei, *Types of Christian Theology*, p. 121.

53 Frei, *Types of Christian Theology*, p. 124.

54 Frei, *Types of Christian Theology*, pp. 20–1, 124; 'Theology and the interpretation of narrative', p. 96; 'The "literal reading"', p. 147.

55 Frei, *Types of Christian Theology*, p. 21.

56 Frei, *Types of Christian Theology*, p. 126.

57 'Theology and the interpretation of narrative', p. 96. This practical setting and function of Christian theology is basic to Frei's construction of the typology. For that reason, Fergus Kerr's characterization of it as 'pervaded by the idea that it is with some metaphysical system that theologians first have to come to terms', whereas in fact Christian theology primarily interacts with life, seems rather wide of the mark ('Frei's Types', *New Blackfriars* 75:881 (1994), p. 193).

58 According to Frei's editors, Hunsinger and Placher, the texts here come from his Princeton lectures (Frei, *Types of Christian Theology*, p. x). According to David Ford, they also formed the substance of Frei's first, second and third Cadbury lectures (David Ford, 'On being theologically hospitable to Jesus Christ: Hans Frei's achievement', *The Journal of Theological Studies* 46: 2 (1995), p. 534).

59 Frei, *Types of Christian Theology*, p. 97.

60 Frei, *Types of Christian Theology*, p. 98.

61 Frei, *Types of Christian Theology*, pp. 98–9.

62 Frei, *Types of Christian Theology*, p. 102.

63 Frei, *Types of Christian Theology*, p. 102.

64 Frei, *Types of Christian Theology*, pp. 95, 102.

65 Frei, *Types of Christian Theology*, pp. 111–16.

66 Frei, *Types of Christian Theology*, p. 117.

67 Frei, *Types of Christian Theology*, p. 118.

68 Frei, *Types of Christian Theology*, p. 18. Frei would have long been familiar with this technical use of 'literal sense'. In the 'Final Discussion Session' of the 1969 Yale Divinity School symposium on Karl Barth, in which Frei was a prominent participant, Brevard Childs describes the substance of what would become his influential article on the *sensus literalis* (in D. L. Dickerman (ed.), *Karl Barth and the Future of Theology* (New Haven, CT: Yale Divinity School Association, 1969), pp. 52–3) and acknowledges a debt to Frei in his understanding of how it had shifted.

69 Frei, *Types of Christian Theology*, pp. 5, 13–16.

70 Frei, *Types of Christian Theology*, pp. 5, 137–40.

71 Frei, *Types of Christian Theology*, p. 15.

72 Frei, *Types of Christian Theology*, pp. 5, 140–41, 142–3. In 'Theology and the interpretation of narrative', Frei's description leans towards simply a literary description of this rule (pp. 111–12). The expanded Schaffer version is significant, I shall argue below.

73 Frei, 'The "literal reading"', pp. 120–1.

74 Frei, 'The "literal reading"', pp. 122–3.

75 Frei, *Types of Christian Theology*, p. 141.

76 Frei, *Types of Christian Theology*, p. 142.

77 Frei, *Types of Christian Theology*, p. 15.

78 Frei, *Types of Christian Theology*, p. 56.

79 Frei, *Types of Christian Theology*, pp. 2–3, 28.

80 Frei, *Types of Christian Theology*, pp. 28–9.

81 Frei, *Types of Christian Theology*, p. 30.

82 Frei, *Types of Christian Theology*, p. 5.

83 Frei, *Types of Christian Theology*, pp. 58–9.

84 Frei, *Types of Christian Theology*, p. 59.

85 Frei, *Types of Christian Theology*, p. 59.

86 Frei, *Types of Christian Theology*, p. 3. In the Princeton lectures, Frei clarifies that, for Fichte, theology as a distinct discipline could only be reconciled to the ideal of *Wissenschaft* and admitted to the university by renouncing its claims that the will of God is irreducibly mysterious and knowable only through special revelation and even then would be inadmissible as a practical subject (Frei, *Types of Christian Theology*, pp. 105–6).

87 As Fergus Kerr shows, 'Frei's Types', pp. 190–93.

88 Frei, *Types of Christian Theology*, pp. 4, 47–9.

89 Frei, *Types of Christian Theology*, p. 4; see also p. 51.

90 Frei, *Types of Christian Theology*, pp. 49–50.

91 Frei, *Types of Christian Theology*, p. 52.

92 Frei, *Types of Christian Theology*, pp. 4–5, 51. On p. 51 Frei is more circumspect about whether Phillips in principle excludes the possibility of overlap between the rules specific to different concepts.

93 Frei, *Types of Christian Theology*, pp. 5, 51.

94 Frei, *Types of Christian Theology*, p. 54.

95 Frei, *Types of Christian Theology*, pp. 54–5.

96 Frei, *Types of Christian Theology*, p. 6.

97 Frei, *Types of Christian Theology*, p. 55.

98 Frei, *Types of Christian Theology*, p. 30.

99 David Tracy, *Blessed Rage for Order: The New Pluralism in Theology* (New York: The Seabury Press, 1975); Frei, *Types of Christian Theology*, pp. 3, 30. Thus alongside Tracy and Bultmann, Frei also lists Wolfhart Pannenberg and Carl F. H. Henry as examples of Type Two theology.

100 Frei, *Types of Christian Theology*, pp. 3, 30–1.

101 Frei, *Types of Christian Theology*, pp. 31–4.

102 Frei, *Types of Christian Theology*, pp. 32–33, 61.

103 Frei, *Types of Christian Theology*, pp. 33, 61–2.

104 Frei, *Types of Christian Theology*, p. 63.

105 Frei, *Types of Christian Theology*, p. 62.

106 Frei, *Types of Christian Theology*, p. 63. Alternatively, Frei thought, where Type Two theology seeks to maintain some focus on Jesus Christ, for example as a historical figure, it does so at the price of hermeneutical coherence (*Types of Christian Theology*, pp. 6, 82). He thought this was the case with David Tracy's *The Analogical Imagination: Christian Theology and the Culture of Pluralism* (New York: Crossroad Publishing Company, 1981). Even here, he argued, Tracy ends up prioritizing

the universal meaningfulness of the stories as their referent and real subject matter, so that his hermeneutic tends towards allegorization ('The "literal reading"', n. 16, pp. 150–1).

107 Frei, *Types of Christian Theology*, p. 64.

108 A key burden of Frei's argument in 'The "literal reading"' is that the literal sense would not survive being defended by means of this sort of hermeneutical treatment.

109 Frei, *Types of Christian Theology*, p. 70.

110 Frei, *Types of Christian Theology*, p. 35.

111 Frei, *Types of Christian Theology*, pp. 3, 111–12; 'Barth and Schleiermacher', in *Theology and Narrative*, pp. 188–91.

112 Frei, *Types of Christian Theology*, pp. 35–6, 114–15.

113 Hans W. Frei, 'Epilogue: George Lindbeck and *The Nature of Doctrine*', in Bruce Marshall (ed.), *Theology and Dialogue: Essays in Conversation with George Lindbeck* (Notre Dame, IN: University of Notre Dame Press, 1990), pp. 279–80.

114 Frei, *Types of Christian Theology*, pp. 36, 70–1.

115 Frei, *Types of Christian Theology*, p. 73. Frei explicates this suggestion more fully here with reference to the paired concepts of 'sin' and 'Redeemer', which are mutually implicated concepts in the logic of Christian belief, and are correlated but not identical with the universally intelligible experience of pain and pleasure in the feeling of absolute dependence, and so may be understood.

116 Frei, *Types of Christian Theology*, pp. 36–7.

117 Frei, *Types of Christian Theology*, p. 36.

118 Frei, *Types of Christian Theology*, pp. 36–7.

119 DeHart, *The Trial of the Witnesses*, pp. 234–5.

120 Frei, *Types of Christian Theology*, p. 38.

121 Frei, *Types of Christian Theology*, pp. 65–6.

122 Frei, *Types of Christian Theology*, p. 66.

123 Frei, *Types of Christian Theology*, pp. 67, 74–5.

124 Frei, *Types of Christian Theology*, pp. 67, 72–3; his emphasis.

125 Frei, *Types of Christian Theology*, p. 68.

126 Frei, *Types of Christian Theology*, p. 68.

127 'David Friedrich Strauss', pp. 232, 234–5.

128 Frei, *Types of Christian Theology*, p. 68; see also p. 6.

129 'David Friedrich Strauss', pp. 240, 250–3.

130 'David Friedrich Strauss', pp. 239–40.

131 Frei, *Types of Christian Theology*, pp. 68, 72, 82–3. Frei thought Tillich, Fuchs, Ebeling, Käsemann and Robinson might be contemporary examples of this type, which implies at least a mitigation of the criticisms he levelled at them in the 1960s.

132 Frei, *Types of Christian Theology*, p. 4.

133 Frei, *Types of Christian Theology*, p. 38.

134 Frei, *Types of Christian Theology*, pp. 39, 45.

135 DeHart rightly observes that one effect of Frei's bringing Schleiermacher and Barth together at the centre of the typology is to contrast Barth's Type Four with Type Five (*The Trial of Witnesses*, p. 216).

136 Frei, *Types of Christian Theology*, pp. 40–5.

137 Frei, *Types of Christian Theology*, pp. 42–3, 81.

138 Frei, *Types of Christian Theology*, pp. 46, 81.

139 Frei, *Types of Christian Theology*, pp. 41–3.
140 Frei, *Types of Christian Theology*, p. 43.
141 Frei, *Types of Christian Theology*, p. 42.
142 Frei, *Types of Christian Theology*, pp. 4, 43.
143 Frei, *Types of Christian Theology*, p. 51.
144 Frei, *Types of Christian Theology*, p. 90.
145 Frei, *Types of Christian Theology*, pp. 80–81.
146 Frei, 'The "literal reading"', p. 142.
147 Frei, 'The "literal reading"', p. 142; his emphasis.
148 Frei, 'The "literal reading"', p. 142.
149 Frei, *Types of Christian Theology*, p. 86; his emphasis.
150 Frei, *Types of Christian Theology*, pp. 78–9. Bruce McCormack criticizes Frei here for flattening the dialectical character of Barth's approach to theological language, as well as ignoring how reference was a vital concern for Barth, and not acknowledging the extent to which Frei's reading of Barth is a use of him for his own purposes (*Orthodox and Modern: Studies in the Theology of Karl Barth* (Grand Rapids, MI: Baker Academic, 2008), pp. 122–7). The complaint about dialectic seems fair (Frei's dissertation is less vulnerable to it, however). The question of reference and realism is a live one in the typology, as in this passage, where Frei also acknowledges that to an extent he is making Barth suit his purposes.
151 Frei, *Types of Christian Theology*, p. 86.
152 Frei, *Types of Christian Theology*, p. 87.
153 Frei, *Types of Christian Theology*, p. 87.
154 Frei, *Types of Christian Theology*, p. 87.
155 Frei, *Types of Christian Theology*, p. 83.
156 Frei, *Types of Christian Theology*, pp. 81, 85.
157 Frei, *Types of Christian Theology*, p. 85.
158 Frei, *Types of Christian Theology*, pp. 46, 90.
159 Frei, *Types of Christian Theology*, p. 87.
160 Frei, *Types of Christian Theology*, p. 87.
161 Frei, *Types of Christian Theology*, pp. 88–9, drawing on Bruce Marshall's account of this approach in *Christology in Conflict: The Identity of a Saviour in Rahner and Barth* (Oxford: Basil Blackwell, 1987).
162 Frei, *Types of Christian Theology*, p. 84.
163 Frei, *Types of Christian Theology*, p. 81.
164 Frei, *Types of Christian Theology*, p. 79.
165 Frei, letter to Elizabeth Hilke, 5 August 1974 (YDS 76 I 2-42).
166 Frei, *Types of Christian Theology*, pp. 84–5.
167 Frei, *Types of Christian Theology*, p. 119.
168 Frei, *Types of Christian Theology*, p. 120.
169 Frei had originally planned to contextualize Strauss in this way in his essay on him. See Frei's correspondence with Philip Clayton (YDS 76 I 1-14 Clayton, John Philip Clayton, 1973–84). With reference to Frei's attention to the case of Berlin, David Ford notes Frei's increasing focus, in his later thinking, on 'the importance of the way a discipline is institutionalized' (David F. Ford, 'Hans Frei and the future of theology', *Modern Theology* 8:2 (1992), p. 206).
170 Frei, *Types of Christian Theology*, pp. 115–16.
171 Frei, *Types of Christian Theology*, pp. 95, 102.
172 Frei, *Types of Christian Theology*, p. 96. See also Frei's imagination of the

end of academic theology in the last of the Cadbury materials (*Types of Christian Theology*, p. 94).

173 Frei, *Types of Christian Theology*, p. 96.

174 Frei, *Types of Christian Theology*, p. 120.

175 Frei, *Types of Christian Theology*, p. 96.

176 Frei, *Types of Christian Theology*, p. 6.

177 Campbell, *Preaching Jesus*, pp. 63–113. On similar lines, see Hunsinger's epilogue to his 'Afterward' in Frei, *Theology and Narrative*, pp. 257–64.

178 Higton, *Christ, Providence and History*, pp. 177–213.

179 Springs, *Toward a Generous Orthodoxy*, pp. 43–62.

180 Although I think there are other important concerns driving Frei's development besides an unfolding of Wittgensteinian insights, as I argue above.

181 Frei, *Types of Christian Theology*, p. 6.

182 Frei, 'Theology and the interpretation of narrative', p. 111.

183 Frei, 'Theology and the interpretation of narrative', p. 112.

184 Frei, 'The "literal reading"', p. 143.

185 See Campbell, *Preaching Jesus*, pp. 102–3.

186 Frei described them as the typology's 'chief topical center' in his NEH grant proposal (*Types of Christian Theology*, p. 6). For a careful reading of Frei on Barth and Schleiermacher and his own placement in the typology, see DeHart, *The Trial of the Witnesses*, pp. 138–42, 211–24.

187 In Frei, *Theology and Narrative*, pp. 178–99.

188 Frei, 'Barth and Schleiermacher', p. 194.

189 As David Kamitsuka observes, Frei here valorizes fully critical reflection in theology (David Kamitsuka, *Theology and Contemporary Culture* (Cambridge: Cambridge University Press, 2000), p. 25).

190 Frei, *Types of Christian Theology*, p. 77.

191 Frei, *Types of Christian Theology*, pp. 77–8.

192 Frei, *Types of Christian Theology*, pp. 44, 90.

193 Frei, *Types of Christian Theology*, pp. 6, 90–1.

194 See Frei's letter to Comstock, 5 November 1984 (YDS 76 I 12-184).

195 As Frei indicates near the beginning of his letter to William Placher, 3 November 1986 (YDS 76 I 4-78).

196 Ford, 'On being theologically hospitable to Jesus Christ', p. 57.

197 Henry, 'Narrative theology: an Evangelical appraisal', p. 19; Frei, *Types of Christian Theology*, pp. 209–10. In this sense Frei was 'mildly anti-foundationalist' about the availability of neutral, transhistorical categories for discussing truth and reference, as he put it in a letter to Gary Comstock on 5 November 1984 (YDS 76 III 12-184).

198 Frei, 'The "literal reading"', p. 119.

199 Frei, 'The "literal reading"', p. 139.

200 Frei, 'The "literal reading"', p. 144.

201 To this extent I demur from those who align Frei's position with Type Four, for example, Higton (*Christ, Providence and History*, p. 213) and Springs ('Frei's later Christology: radiance and obscurity', *Pro Ecclesia* 24:1 (2015) p. 51), but also from Shin, for whom the later Frei seems to lean more towards Schleiermacher than Barth (*Theology and the Public*, pp. 131–3).

202 Frei, *Types of Christian Theology*, pp. 11–12; Frei, 'Theology and the interpretation of narrative', p. 97.

203 Frei, 'Theology and the interpretation of narrative', pp. 97–8.

204 Frei, *Types of Christian Theology*, pp. 12–13; Frei, 'The "literal reading"', pp. 146–7.

205 Frei, 'The "literal reading"', p. 147; Frei, *Types of Christian Theology*, pp. 11–12.

206 Frei, 'Epilogue', p. 280.

207 Frei, *Types of Christian Theology*, p. 128.

208 Frei, 'The "literal reading"', p. 143.

209 Frei, 'The "literal reading"', p. 143; his emphasis.

210 Frei, 'The "literal reading"', p. 141.

211 Frei, 'Conflicts in interpretation: resolution, armistice, or co-existence?', in *Theology and Narrative*, p. 163.

212 Letter to Placher, 3 November 1986 (YDS 76 I 4-78).

213 Letter to Comstock, 5 November 1984 (YDS 76 III 12-184).

214 Frei, 'The "literal reading"', p. 142.

215 Frei, 'The "literal reading"', p. 142.

216 Letter to Comstock, 5 November 1984; letter to Placher, 3 November 1986.

217 Frei, 'Conflicts in interpretation', pp. 163–4.

218 Hans W. Frei, 'Response to "Narrative theology: an Evangelical appraisal"', in Frei, *Theology and Narrative*, p. 209.

219 Frei, 'Response to "Narrative theology"', pp. 211–12.

220 Frei, 'Response to "Narrative theology"', p. 209, 212.

221 Frei, 'Response to "Narrative theology"', p. 212.

222 Frei, *Types of Christian Theology*, pp. 134–5.

223 Frei, *Types of Christian Theology*, pp. 143–6.

224 Letter to Placher, 3 November 1986.

225 Frei, 'Response to "Narrative theology"', p. 210.

226 I will develop this concept in the context of Frei's theology in the next chapter.

227 Frei, 'Response to "Narrative theology"', p. 210; letter to Placher, 3 November 1986.

228 Higton, *Christ, Providence and History*, p. 204.

229 William Werpehowski, 'Ad Hoc Apologetics', *Journal of Religion* 66:3 (1996), pp. 282–301. In using Werpehowski to draw out the significance of Frei's position I am following Shin, *Theology and the Public*, pp. 40–44.

230 Frei, *Types of Christian Theology*, pp. 137–43.

231 See Frei, 'The "literal reading"', pp. 139–43.

232 Frei, *Types of Christian Theology*, p. 140.

233 Frei, *Types of Christian Theology*, p. 124. This continuity is arguably more minimal than the continuity of regulative grammar that George Lindbeck ascribes to Christianity across its divisions. See G. Lindbeck, *The Nature of Doctrine: Religion and Theology in a Postliberal Age* (Louisville, KY: Westminster John Knox Press, 1984).

234 Hans W. Frei, 'The encounter of Jesus with the German academy', in Frei, *Types of Christian Theology*, p. 143.

235 Frei, *Types of Christian Theology*, p. 1.

236 Ford, 'On being theologically hospitable to Jesus Christ', p. 540.

237 Ford, 'On being theologically hospitable to Jesus Christ', p. 545.

238 See Frei, 'Theology and the interpretation of narrative', p. 105, and Frei, *Types of Christian Theology*, p. 140.

239 Frei, *Types of Christian Theology*, p. 140.

240 But see also Charles Campbell, who notes this affirmation of the 'polyphonic character of biblical interpretation in the church' in Frei's Christological essays (*Preaching Jesus*, pp. 110–11).

241 On allegorical reading of these terms, see Frei, 'The "literal reading"', pp. 121–2, and 'Conflicts in interpretation', p. 166.

242 Frei, '"Narrative" in Christian and modern reading', in Bruce Marshall (ed.), *Theology and Dialogue: Essays in Conversation with George Lindbeck* (Notre Dame, IN: University of Notre Dame Press, 1990), pp. 149–63, at p. 152.

243 See Springs, *Toward a Generous Orthodoxy*, pp. 145–8.

244 Frei, *Types of Christian Theology*, pp. 86–7.

245 Springs, *Toward a Generous Orthodoxy*, p. 164.

246 See also Springs, 'Frei's later Christology', pp. 42–5.

247 Frei, 'Response to "Evangelical theology": an Evangelical assessment', in *Theology and Narrative*', p. 208.

248 Mike Higton, 'Hans Frei', in J. Holcomb (ed.), *Christian Theologies of Scripture: A Comparative Introduction* (New York: New York University Press, 2006), p. 230.

249 William Young III, 'The identity of the literal sense: Midrash in the work of Hans Frei', *The Journal of Religion* 85:4 (2005), p. 632. Young notes that for Frei, the Jewish practice of Midrash models this hospitality to a plurality of readings.

250 See Kathryn Tanner, *Theories of Culture: A New Agenda for Theology* (Minneapolis, MN: Augsburg Fortress, 1997), pp. 38–58.

251 Tanner, *Theories of Culture*, pp. 104–19. In his book published the same year as *Theories of Culture*, Campbell independently made a very similar point, drawing on Raymond Williams (*Preaching Jesus*, pp. 80–2).

252 Tanner, *Theories of Culture*, pp. 138–43.

253 Tanner, *Theories of Culture*, pp. 72–90.

254 Tanner, *Theories of Culture*, p. 149.

255 Tanner, *Theories of Culture*, pp. 110–14, 135–7, 149–50.

256 Tanner, *Theories of Culture*, pp. 63–92.

257 Frei, 'The "literal reading"', pp. 147–8; his emphasis.

258 Springs, *Toward a Generous Orthodoxy*, pp. 146–7.

259 For a similar reading here, see Higton, *Christ Providence and History*, p. 202.

260 Hans W. Frei, *The Identity of Jesus Christ* (Philadelphia, PA: Fortress Press, 1975), p. 160.

261 Frei, *Types of Christian Theology*, p. 136; see DeHart, *The Trial of the Witnesses*, pp. 146–7.

262 Springs contrasts this single use with Frei's use of 'embrace' in *The Eclipse of Biblical Narrative*, which reflects the way his position 'permits an openness and underdetermination of the specific results' (Springs, *Toward a Generous Orthodoxy*, p. 82). His careful distinction of Frei and Lindbeck on this question in his third chapter is worth reading.

263 Frei, 'Epilogue', p. 281.

264 Young, 'The identity of the literal sense', p. 631.

265 DeHart makes a similar point against the applicability of Tanner's critique to Frei in *The Trial of Witnesses*, pp. 145–6.

266 C. Gunton, 'Types of Christian theology. By Hans W. Frei. Edited by George Hunsinger and William C. Placher, New Haven and London, Yale University Press, 1992. Pp. xi 180', *Scottish Journal of Theology* 49:2 (1996), p. 234.

267 Paul DeHart offers a similar but fuller, careful constructive development of Frei in response to a similar worry in *The Trial of the Witnesses*, pp. 251–76, which builds on what he takes to be Frei's hints of ways to take forward aspects of H. R. Niebuhr's approach to culture.

268 Hans W. Frei, 'Niebuhr's theological background', in *Faith and Ethics: The Theology of H. Richard Niebuhr*, ed. Paul Ramsey (New York: Harper & Row, 1957), pp. 59–61.

269 For a more developed account along similar lines, see Mike Higton, *The Life of Christian Doctrine* (London: T & T Clark, 2020), chapter 7, which has helped prompt these reflections.

270 Frei, 'The "literal reading"', p. 149.

271 Frei makes a similar point in one of his Princeton lectures (see *Types of Christian Theology*, pp. 123–4). His own understanding of the literal sense as a consensus mode of reading has been informed by his reading of Raphael Loewe's essay, 'The "plain" meaning of Scripture in early Jewish exegesis', in Joseph G. Weiss (ed.), *Papers of the Institute of Jewish Studies London* (Jerusalem: Magnes Press, 1964), pp. 141–85. See Frei, 'Theology and the interpretation of narrative', in *Theology and Narrative*, p. 105; Frei, *Types of Christian Theology*, p. 15. Along with Lindbeck, Frei would later be involved in conversations with the Jewish scholars Peter Ochs and Steven Fraade, comparing Frei's interpretive method with that of the rabbi and biblical scholar Moshe Greenberg (as Ochs relates in *The Return to Scripture in Judaism and Christianity: Essays in Postcritical Scriptural Interpretation* (Eugene, OR: Wipf & Stock, 2008), pp. 5–9). For an illuminating discussion of Frei's discussions of Midrash in relation to the literal sense, see Young, 'The identity of the literal sense'.

272 Frei, 'The "literal reading"', p. 149.

273 Frei, 'The "literal reading"', p. 149.

274 Frei, 'The "literal reading"', p. 149.

275 Frei, 'The "literal reading"', p. 149.

276 Young, 'The identity of the literal sense', pp. 629–30. This concern to nurture the Christian identity of Christian communities so they might contribute to western culture and its quest for justice and freedom was, as David Kamitsuka says, Frei's 'focal value' (Kamitsuka, *Theology and Contemporary Culture*, p. 18).

277 Frei, 'Epilogue', p. 280.

278 Frei, 'Epilogue', p. 280.

279 Frei, 'Epilogue', p. 280.

280 Frei, 'Epilogue', p. 280.

281 Frei, 'Epilogue', p. 281.

282 Frei, 'Epilogue', p. 281.

283 Indeed, he describes it in just these terms in his Princeton lectures; see Frei, *Types of Christian Theology*, pp. 140–43.

284 Frei, 'Epilogue', p. 281.

285 Frei, 'Epilogue', p. 281.

286 Frei, 'Epilogue', p. 281.

287 Frei, 'Epilogue', p. 281.
288 Frei, *Types of Christian Theology*, p. 134.
289 Frei, *Types of Christian Theology*, p. 134.
290 Frei, *Types of Christian Theology*, pp. 134, 136.
291 To this extent Frei adheres to what Ulrich Luz calls the predominant modern 'universal interpretation' of this passage, which identifies the least of the brethren with the poor and marginalized of the world. See Ulrich Luz, *Matthew 21–28* (Minneapolis, MN: Fortress Press, 2005), pp. 267–71. Notably, Luz thinks this reading isn't exegetically justified as Matthew's intention but is a legitimate theological way of reading the passage because it corresponds to significant aspects of the story of Jesus, facilitates a de-absolutizing of the church present in the passage and because it produces love: a hermeneutical judgement consistent with Frei's own approach (*Matthew 21–28*, pp. 283–4).
292 Frei, *Types of Christian Theology*, p. 136.
293 Frei, *Types of Christian Theology*, p. 136.
294 Frei, *Types of Christian Theology*, pp. 136–7.
295 Frei, *Types of Christian Theology*, p. 8.

6

God's Patience and the Work
of Reconciliation

We have seen that Frei's life and thought bear out the adage he frankly and fully acknowledged, that all theology is political.[1] We have traced the political orientation and implications of his theology and ethics from his early Christology essays through *The Eclipse of Biblical Narrative*, to his typological lectures and other associated writings from the last decade of his life. We have seen something of the significance and potential of his understanding of Christ's unsubstitutable and inclusive identity and how it clarifies the manner of his presence in the church and to human history in such a way as to orientate the church's service and witness, not least by the figural reading of history. We have seen how his proposed recovery of a literal reading of biblical narrative and a figural secular imagination frames an implied account of the ethics of responsibility. We have seen how Frei's typology reframes that ethics with a more subtle, complex and historical account of the essence of Christianity and a more robust account of the publicness of Christian theology. We have seen how he proposed a way of doing theology that would foster the political vocation of Christianity in post-Christian societies and a Christian liberal humanism warranted by the identity of Jesus Christ and the pattern of his presence among the marginalized and oppressed.

In this final chapter, I bring the argument of the book to a conclusion by examining several of Frei's writings from the final years of his life, which develop his thinking on political theology and ethics in ways that are coherent with and complementary to the ideas we have examined so far, but which also extend his thinking further. I make the case that his insights have a significant contribution to make to political theology and ethics. I will argue that Frei develops his ethics of responsibility by way of the theme of discipleship, the communal and individual following of Christ 'at a distance'. He characterizes that discipleship by a distinctive and valuable 'particularistic' understanding of generous, reconciliatory neighbour-love, which at the level of Christian communities is expressed in the work of costly penultimate reconciliation and the struggle for justice amid the structural divisions erected by the social sin of dominant groups. I also expound the way Frei came to frame that work of reconciliation and the element of tragedy involved in political struggle by adding to his doctrine of providence and theology of social sin an account of divine patience. I conclude by arguing that the significance of his realist, hopeful political theology can be seen first as carrying forward the appeal to providence in interpreting history found in H. Richard Niebuhr's political theology in contrast to Reinhold Niebuhr's, and second, by bringing it alongside the liberation theologies of some of his contemporaries. For while Frei lacks their contextual, theological attention to the activity and struggles of oppressed groups, his account offers an alternative way to frame divine and human action, and the hope that orientates Christian political engagement, that avoids a key tension in some liberationist accounts.

Responsibility as discipleship

Frei's implicit advocacy, in *The Eclipse of Biblical Narrative*, of an ethics of responsibility coheres with and illumines the way he understands the Christian life in terms of discipleship in both his earlier Christological writings and in the Christological section of his Princeton lecture on 'The encounter of Jesus with the German academy'. In both texts, discipleship in conformity to Christ is the form taken by responsibility to God's command in Christ. Neighbour-love, characterized by a mutuality of service and reciprocity and a reconciliatory, non-dominating delight in the other, is the character of that conformity.

In his account of the mystery of the presence of Jesus Christ, reproduced in *The Identity of Jesus Christ*, Frei describes the church not only as the communal form of his indirect presence but also as a 'collective disciple', following its Lord at a distance.[2] The collective life of Christian communities, therefore, is to be one of practical obedience in conformity to the one whose identity, given in the Gospels, makes him its living Lord. By characterizing the church as following Christ 'at a distance', it marks an abiding and fundamental distinction between the pattern of that conformity and his unrepeatable identity, which unites unrepeatable singularity and universal saving significance. The church as disciple follows at a distance the 'pattern of exchange', not repeating his vicarious historical human destiny and inseparability from God's identity and presence but serving its human neighbour, the world at large, while also being open to it in gratitude and accepting of the enrichment it brings, 'without forsaking its own mission and testimony'.[3]

This non-triumphalist ecclesiology combines the imperative of faith-fulness to the church's distinct testimony to God in Christ with both service of, and receptive, grateful openness to, the world, as we saw in Chapter 3. That posture reflects the logic of Christ's presence within and through the church but also to human history, by commending the holding of the integrity of word and sacrament together with 'passion-ate commitment to the fulfillment of human hopes and aspirations in history'.[4] This passionate concern, we may infer, belongs to the complete commitment characterized by grateful love of God and neighbour that went inseparably, Frei thought, with faith and trust in Christ.[5] There is a clear political dimension to this passionate commitment, whose proper orientation as discipleship depends on its articulation with commitment to the verbal and bodily forms of testimony and bases for Christ's pres-ence in the church. The political dimension of that commitment and its Christological orientation are indicated when Frei implies that it involves the risks of nonconformity in solidarity with the rejected, because Christ made his lot with them.[6]

In the context of that ecclesiology, Frei offers a very similar picture of individual discipleship in the sermon attached to the essay on Christ's presence as the epilogue to *The Identity of Jesus Christ*.[7] There he argues that the significance of the story of Jesus Christ to the believer does not depend on its capacity to be repeated in their imagination and sensibil-ity, collapsing the temporal gap between them and the events of his life. Rather, it becomes the truth for them by their 'hammering out a shape of life patterned after its own shape'.[8] They do not repeat those events literally, but their lives 'reflect the story as in a glass darkly'; it is mean-ingful for them as its shape is 'mirrored in the shape of our lives'. Here the Pauline trope from 1 Corinthians 13.12 complements the metaphor of following at a distance, amplifying the element of similarity of form or pattern of life and carrying forward the qualifying dissimilarity, albeit without the temporal connotations of following in another's footsteps.[9]

In the epilogue to *The Identity of Jesus Christ*, Frei quotes the final paragraph of Albert Schweitzer's *The Quest of the Historical Jesus* to develop his point about discipleship and the meaningfulness of the Easter story. Here Schweitzer speak of Jesus as the One unknown who calls us now as once he called the fishermen to be his disciples of old by the lakeside. He 'speaks to us the same word: "Follow thou me!" and sets us to the tasks which He has to fulfil for our own time'.[10] He commands, says Schweitzer, and reveals himself in the toils, conflict and sufferings of those who obey him and accompany him: they will learn who he is in their own experience, 'as an ineffable mystery'.[11] By quoting Schweitzer approvingly, in this way, Frei does not mean here to take back what he had argued about the way in which Christ's identity is publicly set forth in the narrative patterns by which the Gospels identify him. Rather, he underscores the point that the meaningfulness of the story for anyone is discovered in the experience of obeying Christ's command. It is found in discipleship. Romans 6.4, 12–14 indicates that the 'embodiment of the Easter story's pattern in our lives means ... a new way of governing our bodies'.[12] The meaningfulness of the story is experienced as we let it shape the way we live (our ethos): 'To know this story [in this sense] is to adopt a way of life consequent upon hearing it.'[13] Elsewhere, Frei writes of the Christian life as a pilgrimage, involving a partial figural re-presentation of Christ in quest of his presence, which brings out two further dimensions to his account.[14] First, it introduces the note of the disciple's desire for the fuller presence of the indirectly present Lord to the character of their obedience. Second, it integrates his understanding of discipleship and responsibility into his Christocentric figural imagination. Disciples, in patterning their lives after Christ, become figures of him and so (if we read this in the light of Frei's account of figuration) at once more fully themselves and more fully intelligible in that relation. For Frei, this qualified patterning after, or mirroring in response to, Christ's command to follow – this partial, figural re-presenting of Christ in quest of his presence – is the basic grammar of Christian ethics.

Frei also notes that Schweitzer says that Christ comes to us 'as One unknown, without a name'.[15] Christ does so because, Frei argues (with reference to Romans 6.10), he lives to God, not to time or its overcoming, or by his relation to us. Frei's point again is about the abiding distinction, the distance and unlikeness between Christ and our lives patterned after him, which mean that they can never be 'the final clue to his identity'.[16] But we may also note the clear implication that patterning our lives, governing our bodies, after Christ's identity, is a response to the present command of the living Christ to follow him, the command of one who comes to us (and, presumably, keeps coming and commanding). Here we find the clear echoes of Barth's account of responsibility in Frei's account of the nature of discipleship and continuity between the implied ethics of responsibility in this essay and in *The Eclipse of Biblical Narrative*.[17] Indeed, it gives sharper focus to Frei's implied account there of the intelligibility of the divine command in any given situation.

This command and this responsible discipleship is, presumably, what Frei had in mind when he remarked, in the essay on the mystery of Christ's presence, that 'the New Testament will ask just this of all men: To identify themselves by relation ... to Jesus of Nazareth, who has identified himself with them and for them.'[18] It is a demand made by who Christ is for us and on the basis of his finished work, his justifying grace.

240

As Frei notes in his final Princeton lecture, Schweitzer's imperious Christ is the same as Karl Barth's Judge who is judged in our place, the man who permits us, his poor brothers and sisters, to identify ourselves with him, though we are anything but identical with him, because he identifies himself with us, in the words of Romans 5.8 (KJV): 'while we were yet sinners, Christ died for us.'[19]

Living out this faithful, hopeful and loving responsibility is likewise dependent on God's Spirit. Frei was fully aware that Christian disciples are justified sinners. Believers, he notes, tend to seek refuge from the demands and risks of love of neighbour in response to Christ in uneasy, defensive, dogmatic assertions and from the demands of faith in appropriating the causes of the disinherited for themselves, ironically making that commitment forced or half-hearted.[20] The unity of faith and love in response to Christ, he affirmed, is a work of the Spirit. For Frei, this work is one of personal liberation from sin. The triune God's transforming shaping of life consequent on the full, completed redemptive work of Christ, he wrote in an exposition of the fifth Article of Religion, 'Of the Holy Ghost', is fittingly appropriated to the Holy Spirit because the Spirit, God's living, sustaining presence to his pilgrim people, 'is both spontaneous, presently living freedom in himself and moves us also in the same way; he is God as our life and liberty (John 3:8; 6:63; 1 Cor. 2:4; 2 Cor. 3:17)'.[21] The turn from sin understood, as 'self-enclosed, enslaving sloth and arrogance', towards God and neighbour within the Christian life, this transformation and reversal of dispositions, 'is ... the gift of liberty in and by God the Spirit'.[22]

Generous, non-dominating love of neighbour

As we have seen, Frei cites the same passage from Schweitzer again in his final Princeton lecture in *Types of Christian Theology*. There he also develops his account of neighbour-love in explicating Christ's compassionate humanity as the complement to his compelling call to demanding discipleship. Here we need to return to Frei's emphasis on Christ's self-identification with and contemporary incognito presence among 'the poor, the undeserving, the spiritual and economic underclass' in the context of the saying in Matthew 25.40, that what his disciples do to the least of his brothers and sisters, they do to him.[23] The clear implication, clearer still in the light of what we have seen him say about neighbour-love and the risks of nonconformity in solidarity with the rejected, is that Frei takes Christ's identification with the poor to require believers to follow him in active solidarity with marginalized and disadvantaged people and to seek his presence among them. Indeed, drawing on his own experience of Nazi oppression, Frei commended just such a stance towards any victimized groups in his Holocaust testimony in 1980.[24] In this respect, Frei is quite close to Gustavo Gutiérrez's sketch of a 'theology of the neighbour', also based on Matthew 25, in his *A Theology of Liberation*.[25]

Frei identifies a second aspect of Christ's compassion, however, and develops further insights about love of neighbour, through a remarkable exegesis of Jesus' saying from the Sermon on the Mount counselling his hearers to be reconciled to their brother or sister before offering their gift at the alter (Matt. 5.24). The text, Frei explains, recommends reconciliation 'as a form of celebrating co-humanity' or loving one's neighbour as oneself.[26] The basic orientation of reconciliation is the love of neighbour.[27] Frei thus interprets this reconciliation as much more than patching up a quarrel. It is the renewed pursuit of neighbour-love.

In a way, this should not surprise us. Frei's remarks about neighbour-love are made in the context of acknowledging Christ's identity, which includes his saving work and its reconciliatory aspect, as the enactment of love for humanity. Frei derives his account of Christ's identity from his reading of the way it is rendered by the structure of the Gospel narratives. What this exegetical nugget shows is that Frei reads Jesus' teaching, much as he proposed doing with Jesus' parables, in the light of the identity of the teacher as given in the New Testament stories about him.

What is also interesting about Frei's exegesis here is his understanding of what reconciliatory neighbour-love involves: the service of Christ *in the enjoyment of one's neighbour*, 'in her and his peculiar character, religion, lifestyle, and work – the enjoyment of just the way she or he is'.[28] In this way, 'ordinary kindness and natural gentleness' become forms taken by the extraordinary extravagance of divine love.[29] This is a remarkable and unusual way of parsing neighbour-love in Christian tradition. There are clear echoes – and probable influence – in H. Richard Niebuhr's treatment of neighbour-love, though Frei brings out the coherence with his own Christology more fully and deeply than does Niebuhr.[30] There is a fainter echo in the emphasis on particularity in Karl Barth's treatments of neighbour-love, though Barth seems to lack these notes of ordinary, gentle kindness and rejoicing in the neighbour.[31] But there is more of a contrast with some of Frei's other contemporaries who espouse what Outka calls 'the principle of equal regard', whereby one's attitudes towards others should not be determined by the disparities between them in talent, achievement, attractiveness or social rank.[32]

Rudolf Bultmann had argued that the neighbour-love Christ commands is defined not relative to some quality in the other but by loving obedience towards the God who first loved us in Christ, in the renunci-ation of one's own claims for the good of another.[33] This is the neighbour whom love discloses to us in a concrete situation and whose need is evi-dent to anyone who loves themselves. Here the demand of the moment is the demand of God. Indeed, for Bultmann, neighbour-love is the content of radical obedience to God's eschatological demand.[34]

Frei's friend Paul Ramsay argued along similar lines that the parable of the good Samaritan demands a shift away from asking as to the qualifi-cations that allow us to identify the neighbour whom we are commanded to love, to the requirement of neighbourly love towards others.[35] People are not to be loved as neighbours on account of some hidden worthiness, such as the inherent value of human personality (so that love might be measured to the proportion of worthiness discovered in another). Rather, neighbour-love loves another person for their own sake, and discovers the neighbour in every human being, rather than the humanity in their neighbour. Frei, I suggest, is saying something a little similar but inten-sifying it and adding the note of enjoyment, which Ramsay, I suspect, would think quite superfluous. For him, neighbour-love is disinterested in view of the Messianic judgement of the coming kingdom of God, which makes prudential calculation obsolete.[36] For him, as for Bultmann, it is about the neighbour's *needs*.[37] For Frei, however, it is really about the neighbour themselves, even prior to any needs they might have – for their own sake in a more radical sense – and that means the neighbour in their particular identity, their characteristic dispositions and activities.

Frei, Bultmann and Ramsey all take Christocentric approaches to Christian ethics. The difference in Frei's approach to neighbour-love has to do with the way he understands the logic of Christ's teaching in the light of his identity. Earlier in part of the lecture, Frei had returned to the theme from his earlier Christological essays of the universal vicarious inclusivity of Christ's unsubstitutable identity:

> Jesus is a very specific person as he emerges from the [Gospels'] frag-mentary and diverse fourfold description in which he is rendered for us, yet in that variety there is also the claim of unity which allows people of great diversity access to him, and him access to them.[38]

In those portraits, Jesus is himself and no one else, a distinct, recognizable individual, yet their portrayal of his specificity moves, by the combination in him of fragmentary, even contradictory, contrasts, towards his repre-sentative universality as this specific individual, encompassing 'Jew and Greek, bond and free, male and female … in the universality of this spe-cific person', this man, alone of all men or women.[39] It is this inclusion of all humanity in all their variety in the textual Jesus that explains, Frei now adds, the phenomenon of disciples who practise this reconciling neighbour-love, taking 'a simple pleasure in ... all sorts and conditions of them, the dispossessed and the disadvantaged, but not only them – for their own sake and do so not compulsively ... but with simple and delighted generosity'.[40]

The breadth of that inclusivity meets an objection Bultmann and Ramsey might make. For if neighbour-love for the sake of the neighbour is a delight in the neighbour's characteristic dispositions and activities, then is it not dependent on the inclinations and dispositions of the one who loves? And in that case, does it not return in the end to seeking some qualifying quality in the neighbour or some way in which they meet my needs? To press the point further on Ramsey's terms, how can this approach meet the test Jesus sets for disinterested neighbour-love, namely, love of enemy, from whom one can expect no good in return, only hostility?[41]

Frei, however, interprets neighbour-love to require taking delight in all sorts and conditions of people. In other words, it does not begin with any attractive qualities of the neighbour; it begins with each neighbour and attends to them 'with simple and delighted generosity'.[42] There is a basic gratuity to it, rooted in the gracious, compassionate inclusivity of Christ's identification with all human beings. Although he does not explicitly mention love of enemies, it is clearly in view where Frei is exegeting a passage about reconciliation in the context of divine–human reconciliation in Christ. On this approach, neighbour-love is not partial – it is disinterested in that sense – but it is also not indifferent. Frei's characterization of it as generous indicates that he is not proposing that neighbour-love delights in the neighbour's sins. It clearly includes marginalized and oppressed neighbours but does not propose delighting in or romanticizing their oppression or marginalization and it must mean learning to perceive and value them in terms other than those under which they are marginalized or oppressed.

Such love for neighbour, for themselves, not their attributes, capacities or even their needs, is non-dominating. It is a 'generous unobsessive love of the neighbor', that does not hound them with Christ's image, Frei adds, which marks the line in Christianity between devotion and fanatical imperialism in religious service.[43] Rather than being based in another's need, as if that were their identity – so emphasizing any differential of power in the constitution of the relationship – this generous, delighting love is the ground for what Frei elsewhere describes as 'a quiet nonoppressive dedication to the good of other human beings for their own sake under God'.[44] Its generosity has to do in part with relinquishing the desire to determine who they are ('unobsessive', 'nonoppressive'), to be their judge, to fix the terms on which, or the extent to which, we will value their humanity. It does not dominate because it is genuinely about the neighbour themselves, in their particularity.

It is also notable that Frei's account of neighbour-love, like his account of discipleship in general, does not seem to follow the trait of mainstream, mid-century (male, white) Protestant ethicists, identified by their feminist critics in Frei's time, of defining neighbour-love in terms of self-sacrifice.[45] For this norm, they argue, responds to a typically male sin of pride in response to male experiences of anxiety. When enjoined as a norm of love for everyone, it tends to reinforce the typical sins of women in those structures of 'destructive self-abnegation'.[46] Frei's emphasis on its non-dominating character could certainly imply, for those formed by social structures and cultures that assign them greater power into dominating habits of relation with others, a kind of mortification of a kind of sin, a kind of cross-bearing in that Pauline sense. He also implies clearly that solidarity with the marginalized, after the pattern of Christ's identity, will be costly, implying that love may require self-sacrifice. But he does not make self-sacrifice the defining norm of love. Indeed, in its non-dominating character, its concern for reconciliation and the inclusivity of its call for the celebration of the full humanity of the neighbour in their particularity, Frei's account seems open to the call in feminist theological work on love contemporary with Frei for full mutuality and justice (respecting the full personhood of the neighbour and what they need to live as full persons) in interpersonal relationships.[47] Nevertheless, Frei's account is not fully worked out and does not consider what generous neighbour-love, as characterizing responsibility, would look like in a variety of situations and relationships, especially for those more vulnerable in relationships of unequal power.[48] We should not expect too much of a brief passage in a lecture on the history of Christology, but this limitation flags up a more generic issue about how far Frei's approach to theology and ethics is ready to take account of the socially constructed experience of people in given situations.[49] It does not exclude them – indeed, his account of figural reading and responsibility seems to promise to include them – but there is a question here about the posture of readiness to inquire about such experiences, without returning to the apologetic methodology of Frei's post-liberal forebears.

Group sin, the Spirit and the work of reconciliation

Frei's account of neighbour-love is framed in terms of reconciliation, as we have seen. It assumes that we are basically alienated from our neighbours and that neighbour-love is a reconciling love framed and normed by the reconciling work of Jesus Christ in his life, death and resurrection. For the same reason, Frei also tends to emphasize reconciliation in the ministry of the church, only here with a recognition that human beings are alienated from one another also by the assertion of group interests and superiority and by structures of exploitation and oppression in society. He indicates this role and its rationale in two of his later pieces on the Articles of Religion, specifically 'On the resurrection' and 'Of the Holy Ghost', which can be usefully read alongside another passage in his Princeton lectures, which, like them, were written in 1987.[50]

In 'On the resurrection', Frei concludes his exposition with an interpretation of the Article's reference to the ascension of Christ. He argues that the ascension is best understood in terms of the abiding solidarity of Christ 'in his eternal rule' with human beings, such that we are judged by our Saviour.[51] Thus our comfort is that 'our common Judge is no ruthless stranger appearing suddenly out of an eternal nowhere but the one who bore the universal burden on our behalf, both when we were victimized and when we were victimizers'.[52] Frei follows this emphasis on the assuring universal breadth of Christ's saving work, encompassing the oppressed and their oppressors, by contrasting it with the claims to moral superiority of individuals and groups to justify their pursuit of their self-interest: 'Compared to that universal Judge and the scope and depth of his juridical work, how feeble is the pretense to righteousness, and how hypocritical the pride of individuals, nations, races, classes, interest groups and the like.'[53] The implication of the universality of Christ's saving work is that no group can sustain such a claim to superiority. What Frei's remark does not consider, however, is the formation and invocation of group identity in resistance to oppression and its effects, like the effects of Nazi anti-Semitic propaganda and oppression, which Frei himself felt as a Jewish youth in Berlin. Frei's endorsement, examined in Chapter 3, of Barth's celebration of black self-consciousness in the 1960s, as a figure of Christ as incarnate reconciliation and the fulfilment of human being, gives us grounds to think there is room in his thought for such recognizing and affirming of such group identities, provided they do not in turn claim superiority over others in the furtherance of self-interest.[54]

Frei's reference to the sinful, hypocritical pride of national, class and racial groups seems a clear echo of Reinhold Niebuhr's account in *Moral*

Man and Immoral Society of the imperialistic tendency of group egoism as a prevailing factor in society and international relations, and his amplification of this account in terms of group pride in *The Nature and Destiny of Man*.[55] Frei appears to invoke Niebuhr's idea that groups tend to make themselves the centre of existence for their members and subordinate others' lives to their interests, leading to conflicts for resources whereby one group may achieve dominance through coercion, centralizing power, augmenting inequality, evoking social conflict and the formation of distinct classes and racial groups. Yet in keeping with his view of human beings in other works, he does not ever appeal to Niebuhr's underlying anthropology of the self-conscious self's aggravation of selfish impulses in protest against finitude, preferring instead to picture sin, with echoes of Luther, as the inward turn of the self, as we have seen above.

In Frei's second Princeton lecture, he shows a further way in which reflection on the identity and work of Jesus Christ leads – and has led – to the rejection of unequal, oppressive and exploitative arrangements of labour, life and Christian ministry. In context, Frei is arguing that the professionalization of theology is a contingent feature of the practice and institutionalization of teaching in the Christian tradition. For traditions change, and 'social patterns that religions find peripheral or even compatible in interaction with the surrounding social world in past eras, they later reject as going against the grain of the tradition under changed circumstances.'[56] Frei follows this remark with several examples relevant to our topic here, indicating why they came to be thought incompatible with the Christological grain of the tradition:

> Slavery, the ordination of women, the institutional rigidification of the ownership-wage earner structure of industrial and postindustrial capitalism become, each in its day, issues to confront the ongoing tradition of the appropriate service of a Lord who would be a servant, who is equal and not superior to the least of his brothers and sisters, and in whom – so it was recognized early on by at least some of his followers – there can be neither East nor West, slave nor free, male nor female.[57]

The Christian tradition is one of serving Christ, 'the Lord who would be a servant', and its ongoing problematic is about the appropriateness of its service to this Lord, given the pattern of his service, as one 'who is equal and not superior to the least of his brothers and sisters' in his kenotic identification and solidarity with them.[58] That Christ's inclusively vicarious, solidaristic identity entailed, for his followers, the inappropriateness of certain social patterns is a recognition, expressed in the Pauline formula in Galatians 3.27–28, that for those baptized into Christ and identified with him, there is no longer Jew or Greek, slave or free, male or female. At different times, then, Christians have come to the recognition that slavery, the exclusion of women from ordained ministry, the exploitation of workers by the owners of companies in capitalism, the division of the world into East and West (Frei was writing in the closing years of the Cold War) are inappropriate to the service of Christ, at odds with the pattern of his service that his disciples are called to follow. It is clear, in context, that Frei affirms those judgements and this reasoning from Christ's identity to the recognition and rejection of unjust social structures, inside and outside the church. It is also clear that he thought that such recognitions occur and such rejections become imperative for churches depending on the circumstances in which Christians find themselves carrying on their tradition of service to Christ. The relationship of Christian communities to their social, cultural, economic and political contexts does not change the validity of the recognition but it does, he implies, seem to make a big difference to their capacity to see the inappropriateness. Perhaps we might see the incapacity and awakening of some Christian communities to these recognitions, and the cost of the conflicts they endure, as part of the mysterious combination of judgement of societies and their dominant groups for the oppression of human beings, the partial redemption of oppressed groups and the partial reconciliation between oppressor and oppressed (amid that redemption), which sometimes become apparent as figures of Christ's providential presence.

Frei introduces the notion of Christian communities as communities of reconciliation in his late essay on Article Five of the Articles of Religion of the Anglican tradition. Towards the end of the piece, he discusses the distinctive fruit of the Spirit, the indivisibility of the external works of the Trinity and the special appropriation to the Spirit of being 'God's living and sustaining presence to his people as they make their way through the world in living testimony to God's grace and goodness'.[59] The Spirit, he continues, is at once 'presently living freedom himself and moves us also in the same way: he is God as our life and liberty (John 3:8; 6:63; 1 Cor. 2:4; 2 Cor. 3:17)'.[60] Thus the Christian life is 'the gift of liberty in and by God the Spirit'.[61] This gift of liberty shows itself in the love of neighbour we have been examining. It is why Christian people, in all their varieties, evince 'a quiet and nonoppressive dedication to the good of other human beings for their own sake under God'.[62] However, he adds, 'the more orthodox, Trinitarian Christian communions have not often faced up to the fact that liberty in the Spirit also has a communal shape, both within the church and also in the Christian community's work in the world.'[63] It has a communal shape because, and to the extent that, the liberating Spirit binds it together – liberating its members, we may infer, by the 'turn from self-enclosedness toward God and neighbor' that Frei describes just above as the Spirit's work in the Christian life.[64]

This liberation to unity has a missional and political significance for the church's work in the world. The Christian community has been put on earth 'to exercise the painful, glorious work of reconciliation across the terrifying barriers erected all across our communal existences in this world'.[65] To be the community bound together by the liberating Spirit is, first, 'to embody and exhibit the Spirit in its own joint life', but just as much 'to be a community which lives in and works with the faith that God is the God of but also *beyond* all nations, creeds, races, classes and interest groups.'[66] 'It is to live in the hope that Christians are freed to be active in the often apparently (but not truly) hopeless task of reconciliation across these barriers.'[67] The Spirit's liberating work, he argues, not only frees Christians to be bound together, to exhibit to the world that unity as (we may infer) their testimony to God's goodness. It also frees them for their office of reconciliation in the world. Against the way their membership of other groups forms their dispositions, even towards their enemies, they are liberated from such partiality for a 'far wider' compassion, consistent with their faith in God's transcendence of all groups and communities.[68] They are freed to do the work for reconciliation and mutual understanding across terrifying barriers and enmities between nations, religions, racial groups, classes and other groups with particular interests.[69] At the same time, as Christians are freed from partiality to their own interests, they are also lifted to a compassion that is especially for 'those who have never met with justice', consistent with Christ's especial identification and solidarity with the marginalized.[70]

This remarkable statement, the culmination to Frei's fullest articulation of his pneumatology, contrasts with the emphasis of other post-liberal accounts of the church's work in the world. For Stanley Hauerwas, most notably, the recovery of the properly story-formed, ecclesial setting for Christian ethics does not necessarily mean withdrawal from society, but it does mean that the church's main political contribution is its own life, displaying to the world what it is not, 'a place where God is forming a family out of strangers'.[71] It is to be a contradictory and promissory sign by its ethos, a colony witnessing to the strange land in which it lives by the public form of its life, a foretaste of God's kingdom, and just so a social ethic.[72] That is its task, not to make the world more peaceable or just.[73] Frei's pneumatology implicitly refuses that disjunction. For Frei, the logic of the Spirit's identity as it runs through the Spirit's work in the church, in accord with the logic of Christ's identity, means that the church's very distinctiveness goes together with a work of social reconciliation that is attuned and attentive to victims of injustice.

Cheap and costly reconciliation

Any advocacy of reconciliation in society as a central vocation for the church invites scrutiny, especially in contexts where reconciliation has been used to avoid addressing harm and injustice. In *God of the Oppressed*, first published in 1975, James Cone rejected white and African American theologians' demands that he temper his liberationism with a stronger note of reconciliation by calling for white, black and other Americans to work together. These demands amounted, he argued, to asking black people to be nice to white people while enduring humiliation from them.[74] He interpreted biblical reconciliation as the freedom and life that follow God's liberating action overcoming oppressive powers.[75] Appropriating God's reconciling liberation in the United States meant black people refusing what contradicts that freedom: resisting white people dictating the terms of reconciliation; participating in God's liberatory action to change social structures to eradicate differences between rich and poor, oppressor and oppressed; and fighting the power of the oppressor.[76] For white people, he added, reconciliation must be costly. It means a radical repentance, a kind of death to whiteness and rebirth into the struggle for the liberation of the oppressed, a conversion whose authenticity the black community must adjudicate.[77] There could be no cheap reconciliation of fellowship and cooperation with white people on lesser terms, Cone argued, for such reconciliation only undermines the struggle. Because white people think they know what is best for black people and their struggle, black people must develop strategies that do not depend on their goodwill.

More recently, Jennifer Harvey has critiqued what she calls the 'reconciliation paradigm' in the context of racial relationships in the USA, an attempt to challenge white supremacy by emphasizing the need to honour our common humanity more deeply through pursuing deep, mutual togetherness across divisions.[78] The paradigm fails, she argues, because it ignores the reality of racial relationships. What is needed is a reparations paradigm that begins by acknowledging the deep alienation in those relationships of oppressor and oppressed, in the specific structural forms it takes, in order to repair those social structures and offer concrete redress for the harms they do, even if they can only ever be partial.[79] It is an approach that requires repentance of white people in this way, actively opposing white supremacist structures and confronting their own place in them, their whiteness.

Frei's depiction of the church's work of reconciliation in 'Of the Holy Ghost' could be recruited to the 'reconciliation paradigm' Harvey critiques and in service of the 'cheap reconciliation' pattern of cooperation on the terms of the oppressor that Cone rejects. In that short piece he does not attempt the kind of development and qualification of the meaning of reconciliation needed to minimize that vulnerability and direct it more clearly and productively in a more reparative direction. Nevertheless, there are reasons from the analysis of this and earlier chapters to think that a 'cheap reconciliation' reading of Frei would not do justice to the spirit of his thought. We have seen that Frei accentuates Christ's identification and solidarity with the marginalized and oppressed, and the notes of liberation in some of his Christological passages. We have also seen that for him living out the Christian tradition in accordance with Christ's identity means rejecting unequal and oppressive social structures. His doctrine of providence sees figural traces of Christ's presence in historical events whereby partial redemption, as well as reconciliation and resurrection, are achieved, and one can read his own participation in the struggle to desegregate suburban schools in Connecticut – a struggle against a structural form of white supremacy – in that light. Finally, we may note that in 'Of the Holy Ghost' he considered the work of reconciliation to be painful and one that requires the Spirit's liberation from partiality, as well as showing particular compassion to victims of injustice. That seems a position which might be, at the least, very receptive to a call for costly reconciliation by way of repentance and reparation on the part of those complicit in oppressive structures.

Hope, tragedy and God's patience

In 'Of the Holy Ghost', then, Frei urged the church's work of reconciliation, for which it is liberated by the Spirit, with especial compassion for victims of injustice. As we have seen, he considered this task apparently, but not truly, hopeless. His account of providence and the figural reading of history in his essay on the mystery of the presence of Jesus Christ, examined in Chapter 3, helps us to see how it might not be hopeless for him. As I have shown, Frei proposes that, in the light of the pattern of exchange in the Gospel narratives about Jesus Christ, it is possible dimly to discern figures in history (especially political history) in which the eschatological redemption, reconciliation and resurrection of all things is partially, imperfectly, anticipated. Such figural reading and its eschatological reference, I have argued, offers an ultimately hopeful as well as realistic orientation to the life of discipleship, and would do so in particular to the work of reconciliation. But it would also give some hope for that work in the present and the long-term future before the culmination of the eschaton. Indeed, it would do so even in the face of appearances to the contrary. For, as Frei's examples of the US Civil War and Civil Rights movement suggest, through the mysterious ordering in Christ of contingent and complex historical forces and agencies, long-sought but apparently unlikely and surprising developments may come about that may be read as partial, imperfect figures of redemption, liberation and reconciliation, which give hope of further progress even against the run of events and the apparent weight of forces and probabilities.

We can further this analysis of Frei's thinking about the church's role in politics and its work of reconciliation, hope and realism, by examining two sets of texts composed in the final years of his life, neither published in his lifetime: notes, drafts and a paper delivered at a conference celebrating the work of Jürgen Moltmann and Elisabeth Moltmann-Wendel in 1986; and a paper written for a conference in September 1988 in honour of Frei's doctoral supervisor, H. Richard Niebuhr.[80]

Frei's papers for the Moltmann conference have been paid very little attention in the literature on Frei's thought.[81] In them, Frei develops a view of Christian political responsibility grounded in an account of divine patience that is consistent with and complementary to his account of providence, and which on that basis develops and elaborates his ethics of social reconciliation. Frei drafted a paper in advance but rewrote it after having heard the other papers at the conference, summarizing the original content. The two versions are largely congruent and complementary. Frei's delivered paper expresses his dislike of the draft, however, so I will follow him in drawing on the draft in the light of the delivered version.

In his delivered paper, Frei tried to weave together comments on Moltmann's trinitarian theology and on some of the conference papers. What linked them all, he thought, was the theme of the theology of history and the problem of divine freedom and power. Moltmann's trinitarian theology, Frei proposed, characterized the movement of history as something like what he called 'a dialectic of the Spirit'.[82] For Moltmann, he suggested, the history of the world, characterized by suffering, is transformed and becomes one with the history of God by a dialectical motion whose ground and unity is the Spirit. The Spirit is the unity of Father and Son in their mutual surrender and their respective sufferings in the event of the crucifixion. And the Spirit is the one who is their unity, who eschatologically transforms present and historical suffering from surrender to death to surrender to life. He had found the conference's talk of the triumph of love 'the product of a cheerful liberationist confidence' pervasive in their conversations.[83] The conference papers were upbeat about the sureness of God's promises as grounds for optimism and the belief 'that liberation is not so much a miracle but a steady motion toward the kingdom – which will nonetheless come in as a miracle'.[84]

Frei was bothered by the familiar danger he saw, in both Moltmann's thought and the conference papers, of confusing the power and work of the Spirit in history with fate and chance, a danger to which Frei's own proclivities towards fatalism must have alerted him. Hegel exemplified this danger, he thought. Hegel offered the most eloquent articulation of the cosmic triumph of the spirit of love, but his Spirit of Love 'was exactly equivalent to fate ... an impersonal relational necessity that pervades the universe', who loves out of necessity, not freedom.[85] In response to that kind of view of the Spirit and history, Frei urged both that its optimism is misplaced, that in the Christian imagination the Spirit's love must be more powerful – more substantially powerful – than fate, and hence that the future the Spirit brings about, the triumph of love, must really be a miracle 'that now we see in a glass darkly'.[86] A theology of liberation, he suggested, needs something like the tragic and ironic element in human history insisted upon by the ultimately optimistic Puritan covenant theology. Such a vision was exemplified by Lincoln's Second Inaugural address and its sober optimism about the undefeatable purposes of God being achieved through a puzzling, tragic course of events.

This argument recalls Frei's account of the possibility of discerning, by the parable of the pattern of exchange, and in a glass, darkly, figures of ultimate reconciliation and redemption in certain historical events. Here, as there, he evoked the 'painful images of blood sacrifice and blood reconciliation and blood guilt', unpleasant images that he did not want to push very far and yet which seemed part of a theology that combines ultimate optimism and a strong insistence on tragedy and irony in human history (hence Frei's reference to Reinhold Niebuhr in his title).[87] The sense in this text, even more strongly than in the earlier one, is that, in the present, in history, God works towards the ultimate triumph of love through circumstances shaped by human evil, by the conflicts arising from the presence of sin, even in the redeemed people of God, such that some measure of reconciliation often does not come about apart from the spilling of blood, giving rise to a 'mysterious, almost frightening sense of tragic reconciliation', which here, as before, he connected with the conflict in Vietnam.[88] For this reason, political strategy is also touched by 'a sense of tragedy' whereby 'all moves toward liberation' and for the greater good are also provisional, pragmatic choices for lesser evils.[89]

It is not difficult to discern an implied doctrine of providence behind these remarks, one that is filled out by that earlier essay on the mystery of Christ's presence and the piece on history and salvation history, examined above. But Frei also introduces a new element to his theology in his delivered paper for the Moltmann conference and the paper he prepared: a notion, inspired by a passage in Moltmann's *God in Creation*, of the patience of God, which expressed what he was trying to say about the power of divine love working through a history with a strong sense of tragedy.

In the paper he prepared for the conference, Frei drew from Moltmann's claim in *God in Creation* that life systems become more resilient, richer and flexible the more they are able to bear strain, absorb hostile impulses and assimilate them productively without destroying the enemy or itself, and hence that we should see '"God's inexhaustible patience and his active capacity for suffering as the root of his creative action in history"'.[90] This characterization of God as patient, Frei observes, contrasts with Moltmann's typical emphasis on divine suffering, abandonment and self-emptying. For patience speaks of something more than voluntary self-sacrificial suffering at another's hands: 'it implies constancy, or vital and unbroken reserves of strength and steadiness, not weakness, employed in behalf and for the sake of others in the face of their waywardness.'[91] We call someone patient, Frei claimed, because they are themselves 'in undisputed self-application out of self-disciplined freedom and strength'.[92] According to Moltmann's usage in this passage, Frei also noted, the patient person 'acts in selfless devotion out of an abundance to be shared, not out of craving or need'.[93] Frei found support for ascribing patience to God as one of the divine perfections in Paul's letters but especially in Nehemiah 9.17, where God is praised for his patience arising from his strength, as a God '"ready to forgive, gracious and merciful, slow to anger and abounding in steadfast love"'.[94]

Frei notes how, in *God in Creation*, Moltmann quickly balances reference to divine patience with talk of divine suffering, wary, perhaps, of the dangers of indiscriminately recommending patience as a virtue for all people in all circumstances. But once placed in balance with divine patience, divine suffering takes on a different meaning compared with Moltmann's theology elsewhere, Frei thought. For 'the suffering that goes with patience hints at the richness of a god [*sic*] whose deity is the perfection of his or her unicity through the amplitude of each of his attributes'.[95] God's love and grace in creation, redemption and eschatological salvation comes naturally to God for whom relatedness is essential, as triune. So abundantly rich is the unity of divine love as Creator, Redeemer and Sanctifier, Frei suggests, that God can share the suffering of God's creatures. At any rate, following the rule of the doctrine of the Trinity, 'God's suffering love is to be understood both in the light of the patience of his abiding and undisrupted rulership and grace, and in his willingness in his Son to risk abandonment by undertaking ... the risk of a journey into a country far away from home.'[96] Frei has thus found a way to talk about divine patience alongside divine solidarity with suffering creatures

– indeed in such a way as to add to its intelligibility.[97] In so doing, he has also found a way, once again, to distinguish divine action in history from fate. What, though, does divine patience contribute to his political theology and ethics?

Frei is alert to the dangers of the indiscriminate analogical or parabolic application of one isolated divine perfection to human affairs. As he notes, patience is good Christian counsel for the developed rather than for the Third World; likewise, according it primacy among the virtues might be more appropriate for men than for women, given (we may infer) the structural differences of power in each pair. When 'treated univocally across the board, moral virtues become distortions', whereas they require 'the delicacy of imaginative moral artistry' in respect of ourselves as well as God.[98] Instead, Frei considers how the doctrine of God, and this divine perfection in particular, help us think about the political action of the church in different contexts.

In terms echoing Karl Barth's account of that perfection, Frei defines God's patience as 'that aspect of his grace by which he permits and sustains his creatures in being and grants them their own span of time, limited though it be, and their own social location, which is not a universal home'.[99] This gift of a finite and specific life-span and social location is a condition of the Christian life that Christian thinkers from all traditions have affirmed. Christian life includes the acknowledgement 'that every life including one's own [is] a gift of divine grace, and ... nobody has the right to deny any other individual or group their time and space'.[100] It is a life to be lived 'as a gift from God's abundance'.[101]

Frei now develops the significance of this theological commonplace for political ethics in terms of an understanding of the togetherness of God's relationship to the future and to the past, in ways that go far beyond Barth's brief discussion in *Church Dogmatics* II/1.[102] To live the Christian life in response to divine patience is predicated, provisionally (that is, prior to the eschaton), 'on God's *having been active* in the past, both in preservation and transformation, just as he is active in the future, when the barriers, especially the political barriers, on our earth will be overcome'.[103] Now echoing Barth's discussions of God's eternity and of providence, Frei proposes we think of this togetherness in terms of the fullness of God's temporality, whereby (I infer) God simultaneously precedes, accompanies and goes before our time.[104] In consequence, Frei reasons, we must affirm God's prevenient election of humanity to salvation, the openness and ambiguity of the Christian life 'in the human and political present', and the future reality of God's kingdom.[105]

In consequence of God relating to us in this triune way, the present is shaped not only by God's promised future but also by the reality of the past. Hence, we live 'in a world both of enduring structure *and* of revolutionary transformation – and not of one without the other'.[106] Furthermore, Frei's characteristic epistemic reserve led him to be cautious about what we can know of that future, just as it did in his article on 'The mystery of the presence of Jesus Christ'. The divine promise of the future kingdom is a promise, rather than a programme; we do not know how God's kingdom will supersede the present. 'The promise of God is a miracle or the anticipation of a miracle rather than the fulfilment of a blueprint.'[107] All this is both consistent with Frei's earlier account of God's mysterious, providential ordering of history in Christ in anticipation of the eschatological consummation of all things in him in 'The mystery of the presence of Jesus Christ' and with its hopeful orientation of Christian discipleship, individual and communal. But it adds to it a much more developed doctrine of God and of God's creative and sustaining relationship to human creatures in their contexts, to help frame the church's political engagement.

Furthermore, we can put together Frei's remarks about sin, and the consequent element of tragedy in history and political strategy, with his remarks about the patience of a God 'gracious and merciful, slow to anger and abounding in steadfast love'. By doing so we may draw the further conclusion, consistent with Frei's thought and strengthening its coherence, that God, by patiently preserving the limited times and spaces in which we dwell, and the people who dwell in them, sustains the fabric on which unjust, exploitative and oppressive structures – barriers – are parasitic. Yet by doing so God also keeps open a history in which human beings may pursue humanistic projects, love their neighbours generously, give and receive from one another, and work for justice and equality; a history in which the church may participate in all this and bear witness amid it all to Jesus Christ, to the coming kingdom inaugurated in him and to its mysterious providential anticipation.

For Frei, then, human beings live between the patience and impatience of God, between God's gift of enduring structure and God's promise of a revolutionary future. Christians act, therefore, within the givens of a limited space and time, through which human beings are mutually limited, while holding on to God's promise.[108] As long as these provisional conditions and limitations pertain, Frei added in his delivered paper, 'God works through our mutual limitations'.[109] God, as both the giver of our past and the one who promises God's future kingdom, is free and able in the present to work through the mutual limitations of human creatures towards that promised future, a future that will arrive as miracle, not the culmination of a process nor by any path we can predict.

Indeed, we can go a little further and connect this train of thought with the argument of the previous paragraph to add another strand of coherence to Frei's political theology. God, by patiently preserving the limits of time and space, by working in and through our mutual limitations, mysteriously anticipating the revolutionary transformation of God's future in and through the enduring structures of creaturely life, works in and through the conflicts arising from the assertion and resistance of group interests, so there is a tragic element even where we see signs of God's providential presence and anticipations of God's kingdom.

Frei's account of divine patience then frames a brief ecclesiological statement that extends the implicitly political character of the ecclesiology of his Christological essays in the direction of the political Christology he would go on to deliver at Princeton. The global church's calling, freed from Northern predominance, he argued, was to be God's servant on behalf of all humanity, 'a paradigm, a beacon among the nations for the cause of justice, mercy, and human equality'.[110] It is to set forth for the nations God's bias and promise for the poor and oppressed enacted in Christ becoming poor for our sake. No church is a true church 'if it is not a church *on behalf of* the poor and the oppressed', responding with public action to the public, overriding imperative of Jesus, 'God's self-denying servant', to do for the least of his brothers and sisters as for him.[111] In his response to Elisabeth Moltmann-Wendel he likewise affirmed that, in recognition of femininity as a limited good, granted by God's grace (like masculinity), 'feminine liberation is simply a matter of justice', and endorsed Moltmann-Wendel's use of the doctrine of justification by faith to affirm women's legitimate self-acceptance and self-expression in affirmation of their goodness, wholeness and beauty, and the rejection of patriarchal negative stereotypes of femininity.[112]

To that extent, Frei saw himself in full agreement with the other speakers at the conference and with liberation theologians in general. However, his account of divine patience inflects his account of the church's calling and task. The church faces the real but provisional limits of time and space, given and sustained in God's abundant patience. It exists in a worldly space bordered (by which I take Frei to mean: conditioned) by God's revolutionary action in the cross and resurrection of Jesus Christ. But it is not able to predict the future. In that circumstance, Frei argues, the church should affirm the possibility of extending hands across the barriers, in the hope that some of these may be lowered, without having anticipatory knowledge about their miraculous, full eschatological removal.

This trope of extending hands across barriers is Frei's language for the ministry of reconciliation. In his delivered paper, he spoke of the ecumenical church being called to do the work of human and Christian unity 'across the barriers of our limitations'.[113] In this context it is much clearer than in 'Of the Holy Ghost' how reconciliation and working for justice go hand in hand in Frei's understanding. It is explicit in the latter text and implied in Frei's prepared text for the Moltmann conference, that the barriers in question are barriers between nations, classes, racial groups and interest groups; barriers that divide human beings against one another and maintain structures of oppression, marginalization and inequality. To talk of lowering these barriers in that context, I suggest, can and should be read as talk of overcoming, in some significant measure, the structures that maintain the disparities of power between groups and the systems of oppression and exploitation they facilitate and sustain. That our history is bounded and shaped by what God has done in the crucifixion and resurrection of Jesus Christ, as well as being structured by the gift of limited time and space, means the church can hope for the lowering of these barriers in history, for some degree of revolutionary transformation in the present, short of its full eschatological realization.

But what of the element of reconciliation in Frei's metaphor? The structure of Frei's writing here places the reaching of hands across barriers in the context of the overriding imperative for the church to show forth God's bias to the poor and the oppressed in obedience to Christ's injunction to do for the least of his brothers and sisters as for him. It suggests that reaching hands across barriers, the ministry of reconciliation, is an activity embodying God's bias; that acts on behalf of the poor and oppressed but also – the metaphor clearly implies – with them. What we might call the ministry of penultimate reconciliation involves the church reaching across the barriers, deepening mutual understanding, but also modes of cooperation between those divided by oppressive structures in order to address those structural obstacles to justice, mercy and human equality. As a response to the commanding presence of Christ in and beyond the church, including in the poor and oppressed, we can see this ministry as a form of responsibility, for Frei, though he is clear that only God has ultimate responsibility for the history and its revolutionary transformation.[114]

Such work is done, however, within the limited gift of time and space we receive from God's abundant patience and without having any blueprint or programme for the ultimate removal of those barriers, only the promise and the hope it evokes. It is also conditioned by the specific character of our limited historical existence. By that Frei meant at once the contingency of any polity, whose policies and existence 'are subject to radical transformation and the contingencies of time' with their ambiguous effects; the abiding deformation of the world and the sinfulness of the church; and the hidden yeast of God's promise, 'who was incarnate in

Jesus and who moves the world toward unity despite itself'.[115] In consequence, the church is at best an imperfect parable of the kingdom and the civil community never more than an imperfect parable of that ecclesial parable. Frei's overriding note in these texts is one of realistic caution, but it is a realism qualified by hope, a hopeful realism.

For all these reasons, therefore, Frei argued for a pragmatic, realist participation of the church in political life, in limited and specific ways appropriate to the situation in which it finds itself.[116] It should frame short- and middle-range goals in support of a just society, 'in which the legitimate use of authority is to be balanced with the rights of those who are disenfranchised, and opportunities for peaceful change and redress of grievances remain a live possibility'.[117] But what this means strategically would vary depending on the political situation. In present-day western society, there was, he thought, a natural affinity between Christian commitment and left-of-centre liberalism or democratic socialism. Those holding such a pragmatic stance stood between the extremes of neo-conservative, nationalist Christianity and intolerant varieties of revolutionary political Christianity, and resist the 'politics of Manicheanism' in which social, economic and political history is the fight of pure good versus pure evil, because they believe the world to be the world of the one God 'who both rules over and yet suffers with his creatures'.[118] Hence they seek 'temporary accommodation between the greatest imperfect good and the lesser yet less-than-total evil, with the least possible bloodshed and cruelty'.[119] In similar terms, he counselled a moderate, worldly, pragmatic path for feminist liberation, framed by a similar sense of receiving 'our being and goodness from God's abundant and constant grace', and a respect for the space God has given to others, rather than a perfectionist drive towards unlimited self-assertion and complete self-shaping.[120]

Frei gives us a sense of what this pragmatic stance meant for Christians in the United States (he does not presume to dictate what it would mean for those in other contexts). When he wrote in the mid-1980s, it meant opposing 'imperialist and cruel North American interference in Latin America', together with tentative, provisional support for revolutionary socialists as having the better cause than their reactionary opponents.[121] It meant scepticism for those revolutionaries' ideological pretensions and the political naivety of those Christians supporting them 'with total commitment', in contrast to the political scepticism and irony of East German Christians' conditional support for their socialist state. Yet it also meant humility and receptivity: not imposing their views but listening respectfully to and seeking instruction from more radical brothers and sisters 'who know far more ... about suffering under poverty and injustice' in their context, in order to stand with them.[122] Such mutual instruction, he added, is a form of the ecumenical conversation across barriers, and its orientation to solidarity shows again that for Frei reconciliation and political action for the poor and oppressed go closely together.

Providence, America and a carefully circumscribed progressive politics

Frei developed these reflections further in a piece on his former teacher, H. Richard Niebuhr, written shortly before his death in 1988. Here Frei explores Niebuhr's theology and theological method, how he addressed the expanding global role of the United States in the 1930s and 40s, and how his theology of political history spoke still to US imperial policy in the 1970s and 80s. Frei presents the younger Niebuhr as retrieving the Reformed tradition in America and the story it told of 'God's active universal governance of all that he has made, and of his own unlimited, gracious, prevenient initiative toward all creatures'.[123] Niebuhr took up the tradition of inquiry, in the form of narrative, into patterns in the history of American Christianity and in the history of the nation, and of the relationship between them. For him this particular, Christocentric confessional story was one fragment alongside others of a larger, only partially known and unfinished universal narrative of the one, infinite God's transcendent, mysterious governance of and activity in all things. It guides human action in response, in their own time, 'to the creating, judging and redeeming work of God' in history.[124]

Frei shows evident sympathy in his treatment of Niebuhr's 'radical realism' as to the gracious glory of God and his 'somber ... agonizing theodicy' in affirmation of God's goodness and presence in the face of 'the lack of power of the good, and the lack of goodness of temporal power'.[125] He admires his teacher's refusal of speculative, apologetic forms of theodicy in favour of a more austere, agnostic account of a 'mysterious pattern of coherence' of images of God's creating and universal governance, of judgement and crucifixion, and of redemption, in which each divine action carried echoes of the other two, together with the total revolution of lifelong repentance, initiated by God, by which that coherence becomes manifest to the Christian.[126] He welcomed Niebuhr's subordination of his critically idealist theological methodology to the radical theological realism, also reflected in the anthropology of his account of responsibility, that reaffirmed his central concern with 'the prevenient initiatory action of God in time and in human events'.[127] He was even hopeful amid his unease at the ambiguities of the methodological path Niebuhr took between his brother's liberal theology of 'undisrupted ... human initiative' and Barth's 'consistently Christocentric divine prevenience', distinguishing and holding together universal divine action and divine action in Christ, a universal phenomenology of faith and an image and story-shaped confessional theology, a universal anthropology and ethics, and an image- and story-shaped ethics.[128] For, Frei argued, Niebuhr's use of traditioned images like the Kingdom of God as ways of understanding a tradition so as to shape action for a common future, gave a clue to his priorities. Such images 'bridged the gap between the reality of divine agency in history, as course of human events, and the symbolic part played by our own faith's constructive act'.[129] They gave priority to 'the radical realism of divine action' so that Niebuhr's critical idealist method tended to become a 'qualifying safeguard' of the limits of human knowledge which has always accompanied Christian confessions of God's universal activity.[130] This choice of priority was reflected in Niebuhr's anthropology of the responsible self. As interpreter of what has been and as agent 'in present social process', we are 'responding rather than initiating persons'.[131] This response, moreover, is located 'in a logically different plane to that of the divine initiation'.[132] For God acts as primary cause 'in, with, and through its secondary causal agencies'.[133] Faith's creative causality, then, is not equally matched with divine causation but is, 'simply, a gift of God in repentance'.[134]

Frei's judgements here reveal his own concern for the gracious freedom, the prevenience of God in human affairs and situating human agency as responsible to it within a non-competitive account of the relationship between them founded on the grammar of the transcendence of divine action in history. This concern is also reflected in his account in this piece of the differences between H. Richard Niebuhr's theology and ethics and those of his brother Reinhold, an assessment that offers one way of interpreting the significance of Frei's own position in American social ethics.

Frei and the Niebuhrs

Frei recalls the famous argument between the Niebuhrs, in the pages of *The Christian Century*, over the Japanese army's invasion of Manchuria in 1932 and whether the United States should intervene, militarily or otherwise. H. Richard Niebuhr argued for a constructive inaction on the part of Christians in the USA.[135] In part, he did so on the grounds that there was no constructive intervention available. Japan was following the example of the United States; the faults of the USA, the country for which

US Christians bore responsibility as citizens, were so evident and similar to those of Japan that any intervention would be perceived in the same way and indeed would probably be to advance its own interests.[136] But he proposed an active inactivity that would, alongside palliative works of mercy towards those suffering for sins of the USA and the whole world, take an indirect approach to the situation by seeking 'to create the conditions under which a real reconstruction of habits is possible'.[137] Such a reconstruction would have to begin with American self-analysis, he argued. Such analysis would disclose that a great deal of renunciation of self-interest by the nation and by its Christians before it would be in a position to intervene effectively in any way.

This inactivity, H. Richard Niebuhr argued, was that of 'a patience that is full of hope, and is based on faith'.[138] Specifically, it was based on faith in the reality of God, that God would bring historical transformation, 'a different kind of world with a lasting peace', working through apparently impersonal mundane social and historical forces to effect redemption in history. Such redemption, however, would only come after judgement and considerable destruction. For, as he explained in a subsequent letter to the editor of *The Christian Century*, the divinely willed structure of the universe is such that, when we bring war and (economic) depression on ourselves, out of the conflicts arising from the clash of self-interest between groups and nations, God brings them and their tragic outcomes upon us as judgement.[139] Yet history was more than tragedy and God by that same structure brings some fulfilment, love and fellowship beyond the tragic outcomes of social and international conflict, in anticipation of a greater judgement and a new era.[140] Those with such apparently foolish faith, he proposed, might prepare for the future by forming little cells in each nation, 'who, divorcing themselves from the program of nationalism and of capitalism, unite in a higher loyalty which transcends national and class lines of division and prepare for the future'.[141]

In response, Reinhold Niebuhr agreed with his brother's analysis of US self-interestedness and responsibility for Japanese aggression but argued that the consequence of his position would be perpetual inaction: no nation or human group, not even a human individual, would ever become sufficiently disinterested 'to save another nation purely by the power of love'.[142] Justice, rather than love, was 'probably the highest ideal toward which human groups can aspire'.[143] And it 'inevitably involves the assertion of right against right and interest against interest until some kind of harmony is achieved', for justice aims at the adjustment of right to right.[144] A spiritual note of humility, love and repentance could only qualify and temper such social conflicts, not abolish them. He found what he took to be Richard's idea that the God who presided over brutal social conflicts would somehow bring a kingdom of pure love out of them implausible. While humans are enmeshed in history, social struggle would continue and the highest ideals of human beings, tragically, could never be realized socially and collectively. Human progress in history, therefore, would always 'depend upon the judicious use of the forces of nature in the service of the ideal'.[145] So it was with Japan: the USA must dissuade Japan from its military adventure using the minimum coercion necessary (preferably none), with constant self-analysis and bringing to bear its ethical ideals as far as possible. As Frei notes, Reinhold thus brushed aside Richard's 'central concern, his most powerful persuasion of the prevenient initiatory action of God in time and in human events'.[146] He turned the dispute from a question of the dependence of Christian ethics on prevenient, 'active, divine governance in history' to one of 'an ethical imperative under a practical injunction'.[147] And, Frei adds, whereas Richard subordinated the ethical imperative to an eschatological one, qualifying human agency and freedom as contingent, limited, 'always governed by some compelling motive force', Richard did the opposite.[148] He subjected eschatology to the ethical imperative and an anthropology in which even our finitude and self-interest are aspects of our freedom.

Richard would develop his perspective, founded on his faith in God's providence of judgement and redemption, in further articles in *The Christian Century*, during the Second World War, which anticipate his ethics in *The Responsible Self*. He argued that when we interpret the war through the image of the crucifixion of Christ, we see the indiscriminate mixture in war of justice and injustice in the distribution of suffering on both sides and are confronted with 'the tragic consequences of moral failure' in the sacrifices people make in conflicts.[149] But the cross also shows that the order of the universe is not one of retribution but of graciousness, which is God's righteousness. It shows us that the pursuit of human justice as retribution and vengeance is wrong and calls us to repentance from the pursuit of death and to act in hope in God's continued grace amid human ungraciousness. We should ask what we should do in the light of what God is doing in the war, he wrote the following year, recommending again the interpretation of war as crucifixion and so tragedy, in which the humble, ordinary people and the smaller nations suffer at the hands of and for the remaking of the guilty.[150] Accepting God's judgement there in repentant political action meant forgoing national self-centredness and passing judgement on the combatants while accepting continuous responsibility for their neighbours in dutifully resisting the aggression of some against others and seeking a just peace.[151] It should be a trusting response, hopeful of redemption and resurrection for all participants amid judgement and for the emergence of a better order amid tragedy.

Reinhold's contrasting response also anticipated the argument of later works, including *Moral Man and Immoral Society*, and especially his Gifford lectures, *The Nature and Destiny of Man*. Reinhold's theology in the latter work seems to echo some themes of his brother's thought. He presents God as the transcendent yet present creative ground of human form and vitality, a transcendent will to which human wills are to be subordinated, whose judgement and mercy frame, as limits, the context for human freedom.[152] This God is known as an overtone in all experience, a feeling both of absolute dependence and of conscience, which is clarified by biblical interpretation of that experience of God as Creator, Judge and Redeemer.[153] God is also revealed as Judge, according to biblical faith, in those catastrophes in which nations and civilizations bring upon themselves the consequences of exceeding their creaturely limits. God as Judge is 'the source and centre of the created world against which the pride of man destroys itself in vain rebellion'.[154] Christ's cross, finally, was the revealed assurance that judgement was not God's last word to human beings, but that God is free to overcome sinfulness by assuming it, and thus of a transcendent love which is the final and only adequate norm of human freedom.[155]

Yet for Reinhold, the cross was not, as it was for Richard, a lens by which to interpret God's providential activity in human conflict so as to guide human responsibility to what God was doing there. Christ's cross and resurrection are no less central to Reinhold's theological vision, but as a transcendent ethical norm, not a paradigm of God's providential presence or a pattern for achievable moral action. For him, God's freedom in cross and resurrection to assume and overcome human sinfulness establishes a transcendent, disinterested, self-sacrificial love, one that ends tragically 'because it refuses to participate in the claims and counterclaims of historical existence'.[156] It is a love that cannot maintain itself over against others' counter-assertions or in the balance of interests that is historical justice. Christ's cross reveals God's perfection in the tragedy of historical suffering, symbolizing the perfect coincidence of power and goodness under the historical form of the complete refusal of power amid competing wills and interests that constitute history.[157] It is an ideal and norm of divine–human love, conforming to 'the divine and eternal agape, the ultimate and final harmony of life with life'.[158]

Such purely self-sacrificial love, made possible by a transhistorical dimension of existence, transcends human historical possibilities.[159] It symbolizes something we cannot attain, for perfect goodness and power cannot coincide in history since to exercise power amid historic rivalries is to assert ego. It is not a strategy that can receive historical vindication. We cannot expect that every Christian action should conform to this love rather than to the relative justice and mutual love by which life is maintained and conflicting interests are arbitrated in history. Rather, the cross reveals divine love as the measure, fulfilment, source and term of mutual love in history, which relativizes every achievement of human mutuality in history. At the same time, it also makes mutuality possible as an approximation of that love, relieving us of the anxiety of non-reciprocation by the gift of a telos beyond mutuality. It makes sense of the practical faith involved in those imperfect endeavours. In a similar way, it relativizes and measures achievements of historical justice and social structures, which can only at best approximate the ideal of perfect love in God's kingdom, because (again) contradicting this ideal is 'the contingent and finite character of rational estimates of rights and interests and by the taint of passion and self-interest upon calculations of the rights of others'.[160] Such factors necessitate governmental coercion for attainment of historical justice.[161] Reinhold Niebuhr's account maintains a transcendent norm and goal for human justice in a realist vision of history at the expense of divine transformative presence there. It thus enables him to distance God from any responsibility for the order of things and enthrone God instead as the pure criterion of all, a distant regulative power.

Finally, the norm enshrined in the eschatological symbols of cross and resurrection expresses a hope in the final meaningfulness of our historical struggles and social or cultural attainments, and the supremacy of love over countervailing forces beyond our finite lives and historical possibilities and the partial achievements of civilizations.[162] In this way, the symbols allow us provisionally to discern partial realizations and fulfilments of the meaning of history in history.[163] God's gracious judgements may be seen in moments of civilizational decline and the creative renewal that can follow, for example.[164] That hope of final meaningfulness bestows eternal significance on 'the struggles in which men engaged to preserve civilisations, and to fulfil goodness in history'.[165] Nevertheless, it seems such hope is not meant to temper and reform the repentant way the struggle is conducted as a response to divine judgement, as in Richard's reflections.

Frei's careful, qualified affirmation of Richard's choice of priorities in favour of the realist theological affirmation of God's governing providential presence and human agency as responsive to it, and his clear sympathy for the younger Niebuhr's stance in the controversy with his brother about the interpretation of history and the ethics of war and peace, show where he stood on these differences. It reminds us how limited is Frei's substantive (as distinct from rhetorical) appeal to the elder Niebuhr's theology in his response to the papers at the conference for the Moltmanns in 1986.

It also indicates one way of interpreting the significance of his own political theology and ethics. There are differences between Frei's theology and H. Richard Niebuhr's, indicated by the caution and unease he expresses in the essay. These extend even to the doctrine of providence: Frei's is less inclined to fatalism, to identify God's will with structures of reality or to go so far towards agonized theodicy in his application of the language of sacrifice to human conflict, for example. He is also more firmly Christocentric in his understanding of God's presence to history. Nevertheless, there is a strong affinity between his account and that of his teacher. Despite his invocation of Reinhold Niebuhr's tragic realism, he is closer to Richard's understanding of 'the tragic element' in history and progressive change and to his eschatological hopefulness about historical transformation. If his paper to the Moltmann conference qualified hope with realism, his reading of H. Richard Niebuhr here qualifies realism with hope and, indeed, reminds us that his realism follows a very different understanding of God's action in history from that of Reinhold Niebuhr. In that perspective, Frei's political theology of God's patience, the providential ordering of history in Christ's life, death and resurrection, and of the discernment of figures of that providential presence; his understanding of human responsibility and Christian discipleship; his advocacy of a hopefully realist, pragmatic, contextualized approach to the witness of the church in solidarity with the marginalized and oppressed, combining the pursuit of justice and reconciliation, reaching across barriers of sinful structural division while seeking to lower them: all these mark him as offering, in significant continuity with H. Richard Niebuhr, an awkward alternative to the realism of Reinhold Niebuhr and its influence in American social ethics; one founded on an unfashionable affirmation of 'God's active lordship in our midst'.[166]

Renewing reformed public theology and a call for restraint

In so doing, Frei also took a stance against the neo-conservatism in that tradition and in US politics in the 1970s and 80s. Reinhold Niebuhr's anthropology, even beyond his own realism of collective self-interest, was an affirmation of uninterrupted, self-originating human freedom that leant itself to appropriations from both liberals and neo-conservatives.[167] Frei thought it impossible, however, that H. Richard Niebuhr's theology and ethics might lead to neo-conservatism, for two reasons. First, H. Richard Niebuhr had a firm sense of the contingency and limited character of human agency as God's creature. He saw human actions in history as short-range in their aims, and limited by divine governance 'in, with, and through agencies other than our own, and they by ours'.[168] Second, H. Richard Niebuhr's understanding of where God acts precluded seeing any political community and its culture, or the church and its cultures, as the centre of God's presence and action in the world and hence of special importance. For he located divine agency in the 'at first sign almost ludicrously ill-balanced "polarity" ... between the nation, or other assorted social collectivities, and the church'.[169] He did so because both sorts of group assert their universality, which is what he called 'henotheism': 'that social faith which makes a finite society, whether cultural or religious, the object of trust as well as of loyalty' rather than God, whether in the assertion of the universality of a particular civilization, or the replacement of the history of God's deeds with church history.[170] For Frei, it is H. Richard Niebuhr who has the more robust theological condemnation of group pride of the two brothers.

That Frei aligned himself with the critical force of that theocentric stance is clear from his postscript to the essay, in which he ventured to speak for H. Richard Niebuhr to Frei's theological contemporaries in 1988. In so doing, Frei interjects direct statements in his own voice and explicit affirmations of the three points he advances on Niebuhr's behalf, as it were, so that it is clear that what he says on behalf of Niebuhr is also his own view. Indeed, the third of these points picks up an argument that Frei, setting out from Niebuhr's 1943 lecture, makes in the opening paragraphs. All three resonate closely with the analysis of Frei's political ethics I have been advancing in this chapter, and they indicate one contextual application of them to public theology in the USA.

First, Frei called on theologians in mainstream Protestantism to carry on, in more modest scope and more difficult cultural circumstances, affirming God's glory and 'active lordship in our midst'.[171] It would bear witness to the 'almost lost Puritan heritage of the universal governance of God', which can only be attested by talking in terms of the polarity of church and nation, which is responsible to both and concerned with their interaction under God's 'mysterious, divine prevenience'.[172] Frei's own accounts of divine patience and of God mysteriously ordering human history in Christ's life, death and resurrection, and his proposal for the figural reading of political history, fit this description and fill out what he meant by God's active lordship. The modesty of the scope of this endeavour had to do in part with rejecting 'the notion of a special covenant between God and the American nation', as Frei thought H. Richard Niebuhr would have done, including the Puritans' version of this claim in the jeremiad.[173]

Second, Frei argued that, in parallel with the renewal of this tradition, Niebuhr would have argued for 'the possibility of a new, far more limited role for the American nation'.[174] Frei's essay had begun by recalling H. Richard Niebuhr's evaluation that the United States was, in 1943, now a worldwide empire, and could exercise that power 'with restraint, or recklessly, with a heavy hand that could not rest until it had encircled the globe'.[175] In reviewing the development of the United States' foreign policy in the decades that followed, Frei argued that the proxy conflicts of the Cold War, and the growth and global breadth of US military deployment, international engagement and resourcing of economic and military allies in proportion to its growing power, confirmed that self-restraint had become increasingly difficult.[176] Indeed, the USA had not found any restraints short of 'those encircling the whole globe'.[177] With its heavy debts to overseas investors and the growing power of 'rising demographic epicenters' raising the prospect of American imperial decline; with decreasing economic competitiveness and industrial efficiency; with an imbalance of military and non-military expenditure, might not the United States be 'most dangerous to the balance of the world's precarious equation of power'?[178] Indeed, the difficulty of reversing foreign policy in an open society, as illustrated by the 'agony and bitter conflict of the U.S. reversal on Vietnam', amplified that danger.[179] Restraint in US foreign policy might be both imperative and very difficult to achieve without 'a world of genuinely independent power structures', though Frei seemed to see the prospect of that world.[180] Frei expresses similar anxieties in his delivered lecture at the Moltmann conference, mentioning the airstrikes conducted by United States forces against targets in Libya in retaliation for the bombing of a West Berlin disco frequented by US service personnel.[181]

Against that background, Frei thought H. Richard Niebuhr would have welcomed a 'sobering call' to US Americans 'to take our place in an increasingly pluralistic world with a humanitarianism modified by Christian hope, and to restrain the global anxieties unleashed by global power'.[182] The advocacy of a 'more modest mission' for the nation as an 'internationally useful people' was one that a renewal of the Reformed tradition in America and its doctrine of providence could resource; it was one that, we might add, Frei's doctrine of providence could inform.[183] Indeed, I suggest that Frei's doctrine of providence is precisely what enables him to imagine and recommend the restraint of US power and a more modest, humanitarian global mission for the nation, in place of the anxious, hasty resort to coercion and expansion of reach.

Finally, Frei thought Niebuhr might have agreed with Barth that 'a gospel of the universal, present, governing glory of God might have more to do with a carefully circumscribed progressive politics than with either a theology of revolution or some other political theology', including neo-conservatism.[184] For the public theology he proposed, it must be 'one step at a time' in pragmatic progressive politics, with 'the protest against national self-aggrandizement and idolatry' always in mind.[185] This point is very much in keeping with Frei's argument at the Moltmann conference, but needs to be read in the light of the affinity of the hopefulness of his realism with that of his teacher and the difference of that hope and realism from the realism of Reinhold Niebuhr. The motto 'one step at a time' expressed Frei's theological hope no less than his caution and characteristic pessimism.

Social sin in liberation theologies

I want to conclude the argument of this chapter, and of the book, by bringing Frei's political theology and ethics into conversation with some examples of liberation theologies in the Americas.[186] As we have seen, while there are elements in Frei's Christology and political theology that echo liberationist themes, he can be quite dismissive of liberation theology in broad, generalizing terms, as unrealistic, impatient and rigidly programmatic.[187] Contrary to those generalizations, however, a good deal of liberation theology contemporary with Frei was far more realistic than he gave it credit for, indeed, in ways that could resource his own realism about social sin, about which his remarks tend to be fairly abstract. At the same time, rather like Moltmann's *Theology of Hope*, such liberation theologians tend to think of God's presence in history in such a way as to focus its power upon the transformation of the subjectivity of the oppressed, to be realized in history solely through their agency. And this understanding, while it limits God's responsibility for evil, turns out to be less hopeful than Frei's theology.

The Peruvian theologian Gustavo Gutiérrez's understanding of social sin, for example, is quite compatible with Frei's. Gutiérrez identifies social sin primarily in the light of Jesus' preaching of the kingdom, seen in the context of the Exodus traditions and prophetic denunciations of the oppression of the poor by the wealthy in ancient Israel. Sin has collective dimensions in biblical traditions, he reminds us, and constitutes a structure that conditions the progress of human history.[188] In the partiality it shows for some over others, Gutiérrez implies, it is contrary to the universal love of God that Jesus preached.[189] Social sin is a rejection and compound fracture of the eschatological human brotherhood and sisterhood Jesus preached and of the filial relationship to God in which it is grounded, resulting in internal personal fracture.[190] It is evident 'in oppressive structures, in the exploitation of man by man, in the domination and slavery of peoples, races, and social classes'.[191] It appears therefore 'as the fundamental alienation, the root of a situation of injustice and exploitation'.[192] It is at once structural and spiritual.[193] Its concrete manifestations can only be understood in the light of this underlying basis, and vice versa, through participation in the process of liberation. There is significant resonance here with both Niebuhrs, but without the reliance on a notion of group consciousness or group pride characteristic of Reinhold Niebuhr's hamartiology. What Gutiérrez also brings is a more developed analysis than that of either Niebuhr or Frei of the structural character of social sin at a global level, and of its impact on Latin America.

Gutiérrez notes that the social and economic situation of Latin American nations is a consequence of the structuring of the global economy around a central group of capitalist countries whose more advanced development, wealth and social progress is integrally connected to the political instability and socio-economic inequality of a much larger periphery of poorer nations. This systemic relationship produces relations of dependence of the peripheral countries on, and domination by, those at the centre. It so shapes structures within the dependent country that the relationship of dependency and domination is experienced as internal to it, between dominant classes and the poor.[194]

It is, Gutiérrez argues, a continuation of a long history of colonial domination that began with the conquest and exploitation of Amerindians in the sixteenth century.[195] Some of the forms inherited from that past also persist in mines and plantations.[196] Others are bound up with new foreign investment in local industry, leading to rationalization of the economy in the interests of multinational corporations and the exploitation of the local labour force through high production at low wages for short-term profit, with the capital used to shore up or develop more developed economies.[197] The consequence is lethal poverty, a situation maintained by institutionalized violence, repression of movements of liberation and the restriction of democracy: an experience, for the conscientized, of alienation and exile in land that ultimately belongs to God alone.[198] Gutiérrez thus adds specificity to the Niebuhrs' and Frei's gestures towards international dimensions of social sin in respect of the legacies and new forms of immiserating, extractive neo-colonial global economic structures between a capital-owning centre and the labour force and natural resources of peripheral countries. Gutiérrez briefly acknowledges two other structural factors in social sin, namely race and gender (and their intersection), but for a deeper understanding of them we need to turn elsewhere.[199]

Frei's contemporary, Rosemary Radford Ruether, offers an account of sexism that also echoes Reinhold Niebuhr but goes beyond the well-known masculine bias of his hamartiology.[200] Frei was sceptical about the neatness of the gendering of typical sins in some of the classic feminist critiques of Niebuhr (as he was of very sharply contrastive accounts of sexual difference), but even with that caution in mind, there is much to be appreciated in Ruether's careful account.[201]

For Ruether, differences between masculinity and femininity cannot be explained by biological sexual differentiation. They are 'reproductive role specializations', which, as sets of qualities, are the product of culture and socialization rather than innate traits based in biology.[202] Ruether argues that human beings' capacity for non-manipulative, non-self-abnegating I–Thou relationality between the sexes (the *imago Dei*) has been perverted in history into an oppressive relationship wherein women are victimized and men become tyrants, one that is reflected in other kinds of alienation (from the body-self, from others, from non-human nature, from the God/ess).[203] As in Reinhold Niebuhr and Frei, group dynamics amplify her account.

Groups, she argues, tend to centre their understanding of authentic humanness on themselves, and describe other groups negatively relative to themselves, so that they become the cultural carriers of rejected qualities.[204] This perception of inferiority and evil then rationalizes the exploitation, abuse (and extermination) of other groups when the opportunity arises.[205] Subjugated groups tend to internalize the dominant ideology and the negative perception of themselves, filling it with 'fear and ambiguity about its own humanity'.[206] The distortion of the male–female duality into a hierarchy is the primary form of this phenomenon, she argues.[207] Men and women are socialized into this perception and a passive relation to the dominant male group ego, a passivity that men project onto women and others, and in which women (and some men) passively acquiesce.[208] Through the translation of distorted relationships into means of exploitation, a powerful counter-reality is established, which 'perpetuates itself, both through socioeconomic and political structures and through ideology that shapes education and socialization at every level'.[209]

Ruether also adds a cultural and religious dimension to her analysis of social sin. The aetiology of male status in terms of the female origins of evil in various stories in European culture, including that of Eve, helps legitimate male power and the structural and quotidian practical subjugation and continual repression of women as perennial source of potential threat to the male spirit.[210] Male monotheism performs a parallel function, on Ruether's analysis, projecting a patriarchal hierarchy onto the divine and reinforcing patriarchal, and sometimes racial, rule over subject or colonized groups by the analogy, paternity and partnership between divine male rule and its male human representatives.[211]

These distorted gender relationships and group self-understandings in turn distort men and women, especially as a result of the structural influence role of gender stereotypes.[212] Men project onto women the negative parts of the male psyche and repress rather than integrate those aspects in themselves, while claiming monopoly of other traits, like rationality.[213] This projection in turn objectifies women in a negative stereotype, which is used to legitimate the denial of their capacities for autonomy and critical intelligence. These constructed differences then structure and distort relations between the sexes into a pathological interdependence: women on men for their access to public power, resources and the skills developed for that sphere; men on women as domestic, child-rearing and sexual servants.[214]

Ruether is also far more concrete, in respect of sexism, than Reinhold Niebuhr, Frei or even Gutiérrez tend to be about the effects of social sin. She argues that this distorted gender relation reduces women, by way of a vast network of control (above all in respect of reproductive agency), upheld by the ultimate resort of violence, to a passive, objectified body for men's use, and starved of real communication.[215] This objectification involves the mutilation and commodification of their bodies as objects of display rather than self-actualizing agents.[216] Where women participate in employed work, domestic role segregation is extended to the workplace through low-status, poorly paid, menial jobs, with a merely tokenistic presence in prestigious male-dominated professions.[217] Men are also distorted by these relations 'into a fundamental proneness to translate all relationships into aggressive, assaultive modes of behavior' that reduce others to objects of control and deny the possibilities for mutually enriching relations.[218]

Finally, Ruether, like Valerie Saiving, Judith Plaskow and others, offers a richer analysis than Reinhold Niebuhr, Frei or Gutiérrez of how specific structures of social sin coopt the attitudes and agency of those whom they oppress. Women and subjugated men's opportunities for evil tend to be limited by their positions in a patriarchal social hierarchy. Nevertheless, women 'sin by cooperating in their own subjugation, by lateral violence to other women who seek emancipation, and by oppressing groups of people such as children and domestic servants under their control'.[219] They can be 'racist, classist, self-hating, manipulative toward dominant males, dominating toward children'.[220] In this way they help perpetuate 'an overall system of distorted humanity in which ruling-class males are the apex'.[221] Sexism, as historic, inherited systemic social sin, is thus a power and principality which precedes and shapes individual evil actions while preventing us understanding its influence upon them.

We could go on. The contributions of Gutiérrez and Ruether are complemented by, for example, James Cone's analysis of white supremacy, which echoes Niebuhr's account of group egoism (which it corrects on race), Gutiérrez's theocentric reference and Ruether's analysis of the effects of social sin on the subjugated. For Cone, white supremacy is the systemic attempt to realize white people's irrational desire for total domination of others in contravention to God's liberating work revealed in Israel and in Jesus.[222] It is born of their idolatry towards their racialized self-image as definitive of the human. It occludes itself; it recruits black people into the sin of accepting the normative status of whiteness, distorting their self-knowledge; it resists God's liberative work.[223] Despite his practical opposition to segregated education (and probably to segregated housing), his characterization of slavery in the USA as a curse and as sin, his sensitivity towards double consciousness among African Americans from his own, parallel experience as a Jew in Germany, his celebration of black consciousness and his understanding of group pride, Frei offered no analysis of white supremacy or of its impact on institutions like Yale or the shaping of western theology and the formation of academic theologians. He is as guilty as anyone of the great sin of silence on this subject, which James Cone identified, though he was engaged for a time at least in opposing white supremacist structures.[224]

Or again, there is Delores Williams' analysis, more ambiguously referenced to God rather than to the ministry of Jesus Christ, of the intersection of class, racial and gender oppression in the sexual surrogacy, and her concept of demonarchy, denoting the racial dynamic that intersects with class and patriarchy in the experience of African American women.[225] Like Ruether, she too draws attention to the role of cultural stereotypes and religious doctrines in socializing people, both oppressor and oppressed, into sin and normalizing and legitimizing it: what Emilie Townes calls the cultural production of evil.[226]

On the side of understandings of sin and its social and structural dimensions and power, then, Frei's liberationist contemporaries seem to have well-developed realistic accounts of social sin from which he has much to learn, much that could be incorporated into his account of group sin if it could be orientated around his Christ-centred theological way of thinking. But what about liberationist understandings of God's relationship to history and the transformation of history?

God's presence and the diminishment of progressive hope

Liberation theologians like those mentioned above do tend to take account of the roles and interactions of various social and historical forces in shaping and sustaining unjust social structures and to be alive to their strength of resistance to attempts to transform social orders. They also tend to want to avoid attributing the existing, unjust social structure to divine providence and yet (in most cases) want to uphold some divine promise of liberation from those structures and their effects. How can God have the comprehensive transhistorical agency to keep those promises without being the agent responsible for the present order of things, whose power and agency legitimates them? In some cases, liberation theologians like those we have discussed respond by focusing divine presence and empowerment on the transformation of the subjectivity of the oppressed, primarily, and focus the hope of liberation on the organized, divinely empowered agency of the oppressed. This stance then raises further questions about the realism of that hope given the power of the structures and forces against which it is assembled, to which one answer is to scale back the hope for historical change prior to the eschaton. An alternative to this approach, which confirms the problematic, is to scale back hope from the outset, with a diminished divine presence or divine commitment to liberation. One way to see the significance of Frei's political theology and ethics, I will argue, is as another alternative to these options and to this dilemma.

Gustavo Gutiérrez's *A Theology of Liberation* is a good example of the first alternative, which accords with the literal sense and centres Christology and pneumatology, like Frei. For Gutiérrez, salvation is a dynamic process of liberation taking place at the heart of history, which is continuous with creation, driven by divine promises and fulfilled in Christ. It is 'the communion of men with God and the communion of men among themselves – which orientates, transforms, and guides history to its fulfilment'.[227] It is a history at the very heart of history that embraces and fulfils every dimension of human existence.[228] Its paradigm is the Exodus as an event in which God liberates God's people from the alienation, misery and oppression arising from sin for the holiness of covenant life with God in establishing a just society.[229] Humans participate in it by their non-alienated labour and their struggle against exploitation to build a just society.[230]

For Gutiérrez, following Moltmann, divine promise is the form of God's self-communication in history. Together with its partial liberatory and promissory fulfilments, it gives liberation as a historical process its dynamic teleology, projecting itself into the future, dominating history.[231]

These historical promises and fulfilments exist in dialectical relation to Christ as Incarnate Promise, in whom they are fulfilled and explicated, and who thus accelerates history towards its eschatological goal of total reconciliation. The partial fulfilments of those promises in history are signs of the coming kingdom with transformative social consequences in the anticipation of the establishment of justice, the defence of the rights of the poor and the liberation of the oppressed in that kingdom. They are an encounter with the presence of the Lord. They open up further possibilities, but their partial character means they impel human becoming towards the eschatological encounter with Christ.

Jesus Christ, therefore, is central to this theology, for in him the divine Word takes on the history of liberation focused on the people of Israel and opens it to all people. His ministry and preaching were aimed at a universal, integral, total liberation from the very basis of social injustice, with radical social and political implications, for which he was executed, and his resurrection establishes its universal significance.[232] In him the divine presence accompanying God's people is manifest and by the Spirit indwells all who accept it, Christian or not, in their historical, material circumstances, but above all in the poor and exploited.[233]

Gutiérrez's theology of liberation emphasizes divine initiative, purpose and presence in the process of liberation at all levels. It admits of incompleteness, limits to progress in particular events, and affords a critical denunciation of the limitations and ambiguities of political liberation from the perspective of the kingdom, but its basic logic of hope is of a punctuated linear progress.[234] Gutiérrez is clear that the human agents of liberation will be the poor and oppressed, in whom the Lord 'saves history'.[235] The poor masses 'are history's transforming power, the agents of a liberating praxis'.[236] The call of Christ for those in dominating classes is to join them: to conversion to the neighbour in respect of the poor so understood.[237]

The church has a particular role here, which sheds more light on Gutiérrez's understanding of where agency lies and divine presence is focused. According to Gutiérrez's strong reading of *Lumen Gentium*, the church is constituted by the Spirit as a sacrament of the Spirit's Christ-centred work of salvation that extends beyond it, and therefore fulfils that function in a dialectical relationship with the world. It is to be evangelized and inhabited by the world (and specifically the poor) in which the kingdom of God is already breaking in through the work of Christ and the Spirit, so that it can understand the gospel's societal and political implications in history and so the poor can reclaim the gospel from their oppressors.[238] In turn, as a portion of humanity explicitly accepting of and attentive to Christ's Word and orientated to the future he promises, it is called to be an effective, visible sign, in its own structures and practices, of the liberation it announces and of Christ's presence in the struggle for liberation.[239]

In this way it enables the world to know 'the ultimate meaning of its historical future and the value of every human act'.[240] It does so by announcing, in the context of effective, concrete solidarity with exploited classes, the coming kingdom of the love of God and communion of God and human beings with one another. Such evangelization reveals the fundamental alienation at the root of every human alienation and social injustice, reveals God's present work and opens human history to God's promised future.[241] It frames every step towards brotherhood and sisterhood and justice as a step towards total communion with God and neighbours and the partial and provisional character of such steps.[242] It thus 'has a conscientizing function ... a politicizing function'.[243] It can help undermine in society the perceived legitimacy of the present order, and it can personalize, bringing those who are oppressed who hear it to understand 'the profound meaning of their historical existence [and] ... to perceive themselves as oppressed and feel impelled to seek their own liberation', living out an active, creative hope to work for the fulfilment of human brotherhood and sisterhood.[244] It can and should shape, we may infer, utopian thinking which carries forward the denunciation of the existing order and the annunciation of a different social order according to different values, so mobilizing people and supplying goals for political action.[245] The church's pastoral work, therefore, should be addressed primarily to, and undertaken by, the oppressed, whose presence in the church would transform its structures, values and actions.[246]

The focus of divine presence and action, then, is entirely on the agency of the oppressed and of the church among them and towards them, and the transformation of their consciousness, which frees and empowers them for that struggle.[247] Although Gutiérrez's theology of history attributes liberatory agency to God on a large scale, the most detailed account of the working of divine presence focuses on this psychological transformation of the oppressed by means of the gospel message. Indeed, it does not seem to require that Christ's presence make any more difference than the difference of evangelizing conscientization itself, multiplied across many individuals and communities to mass effect.

This focus has the effect of appearing to minimize divine responsibility for the structural situation of oppression. It also appears to limit divine agency to a mode of presence whose end is to evoke and empower the collective agency of the oppressed. Elsewhere, Gutiérrez appears to confirm this reading by arguing that God graciously and freely limits divine power to allow for human freedom, since there is no justice without it. God so values human beings as to stop 'at the threshold of their freedom and ask for their collaboration in the building of the world and in its just government'.[248] This passage also exposes an important feature of Gutiérrez's theology on these questions: an essentially zero-sum view of the relationship between divine and human power. Human freedom can only exist where divine power limits itself and so it must be a freely limited divine power that evokes the agency of the oppressed (and the conversion of their oppressors). To make this observation is not to belittle the remarkable transformations that conscientization can effect in oppressed people, nor that it may be a proper and vital effect of the announcement of the gospel. But is it, and the power it liberates, enough for the hope Gutiérrez articulates?

Gutiérrez's theology, and perhaps the circumstances of the mass movements of the 1960s and 70s, led him to articulate hope, even in the face of violent repression, for linear progressive change in stepwise anticipation of the eschaton.[249] The centrality of the agency of the oppressed, together with this greater historical hope, means that for him much is staked on the liberated power of the poor in history. In the right circumstances, such power can overturn oppressive regimes or force significant political change or win concessions from governments and others. Such revolutionary power may in some contexts be correlated with the conscientizing evangelistic activity of base ecclesial communities, as in the Sandinista revolution in Nicaragua in 1979, El Salvador in the 1970s and the Civil War of 1981–93, the election of Jean-Bertrand Aristide as President of Haiti in December 1990, the Zapatista uprising in Chiapas, Mexico, in January 1994, and the Quechua insurrection against a neo-liberal agrarian law in June 1994.[250]

However, in circumstances where the power of mass movements to effect progressive change is mismatched with the power of the structural forces of social sin, a gap threatens to yawn between the scale of the hope Gutiérrez articulates and the power of God's liberatory action to realize that change through the evangelical conscientization of the poor. For example, Manuel Vásquez's analysis of a base community on the outskirts of Rio de Janeiro exposes the possibilities of such groups and the limitations of their agency, especially when confronted with a changing economic model.[251] Informing and informed by theologies by Gutiérrez and others, they could sustain long campaigns to bring incremental change in their locality, to participate in the successful campaigns of unions, and to resist the repression of authoritarian regimes. But they have not been effective in contributing to wider structural transformation, and their cohesion and efficacy has been dissipated by the effects on their time and energies of the neo-liberal intensification of the extraction of labour value by transnational corporations.

Not all liberation theologies that focus God's presence in Christ on the transformation of the subjectivity of the oppressed, and focus liberatory hope on their agency, produce a gap in this way or to the same extent. James Cone's black liberation theology, for example, is similarly Christocentric in interpreting the Christ who is present in black experience and the source of black people's empowerment in their struggle for freedom (indeed it also resonates with Frei's procedure in his Christological essays to this extent). For Cone, Christ is God's freedom breaking into our history in identification with the materially poor in first-century Judaea and in twentieth-century America, and beyond. He discloses God's election and liberation of the poor. He fulfils and transcends the Exodus, Davidic, prophetic and wisdom traditions by his assumption of the condition of enslavement on the cross and by his vicarious liberating judgement upon their condition of slavery in his resurrection, transforming it 'into the battleground for freedom'.[252] Jesus' past Jewish identity attested in the Scriptures becomes the clue to his presence with the oppressed today and the revelation of their humanity in his person, crucified and resurrected.[253] The actualization of the combination of his Jewish particularity and its universal applicability for all the oppressed in the situation of black people in the United States is his blackness, his profound solidarity with the struggles and pain of black Americans, symbolic of his solidarity with the oppressed everywhere.[254] That this same one is the risen Lord secures the liberating character of his historical identity, for he creates a new future for the poor.[255] That identity in turn provides the clue to his present involvement made possible by his divinity: his presence with the black people in the struggle for freedom and meaning in life, empowering their survival and dignity through slavery, Jim Crow, police brutality and other forms of everyday discrimination and oppression.[256] Christ's lordship, Cone writes, 'emphasizes his present rule in the lives of the people, helping them to struggle for the maintenance of humanity in a situation of oppression ... moving the people toward the future realization of their humanity'.[257] In this respect, Cone offers a salutary challenge to Frei to develop more concretely the solidaristic themes of his later Christological reflections, as Cone does through the affirmation of Christ's blackness.

Cone's account of Jesus' identity and presence with the oppressed seems to imply an account of providence whereby God is active in history to liberate the oppressed from their oppressors. Certainly, liberation its firmly theocentric for Cone. It has its beginning and end in fellowship with God.[258] It is important to note, though, how focused the divine presence in Christ is in Cone's account. Jesus is present with, identifies with, is in solidarity with, and empowers the oppressed. The risen Christ in his historic solidarity and contemporary presence with the oppressed discloses to them that their poverty is contrived and calls them to political action against the social and economic structures that impoverish them.[259] This focused divine presence, disclosing eschatological liberation, empowers oppressed people in the sense that it raises consciousness; it frees up people to struggle for their freedom by disclosing their dignity and true humanity in the liberated Christ and hence the injustice and contingency of their situation and suffering.[260] There is no clear sense, however, that his presence somehow governs or disrupts the wider social context by which they are oppressed and others are privileged, except by their actions. Indeed, this focus may reflect Cone's rejection of appeals to providence to interpret the historic and contemporary sufferings of the black community as though divinely willed.[261] Instead, he sees the presence of God in Christ as focused on empowerment by the transformation of the subjectivity of the oppressed, as in Gutiérrez.

The note of Christ's presence to empower the oppressed *for struggle* is significant here, however, and helps us identify a degree of contrast with Gutiérrez's liberation theology. Cone's is indeed a theology of hope, of orientated struggle towards its eschatological fulfilment. Christ is also the Lord who is expected to come and consummate this liberation, towards which he moves people by his present reign. Their struggle for freedom is the enactment of this hope, by their living as if his future presence were already realized, in contradiction to their present status and so expressing eschatological judgement upon a white supremacist society.[262]

But Cone has a greater note of realism about what this struggle may achieve, compared with Gutiérrez. In his earlier work, Cone had at times seemed to entertain the possibility of violent revolution as a legitimate means of liberation or at least of dignifying struggle.[263] In *God of the Oppressed* he attributes to black American Christians a more realistic perspective. They knew they could not end slavery; they know they cannot defeat the Pentagon (as Martin Luther King Jr had also argued).[264] Only their hope transforms their struggle from desperation to a sign of Jesus' presence and of his coming. Short of the eschaton, Cone goes so far as to say, 'the measure of liberation achievable is limited to the consciousness of freedom as defined by the oppressed and downtrodden in their fight for justice'.[265] The prospects for anticipations of eschatological liberation in history beyond the agency to struggle, however, appear bleaker.

It is also worth noting Delores Williams' theology here, for it represents another step along this trajectory, and resolves the problematic I am trying to identify in another way. She questions the significance of liberation as the sole paradigm of divine and human agency.[266] Her account, based on the Hagar cycle in Genesis 16 and 21 in dialogue with black women's history and experiences, focuses instead on the transformed God-consciousness and God-dependence of non-middle-class African American women.[267] God's wilderness presence and the women's God-consciousness informs their capacity and strategies to resist oppression and secure survival for themselves and those they protect, provide for, nurture and endeavour to emancipate, in a cold, wide world. The communal manifestation of that divine presence and that God-consciousness in the ideal black church or 'Godforce' infuses the black community with compassion and power in its struggle for survival, flourishing and justice.

In understanding divine presence as empowering African American women in their struggle to survive and obtain a better quality of life in that context, Williams focuses divine presence and empowerment in a manner that resembles many of the other thinkers we have examined in this chapter. Like Cone, her realism about social sin is reconciled with faith in God by her focusing of God's presence in this way. Yet while Williams affirms liberation as the ultimate goal for black and womanist theologies, her emphasis is firmly upon survival and quality of life in a context in which white people continue to control the power structures under which black people suffer.[268] For this reason, her resolution of realism with faith in God's presence does not entail a further tension with claims about divine initiative, promise or empowerment of historical liberation that several of the other thinkers we have examined evince.[269]

The common features of Gutiérrez's, Cone's and Williams' theologies of divine presence and the empowerment of oppressed people provide a helpful comparison with Frei. Their contrasting extent and modes by which they address the tension between hopeful, liberatory affirmations about the empowering presence of God and Jesus Christ and a realistic appraisal of the strength of the empowered agency of the oppressed and the prospects for liberative structural transformation in history, offer a way to frame the significance of Frei's political theology and ethics.

Frei's account, of God's patience, in upholding the times and spaces in which we dwell, and of God's providential presence in Christ, shaping historical events in figural anticipation of the revolution of his eschatological consummation of all things, reconciling and redeeming and liberating them; offers another approach to these issues. Here, the pessimistic realism entailed by the structures of social sin and by God's patient commitment to work through the mutual limitations of creatures is met by the hopeful anticipation and promise in history of revolutionary transformation through Christ's presence, as they come together in figures of reconciliation and redemption marked by tragedy. In this way, although he lacks an account of conscientization, Frei seems to be able to envisage not the complete overthrow of systems of social sin but moments of significant structural change that give hope and create the impetus for renewed struggle amid reactionary responses.

To put it another way: Frei's account of God's providential presence to history in Christ is less revolutionary in its overall cast and rhetoric because it is qualified by his affirmation of divine patience alongside the realism about social sin that he shares with liberation and womanist theologians. Frei was cautious about the prospects for progressive change in society in history. But in Frei that realism coheres with hope for penultimate figures of reconciliation and redemption, as well as their ultimate eschatological realization, through the affirmation that God works (non-competitively) through our mutual limitations, according to the form of Christ's identity, in a manner that may be partially discerned according to part of the pattern of that identity.

Questions of the meaning of suffering are no less fraught for him than for Gutiérrez, Cone or Williams, and he does not attempt to rationalize it. Nor does he offer the rich accounts of the oppression and divine empowerment of particular groups of people in the struggles, as do those other thinkers. But he does avoid the tension we have seen and the logical tendency towards the reduction of hope to the shape and size of the agency of the oppressed that we have traced in Gutiérrez, Cone and Williams. And this observation suggests the possibility of further, constructive conversation between his work and perspectives like these than has been the case to date – more, indeed, than some of Frei's own rhetoric would encourage.

Conclusion

Frei wrote relatively little on political theology and political ethics. Some of his most extensive writings on these topics were not prepared for publication; much of what else he wrote on them was in passages in pieces on other topics. Nevertheless, from his writings we can reconstruct an account deeply coherent with his Christology, doctrines of God and of providence, and his ethics of responsibility and discipleship. And what he has to say makes a distinctive contribution to political theology, which I have tried to show in respect of the Niebuhrs and of select theologians of liberation and survival. Perhaps Frei was overly moderate and cautious about a carefully circumscribed progressive politics, at least as a stance for all contexts, though he was thinking primarily of his own context in the United States in the late twentieth century. Nevertheless, his particularistic understanding of the generous, non-obsessive love of neighbour has wide pertinence. His account of the church's ministry of penultimate reconciliation and working towards greater justice, in solidarity with the oppressed and marginalized, as framed by his account of divine patience and providence, seems relevant still. Indeed, it seems set to remain pertinent to a world in which conflicts within and between churches and between groups within societies and between nations proliferate in complex ways, and will intensify with the likelihood of growing competition for resources and habitable spaces in the circumstances of a burning planet and the enduring propensity of human beings to exploit other human and non-human creatures, even in the depths of planetary crisis. Indeed, as fundamental as conflicts around hierarchies of class, gender or sexuality, and thoroughly intertwined with them, is the conflict between dominant human groups and the structures built around their interests, and the wider non-human environment and its non-human inhabitants. Perhaps one of the greatest challenges facing any theologian wanting to pursue Frei's insights in this area is to attend to what it means to pursue hopeful, realistic penultimate reconciliation in that multi-faceted, multi-conflictual context.

Notes

1 Hans W. Frei, 'Reinhold Niebuhr, where are you now that we need you?', in *Reading Faithfully: Writings from the Archive, vol. 1, Theology and Hermeneutics* (Eugene, OR: Wipf & Stock, 2015), p. 182.

2 Hans W. Frei, *The Identity of Jesus Christ* (Philadelphia, PA: Fortress Press, 1975), p. 160.

3 Frei, *The Identity of Jesus Christ*, p. 160.

4 Frei, *The Identity of Jesus Christ*, p. 158.

5 Frei, *The Identity of Jesus Christ*, p. 157.

6 Frei, *The Identity of Jesus Christ*, p. 156.

7 There are echoes here of Barth's account of discipleship in §66.3, *Church Dogmatics* (hereafter CD) (Edinburgh: T & T Clark, 1957) IV.2, pp. 533–53. See also Gene Outka's perceptive commentary on discipleship and ethics in *The Identity of Jesus Christ* ('Following at a distance: ethics and the identity of Jesus', in Garrett Green (ed.), *Scriptural Authority and Narrative Interpretation* (Philadelphia, PA: Fortress Press, 1987)).

8 Frei, *The Identity of Jesus Christ*, pp. 170–1.

9 Here and elsewhere, I would suggest, Frei has more to say about the transformation of disciples and their bodies than David Dawson thinks. See David Dawson, *Christian Figural Reading and the Fashioning of Identity* (Berkeley, CA: University of California, 2002), pp. 212–14.

10 Frei, *The Identity of Jesus Christ*, p. 171, citing Albert Schweitzer, *The Quest of the Historical Jesus* (New York: Macmillan, 1956), p. 403.

11 Frei, *The Identity of Jesus Christ*, p. 171.

12 Frei, *The Identity of Jesus Christ*, p. 171.

13 Frei, *The Identity of Jesus Christ*, p. 171.

14 Hans W. Frei, 'Sinner, saint and pilgrim', in *Reading Faithfully, vol. 1*, pp. 123–5.

15 Frei, *The Identity of Jesus Christ*, pp. 171–2.

16 Frei, *The Identity of Jesus Christ*, p. 172.

17 Here Outka in effect extrapolates a greater element of individual judgement, without specific guidance, in Frei's ethics about what loving actions are fitting responses to what Christ has done for us, given our condition of reciprocity with our neighbours, than my comparison with Barth's ethics of responsibility might encourage. See Outka, 'Following at a distance', p. 157.

18 Frei, *The Identity of Jesus Christ*, p. 149.

19 Frei, *The Identity of Jesus Christ*, p. 143.

20 Frei, *The Identity of Jesus Christ*, pp. 156–7.

21 Hans W. Frei, 'Of the Holy Ghost', in *Reading Faithfully, vol. 1*, pp. 193–4.

22 Frei, 'Of the Holy Ghost', pp. 193–4.

23 Hans W. Frei, *Types of Christian Theology* (New Haven, CT: Yale University Press, 1992), p. 136.

24 Hans F. Holocaust Testimony HV 170, Fortunoff Video Archive for Holocaust Testimonies, Yale University, 1980, from 1 hr 32 minutes.

25 Gustavo Gutiérrez, *A Theology of Liberation: History, Politics and Salvation* (London: SCM Press, 1974), pp. 196–203. According to Serene Jones, Frei told her that the logical implication of *The Identity of Jesus Christ*, were he to write a sequel to it, would take him 'straight into the realm of liberation theology' (interview with Serene Jones, part 1, 18 December 2015). This passage in his Princeton lecture gives us some idea of the direction he might have taken had he done so.

26 Frei, *Types of Christion Theology*, p. 136.

27 Günther Bornkamm had already made a similar connection in finding both the love command and the demand to reconcile rooted in God's will and action, and in connecting this to the command to love enemies (*Jesus of Nazareth* (London: Hodder & Stoughton, 1960), p. 114).

28 Frei, *Types of Christian Theology*, p. 136.

29 Frei, *Types of Christian Theology*, p. 136.

30 See H. Richard Niebuhr, 'The church and its purpose', in *The Purpose of the Church and its Ministry: Reflections on the Aims of Theological Education* (New York, Evanston, IL, and London: Harper & Row, Publishers, 1956), pp. 33–4.

31 Barth, *CD* IV/2, pp. 802–40.

32 Gene Outka, *Agape: An Ethical Analysis* (New Haven, CT: Yale University Press, 1972), p. 262.

33 Rudolf Bultmann, *Jesus and the Word* (London: Ivor Nicholson & Watson, 1982), pp. 108–18; Thomas Oden, *Radical Obedience: The Ethics of Rudolf Bultmann* (London: Epworth Press, 1965), pp. 34–9, 107–12.

34 Oden, *Radical Obedience*, pp. 27–8.

35 See Paul Ramsay, *Basic Christian Ethics* (London: SCM Press, 1950), pp. 93–7. Bornkamm's approach to neighbour-love owes a great deal to Bultmann and also involves a similar reading of this parable. See his *Jesus of Nazareth*, pp. 109–15.

36 Ramsay, *Basic Christian Ethics*, pp. 37–45, 98–100.

37 Ramsay, *Basic Christian Ethics*, pp. 56–9, 78–9.

38 Frei, *Types of Christian Theology*, p. 134.

39 Frei, *Types of Christian Theology*, p. 135.

40 Frei, *Types of Christian Theology*, pp. 136–7.

41 Ramsay, *Basic Christian Ethics*, pp. 98–9.

42 Frei, *Types of Christian Theology*, p. 137.

43 Frei, *Types of Christian Theology*, p. 137.

44 Frei, 'Of the Holy Ghost', p. 194.

45 See the overview of these critiques in Barbara Hilkert Andolsen, 'Agape in feminist ethics', *The Journal of Religious Ethics* 9:1 (1981), pp. 69–83.

46 Andolsen, 'Agape in feminist ethics', p. 74.

47 See, for example, Frei's colleague Margaret Farley's call for a moral revolution on these terms in her 'New patterns of relationship: beginnings of a moral revolution', *Theological Studies* 36:4 (1975), pp. 627–46; and Beverly Wildung Harrison, 'The power of anger in the work of love: Christian ethics for women and other strangers', in B. W. Harrison, *Making the Connections: Essays in Feminist Social Ethics*, ed. Carol S. Robb (Boston, MA: Beacon Press, 1985), pp. 15–20. Frei, Farley and Harrison arrive at their accounts of love, however, in quite different ways. Harrison's call for radical, relational mutuality is premised on de-centring Christ's crucifixion in favour of his ministry; Frei's generous neighbour-love is normed by the love of Christ climactically enacted in his passion. Farley emphasizes intra-trinitarian love as a norm, in contrast to both.

48 For example, for women in heterosexual relationships in the cultures where sexuality is linked with violence through the eroticization of domination. See Karen Lebacqz, 'Love your enemy: sex, power, and Christian ethics', *The Annual of the Society of Christian Ethics* 10 (1990), pp. 3–23.

49 As Lebacqz argues, we must, invoking Beverly Wildung Harrison ('Love your enemy', p. 6).

50 See Mike Higton, *Christ, Providence and History* (Edinburgh: T & T Clark, 2004), pp. 267–8.

51 Hans W. Frei, 'Of the resurrection', in G. Hunsinger and W. Placher (eds), *Theology and Narrative: Selected Essays* (Oxford: Oxford University Press, 1993), p. 206.

52 Frei, 'Of the resurrection', p. 206.

53 Frei, 'Of the resurrection', p. 206.

54 Hans W. Frei, 'Karl Barth: theologian', in *Theology and Narrative*, pp. 172–3.

55 See Reinhold Niebuhr, 'Moral man and immoral society: a study in ethics and politics', in E. Sefton (ed.), *Reinhold Niebuhr: Major Works on Religion and Politics* (New York: Library Classics of the United States, 2015), pp. 139–350; and Reinhold Niebuhr, *The Nature and Destiny of Man: A Christian Interpretation. Volume 1: Human Nature* (London: Nisbet & Co., 1941), especially pp. 1–253.

56 Hans W. Frei, 'Types of academic theology', in *Types of Christian Theology*, p. 126.

57 Frei, 'Types of academic theology', pp. 126–7.

58 As David Kamitsuka observes, the value of solidarity with the oppressed is unfocused in Frei but this passage, where Frei is poised to reflect on it, shows that the impetus for attention to the needs and theological reflection of the oppressed is so deeply embedded 'in the plain sense of Jesus' identity as to be unavoidable' (D. Kamitsuka, *Theology and Contemporary Culture* (Cambridge: Cambridge University Press, 2000), p. 42).

59 Frei, 'Of the Holy Ghost', pp. 193–4.

60 Frei, 'Of the Holy Ghost', p. 194.

61 Frei, 'Of the Holy Ghost', p. 194.

62 Frei, 'Of the Holy Ghost', p. 194.

63 Frei, 'Of the Holy Ghost', p. 194.

64 Frei, 'Of the Holy Ghost', p. 194.

65 Frei, 'Of the Holy Ghost', p. 194.

66 Frei, 'Of the Holy Ghost', p. 194; his emphasis.

67 Frei, 'Of the Holy Ghost', p. 194.

68 Frei, 'Of the Holy Ghost', p. 194.

69 Frei, 'Of the Holy Ghost', pp. 194–5.

70 Frei, 'Of the Holy Ghost', pp. 194–5.

71 Stanley Hauerwas, *Resident Aliens: Life in the Christian Colony*, expanded 25th anniversary edn (Nashville, TN: Abingdon Press, 2014), pp. 82–3.

72 Hauerwas, *Resident Aliens*, pp. 91–2; Stanley Hauerwas, *The Peaceable Kingdom: A Primer in Christian Ethics* (Notre Dame, IN: University of Notre Dame Press, 1991), p. 97.

73 Hauerwas, *The Peaceable Kingdom*, p. 99.

74 James Cone, *God of the Oppressed* (Maryknoll, NY: Orbis Books, 1997 [1975]), pp. xi–x, 207.

75 Cone, *God of the Oppressed*, pp. 207–10. See also his later *The Cross and the Lynching Tree* (Maryknoll, NY: Orbis Books, 2013).

76 Cone, *God of the Oppressed*, pp. 213–18.

77 Cone, *God of the Oppressed*, pp. 219–22.

78 Jennifer Harvey, *Dear White Christians: For Those Still Longing for Racial Reconciliation*, 2nd edn (Grand Rapids, MI: Eerdmans, 2020).

79 For congruent approaches to reconciliation in the context of South Africa, see John W. De Gruchy, *Reconciliation: Restoring Justice* (London: SCM Press, 2002), and Allan Aubrey Boesak and Curtiss Paul DeYoung, *Radical Reconciliation: Beyond Political Pietism and Christian Quietism* (Maryknoll, NY: Orbis Books, 2012).

80 Hans W. Frei, 'God's patience and our work', 'To give and to receive', 'Response to Elisabeth Moltmann-Wendel' and 'Reinhold Niebuhr, where are you now that we need you?', published in Frei, *Reading Faithfully, vol. 1*, pp. 161–3, 163–72, 173–5, 176–82, and available online (http://divinity-adhoc.library.yale.edu/HansFreiTranscripts/Freitranscripts/Frei07-Patience.pdf, accessed 15.11.2023); 'H. Richard Niebuhr on history, church, and nation', in Frei, *Theology and Narrative*, pp. 214–33.

81 Higton, *Christ, Providence and History*, pp. 170–3, is a notable exception.

82 Frei, 'Reinhold Niebuhr', p. 177.

83 Frei, 'Reinhold Niebuhr', pp. 180–1.

84 Frei, 'Reinhold Niebuhr', p. 178.

85 Frei, 'Reinhold Niebuhr', p. 179.

86 Frei, 'Reinhold Niebuhr', pp. 178–9, 181.

87 Frei, 'Reinhold Niebuhr', p. 180. See Reinhold Niebuhr, 'The irony of American history', in *Reinhold Niebuhr: Major Works on Religion and Politics*, pp. 459–589. Niebuhr writes here about tragedy and irony in the situation of the United States confronting communism early in the Cold War. The USA had to make tragic choices, he argued, in the exercise of its global power: conscious choices to do evil for the sake of good, sacrificing one high value for a higher one. The irony of the situation of the USA in the early 1950s had to do with the way exceptionalist liberal American ideals about the USA were being refuted by the way

the very rationalistic-technical advances they celebrated had augmented its power so that it had been drawn into global responsibilities through self-interest, necessitating the tragic (and risk-laden) choices like the threat of nuclear war to maintain peace. Immature US ideologies and their illusions – not least their own innocence about the USA's own imperialistic group pride – meant the nation had not come to terms with the complexities of international social conflict and was not ready for its new responsibilities. Its dreams of mastering history were undergoing ironic refutation through its vast entanglement with other wills and recalcitrant historical forces. This innocence could only be dissipated if American idealism came to terms with 'the limits of all human striving, the fragmentariness of all human wisdom, the precariousness of all historic configurations of power, and the mixture of good and evil in human virtue' (p. 560). Frei's more qualified notion of tragic choices, however, is not as extreme as Niebuhr's and, as we shall see, he was more dubious about the global power and role of the USA.

88 Frei, 'Reinhold Niebuhr', pp. 180–1. I am reading Frei's comments about sacrifice here in connection with his remarks about the doctrine of sin, the irony of history and the characterization of political choices towards liberation as choosing a greater good that is a lesser evil (p. 181). Frei seems to make the connection when he summarizes that latter discussion by reiterating that the promise of God is a miracle we see now only in a glass darkly.

89 Frei, 'Reinhold Niebuhr', p. 181.

90 Hans W. Frei, 'To give and to receive', p. 163, quoting Jürgen Moltmann, *God in Creation: An Ecological Doctrine of Creation* (London: SCM Press, 1985), p. 210.

91 Frei, 'To give and to receive', p. 164.

92 Frei, 'To give and to receive', p. 164.

93 Frei, 'To give and to receive', p. 164.

94 Frei, 'To give and to receive', p. 165

95 Frei, 'To give and to receive', p. 166.

96 Frei, 'To give and to receive', p. 167. Frei acknowledges the allusion here to Karl Barth's phrase in the title of paragraph 59 of *CD* IV/1: 'The way of God into the far country'.

97 We might recall here Frei's account of divine impassibility in the epilogue to *The Identity of Jesus Christ*, p. 173.

98 Frei, 'To give and to receive', p. 165.

99 Frei, 'To give and to receive', p. 168. See Barth, 'The perfections of the Divine Loving', §30.3, 'The patience and wisdom of God', *CD* II/1, pp. 406–22.

100 Frei, 'To give and to receive', p. 168.

101 Frei, 'To give and to receive', p. 168.

102 See, however, Paul Dafydd Jones' analysis of how the theme of divine patience, as expounded in *CD* II/1, underlies Barth's account of the church's mission, including its political dimensions. See P. D. Jones, 'On patience: thinking with and beyond Karl Barth', *Scottish Journal of Theology* 68:3 (2015), pp. 292–3.

103 Frei, 'To give and to receive', p. 168; his emphasis.

104 Compare Barth on 'The eternity and glory of God', §31.3, *CD* II/1, pp. 608–40; and §49, 'God the Father as Lord of his creature', *CD* III/3 (Edinburgh: T & T Clark, 1961), pp. 58–288.

105 Frei, 'To give and to receive', p. 169.

106 Frei, 'To give and to receive', p. 168; his emphasis.

107 Frei, 'To give and to receive', p. 169.

108 Frei, 'To give and to receive', p. 169; Frei, 'Reinhold Niebuhr', p. 182.

109 Frei, 'Reinhold Niebuhr', p. 182.

110 Frei, 'To give and to receive', p. 169.

111 Frei, 'To give and to receive', p. 170; Frei, 'Reinhold Niebuhr', p. 182; his emphasis.

112 Frei, 'Response to Elisabeth Moltmann-Wendel', pp. 173–4.

113 Frei, 'Reinhold Niebuhr', p. 182.

114 Frei, 'To give and to receive', p. 172.

115 Frei, 'To give and to receive', p. 170.

116 Frei, 'To give and to receive', p. 170; Frei, 'Reinhold Niebuhr', p. 182.

117 Frei, 'To give and to receive', p. 170.

118 Frei, 'To give and to receive', p. 171.

119 Frei, 'To give and to receive', p. 171.

120 Frei, 'Response to Elisabeth Moltmann-Wendel', pp. 173–5. He took Moltmann-Wendel to reject such self-assertion.

121 Frei, 'To give and to receive', p. 171.

122 Frei, 'To give and to receive', p. 171.

123 Frei, 'H. Richard Niebuhr', pp. 218–20.

124 Frei, 'H. Richard Niebuhr', p. 219.

125 Frei, 'H. Richard Niebuhr', p. 222.

126 Frei, 'H. Richard Niebuhr', pp. 222–3.

127 Frei, 'H. Richard Niebuhr', pp. 223–5.

128 Frei, 'H. Richard Niebuhr', pp. 228–9.

129 Frei, 'H. Richard Niebuhr', p. 229.

130 Frei, 'H. Richard Niebuhr', pp. 229–30.

131 Frei, 'H. Richard Niebuhr', p. 230.

132 Frei, 'H. Richard Niebuhr', p. 230.

133 Frei, 'H. Richard Niebuhr', p. 230.

134 Frei, 'H. Richard Niebuhr', p. 230.

135 H. Richard Niebuhr, 'The grace of doing nothing', in Richard. B Miller (ed.), *War in the Twentieth Century: Sources in Theological Ethics* (Louisville, KY: Westminster John Knox Press, 1992), pp. 6–11.

136 Niebuhr, 'The grace of doing nothing', pp. 10–11.

137 Niebuhr, 'The grace of doing nothing', p. 11.

138 Niebuhr, 'The grace of doing nothing', p. 11.

139 H. Richard Niebuhr, 'A communication: the only way into the kingdom of God', in Miller, *War in the Twentieth Century*, p. 20.

140 Niebuhr, 'The grace of doing nothing', p. 9; Niebuhr, 'A communication', p. 20.

141 Niebuhr, 'The grace of doing nothing', p. 10.

142 Reinhold Niebuhr, 'Must we do nothing?', in Miller, *War in the Twentieth Century*, pp. 12–18, at p. 14.

143 Niebuhr, 'Must we do nothing?', p. 14.

144 Niebuhr, 'Must we do nothing?', p. 15.

145 Niebuhr, 'Must we do nothing?', p. 17.

146 Frei, 'H. Richard Niebuhr', p. 226.

147 Frei, 'H. Richard Niebuhr', p. 226.

148 Frei, 'H. Richard Niebuhr', pp. 226–7.

149 H. Richard Niebuhr, 'War as crucifixion', in Miller, *War in the Twentieth Century*, pp. 65–7 (first published in May 1942).

150 H. Richard Niebuhr, 'War as the judgment of God', in Miller, *War in the Twentieth Century*, pp. 47, 50–1 (originally published in April 1943).

151 Niebuhr, 'War as the judgment of God', pp. 52–5.

152 Niebuhr, *The Nature and Destiny of Man*, vol. 1, pp. 135ff.

153 Niebuhr, *The Nature and Destiny of Man*, vol. 1, p. 142.

154 Niebuhr, *The Nature and Destiny of Man*, vol. 1, p. 151.

155 Niebuhr, *The Nature and Destiny of Man*, vol. 1, pp. 152–9.

156 Niebuhr, *The Nature and Destiny of Man: A Christian Interpretation. Volume 2: Human Destiny* (London: Nisbet & Co., 1943), p. 74.

157 Niebuhr, *The Nature and Destiny of Man*, vol. 2, p. 74.

158 Niebuhr, *The Nature and Destiny of Man*, vol. 2, p. 84.

159 Niebuhr, *The Nature and Destiny of Man*, vol. 2, pp. 71–3.

160 Niebuhr, *The Nature and Destiny of Man*, vol. 2, p. 261.

161 Niebuhr, *The Nature and Destiny of Man*, vol. 2, pp. 266–96.

162 Niebuhr, *The Nature and Destiny of Man*, vol. 2, pp. 297–309.

163 Niebuhr, *The Nature and Destiny of Man*, vol. 2, pp. 309–11. See also Reinhold Niebuhr, *Faith and History: A Comparison of Christian and Modern Views of History* (London: Nisbet & Co., 1949), p. 243.

164 Niebuhr, *The Nature and Destiny of Man*, vol. 2, pp. 312–18. In *Faith and History*, Niebuhr highlights a community's concern for those outside its borders, and moments where the interests of rulers and the total community coincide as examples of the virtuous moments possible for historical communities (*Faith and History*, pp. 251–2).

165 Niebuhr, *The Nature and Destiny of Man*, vol. 2, p. 323.

166 Frei, 'H. Richard Niebuhr', p. 233. For Reinhold Niebuhr's significance for the tradition of American social ethics, see G. Dorrien, *Social Ethics in the Making: Interpreting an American Tradition* (Chichester: Wiley-Blackwell, 2009).

167 Frei, 'H. Richard Niebuhr', p. 230.

168 Frei, 'H. Richard Niebuhr', p. 231.

169 Frei, 'H. Richard Niebuhr', p. 231.

170 H. Richard Niebuhr, *Radical Monotheism and Western Culture* (Louisville, KY: Westminster/John Knox Press, 1970), p. 11.

171 Frei, 'H. Richard Niebuhr', pp. 231, 233.

172 Frei, 'H. Richard Niebuhr', p. 232.

173 Frei, 'H. Richard Niebuhr', p. 231.

174 Frei, 'H. Richard Niebuhr', p. 232.

175 Frei, 'H. Richard Niebuhr', p. 214.

176 Frei, 'H. Richard Niebuhr', p. 214.

177 Frei, 'H. Richard Niebuhr', p. 215.

178 Frei, 'H. Richard Niebuhr', p. 215.

179 Frei, 'H. Richard Niebuhr', pp. 215–16.

180 Frei, 'H. Richard Niebuhr', p. 216.

181 Frei, 'Reinhold Niebuhr', p. 180. Frei noted at the conference that the bombing was not the only choice available to the USA in the situation (untitled notes, Yale Divinity School archive (YDS) 76 III 11-173).

182 Frei, 'H. Richard Niebuhr', pp. 216, 231.

183 Frei, 'H. Richard Niebuhr', p. 232.

184 Frei, 'H. Richard Niebuhr', p. 232.

185 Frei, 'H. Richard Niebuhr', pp. 232–3.

186 As Lillian Calles Barger has shown, the history of liberation theologies in North and Latin America, and the traditions from which they emerged, are closely interconnected and there is considerable conversation and influence between different strands across the Americas. See L. C. Barger, *The World Come of Age: An Intellectual History of Liberation Theology* (New York: Oxford University Press, 2018).

187 See above and also Hans W. Frei, 'Conflicts in interpretation', in *Theology and Narrative*, p. 166.

188 Gutiérrez, *A Theology of Liberation*, p. 175.

189 Gutiérrez, *A Theology of Liberation*, p. 232.

190 Gutiérrez, *A Theology of Liberation*, pp. 175, 198, 269.

191 Gutiérrez, *A Theology of Liberation*, p. 175.

192 Gutiérrez, *A Theology of Liberation*, p. 175.

193 Gutiérrez, *A Theology of Liberation*, p. 35.

194 See also Gutiérrez's account of this 'internal colonialism' in Gustavo Gutiérrez, *The Power of the Poor in History: Selected Writings* (Maryknoll, NY: Orbis Books, 1983), p. 28.

195 Gutiérrez, *The Power of the Poor in History*, pp. 77–8; Gustavo Gutiérrez, *We Drink from Our Own Wells: The Spiritual Journey of a People* (London: SCM Press, 2005), p. 11.

196 Gutiérrez, *A Theology of Liberation*, p. 85.

197 Gutiérrez, *A Theology of Liberation*, p. 85; Gutiérrez, *The Power of the Poor in History*, pp. 83–5.

198 Gutiérrez, *The Power of the Poor in History*, p. 86; Gutiérrez, *We Drink from Our Own Wells*, pp. 9–11.

199 See Gutiérrez, *We Drink from Our Own Wells*, p. 10.

200 See the classic feminist critique of Niebuhr on sin in Valerie Saiving Goldstein, 'The human situation: a feminine view', *Journal of Religion* 40:2 (1960), pp. 100–12. See also, among others, Judith Plaskow, *Sex, Sin and Grace: Women's Experience and the Theologies of Reinhold Niebuhr and Paul Tillich* (Lanham, MD and London: University of America Press, 1980).

201 See Frei, 'Response to Elisabeth Moltmann-Wendel', pp. 173–4, where he instances Saiving and Plaskow's 'fine analysis' of Niebuhr and Tillich. Frei was one of those who read through the Yale doctoral dissertation on which Plaskow's book was based. See the Preface to the book (p. vii).

202 Rosemary Radford Ruether, *Sexism and God-Talk: Towards a Feminist Theology* (London: SCM Press, 1983), p. 111.

203 Ruether, *Sexism and God-Talk*, pp. 113–14, 161. 'God/ess' is Ruether's term for a reconstructed, liberative feminist understanding of the divine that is guided by biblical anti-hierarchical, anti-patriarchal and anti-idolatry traditions and biblical female metaphors for God, to deprivilege male God-talk, and which draws on female roles and experiences and those of other people at the bottom of society (pp. 56–71).

204 Ruether, *Sexism and God-Talk*, pp. 161–2.

205 Ruether, *Sexism and God-Talk*, pp. 162–3.

206 Ruether, *Sexism and God-Talk*, p. 162.

207 Ruether, *Sexism and God-Talk*, p. 165.

208 Ruether, *Sexism and God-Talk*, p. 164.

209 Ruether, *Sexism and God-Talk*, p. 164.

210 Ruether, *Sexism and God-Talk*, pp. 165–70. See also the analysis in Mary Daly, *Beyond God the Father: Toward a Philosophy of Women's Liberation* (Boston, MA: Beacon Press, 1973), pp. 46–9, where Daly notes the pervasive influence of the myth of the fall of Adam and Eve on laws concerning women's social status (especially in relation to reproductive rights) and cultural representations of women in the mass media.

211 Ruether, *Sexism and God-Talk*, pp. 53–5, 61. Daly's statement of this critique is now classic, of course. See Daly, *Beyond God the Father*, p. 13. Ruether, however, provides a much more historically nuanced analysis of the development of male monotheism in the Ancient Near East, including in Israelite religion; of the anti-patriarchal strands of God-talk in the Hebrew Bible and New Testament, as well as of the co-option of some of these (especially God as father and king) in Christianized but still patriarchal societies (Ruether, *Sexism and God-Talk*, pp. 47–66).

212 Though, as Beverly Wildung Harrison notes, gender oppression does not always need to depend on explicit sexual stereotypes; the exclusion of women's experience, modes of being and culture from male-dominated culture has the same effect of reinforcing a gender dualism basic to the structural oppression of women (*Making the Connections*, p. 31).

213 Ruether, *Sexism and God-Talk*, p. 174. Daly also notes the logical dependence of the male stereotype on there being a corresponding contrasting negative female stereotype (*Beyond God the Father*, pp. 9–10).

214 Ruether, *Sexism and God-Talk*, pp. 174, 176–7.

215 Ruether, *Sexism and God-Talk*, p. 175.

216 Ruether, *Sexism and God-Talk*, pp. 175–6.

217 Ruether, *Sexism and God-Talk*, pp. 177–8. Ruether's account here is of the society of her time. Harrison offers a more historically contextualized analysis of this situation in *Making the Connections*, pp. 42–53.

218 Ruether, *Sexism and God-Talk*, pp. 178–80.

219 Ruether, *Sexism and God-talk*, p. 180.

220 Ruether, *Sexism and God-Talk*, p. 180.

221 Ruether, *Sexism and God-Talk*, p. 180.

222 James Cone, *A Black Theology of Liberation* (Maryknoll, NY: Orbis Books, 1990), pp. 11–18, 24–26, 55, 103–7. In *The Cross and the Lynching Tree*, Cone is more emphatic in making Jesus Christ normative for the identification of white supremacy as sin.

223 Cone, *A Black Theology of Liberation*, pp. 8, 106–7.

224 See James Cone, 'Theology's great sin: silence in the face of white supremacy', *Black Theology* 2:2 (2004), pp. 139–52.

225 See Delores Williams, *Sisters in the Wilderness: The Challenge of Womanist God-Talk* (Maryknoll, NY: Orbis Books, 1993); and Delores Williams, 'The color of feminism: on speaking the black woman's tongue', *The Journal of Religious Thought* 43:1 (1986), pp. 42–58.

226 Williams, *Sisters in the Wilderness*, pp. 74–81. See Emilie Townes, *Womanist Ethics and the Cultural Production of Evil* (New York: Palgrave Macmillan, 2006), which offers a sophisticated analysis of this dynamic in respect of stereotypes of black femaleness.

227 Gutiérrez, *A Theology of Liberation*, p. 152.

228 Gutiérrez, *A Theology of Liberation*, pp. 153, 159–60, 173.

229 Gutiérrez, *A Theology of Liberation*, pp. 154–6.

230 Gutiérrez, *A Theology of Liberation*, pp. 158–9. See also Gutiérrez, *The Power of the Poor in History*, p. 32.

231 Gutiérrez, *A Theology of Liberation*, pp. 160–7.

232 Gutiérrez, *A Theology of Liberation*, pp. 226–32; Gutiérrez, *The Power of the Poor in History*, p. 15.

233 Gutiérrez, *A Theology of Liberation*, pp. 189–94, 201–2. Gutiérrez appeals to the story of Cornelius in Acts 10 as warrant for this universalization of the Johannine notion of the indwelling of Christ and the Father by the Spirit (p. 193), and to Matthew 25.31–45 for the emphasis on Christ's presence in the poor (see below).

234 On critical denunciation, see Gutiérrez, *A Theology of Liberation*, p. 177.

235 Gutiérrez, *A Theology of Liberation*, p. 208.

236 Gutiérrez, *The Power of the Poor in History*, p. 105.

237 Gutiérrez seems implicitly to address those not being oppressed in *A Theology of Liberation*.

238 Gutiérrez, *A Theology of Liberation*, pp. 260–1, 269. See also *The Power of the Poor in History*, pp. 21–22, 105, where the poor are specified as those who evangelize the church.

239 Gutiérrez, *A Theology of Liberation*, pp. 260–2.

240 Gutiérrez, *A Theology of Liberation*, p. 260.

241 Gutiérrez, *A Theology of Liberation*, pp. 268–9, 272.

242 Gutiérrez, *A Theology of Liberation*, p. 272.

243 Gutiérrez, *A Theology of Liberation*, p. 269. See also *The Power of the Poor in History*, p. 18.

244 Gutiérrez, *A Theology of Liberation*, p. 269.

245 Gutiérrez offers this account of utopian thought in *A Theology of Liberation*, pp. 232–4.

246 Gutiérrez thus offers a theological transformation of Paulo Freire's model of conscientization in Paulo Freire, *Pedagogy of the Oppressed* (London: Penguin Books, 1970).

247 It is relevant here that in Gutiérrez's account of 'God's revelation and proclamation in history' in *The Power of the Poor in History*, he advances an account of the biblical God as one who liberates, and de-emphasizes any wider providential governance. See *The Power of the Poor in History*, pp. 4, 7. Gutiérrez in effect is close here to identifying God's revelatory works in history entirely with God's liberating acts. But as he notes in respect of the moves to universalize this view in the prophets, to be this powerful God must be creator of all things (p. 11).

248 Gustavo Gutiérrez, *On Job: God-Talk and the Suffering of the Innocent* (Maryknoll, NY: Orbis Books, 1987), p. 79.

249 For the resilience of his hope in the face of repression, see his 1978 retrospect, 'The historical power of the poor', in Gutiérrez, *The Power of the Poor in History*, especially pp. 75–82.

250 See Michael Löwy, *The War of Gods: Religion and Politics in Latin America* (London: Verso, 1996), pp. 94–8, 102–7, 125–31.

251 Manuel Vásquez, *The Brazilian Popular Church and the Crisis of Modernity* (Cambridge: Cambridge University Press, 1998). See also Goetz Frank Ottmann's

account of liberationism in the Brasilândia region of Brazil: Goetz Frank Ottmann, *Lost for Words? Brazilian Liberationism in the 1990s* (Pittsburgh, PA: University of Pittsburgh Press, 2002).

252 Cone, *God of the Oppressed*, pp. 74, 123–4.

253 Cone, *God of the Oppressed*, pp. 106, 109.

254 Cone, *God of the Oppressed*, pp. 123–6.

255 Cone, *God of the Oppressed*, pp. 110, 128.

256 Cone, *God of the Oppressed*, pp. 111–12.

257 Cone, *God of the Oppressed*, p. 115.

258 Cone, *God of the Oppressed*, p. 130.

259 Cone, *God of the Oppressed*, p. 115.

260 Cone, *God of the Oppressed*, pp. 74, 146–7, 161–2.

261 On providence and suffering, see Cone, *A Black Theology of Liberation*, pp. 16–17, 78–81. See also James Cone, '"Calling the oppressors to account": justice, love and hope in black religion', in Quinton Hosford Dixie and Cornel West (eds), *The Courage to Hope: From Black Suffering to Human Redemption* (Boston, MA: Beacon Press, 1999), p. 77.

262 Cone, *God of the Oppressed*, pp. 115, 118–20, 138.

263 See the theme of God's revelation in Christ justifying black people pursuing their complete emancipation by whatever means they deem necessary, including rebellion, in James Cone, *Black Theology and Black Power* (New York: The Seabury Press, 1969), pp. 6, 22. See also Cone, *A Black Theology of Liberation*, pp. 45–6.

264 Cone, *God of the Oppressed*, p. 121.

265 Cone, *God of the Oppressed*, p. 135; see also p. 138.

266 Williams, *Sisters in the Wilderness*, p. 151.

267 Williams, *Sisters in the Wilderness*, pp. 5–6, 39–58, 108–20, 127–39, 159.

268 Williams, *Sisters in the Wilderness*, pp. 195–9.

269 One further position, in some disjunction from this trajectory, would be a more purely imminentist construal of the power of love and realist construal of prospects for social justice and transformation, as seen in, for example, Harrison, *Making the Connections*.

Bibliography

Ahlstrom, S. E., 'The Radical Turn in Theology and Ethics: Why it Occurred in the 1960's', *The Annals of The American Academy of Political and Social Science* 387:1 (1970), pp. 1–13.

Andolsen, B. H., 'Agape in Feminist Ethics', *The Journal of Religious Ethics* 9:1 (1981), pp. 69–83.

Aschheim, S. E., 1982, *Brothers and Strangers: The East European Jew In German and German Jewish Consciousness, 1800–1923*, Madison, WI: The University of Wisconsin Press.

Auerbach, E., 1959, *Figura*, from Auerbach, *Scenes from the Drama of European Literature*, New York: Meridian Books, pp. 11–76.

——, 1953, *Mimesis: The Representation of Reality in Western Literature*, Princeton, NJ: Princeton University Press.

August, S. and M. Levy, *Project Concern in Cheshire. A Preliminary Report*, Department of Education, Cheshire (January 1970).

Barger, L. C., 2018, *The World Come of Age. An Intellectual History of Liberation Theology*, New York: Oxford University Press.

Barth, K., 1972, 'Bultmann – an attempt to understand him' in H.-W. Bartsch, *Kerygma and Myth. A Theological Debate*, tr. R. H. Fuller, London: SPCK, pp. 83–132.

Barth, K., 1979 (1963), *Evangelical Theology*, Grand Rapids, MI: Eerdmans.

——, *Church Dogmatics*

——, 1954, 'The Christian Community and the Civil Community' in K. Barth, *Against the Stream. Shorter Post-War Writings 1946–52*, London: SCM Press, pp. 15–50.

——, 1928, *The Word of God and the Word of Man*, tr. D. Horton, Boston and Chicago, IL: Pilgrim Press.

Bartsch, H.-W., 1972, *Kerygma and Myth. A Theological Debate*, tr. R. H. Fuller, London: SPCK.

Benner, S.A. et al., 'Report of the Committee on Freedom of Expression at Yale' (December 1974), https://yalecollege.yale.edu/get-know-yale-college/office-dean/reports/report-committee-freedom-expression-yale, accessed 15.03.2022.

Bettis, P., 2017 (1976), 'Political Theology and Social Ethics: The Socialist Humanism of Karl Barth', in G. Hunsinger (ed.), *Karl Barth and Radical Politics*, Eugene, OR: Wipf & Stock, pp. 117–34.

Biggar, N. J., 1993, *The Hastening that Waits: Karl Barth's Ethics*, Oxford: Clarendon Press.

Boesak, A. A. and C. P. DeYoung, 2012, *Radical Reconciliation. Beyond Political Pietism and Christian Quietism*, Maryknoll, NY: Orbis Books.

Bonastia, C., 2006, *Knocking on the Door. The Federal Government's Attempt to Desegregate the Suburbs*, Princeton, NJ: Princeton University Press.

Boniface, T., 2018, *Jesus, Transcendence, and Generosity. Christology and Transcendence in Hans Frei and Dietrich Bonhoeffer*, Lanham, MD: Lexington Books/Fortress Press.

Bornkamm, G., 1960, *Jesus of Nazareth*, London: Hodder and Stoughton.

Boyle, N., 2004, *Sacred and Secular Scriptures: A Catholic approach to Literature*, London: Darton, Longman & Todd.

Bultmann, R. K., 1984, 'New Testament and Mythology: The Problem of Demythologizing the New Testament Proclamation (1941)' in R. K. Bultmann and Schubert M. Ogden (eds), *New Testament Mythology and Other Basic Writings*, Philadelphia, PA: Fortress Press, pp. 1–44.

——, 'The Problem of Hermeneutics' in R. K. Bultmann and S. Ogden (ed., tr.), *New Testament and Mythology and Other Basic Writings*, pp. 69–94.

——, 1969 (1924), 'Liberal Theology and the Latest Theological Movement' in R. W. Funk (ed.), *Faith and Understanding. Collected Essays*, tr. Louise Pettibone Smith, London: SCM Press, pp. 53–7.

——, 1969 (1925), 'What does it mean to speak of God?' in *Faith and Understanding*, pp. 45–6.

——, 1969 (1928), 'The Significance of "Dialectical Theology" for the Scientific Study of the New Testament' in *Faith and Understanding*, pp. 145–64.

——, 1960, *Jesus Christ and Mythology*, London: SCM Press.

——, 2007 (1951), *Theology of the New Testament* vol. 1, Waco, TX: Baylor University Press.

——, 1935 (1926), *Jesus and the Word*, tr. Louise Pettibone Smith, Erminie Huntress, London: Ivor Nicholson & Watson.

Calvin, J., 1960, *Institutes of the Christian Religion*, tr. Ford Lewis Battles, Philadelphia, PA: Westminster Press.

Campbell, C., 1997, *Preaching Jesus: New Directions for Homiletics in Hans Frei's Postliberal Theology*, Grand Rapids, MI: William B Eerdmans.

Chauncey, H., J. T. Hill, T. Strong and H. L. Gates Jr., 2016, *May Day at Yale, 1970: Recollections. The Trial of Bobby Seale and the Black Panthers*, Westport: Prospecta Press.

Childs, B. S., 1977, 'The Sensus Literalis of Scripture: An Ancient and Modern Problem' in W. Zimmerli, H. Donner, R. Hanhart and R. Smend (eds), *Beiträge zur alttestamentlichen Theologie: Festschrift für Walther Zimmerli zum 70. Geburtstag*, Göttingen: Vandenhoeck & Ruprecht, pp. 80–93.

Childs, B.S. et al., 1969, 'Final Discussion' in D. L. Dickerman (ed.), *Karl Barth and the Future of Theology: A Memorial Colloquium Held at the Yale Divinity School, January 28, 1969*, New Haven, CT: Yale Divinity School Association, pp. 52–3.

Cobb, J. B., 'The Post-Bultmannian Trend', *Journal of Bible and Religion* 30:1 (1962), pp. 3–11.

Collins, D., 2021, *The Unique and Universal Christ. Refiguring the Theology of Religions*, Waco, TX: Baylor University Press.

Comstock, G., 'Truth or Meaning: Ricoeur versus Frei on Biblical Narrative', *Journal of Religion* 66 (2) 1986, pp. 117–40.

Cone, J. H., 2013, *The Cross and the Lynching Tree*, Maryknoll, NY: Orbis Books.

——, 'Theology's Great Sin: Silence in the Face of White Supremacy', *Black Theology*, 2:2 (2004), pp. 139–52.

——, 1999, '"Calling the Oppressors to Account": Justice, Love and Hope in Black Religion' in Quinton Hosford Dixie and Cornel West (eds), *The Courage to Hope. From Black Suffering to Human Redemption*, Boston, MA: Beacon Press, pp. 73–85.

——, 1997 (1975), *God of the Oppressed*, Maryknoll, NY: Orbis Books.

——, 1990, *A Black Theology of Liberation*, Maryknoll, NY: Orbis Books.

——, 1969, *Black theology and Black Power*, New York: The Seabury Press.

Congdon, D. W., 'Deworlded within the World: Bultmann's Paradoxical Politics in an Age of Polarization', *Theology Today* 79:1 (2022), pp. 52–66.

——, 2015, *Rudolf Bultmann: A Companion to His Theology*, Eugene, OR: Cascade Books.

Connecticut State Advisory Committee to US Commission on Civil Rights, *El Boricua: The Puerto Rican Community in Bridgeport and New Haven* (January 1973).

Dahl, N., 1962, 'Der historische Jesus als geschichtswissenschaftliches und theologisches Problem', *Kerygma und Dogma*, 1 (1955), pp. 104–32; trans. in C. Braaten and R. A. Harrisville (eds), *Kerygma and History*, Nashville, TN: Abingdon Press, pp. 138–71.

Daly, M., 1973, *Beyond God the Father. Toward a Philosophy of Women's Liberation*, Boston, MA: Beacon Press.

Dawson, J. D., 2002, *Christian Figural Reading and the Fashioning of Identity*, Berkeley, CA Los Angeles; London: University of California Press.

——, 'Figural Reading and the Fashioning of Christian Identity in Boyarin, Auerbach and Frei', *Modern Theology* 14:2 (1998), pp. 181–96.

De Gruchy, J. W., 2002, *Reconciliation. Restoring Justice*, London: SCM Press.

DeHart, P. J., 2006, *The Trial of Witnesses. The Rise and Decline of Postliberal Theology*, Malden: Blackwell Publishing.

Delmont, M. F., 2016, *Why Busing Failed. Race, Media, and the National Resistance to School Desegregation*, Oakland, CA: University of California Press.

Demson, D. and J. Webster (eds), *Modern Theology* 8.2 (April 1992), pp. 103–220.

Demson, D., 1997, *Hans Frei and Karl Barth: Different Ways of Reading Scripture*, Grand Rapids, MI: Eerdmans.

Dorrien, G., 2009, *Social Ethics in the Making: Interpreting an American Tradition*, Chichester: Wiley-Blackwell.

Du Bois, W. E. B., 1994, *The Souls of Black Folk*, New York: Dover Publications.

Farley, M., 'New Patterns of Relationship: Beginnings of a Moral Revolution', *Theological Studies* 36:4 (1975), pp. 627–46.

Ford, D. F., 'Hans Frei and the Future of Theology', *Modern Theology* 8:2 (1992), pp. 203–14.

Ford, D. F., 'On Being Theologically Hospitable to Jesus Christ: Hans Frei's Achievement', *The Journal of Theological Studies* 46, no. 2 (1995), pp. 532–46.

Frei, H. W., 2015, 'Scripture as Realistic Narrative. Karl Barth as Critic of Historical Criticism' in H. W. Frei, M. Higton and M. A. Bowald (eds), *Reading Faithfully. Vol. 1. Writings from the Archives. Theology and Hermeneutics*, Eugene, OR: Cascade Books, pp. 49–63.

——, 2015, 'On Interpreting the Christian Story' in Frei, Higton and Bowald, *Reading Faithfully. Vol. 1*, pp. 68–93.

——, 2015, 'Sinner, Saint and Pilgrim' in Frei, Higton and Bowald, *Reading Faithfully. Vol. 1*, pp. 122–40.

——, 2015, 'Is Religious Sensibility Accessible to Study?' in Frei, Higton and Bowald, *Reading Faithfully. Vol. 1*, pp. 141–8.

——, 2015, 'History, Salvation-History, and Typology' in Frei, Higton and Bowald, *Reading Faithfully. Vol. 1*, pp. 149–60.

——, 2015, 'God's Patience and Our Work' in Frei, Higton and Bowald, *Reading Faithfully. Vol. 1*, pp. 161–3.

——, 2015, 'To Give and To Receive' in Frei, Higton and Bowald, *Reading Faithfully. Vol. 1*, pp. 163–72.

——, 2015, 'Response to Elisabeth Moltmann-Wendel' in Frei, Higton and Bowald, *Reading Faithfully. Vol. 1*, pp. 173–5.

——, 2015, 'Reinhold Niebuhr, Where Are You Now That We Need You?' in Frei, Higton and Bowald, *Reading Faithfully. Vol. 1*, pp. 176–82.

——, 2015, 'Of the Holy Ghost' in Frei, Higton and Bowald, *Reading Faithfully.*, *vol. 1*, pp. 191–5.

——, 2015, 'Lessing and the Religious Use of Irony' in H. W. Frei, M. Higton and M. A. Bowald (eds), *Reading Faithfully vol. 2. Writings from the Archives. Frei's Theological Background*, Eugene, OR: Cascade Books, pp. 1–48.

——, 2015, 'Kant and the Transcendence of Rationalism and Religion' in Frei, Higton and Bowald, *Reading Faithfully vol. 2*, pp. 49–59.

——, 1993, 'Remarks in Connection with a Theological Proposal' in H. W. Frei, G. Hunsinger and W. Placher (eds), *Theology and Narrative: Selected Essays*, New York: Oxford University Press, pp. 26–44.

——, 1993, 'Theology and the Interpretation of Narrative: Some Hermeneutical Considerations' in Frei, Hunsinger and Placher, *Theology and Narrative*, pp. 95–116.

——, 1993, 'The "Literal Reading" of Biblical Narrative in the Christian Tradition: Does It Stretch Or Will It Break?' in Frei, Hunsinger and Placher, *Theology and Narrative*, pp. 117–52.

——, 1993, 'Conflicts in Interpretation: Resolution, Armistice, or Co-existence?' in Frei, Hunsinger and Placher, *Theology and Narrative*, pp. 153–66.

——, 1993, 'Karl Barth: Theologian' in Frei, Hunsinger and Placher, *Theology and Narrative*, pp. 167–76.

——, 1993, 'Barth and Schleiermacher: Divergence and Convergence' in Frei, Hunsinger and Placher, *Theology and Narrative*, pp. 177–99.

——, 1993, 'Of the Resurrection of Christ' in Frei, Hunsinger and Placher, *Theology and Narrative*, pp. 200–6.

——, 1993, 'Response to "Narrative Theology": An Evangelical Assessment' in Frei, Hunsinger and Placher, *Theology and Narrative*, pp. 207–12.

——, 1993, 'H. Richard Niebuhr on History, Church, and Nation' in *Theology and Narrative*, pp. 214–34.

——, 1992, *Types of Christian Theology*, G. Hunsinger, W. C. Placher (eds), New Haven, CT and London: Yale University Press.

——, 1992, 'Eberhard Busch's Biography of Karl Barth' in Hunsinger and Placher (eds), *Types of Christian Theology*, pp. 158–61.

——, 1990, 'Epilogue: George Lindbeck and *The Nature of Doctrine*' in Bruce Marshall (ed.), *Theology and Dialogue. Essays in Conversation with George Lindbeck*, Notre Dame, IN: University of Notre Dame Press, pp. 275–82.

——, 1985, 'David Friedrich Strauss' in N. Smart, P. Clayton, P. Sherry and S. T. Katz (eds), *Nineteenth Century Religious Thought in the West* vol. 1., Cambridge: Cambridge University Press, pp. 215–60.

——, 1980, Hans F. Holocaust Testimony HV 170, Fortunoff Video Archive for Holocaust Testimonies, Yale University, https://editions.fortunoff.library.yale.edu/essay/hvt-0170, accessed 26.01.2024.

——, 1975, *The Identity of Jesus Christ: The Hermeneutical Bases of Dogmatic Theology*, Philadelphia, PA: Fortress Press.

——, 1974, *The Eclipse of Biblical Narrative. A Study in Eighteenth and Nineteenth Century Hermeneutics*, New Haven, CT: Yale University Press.

——, 1974, 'German theology: Transcendence and Secularity' in Charles E. McClelland and Steven P. Scher (eds), *Postwar German Culture. An Anthology*, New York: E.P. Dutton & Co., pp. 98–112.

——, 'The Mystery of the Presence of Jesus Christ', *Crossroads: An Adult Education Magazine of the Presbyterian Church* 17:2 (1967), pp. 69–96 and 17:3, pp. 69–96.

——, 'Review of Jürgen Moltmann, *The Theology of Hope* (New York: Harper & Row, 1967)', *Union Seminary Quarterly Review* 23.3 (Spring), pp. 267–72.

——, 'Theological Reflections on the Accounts of Jesus' Death and Resurrection', *Christian Scholar* 49:4 (1966), pp. 263–306 and republished in H. W. Frei, G. Hunsinger and W. C. Placher (eds), 1993, *Theology and Narrative: selected essays*, New York: Oxford University Press, pp. 45–93.

——, 1962, 'Religion (Natural and Revealed)' in M. Halverson and A. Cohen, *A Handbook of Christian Theology*, London: Fontana Books, pp. 310–21.

——, 1957, 'Niebuhr's Theological Background' in P. Ramsey (ed.), *Faith and Ethics. The Theology of H. Richard Niebuhr*, New York: Harper & Row, pp. 9–64.

——, 1957, 'The Theology of H. Richard Niebuhr' in P. Ramsey (ed.), *Faith and Ethics. The Theology of H. Richard Niebuhr*, New York: Harper & Row, pp. 65–116.

——, 1956, 'The Doctrine of Revelation in Karl Barth', New Haven, CT: Yale University Press.

Freire, P., 1970, *Pedagogy of the Oppressed*, London: Penguin Books.

Fulford, B., 2020, 'Barth and Hans W. Frei' in G. Hunsinger and K. L. Johnson (eds), *The Wiley Blackwell Companion to Karl Barth* (vol. 2), London: Wiley Blackwell, pp. 645–56.

——, 'Moderating Religious Identity and the Eclipse of Religious Wisdoms: Lessons from Hans Frei', *The Review of Faith and International Affairs* 15 (2017), pp. 24–33.

——, 2016, 'Thinking about marriage with Scripture' in J. Bradbury and S. Cornwall (eds), *Thinking Again About Marriage: Key Theological Questions*, London: SCM Press, pp. 44–61.

——, 'Liberalism versus Postliberalism: The Great Divide in Twentieth-Century Theology. By John Allan Knight', *The Journal of Theological Studies*, 65(1) (2014), pp. 363–7.

——, 2013, *Divine Eloquence and Human Transformation: Rethinking Scripture and History Through Gregory of Nazianzus and Hans Frei*, Minneapolis, MN: Fortress Press.

Gespaire, B., 2013, 'Blockbusting', *Black Past*, https://www.blackpast.org/african-american-history/blockbusting, accessed 13.04.2022.

Goldstein, W., 2004, *William Sloane Coffin Jr. A Holy Impatience*, New Haven, CT and London: Yale University Press.

Gorringe, T. J., 1999, *Karl Barth: Against Hegemony*, Oxford: Oxford University Press.

Graham, E. L., H. Walton, F. Ward, 2013, *Theological Reflections: Methods*, London: SCM Press.

Green, G. (ed.), 1987, *Scriptural Authority and Narrative Interpretation*, Philadelphia, PA: Fortress Press.

Gunton, C., 1992, 'Types of Christian Theology. By Hans W. Frei. Edited by George Hunsinger and William C. Placher. New Haven and London, Yale University Press, 1992. Pp. xi 180. £16.95/$29.00', *Scottish Journal of Theology*, 49:2 (1996), pp. 233–4.

Gustafson, J. M. and J. T. Laney (eds), 1969, *On Being Responsible. Issues in Personal Ethics*, London: SCM Press.

Gutiérrez, G., 1974, *A Theology of Liberation. History, Politics and Salvation*, London: SCM Press.

——, 1983, *The Power of the Poor in History. Selected Writings*, Maryknoll, NY: Orbis Books.

——, 2005, *We Drink From Our Own Wells. The Spiritual Journey of a People*, London: SCM Press.

——, 1987, *On Job. God-Talk and the Suffering of the Innocent*, Maryknoll, NY: Orbis Books.

Harrison, B. W., 1985, *Making the Connections. Essays in Feminist Social Ethics*, Carol S. Robb (ed.), Boston, MA: Beacon Press.

Harvey, V., 'A Christology for Barabbases', *Perkins Journal* 29:3 (Spring 1976), pp. 1–13.

Harvey, J., 2020, *Dear White Christians. For those still longing for racial reconciliation* (2nd edition), Grand Rapids, MI: Eerdmans.

Hauerwas, S. M., 2013, *With the Grain of the Universe. The Church's Witness and Natural Theology*, Grand Rapids, MI: Baker Academic.

——, 2010, *Christian Existence Today. Essays on Church, World, and Living In Between*, Eugene, OR: Wipf & Stock.

——, 1991, *The Peaceable Kingdom. A Primer in Christian Ethics*, Notre Dame, IN: University of Notre Dame Press.

Hauerwas, S. M. and R. Coles, 2008, *Christianity, Radical Democracy and the Radical Ordinary. Conversations between a Radical Democrat and a Christian*, Cambridge: The Lutterworth Press.

Hauerwas, S. M. and W. H. Willimon, 2014, *Resident Aliens*, Nashville, TN: Abingdon Press.

Hays, R. B., 2002, *The Faith of Jesus Christ: The Narrative Substructure of Galatians 3:1–4:11*, Grand Rapids, MI: Eerdmans.

Henry, C. F. H., 'Narrative Theology: An Evangelical Appraisal' in *The Trinity Journal* NS 8:1 (1987), pp. 3–19.

Hertz, D., 2007, *How Jews Became Germans. The History of Conversion and Assimilation in Berlin*, New Haven, CT: Yale University Press.

Higton, M., 2020, *The Life of Christian Doctrine*, London: T & T Clark.

——, 2006, 'Hans Frei' in J. Holcomb (ed.), *Christian Theologies of Scripture: A comparative introduction*, New York: NYU Press, pp. 220–39.

——, 2004, *Christ, Providence and History. Hans W. Frei's Public Theology*, London: T & T Clark.

——, 2004, 'The Fulfilment of History in Barth, Frei, Auerbach and Dante' in J. C. McDowell and M. Higton (eds), *Conversing with Barth*, Aldershot: Ashgate, pp. 120–41.

Hood, R. E., 1985, *Contemporary Political Orders and Christ: Karl Barth's Christology and Political Praxis*, Allison Park: Pickwick Publications.

Hunsinger, G. (ed.), 2017 (1976), *Karl Barth and Radical Politics* (2nd edn), Eugene, OR: Wipf & Stock.

——, 2014, 'The Political Views of Karl Barth' in G. Hunsinger, *Conversational Theology: Essays on Ecumenical, Postliberal, and Political Themes, with Special Reference to Karl Barth*, London: Bloomsbury Publishing, pp. 179–204.

——, 2014, 'Frei's Early Christology: the Book of Detours' in *Conversational Theology*, pp. 129–44.

——, 1993, 'Afterword: Hans Frei as Theologian', in H. W. Frei, G. Hunsinger and W. C. Placher (eds), *Theology and Narrative: selected essays*, New York: Oxford University Press, pp. 235–70.

——, 1991, *How to read Karl Barth. The Shape of his Theology*, New York: Oxford University Press.

——, 'Hans Frei as Theologian: The Quest for A Generous Orthodoxy', *Modern Theology* 8:2 (1992), pp. 103–28.

——, 'Introduction to Theology. Questions to and Discussion with Dr. Karl Barth', *Criterion. A Publication of the University of Chicago Divinity School* 2:1 (1963), pp. 3–11.

Jehle, F., 2002, *Ever Against the Stream: The Politics of Karl Barth*, Grand Rapids, MI: Eerdmans.

Jones, P. D., 'On Patience: thinking with and beyond Karl Barth', *Scottish Journal of Theology* 68:3 (2015), pp. 273–98.

——, 2008, *The Humanity of Christ. Christology in Karl Barth's Church Dogmatics*, London: T & T Clark.

Jonsen, A. R., 1968, *Responsibility in Modern Religious Ethics*, Washington/Cleveland, OH: Corpus Books.

Kabaservice, G., 2004, *The Guardians. Kingman Brewster, His Circle, And the Rise of the Liberal Establishment*, New York: Henry Holt and Company, LLC.

——, 'The Birth of a New Institution. How two Yale presidents and their admissions directors tore up the "old blueprint" to create a modern Yale', *Yale Alumni Magazine* (December 1999), http://archives.yalealumnimagazine.com/issues/99_12/admissions.html, accessed 26.01.2024.

Kamitsuka, D. G., 1999, *Theology and Contemporary Culture. Liberation, Postliberal and Revisionary Perspectives*, Cambridge: Cambridge University Press.

Kaplan, M. A., 1998, *Between Dignity and Despair: Jewish Life in Nazi Germany*, Oxford: Oxford University Press.

Käsemann, E., 1964, 'The Problem of the Historical Jesus' in E. Käsemann, *Essays on New Testament Themes*, London: SCM Press, pp. 15–47.

Kay, J. F., 1994, *Christus Praesens. A Reconsideration of Rudolf Bultmann's Christology*, Grand Rapids, MI: Eerdmans.

Keck, L. E., 'Bornkamm's "Jesus of Nazareth" Revisited', *The Journal of Religion* 49:1 (1969), pp. 1–17.

Kerr, F., 'Frei's Types', *New Blackfriars* 75:881 (1994), pp. 184–93.

King, R. H., 1974, *The Meaning of God*, London: SCM Press.

Knight, J. A., 2013, *Liberalism Versus Postliberalism. The Great Divide in Twentieth-Century Theology*, New York: Oxford University Press.

Kreutzmüller, C., 2017, *Final Sale: The Destruction of Jewish Commercial Activity, 1930–1945*, New York: Berghahn Books.

Lebacqz, K., 'Love your Enemy: Sex, Power, and Christian Ethics', *The Annual of the Society of Christian Ethics* 10 (1990), pp. 3–23.

Lee, D., 1999, *Luke's Stories of Jesus. Theological Reading and the Legacy of Hans Frei*, Sheffield: Sheffield Academic Press.

Lehmann, P., 'Karl Barth: Theologian of Permanent Revolution', *Union Theological Seminary Review* 28:1 (1972/73), pp. 67–81.

Leyden, M. J., 2014, *Responsible Before God: Human Responsibility in Karl Barth's Moral Theology*, University of Chester.

Lindbeck, G., 2011, 'Introduction' to Robert L. Calhoun and George Lindbeck (eds), *Scripture, Creed, and Theology: Lectures on the History of Christian Doctrine in the First Centuries*, Eugene, OR: Wipf & Stock, pp. ix–lxx.

——, 2002 (1990), 'Confession and Community' in *The Church in a Postliberal Age*, London: SCM Press, pp. 1–9.

——, 1984, *The Nature of Doctrine. Religion and Theology in a Postliberal Age*, Philadelphia, PA: The Westminster Press.

——, 1970, *The Future of Roman Catholic Theology*, London, SPCK.

——, 'Ecumenism and the Future of Belief', *Una Sancta* 25:3 (1968), pp. 3–18, republished in *Church in a Postliberal Age*, pp. 91–105.

——, 'The Jews, Renewal and Ecumenism', *Journal of Ecumenical Studies* 2:3 (1965), pp. 471–3.

Locke, J. and P. Laslett (ed.), 1988, *Two Treatises of Government*, Cambridge: Cambridge University Press.

Locke, J. and J. Tully (ed.), 1983, *A Letter Concerning Toleration*, Indianapolis, IN: Hackett Publishing Company.

Loewe, R., 1964, 'The 'Plain' Meaning of Scripture in Early Jewish Exegesis' in Joseph G. Weiss (ed.), *Papers of the Institute of Jewish Studies London*, Jerusalem: Magnes Press, pp. 141–85.

Longenecker, B. W., 2009, 'Narrative Interest in the Study of Paul' in B. W. Longenecker (ed.), *Narrative Dynamics in Paul: A Critical Assessment*, Louisville, KY: Westminster John Knox Press, pp. 3–18.

Löwy, M., 1996, *The War of Gods. Religion and Politics in Latin America*, London: Verso.

Luz, U., 2005, *Matthew 21–28*, Minneapolis, MN: Fortress Press.

Mahan, T. W., *Project Concern – 1966–1968: A Report on the Effectiveness of Suburban School Placement for Inner-City Youth. Hartford Public Schools* (Hartford, Connecticut, August 1968).

Marshall, B. D., 1987, *Christology in Conflict*, Oxford: Basil Blackwell.

McCormack, B. D., 2008, 'Beyond Nonfoundational and Postmodern Readings of Barth' in B. D. McCormack, *Orthodox and Modern. Studies in the Theology of Karl Barth*, Grand Rapids, MI: Baker Academic, pp. 109–65.

Michalson, C., 1959, *The Hinge of History. An Existential Approach to the Christian Faith*, New York: Charles Scribner's Sons.

Moltmann, J., 2002 (1967), *The Theology of Hope*, London: SCM Press.

Mostert, C., 2002, *God and the Future: Wolfhart Pannenberg's Eschatological Doctrine of God*, London: Bloomsbury Publishing.

Neie, H., 2012 (1978), *The Doctrine of the Atonement in the Theology of Wolfhart Pannenberg*, Berlin, Boston, MA: De Gruyter.

Niebuhr, H. R., 1999, *The Responsible Self. An Essay in Christian Moral Philosophy*, Louisville, KY: WJK Press.

——, 1992, 'The Grace of Doing Nothing' in Richard. B Miller (ed.), *War in the Twentieth Century. Sources in Theological Ethics*, Louisville, KY: Westminster/John Knox Press, pp. 6–11.

——, 1992, 'A Communication: The Only Way Into the Kingdom of God' in Richard B. Miller (ed.), *War in the Twentieth Century*, pp. 19–21.

——, 1992, 'War as Crucifixion' in Richard. B Miller (ed.), *War in the Twentieth Century*, pp. 63–70.

——, 1992, 'War as the Judgment of God' in Richard. B Miller (ed.), *War in the Twentieth Century*, pp. 46–55.

——, 1970, *Radical Monotheism and Western Culture*, Louisville, KY: Westminster/John Knox Press.

——, 1956, 'The Church and Its Purpose' in H. R. Niebuhr, *The Purpose of the Church and its Ministry. Reflections on the Aims of Theological Education*, New York, Evanston and London: Harper & Row Publishers.

Niebuhr, R., 2015, 'Moral Man and Immoral Society A Study in Ethics and Politics' in E. Sefton (ed.), *Reinhold Niebuhr: Major Works on Religion and Politics*, New York: Library Classics of the United States, pp. 139–350.

——, 2015, *The Irony of American History* in R. Niebuhr and E. Sifton (eds), *Major Works on Religion and Politics*, New York: Library of America, pp. 459–589.

——, 1992, 'Must We Do Nothing?', in Richard. B Miller (ed.), *War in the Twentieth Century*, pp. 13–15.

——, 1949, *Faith and History. A Comparison of Christian and Modern Views of History*, London: Nisbet & Co.

——, 1941, *The Nature and Destiny of Man. A Christian Interpretation* (2 vols.), London: Nisbet and Co.

Nimmo, P. T., 2011, *Being in Action. The Theological Shape of Barth's Ethical Vision*, London: T & T Clark.

Norris, K., 2020, *Witnessing Whiteness. Confronting White Supremacy in the American Church*, New York: Oxford University Press.

Ochs, P., 2008, 'An Introduction to Postcritical Scriptural Interpretation' in P. Ochs, *The Return to Scripture in Judaism and Christianity: Essays in Postcritical Scriptural Interpretation*, Eugene, OR: Wipf & Stock, pp. 3–51.

Oden, T. C., 1965, *Radical Obedience: the ethics of Rudolf Bultmann*, London: The Epworth Press.

Ogden, S. M., 1962, *Christ Without Myth. A Study Based on the Theology of Rudolf Bultmann*, London: Collins.

Ogden, S. M. and V. Harvey, 1964, 'How New Is the "New Quest of the Historical Jesus"?' in C. E. Braaten and R. A. Harrisville (eds), *The Historical Jesus and the Kerygmatic Christ*, Nashville, TN: The Abingdon Press, pp. 197–242.

Olegovich, G. (ed.), 1999, *Ten Year Commemoration to the Life of Hans Frei (1922–1988)*, New York: Semenenko Foundation.

Oren, D. A., 2000, *Joining the Club. A History of Jews and Yale* (2nd edn), New Haven, CT and London: Yale University Press.

Ottmann, G. F., 2002, *Lost for Words? Brazilian Liberationism in the 1990s*, Pittsburg, PA: University of Pittsburgh Press.

Outka, G., 1987, 'Following at a Distance: Ethics and the Identity of Jesus' in Garrett Green (ed.), *Scriptural Authority and Narrative Interpretation*, Philadelphia, PA: Fortress Press, pp. 144–60.

——, 1972, *Agape. An Ethical Analysis*, New Haven, CT: Yale University Press.

Owens, J. J., 2014, *Making Religion Safe for Democracy: Transformation from Hobbes to Tocqueville*, New York: Cambridge University Press.

Pannenberg, W., 2002, *Jesus – God and Man*, London: SCM Press.

Placher, W. C., 1993, 'Introduction to Frei' in W. C. Placher and G. Hunsinger (eds), *Theology and Narrative. Selected Essays*, New York: Oxford University Press, pp. 3–25.

Plaskow, J., 1980, *Sex, Sin and Grace. Women's Experience and the Theologies of Reinhold Niebuhr and Paul Tillich*, Lanham, MD and London: University of America Press.

Pritchard, E., 2013, *Religion in Public: Locke's Political Theology*, Stanford, CA: Stanford University Press.

Rae, D. W., 2003, *City. Urbanism and its End*, New Haven, CT and London: Yale University Press.

Ramsey, P., 1950, *Basic Christian Ethics*, London: SCM Press.

Robinson, J. M., '*Jesus von Nazareth*, by Günther Bornkamm', *Journal of Biblical Literature* 76:4 (January 1957), pp. 310–13.

——, 1959, *A New Quest of the Historical Jesus*, London: SCM Press.

Ruether, R. R., 1983, *Sexism and God-Talk: Toward a Feminist Theology*, London: SCM Press.

Ryle, G., 1973, *The Concept of Mind*, Harmondsworth: Penguin Books.

Saiving Goldstein, V., 'The Human Situation: A Feminine View', *Journal of Religion* 40:2 (1960), pp. 100–12.

Schner, G. P., 'The Eclipse of Biblical Narrative: Analysis and Critique', *Modern Theology* 8:2 (April 1992), pp. 149–72.

Shin, D., 2019, *Theology and the Public. Reflections on Hans W. Frei on Hermeneutics, Christology, and Theological Method*, Lanham, MD: Lexington Books.

Sölle, D., 1974, *Political Theology*, Philadelphia, PA: Fortress Press.

Sonderegger, K., 'Epistemological Monophysitism in Karl Barth and Hans Frei', *Pro Ecclesia* 22:3 (2013), pp. 255–62.

Springs, J. A., 'Frei's Later Christology: Radiance and Obscurity', *Pro Ecclesia* (2015), 24.1, pp. 37–52.

——, 2010, *Toward A Generous Orthodoxy. Prospects for Hans Frei's Postliberal Theology*, New York: Oxford University Press.

——, 'Between Barth and Wittgenstein: on the availability of Hans Frei's later theology', *Modern Theology* 23:3 (2007), pp. 393–413.

Staden, E. von, 1981, *Darkness over the Valley: Growing Up in Nazi Germany*, New York: Ticknor and Fields.

Sternberg, M., 1987, *The Poetics of Biblical Narrative. Ideological Literature and the Drama of Reading*, Bloomington, IN: Indiana University Press.

Surin, K. J., 1989, *The Turnings of Darkness and Light. Essays in Philosophical and Systematic Theology*, Cambridge: Cambridge University Press.

Tanner, K. E., 1997, *Theories of Culture. A New Agenda for Theology*, Minneapolis, MN: Augsburg Fortress.

——, 1988, *God and Creation in Christian Theology: Tyranny or Empowerment?*, Minneapolis, MN: Fortress Press.

Townes, E., 2006, *Womanist Ethics and the Cultural Production of Evil*, New York: Palgrave Macmillan.

Tracy, D., 1981, *The Analogical Imagination: Christian Theology and the Culture of Pluralism*, New York: Crossroad Publishing Company.

Van Buren, P., 1963, *The Secular Meaning of the Gospel*, London: SCM Press.

Vásquez, M., 1998, *The Brazilian Popular Church and the Crisis of Modernity*, Cambridge: Cambridge University Press.

1997, 'Vossische Zeitung' in H. Garland and M. Garland (eds), *The Oxford Companion to German Literature*, Oxford: Oxford University Press. Retrieved from https://www.oxfordreference.com/view/10.1093/acref/9780198158967 .001.0001/acref-9780198158967-e-5633, accessed 23.08.2023.

Webster, J. B., 2004, 'Freedom in Limitation' in J. B. Webster, *Barth's Moral Theology*, Edinburgh: T & T Clark, pp. 99–123.

——, 2000, *Karl Barth*, London: Continuum.

——, 1995, *Barth's Ethics of Reconciliation*, Cambridge: Cambridge University Press.

Werpehowski, W., 2014, *Karl Barth and Christian Ethics: Living in Truth*, Farnham: Taylor Francis Group.

——, 'Ad Hoc Apologetics', *Journal of Religion* 66:3 (1996), pp. 282–301.

West, C. R., 1988, 'On Hans Frei's *Eclipse of Biblical Narrative*' in C. R. West, *Prophetic Fragments*, Grand Rapids, MI: Eerdmans, pp. 236–9.

Wiles, M., '*The Identity of Jesus Christ* by Hans W. Frei', *Journal of Theological Studies* 27:1 (1976), pp. 261–2.

Williams, D. S, 1993, *Sisters in the Wilderness. The Challenge of Womanist God-Talk*, Maryknoll, NY: Orbis Books.

——, 'The Color of Feminism: On Speaking the Black Woman's Tongue', *The Journal of Religious Thought* 43:1 (1986), pp. 42–58.

Williams, Y., 2008, *Black Politics/White Power. Civil Rights, Black Power, and the Black Panthers in New Haven*, Malden, MA.

Wittgenstein, L., 2009, *Philosophical Investigations* §109, tr. G. E. M. Anscombe, P. M. S Hacker and J. Schulte, rev. 4th edn, Chichester: Wiley-Blackwell.

Wolkoff, A., 'Creating a Suburban Ghetto: Public Housing at New Haven's West Rock, 1945–1979', *Connecticut History Review* 45:1 (2006), pp. 56–93.

Woolverton, J., 'Hans W. Frei in Context: A Theological and Historical Memoir', *Anglican Theological Review* 79:3 (1997), pp. 369–93.

Young III, William W., 'The Identity of the Literal Sense: Midrash in the Work of Hans Frei', *The Journal of Religion* 85:4 (2005), pp. 609–33.

Index

agency, moral *see* Christian freedom
alienation of self 105–7, 129–30n187, 173–4n21, 192, 214
allegory, allegorical 192, 198, 214, 229n106
analogy, analogical 92, 111, 115, 167, 206, 211–12
apologetic theology 80–4
  Hermeneutics and 84–5, 146–8, 201
ascriptive literalism 190–1
Atonement 47, 53–4, 55, 65–6, 93–4, 103–4, 106–7, 114–17, 121, 170, 246
Auerbach, Erich 103, 118, 139–40, 174n42, 174–5n45, 176n87
authorial intention 191, 194

baptism 70, 130n199
Barth, Karl 45, 51–9, 62, 65, 66–7, 71, 72, 82, 99, 100–1, 107, 118–19, 120–1, 137, 156–7, 160–8, 184, 195, 198–202, 205–9, 231n150, 240, 241, 242, 255, 261, 282n7
Berlin, University of 188–9, 192, 195, 231n169
Bornkamm, Günther 60–1, 65, 71, 72, 84, 88, 283n27, 283n35
Brewster, Kingman 16, 19, 20, 21, 29, 40n97, 40–1n99
Bultmann, Rudolf 45, 46–51, 51–2, 53, 54, 56, 57, 59–60, 61–2, 64, 65, 68, 71, 72, 83, 86, 87, 97, 99, 107, 119, 175n68, 229n99, 242–3, 283n25
Burg, Bernard 29, 30, 31, 32–4, 42n115, 43–4n129, 44n144

Chalcedon, declaration of the Council of 100, 200
Christianity
  And culture 187–8, 189, 190, 208, 216–19, 234n262, 235n267
  and Judaism 182, 191, 219, 220–1
  in post-Christian societies 15–16, 182, 185, 220–1, 235n276, 237
Christian life
  as pilgrimage 240
Christology *see* Jesus Christ
Church, Christian community 50–1, 57, 66, 108–13, 117, 121, 253, 259
collective disciple 238
  as community of reconciliation 222, 244–9, 281–2
  Israel-like view of 113, 131n233, 241
  nation and 267–9
  Political engagement and responsibility of 58–9, 67, 80, 119, 121–2, 248–9, 256–7, 259–60, 266, 275–6, 280
  world and 110–11, 112–14, 117, 121, 185, 238–9, 249
Civil Rights movement (US) 7, 15, 16, 17, 18, 20, 24, 27–34, 35, 42n102, 115, 116, 119
Civil War (US) 114–15, 116, 132–3n245
climate change 282
Cocceius, Johannes 144
Collins, Anthony 144–6
command, of God in Jesus Christ 159–67, 240
Cone, James H. 250–1, 273, 278–81, 290n222
Connecticut Housing Investment Fund 33–4